W9-CLW-527

NEW AND

COLLECTED POEMS

1931–2001

SELECTED WORKS IN ENGLISH BY CZESLAW MILOSZ

The Captive Mind

Seizure of Power

Postwar Polish Poetry: An Anthology

*Native Realm: A Search for
Self-Definition*

Selected Poems by Zbigniew Herbert
(translated by Czeslaw Milosz and Peter Dale Scott)

The History of Polish Literature

Selected Poems

Mediterranean Poems by Aleksander Wat
(translated by Czeslaw Milosz)

*Emperor of the Earth:
Modes of Eccentric Vision*

Bells in Winter

The Witness of Poetry

The Issa Valley

Visions from San Francisco Bay

The Separate Notebooks

The Land of Ulto

Unattainable Earth

The Collected Poems 1931–1987

With the Skin: Poems of Aleksander Wat
(translated and edited by Czeslaw Milosz and
Leonard Nathan)

Beginning with My Streets

Provinces

Facing the River

Road-side Dog

A Treatise on Poetry

Milosz's ABC's

CZESLAW MILOSZ

New and

Collected Poems

1931–2001

An Imprint of HarperCollins*Publishers*

HarperCollins books may be purchased for educational,
business, or sales promotional use. For information please
write: Special Markets Department, HarperCollins Publishers,
Inc., 10 East 53rd Street, New York, NY 10022.

Designed by Kate Nichols

Library of Congress Cataloging-in-Publication Data has been
applied for.

ISBN 0-06-019667-X

01 02 03 04 05   DC/RRD   10 9 8 7 6 5 4 3 2 1

CONTENTS

DAYLIGHT   *79*
(Światło dzienne, 1953)

HYMN OF THE PEARL *333*
(Hymn o perle, 1981)

ROAD-SIDE DOG   643
(Piesek przydrozny, 1998)

THIS   659
(To, 2000)

I

INTRODUCTION

A poet at ninety should be wise enough not to write introductions to his work of many decades. Yet my publisher insists, and my resistance to his entreaties is not dogmatic. Therefore, a few words on my poems looked at retrospectively.

I see an inner logic linking my early poems written at age twenty to my latest volume, *This*, which appeared in its original Polish version in 2000 and is included in this book. It is, however, a kind of logic that does not agree with ratiocinations. I strongly believe in the passivity of a poet, who receives every poem as a gift from his daimonion or, if you prefer, his Muse. He should be humble enough not to ascribe what is received to his own virtues. At the same time, however, his mind and his will should be alert. I lived amidst scenes of horror in the twentieth century—that was reality, and I could not escape into a realm of "pure poetry" as some descendants of French symbolism advised. Yet our hot-blooded reactions to inhumanity rarely result in texts artistically valid, even if such poems as my "Campo dei Fiori," written in April 1943 in Warsaw when the ghetto was burning, continue to have some value.

I think that effort to capture as much as possible of tangible reality is the health of poetry. Having to choose between subjective art and objective art, I would vote for the latter, even if the meaning of that term is grasped not by theory but by personal struggle. I hope that my practice justifies my claim.

The history of the twentieth century prompted many poets to design images that conveyed their moral protest. Yet to remain aware of the weight of fact without yielding to the temptation to become only a reporter is one of the most difficult puzzles confronting a practitioner of poetry. It calls for a cunning in selecting one's means and a kind of distillation of material to achieve a distance to contemplate the things of this world as they are, without illusion. In other words, poetry has always been for me a participation in the humanly modulated time of my contemporaries.

Czeslaw Milosz

A POEM
ON FROZEN
TIME

(Poemat o czasie zastygłym)

1933

ARTIFICER

Burning, he walks in the stream of flickering letters, clarinets,
machines throbbing quicker than the heart, lopped-off heads, silk
canvases, and he stops under the sky

and raises toward it his joined clenched fists.

Believers fall on their bellies, they suppose it is a monstrance that
    shines,

but those are knuckles, sharp knuckles shine that way, my friends.

He cuts the glowing, yellow buildings in two, breaks the walls into
    motley halves;
pensive, he looks at the honey seeping from those huge honeycombs:
throbs of pianos, children's cries, the thud of a head banging against
    the floor.
This is the only landscape able to make him feel.

He wonders at his brother's skull shaped like an egg,
every day he shoves back his black hair from his brow,
then one day he plants a big load of dynamite
and is surprised that afterward everything spouts up in the explosion.
Agape, he observes the clouds and what is hanging in them:
globes, penal codes, dead cats floating on their backs, locomotives.
They turn in the skeins of white clouds like trash in a puddle.
While below on the earth a banner, the color of a romantic rose,
    flutters,
and a long row of military trains crawls on the weed-covered tracks.

Wilno, 1931

THREE

WINTERS

(Trzy zimy)

1936

THE SONG

Woman:
Earth flows away from the shore where I stand,
her trees and grasses, more and more distant, shine.
Buds of chestnuts, lights of frail birches,
I won't see you anymore.
With worn-out people you move away,
with the sun waving like a flag you run toward the night,
I am afraid to stay here alone, I have nothing except my body
—it glistens in the dark, a star with crossed hands,
so that I am scared to look at myself. Earth,
do not abandon me.

Chorus:
Ice flowed down the rivers, trees sprouted buoyant leaves,
ploughs went through the fields, doves in the forest are cooing,
a doe runs in the hills and cries her exulting songs,
tall-stemmed flowers are blooming, steam rises from warm gardens,
Children throw balls, they dance on the meadow by threesomes,
women wash linen at streamside and fish for the moon.
All joy comes from the earth, there is no delight without her,
man is given to the earth, let him desire no other.

Woman:
I don't want you, don't tempt me, keep flowing, my tranquil sister.
Your burning touch on my neck, I still feel it.
Nights of love with you bitter as the ash of clouds,
and the dawn after them, red, and on the lakes
first terns circling and such sadness
that I could not cry anymore, just keep counting
the hours of the morning, listen to the cold rustle
of the high, dead poplars. You, God, have mercy on me.
From the earth's greedy mouth deliver me,
cleanse me of her untrue songs.

Chorus:
The capstans are turning, fish toss in the nets,
baked breads smell sweetly, apples roll on the tables,
evenings go down the steps and the steps are live flesh—
everything is begot by the earth, she is without blemish.
Heavy ships are yawing, copper brethren are sailing,
animals sway their backs, butterflies fall to the sea,
baskets wander at dusk, dawn lives in the apple tree—
everything is begot by the earth, to her everything will return.

Woman:
Oh, if there were in me one seed without rust,
no more than one grain that could perdure
I could sleep in the cradle leaning by turns
now into darkness, now into the break of day.
I would wait quietly till the slow movement ceases
and the real shows itself naked suddenly,
till a wildflower, a stone in the fields stare up
with the disk of an unknown new face.
Then they who live in the lies
like weeds at the bottom of a bay's wash
would only be what pine needles are
when one looks from above through the clouds at a forest.
But there is nothing in me, just fear,
nothing but the running of dark waves.
I am the wind that blows and dies out in dark waters,
I am the wind going and not returning,
a milkweed pollen on the black meadows of the world.

The last voices:
At the forge on the lake shore, hammerblows,
a man, bent over, fixes a scythe,
his head gleams in the flame of the hearth.

A resin chip is lit in the hut,
tired ploughboys lay their heads on the table.
A bowl is already steaming and the crickets sing.

Islands are animals falling asleep,
in the nest of the lake they settle down, purring:
above them, a narrow cloud.

Wilno, 1934

THE GATES OF THE ARSENAL

Tender and faithful animals, secretive, very quiet,
Watched the expanse of gardens, half shutting the slits
Of their olive eyes. The statues gleaned
Chestnut leaves for their heads and with a stone scroll
Of laws from long ago or the trace of a sword
Marched, covered with the laurels of new autumns,
To a pond where a paper boat was sailing.
Light grew up from under the ground, a cold glow shone through
The striped fur of the animals in their alert repose,
Through the cellars of buildings sprinkled with the foam of day.
And the wings of trees were flying in the haze.

Flame, o flame, immense musics
Resound, eternal movement stirs the groves,
With their hands tied, on gun-carriages, horseback,
Under immobile wind or blowing silent flutes,
Travelers pass each other, going round and round,
Showing each other their lips locked by frost,
Contorted in a scream, or their eyebrows
Ripped apart by wisdom, or fingers tearing open
Their breasts shorn of ribbons, medals, braids.

A tempestuous noise, the din of waves, the soughing of pianos
Resounds from the abyss. There, do the flocks of birches
Ring the little cloud-bells, or herds of goats
Dip their white beards in the caressing jar
Of the green gorge, or perhaps the weirs
Play to the streams in the calm highland valleys,
And full carts are passing, side by side with the evening,
While the stubble dims, laughter and the clatter of steps subside?

You lunar gardens, dominions of forlorn dreams,
Receive her with a good heart, who comes

From the world where all of living beauty grows.
Even if she is miserable, a handful of gathered ash,
Destined to last no longer than the sun's flight,
Take her, never let her summon love.

Into a bluish distance of lanes, glitters of corteges,
She goes, unaware of the depths of the misty gardens,
A young woman, covering her eyes with her hand.
The animals turn their muzzles from the lawns
And a bearded keeper trots on his crooked horse,
Carrying a golden arrow in the taut string of his bow.

Gravel under her feet, pacing in false silence,
Rustles and a knot of chestnut hair streams
From her brow raised like a small planet.
Silver seeps into her lips, fear bleaches her face,
The breast, two icicles now, restlessly heaves,
The glare strikes. And touched by light, all that lives dies.

Her dress will fall off in flames, the bush of hair will blaze
And reveal her belly like a copper disk.
Her nimble thighs no more rule over dreams,
Naked and pure they smoke like auburn Pompeii.

And if a child is born of that Slavic blood,
White-eyed, it will strike its head hard against the steps
And sleep with its four legs up, day and night,
As a dead horse sleeps amid burned-out pastures.

Choruses, wreaths will entangle her.
Evening will lay shadowy thorns on her brow.
And this will be the eternal rest of tempests,
With a hand pouring grain for hunchback angels.

Rolling yellow hoops, carrying sailboats
Loaded with tin soldiers, boys were returning home.
There was a small rain, a bird sang,
The moon rose slowly, cut in half by a cloud.
With wet eyes the riders were looking straight west.
Tribes of dogs chased each other through the flower beds.
Lovers took their seat above the golden steps.
There was peace on earth. An orchestra, submerged
In the gates of dusk, was falling silent
At the end of a long street, and by the box hedges
The mimosas cooled, bowing to the night.

Paris, 1934

HYMN

There is no one between you and me.
Neither a plant drawing sap from the depths of earth
nor an animal, nor a man,
nor wind walking between the clouds.

The most beautiful bodies are like transparent glass.
The most powerful flames like water washing the tired feet of
    travelers.
The greenest trees like lead blooming in the thick of the night.
Love is sand swallowed by parched lips.
Hatred is a salty jug offered to the thirsty.
Roll on, rivers; raise your hands,
cities! I, a faithful son of the black earth, shall return to the black
    earth.
as if my life had not been,
as if not my heart, not my blood,
not my duration
had created words and songs
but an unknown, impersonal voice,
only the flapping of waves, only the choir of winds
and the autumnal sway
of the tall trees.

There is no one between you and me
and to me strength is given.
White mountains graze on terrestrial plains,
to the sea they go, their watering place,
new and new, suns lean over
a valley of a small, dark river where I was born.
I have no wisdom, no skills, and no faith
but I received strength, it tears the world apart.
I shall break, a heavy wave, against its shores
and a young wave will cover my trace. O darkness!

Tainted by the first glare of the dawn,
like a lung taken out of a ripped-up beast,
you are rocking, you are sinking.
How many times I have floated with you,
transfixed in the middle of the night,
hearing some voice above your horror-stricken church;
a cry of grouse, a rustle of the heath were stalking in you
and two apples shone on the table
or open scissors glittered—
and we were alike:
apples, scissors, darkness, and I
under the same immobile
Assyrian, Egyptian, and Roman
moon.

Seasons come and go, men and women mate,
children in half-sleep run their hands across the wall
and draw lands with a finger wet with saliva.
Forms come and go, what seemed invincible crumbles.

But amid the States rising from the sea,
amid demolished streets where one day
mountains will loom made of a fallen planet,
against what is past and what is to pass
youth defends itself, austere as the sundust,
in love neither with good nor with evil,
all tossed under your immense feet,
so that you may crush it, so that you may step on it,
so that your breath move the wheel
and a frail structure shake with motion,
so that you give to it hunger and to others wine, salt, and bread.

The sound of the horn still is not heard
calling the dispersed, those who lie in the valleys.
On the frozen ground as yet no rumble of the last cart.
There is no one between you and me.

Paris, 1935

DAWNS

A tall building. The walls crept upward in the dark,
Above the rustle of maple leaves, above hurrying feet.
A tall building, dawning with its lights above the square.
Inside hissing softly in the predawn hours,
The elevator moved between the floors. The cables twanged.
A rooster's cry rang in the pipes and gutters
Till a shiver ran through the house. Those awakened heard
This singing in the walls, terrible as the earth's happiness.

Already the screech of a tram. And day. And smoke again.
Oh, the day is dark. Above us, who are shut
High up in our rooms, flocks of birds
Fly by in a whir of flickering wings.
Not enough. One life is not enough.
I'd like to live twice on this sad planet,
In lonely cities, in starved villages,
To look at all evil, at the decay of bodies,
And probe the laws to which the time was subject,
Time that howled above us like a wind.

In the courtyard of the apartment house street musicians
Croon in chorus. The hands of listeners shine at the windows.
She gets up from her rumpled sheets.
In her dreams she thought of dresses and travel.
She walks up to the black mirror. Youth didn't last long.
Nobody knew that work would divide a day
Into great toil and dead rest,
And that the moon would pause every spring
Above the sleep of the weary ones. In our hearts' heavy beating
No spring for us anymore, nor love.

To cover up one's thighs. Let them not,
With their lacing of thin purple veins, remember

This child rushing down the staircase,
This child running down the gray sidewalk.
Laughter can still be heard in the distance—
Anew, everything the child will discover anew
And down an immense, empty, frosty road
Through a space ringing with the thunder of the pulse
Her child will go. And time will howl.
Standing naked in front of her mirror, the woman
Lightly wipes away two tears with her kerchief
And darkens her eyebrows with henna.

Wilno, 1932

SLOW RIVER

There has not been for a long time a spring
as beautiful as this one; the grass, just before mowing,
is thick and wet with dew. At night bird cries
come up from the edge of the marsh, a crimson shoal
lies in the east till the morning hours.
In such a season, every voice becomes for us
a shout of triumph. Glory, pain and glory
to the grass, to the clouds, to the green oak wood.
The gates of the earth torn open, the key
to the earth revealed. A star is greeting the day.
Then why do your eyes hold an impure gleam
like the eyes of those who have not tasted
evil and long only for crime? Why does this heat
and depth of hatred radiate
from your narrowed eyes? To you the rule,
for you clouds in golden rings
play a music, maples by the road exalt you.
The invisible rein on every living thing
leads to your hand—pull, and they all
turn a half-circle under the canopy
called cirrus. And your tasks? A wooded mountain
awaits you, the place for cities in the air,
a valley where wheat should grow, a table, a white page
on which, maybe, a long poem could be started,
joy and toil. And the road bolts like an animal,
it falls away so quickly, leaving a trail of dust,
that there is scarcely a sight to prepare a nod for,
the hand's grip already weakened, a sigh, and the storm is over.
And then they carry the malefactor through the fields,
rocking his gray head, and above the seashore
on a tree-lined avenue, they put him down
where the wind from the bay furls banners

and schoolchildren run on the gravel paths,
singing their songs.

—"So that neighing in the gardens, drinking on the green,
so that, not knowing whether they are happy or just weary,
they take bread from the hands of their pregnant wives.
They bow their heads to nothing in their lives.
My brothers, avid for pleasure, smiling, beery,
have the world for a granary, a house of joy."

—"Ah, dark rabble at their vernal feasts
and crematoria rising like white cliffs
and smoke seeping from the dead wasps' nests.
In a stammer of mandolins, a dust-cloud of scythes,
on heaps of food and mosses stomped ash-gray,
the new sun rises on another day."

For a long time there has not been a spring
as beautiful as this one to the voyager.
The expanse of water seems to him dense
as the blood of hemlock. And a fleet of sails
speeding in the dark, like the last
vibration of a pure note. He saw
human figures scattered on the sands
under the light of planets, falling from the vault
of heaven, and when a wave grew silent, it was silent,
the foam smelled of iodine? heliotrope?
They sang on the dunes, Maria, Maria,
resting a spattered hand on the saddle
and he didn't know if this was the new sign
that promises salvation, but kills first.
Three times must the wheel of blindness

turn, before I look without fear at the power
sleeping in my own hand, and recognize spring,
the sky, the seas, and the dark, massed land.
Three times will the liars have conquered
before the great truth appears alive
and in the splendor of one moment
stand spring and the sky, the seas, the lands.

Wilno, 1936

STATUE OF A COUPLE

Your hand, my wonder, is now icy cold.
The purest light of the celestial dome
has burned me through. And now we are
as two still plains lying in darkness,
as two black banks of a frozen stream
in the chasm of the world.

Our hair combed back is carved in wood,
the moon walks over our ebony shoulders.
A distant cockcrow, the night goes by, silent.
Rich is the rime of love, withered the dowry.

Where are you, living in what depths of time,
love, stepping down into what waters,
now, when the frost of our voiceless lips
does not fend off the divine fires?

In a forest of clouds, of foam, and of silver
we live, caressing lands under our feet.
And we are wielding the might of a dark scepter
to earn oblivion.

My love, your breast cut through by a chisel
knows nothing anymore of what it was.
Of clouds at dawn, of angers at daybreak,
of shadows in springtime it has no remembrance.

And you have led me, as once an angel led
Tobias, onto the rusty marshes of Lombardy.
But a day came when a sign frightened you,
a stigma of golden measure.

With a scream, with immobile fear in your thin hands
you fell into a pit that ashes lie over,
where neither northern firs nor Italian yews
could protect our ancient bed of lovers.

What was it, what is it, what will it be—
we filled the world with our cry and calling.
The dawn is back, the red moon set,
do we know now? In a heavy ship

A helmsman comes, throws a silken rope
and binds us tightly to each other,
then he pours on friends, once enemies,
a handful of snow.

Wilno, 1935

RESCUE

(Ocalenie)

1945

BALLAD OF LEVALLOIS

—barracks for the unemployed in Levallois-Perret, 1935

O God, have mercy on Levallois,
Look under these chestnut trees poisoned with smoke,
Give a moment of joy to the weak and the drunk,
O God, have mercy on Levallois.

All day long they stole and cursed,
Now they lie in their bunks and lick their wounds,
And while the darkness thickens over Paris
They hide their faces in their thieving hands.
O God, have mercy on Levallois.

They followed your commandment every day:
They harvested wheat, tore coal from the earth.
And often they drenched themselves in their brothers' blood
Murmuring the names of Jesus and Mary.

Their insane jabber welled from the taverns.
That was their song in your praise.
They perished in mines, in the snow, in the heat,
In mud and the depths of the seas.

It was they who lifted you above themselves,
Their hands sculpted your face.
So deign to look on your faithful priests,
Give them the joys of table and bed.

Take from them the stigmas of illness and sin.
Set them free. Lead them into Sodom.
Let them adorn their houses with garlands.
Let them learn how to live and die more lightly.

Darkness. Silence. A bridge hums in the distance.
The wind streams through Cain's trees.
On the void of the earth, on the human tribe
No mercy, no mercy on Levallois.

Wilno, 1936

ENCOUNTER

We were riding through frozen fields in a wagon at dawn.
A red wing rose in the darkness.

And suddenly a hare ran across the road.
One of us pointed to it with his hand.

That was long ago. Today neither of them is alive,
Not the hare, nor the man who made the gesture.

O my love, where are they, where are they going
The flash of a hand, streak of movement, rustle of pebbles.
I ask not out of sorrow, but in wonder.

Wilno, 1936

A BOOK IN THE RUINS

A dark building. Crossed boards, nailed up, create
A barrier at the entrance, or a gate
When you go in. Here, in the gutted foyer,
The ivy snaking down the walls is wire
Dangling. And over there the twisted metal
Columns rising from the undergrowth of rubble
Are tattered tree trunks. This could be the brick
Of the library, you don't know yet, or the sick
Grove of dry white aspen where, stalking birds,
You met a Lithuanian dusk stirred
From its silence only by the wails of hawks.
Now walk carefully. You see whole blocks
Of ceiling caved in by a recent blast.
And above, through jagged tiers of plaster,
A patch of blue. Pages of books lying
Scattered at your feet are like fern-leaves hiding
A moldy skeleton, or else fossils
Whitened by the secrets of Jurassic shells.
A remnant life so ancient and unknown
Compels a scientist, tilting a stone
Into the light, to wonder. He can't know
Whether it is some dead epoch's shadow
Or a living form. He looks again
At chalk spirals eroded by the rain,
The rust of tears. Thus, in a book picked up
From the ruins, you see a world erupt
And glitter with its distant sleepy past,
Green times of creatures tumbled to the vast
Abyss and backward: the brows of women,
An earring fixed with trembling hand, pearl button
On a glove, candelabra in the mirror.
The lanterns have been lit. A first shiver
Passes over the instruments. The quadrille

Begins to curl, subdued by the rustle
Of big trees swaying in the formal park.
She slips outside, her shawl floating in the dark,
And meets him in a bower overgrown
With vines. They sit close on a bench of stone
And watch the lanterns glowing in the jasmine.
Or here, this stanza: you hear a goose pen
Creak, the butterfly of an oil lamp
Flutters slowly over scrolls and parchment,
A crucifix, bronze busts. The lines complain,
In plangent rhythms, that desire is vain.
Here a city rises. In the market square
Signboards clang, a stagecoach rumbles in to scare
A flock of pigeons up. Under the town clock,
In the tavern, a hand pauses in the stock
Gesture of arrest—meanwhile workers walk
Home from the textile mill, townsfolk talk
On the steps—and the hand moves now to evoke
The fire of justice, a world gone up in smoke,
The voice quavering with the revenge of ages.
So the world seems to drift from these pages
Like the mist clearing on a field at dawn.
Only when two times, two forms are drawn
Together and their legibility
Disturbed, do you see that immortality
Is not very different from the present
And is for its sake. You pick a fragment
Of grenade which pierced the body of a song
On Daphnis and Chloe. And you long,
Ruefully, to have a talk with her,
As if it were what life prepared you for.
—How is it, Chloe, that your pretty skirt
Is torn so badly by the winds that hurt

Real people, you who, in eternity, sing
The hours, sun in your hair appearing
And disappearing? How is it that your breasts
Are pierced by shrapnel, and the oak groves burn,
While you, charmed, not caring at all, turn
To run through forests of machinery and concrete
And haunt us with the echoes of your feet?
If there is such an eternity, lush
Though short-lived, that's enough. But how . . . hush!
We were predestined to live when the scene
Grows dim and the outline of a Greek ruin
Blackens the sky. It is noon, and wandering
Through a dark building, you see workers sitting
Down to a fire a narrow ray of sunlight
Kindles on the floor. They have dragged out
Heavy books and made a table of them
And begun to cut their bread. In good time
A tank will clatter past, a streetcar chime.

Warsaw, 1941

DAY OF GENERATION

When, once enmeshed in the motions of their legs,
Cyclists on the highway lean into a curve,
In air that is childish, rosy
And already prepared for other forms,
For the outline of non-mortal feet,

When, clipping through the mist with glinting legs,
They enter in the morning some human city,
And roadside sunflowers rush past them in the haze
And the poplar phantoms lilt in space,

A peasant woman bent under her basket,
Walking at dawn, cuts across the crowd
Of invisible dwellers whose towering chambers
Are not to be discovered by her eye.

÷

It's enough to raise your hand to touch
Somebody's cheek, to find a satin dress,
A face wearing the smile of ancient days,
A foam-like chain, a shell-encrusted comb.

A wizard, taking a wand or a chisel,
Will call: *Let it be*, bring forth from the air
A carriage and four in immobile speed
Or a bronze forearm punctured by the rains.

And where there was a circle of white void,
Now little reddish flames are running to and fro.
Thus the air grew thick from being touched,
Layer after layer changed into waterfalls.
They turn, the helices of stone-hard flowers,

The whole earth smells of lightning as in spring.
A wand, a chisel falls from your hands. Perish.

Too late. An unrestrained chorus pushes on.
Ranks of reed-pipes, of adroit fingers.
The smoke of banners claps right over them.
Abysses, struck, go out one by one.
For the sake of the past small as a plaything,
For the doom of wizards sad as fate,
Monuments wet with dew shine on the squares.

÷

Then glints of legs clip through the break of day,
There is also a peasant woman with her basket
And sunflowers sway over the haze.
Now somebody else calls you in,
Now somebody else summons you
Where you are both a self and not a self.

ENVOY

It is your destiny so to move your wand,
To wake up storms, to run through the heart of storms,
To lay bare a monument like a nest in a thicket,
Though all you wanted was to pluck a few roses.

Warsaw, 1942

CAMPO DEI FIORI

In Rome on the Campo dei Fiori
baskets of olives and lemons,
cobbles spattered with wine
and the wreckage of flowers.
Vendors cover the trestles
with rose-pink fish;
armfuls of dark grapes
heaped on peach-down.

On this same square
they burned Giordano Bruno.
Henchmen kindled the pyre
close-pressed by the mob.
Before the flames had died
the taverns were full again,
baskets of olives and lemons
again on the vendors' shoulders.

I thought of the Campo dei Fiori
in Warsaw by the sky-carousel
one clear spring evening
to the strains of a carnival tune.
The bright melody drowned
the salvos from the ghetto wall,
and couples were flying
high in the cloudless sky.

At times wind from the burning
would drift dark kites along
and riders on the carousel
caught petals in midair.
That same hot wind
blew open the skirts of the girls

and the crowds were laughing
on that beautiful Warsaw Sunday.

Someone will read as moral
that the people of Rome or Warsaw
haggle, laugh, make love
as they pass by martyrs' pyres.
Someone else will read
of the passing of things human,
of the oblivion
born before the flames have died.

But that day I thought only
of the loneliness of the dying,
of how, when Giordano
climbed to his burning
he could not find
in any human tongue
words for mankind,
mankind who live on.

Already they were back at their wine
or peddled their white starfish,
baskets of olives and lemons
they had shouldered to the fair,
and he already distanced
as if centuries had passed
while they paused just a moment
for his flying in the fire.

Those dying here, the lonely
forgotten by the world,
our tongue becomes for them

the language of an ancient planet.
Until, when all is legend
and many years have passed,
on a new Campo dei Fiori
rage will kindle at a poet's word.

Warsaw, 1943

THE WORLD

The Road

There where you see a green valley
And a road half-covered with grass,
Through an oak wood beginning to bloom
Children are returning home from school.

In a pencil case that opens sideways
Crayons rattle among crumbs of a roll
And a copper penny saved by every child
To greet the first spring cuckoo.

Sister's beret and brother's cap
Bob in the bushy underbrush,
A screeching jay hops in the branches
And long clouds float over the trees.

A red roof is already visible at the bend.
In front of the house father, leaning on a hoe,
Bows down, touches the unfolded leaves,
And from his flower bed inspects the whole region.

The Gate

Later dense hops will cover it completely.
As for now, it has the color
That lily pads have in very deep water
When you pluck them in the light of a summer evening.

The pickets are painted white at the top.
White and sharp, like tiny flames.
Strange that this never bothered the birds.
Even a wild pigeon once perched there.

The handle is of wood worn smooth over time,
Polished by the touch of many hands.
Nettles like to steal under the handle
And a yellow jasmine here is a tiny lantern.

The Porch

The porch whose doors face the west
Has large windows. The sun warms it well.
From here you can see north, south, east, and west,
Forests and rivers, fields and tree-lined lanes.

When the oaks array themselves in green
And the linden's shade reaches the flower bed,
The world disappears behind the blue bark,
Engraved by leaves into motley patches.

Here, at a tiny table, brother and sister
Kneel, drawing scenes of battle and pursuit.
And with their pink tongues try to help
Great warships, one of which is sinking.

The Dining Room

A room with low windows, with brown shades,
Where a Danzig clock keeps silent in the corner;
A low leather sofa; and right above it
The sculpted heads of two smiling devils;
And a copper pan shows its gleaming paunch.

On the wall a painting that depicts winter.
A crowd of people skate on ice
Between the trees, smoke comes from a chimney,
And crows fly in an overcast sky.

Nearby a second clock. A bird sits inside.
It pops out squawking and calls three times.
And it has barely finished its third and last call
When mother ladles out soup from a hot tureen.

The Stairs

Yellow, creaking, and smelling of wax
The curved steps are narrow. Near the wall
You can place your shoe crosswise
But near the banister they hardly hold your foot.

The boar's head is alive, enormous in shadow.
At first, just the tusks, then as it grows
The snout roams the ceiling, sniffing the stairway vault
While the light dissolves into vibrating dust.

Mother carries down a flickering light.
She walks slowly, tall, her robe tied at the waist,
Her shadow climbs up to the shadow of the boar.
And so she struggles, alone, with the cruel beast.

Pictures

The book is open. A moth with its shaky flight
Flits over a chariot that speeds through the dust.
Touched, it falls down pouring a golden spray
On a Greek army storming a city.

Behind a speeding chariot they drag the hero.
His head bumps against stone slabs.
While the moth, pinned to the page by the slap of a hand,
Flutters and dies on the hero's body.

And here, the sky gets cloudy, thunder resounds,
Ships clear the rocks for the open sea.
On the shore oxen lower their yoked necks
And a naked man ploughs the field.

Father in the Library

A high forehead, and above it tousled hair
On which a ray of sun falls from the window.
And so father wears a bright fluffy crown
When he spreads before him a huge book.

His gown is patterned like that of a wizard.
Softly, he murmurs his incantations.
Only he whom God instructs in magic
Will learn what wonders are hidden in this book.

Father's Incantations

O sweet master, with how much peace
Your serene wisdom fills the heart!
I love you, I am in your power
Even though I will never see your face.

Your ashes have long been scattered,
Your sins and follies no one remembers.
And for ages you will remain perfect
Like your book drawn by thought from nothingness.

You knew bitterness and you knew doubt
But the memory of your faults has vanished.
And I know why I cherish you today:
Men are small but their works are great.

From the Window

Beyond a field, a wood and a second field,
The expanse of water, a white mirror, glitters.
And the golden lowland of the earth
Bathes in the sea, a half-sunken tulip.

Father tells us that this is Europe.
On sunny days you can see it all clearly.
Now it is smoking after many floods,
A home for people, dogs, cats, and horses.

The bright towers of cities shine there,
Streams intertwine their silver threads,
And the moons of mountains are visible in spots,
Something like goose feathers scattered on the ground.

Father Explains

"There where that ray touches the plain
And the shadows escape as if they really ran,
Warsaw stands, open from all sides,
A city not very old but quite famous.

"Farther, where strings of rain hang from a little cloud,
Under the hills with an acacia grove
Is Prague. Above it, a marvelous castle
Shored against a slope in accordance with old rules.

"What divides this land with white foam
Is the Alps. The black means fir forests.
Beyond them, bathing in the yellow sun
Italy lies, like a deep-blue dish.

"Among the many fine cities that are there
You will recognize Rome, Christendom's capital,
By those round roofs on the church
Called the Basilica of Saint Peter.

"And there, to the north, beyond a bay,
Where a level bluish mist moves in waves,
Paris tries to keep pace with its tower
And reins in its herd of bridges.

"Also other cities accompany Paris,
They are adorned with glass, arrayed in iron,
But for today that would be too much,
I'll tell the rest another time."

A Parable of the Poppy

On a poppy seed is a tiny house,
Dogs bark at the poppy-seed moon,
And never, never do those poppy-seed dogs
Imagine that somewhere there is a world much larger.

The Earth is a seed—and really no more,
While other seeds are planets and stars.
And even if there were a hundred thousand,
Each might have a house and a garden.

All in a poppy head. The poppy grows tall,
The children run by and the poppy sways.
And in the evening, under the rising moon,
Dogs bark somewhere, now loudly, now softly.

By the Peonies

The peonies bloom, white and pink.
And inside each, as in a fragrant bowl,
A swarm of tiny beetles have their conversation,
For the flower is given to them as their home.

Mother stands by the peony bed,
Reaches for one bloom, opens its petals,
And looks for a long time into peony lands,
Where one short instant equals a whole year.

Then lets the flower go. And what she thinks
She repeats aloud to the children and herself.
The wind sways the green leaves gently
And speckles of light flick across their faces.

Faith

Faith is in you whenever you look
At a dewdrop or a floating leaf
And know that they are because they have to be.
Even if you close your eyes and dream up things
The world will remain as it has always been
And the leaf will be carried by the waters of the river.

You have faith also when you hurt your foot
Against a sharp rock and you know
That rocks are here to hurt our feet.
See the long shadow that is cast by the tree?
We and the flowers throw shadows on the earth.
What has no shadow has no strength to live.

Hope

Hope is with you when you believe
The earth is not a dream but living flesh,
That sight, touch, and hearing do not lie,
That all things you have ever seen here
Are like a garden looked at from a gate.

You cannot enter. But you're sure it's there.
Could we but look more clearly and wisely
We might discover somewhere in the garden
A strange new flower and an unnamed star.

Some people say we should not trust our eyes,
That there is nothing, just a seeming,
These are the ones who have no hope.
They think that the moment we turn away,
The world, behind our backs, ceases to exist,
As if snatched up by the hands of thieves.

Love

Love means to learn to look at yourself
The way one looks at distant things
For you are only one thing among many.
And whoever sees that way heals his heart,
Without knowing it, from various ills—
A bird and a tree say to him: Friend.

Then he wants to use himself and things
So that they stand in the glow of ripeness.
It doesn't matter whether he knows what he serves:
Who serves best doesn't always understand.

The Excursion to the Forest

The trees so huge you can't see treetops.
The setting sun fixes a rosy flame
On every tree, as on a candlestick,
And tiny people walk a path below.

Let us raise our heads, hold hands
So that we don't lose our way in the tangled grass.
The night has begun to put seals on the flowers,
Color after color is flowing down the sky.

And there, above, a feast. Jugs of gold,
Red wine is being poured in aspen copper.
And an airborne coach carries gifts
For the invisible kings or for the bears.

The Bird Kingdom

Flying high the heavy wood grouse
Slash the forest sky with their wings
And a pigeon returns to its airy wilderness
And a raven gleams with airplane steel.

What is the earth for them? A lake of darkness.
It has been swallowed by the night forever.
They, above the dark as above black waves,
Have their homes and islands, saved by the light.

If they groom their long feathers with their beaks
And drop one of them, it floats a long time
Before it reaches the bottom of the lake
And brushes someone's face, bringing news
From a world that is bright, beautiful, warm, and free.

Fear

"Father, where are you? The forest is wild,
There are creatures here, the bushes sway.
The orchids burst with poisonous fire,
Treacherous chasms lurk under our feet.

"Where are you, Father? The night has no end.
From now on darkness will last forever.
The travelers are homeless, they will die of hunger,
Our bread is bitter and hard as stone.

"The hot breath of the terrible beast
Comes nearer and nearer, it belches its stench.
Where have you gone, Father? Why do you not pity
Your children lost in this murky wood?"

Recovery

"Here I am—why this senseless fear?
The night is over, the day will soon arise.
You hear. The shepherds' horns already sound,
And stars grow pale over the rosy glow.

"The path is straight. We are at the edge.
Down in the village the little bell chimes.
Roosters on the fences greet the light
And the earth steams, fertile and happy.

"Here it is still dark. Fog like a river flood
Swaddles the black clumps of bilberries.
But the dawn on bright stilts wades in from the shore
And the ball of the sun, ringing, rolls."

The Sun

All colors come from the sun. And it does not have
Any particular color, for it contains them all.
And the whole Earth is like a poem
While the sun above represents the artist.

Whoever wants to paint the variegated world
Let him never look straight up at the sun
Or he will lose the memory of things he has seen.
Only burning tears will stay in his eyes.

Let him kneel down, lower his face to the grass,
And look at light reflected by the ground.
There he will find everything we have lost:
The stars and the roses, the dusks and the dawns.

Warsaw, 1943

VOICES OF POOR PEOPLE

A Song on the End of the World

On the day the world ends
A bee circles a clover,
A fisherman mends a glimmering net.
Happy porpoises jump in the sea,
By the rainspout young sparrows are playing
And the snake is gold-skinned as it should always be.

On the day the world ends
Women walk through the fields under their umbrellas,
A drunkard grows sleepy at the edge of a lawn,
Vegetable peddlers shout in the street
And a yellow-sailed boat comes nearer the island,
The voice of a violin lasts in the air
And leads into a starry night.

And those who expected lightning and thunder
Are disappointed.
And those who expected signs and archangels' trumps
Do not believe it is happening now.
As long as the sun and the moon are above,
As long as the bumblebee visits a rose,
As long as rosy infants are born
No one believes it is happening now.

Only a white-haired old man, who would be a prophet
Yet is not a prophet, for he's much too busy,
Repeats while he binds his tomatoes:
There will be no other end of the world,
There will be no other end of the world.

Warsaw, 1944

[56

Song of a Citizen

A stone from the depths that has witnessed the seas drying up
and a million white fish leaping in agony,
I, poor man, see a multitude of white-bellied nations
without freedom. I see the crab feeding on their flesh.

I have seen the fall of States and the perdition of tribes,
the flight of kings and emperors, the power of tyrants.
I can say now, in this hour,
that I—am, while everything expires,
that it is better to be a live dog than a dead lion,
as the Scripture says.

A poor man, sitting on a cold chair, pressing my eyelids,
I sigh and think of a starry sky,
of non-Euclidean space, of amoebas and their pseudopodia,
of tall mounds of termites.

When walking, I am asleep, when sleeping, I dream reality,
pursued and covered with sweat, I run.
On city squares lifted up by the glaring dawn,
beneath marble remnants of blasted-down gates,
I deal in vodka and gold.

And yet so often I was near,
I reached into the heart of metal, the soul of earth, of fire, of water.
And the unknown unveiled its face
as a night reveals itself, serene, mirrored by tide.
Lustrous copper-leaved gardens greeted me
that disappear as soon as you touch them.

And so near, just outside the window—the greenhouse of the worlds
where a tiny beetle and a spider are equal to planets,
where a wandering atom flares up like Saturn,
and, close by, harvesters drink from a cold jug
in scorching summer.

This I wanted and nothing more. In my later years
like old Goethe to stand before the face of the earth,
and recognize it and reconcile it
with my work built up, a forest citadel
on a river of shifting lights and brief shadows.

This I wanted and nothing more. So who
is guilty? Who deprived me
of my youth and my ripe years, who seasoned
my best years with horror? Who,
who ever is to blame, who, O God?

And I can think only about the starry sky,
about the tall mounds of termites.

Warsaw, 1943

The Poor Poet

The first movement is singing,
A free voice, filling mountains and valleys.
The first movement is joy,
But it is taken away.

And now that the years have transformed my blood
And thousands of planetary systems have been born and died in my
    flesh,
I sit, a sly and angry poet
With malevolently squinted eyes,
And, weighing a pen in my hand,
I plot revenge.

I poise the pen and it puts forth twigs and leaves, it is covered with
    blossoms
And the scent of that tree is impudent, for there, on the real earth,
Such trees do not grow, and like an insult
To suffering humanity is the scent of that tree.

Some take refuge in despair, which is sweet
Like strong tobacco, like a glass of vodka drunk in the hour of
    annihilation.
Others have the hope of fools, rosy as erotic dreams.

Still others find peace in the idolatry of country,
Which can last for a long time,
Although little longer than the nineteenth century lasts.

But to me a cynical hope is given,
For since I opened my eyes I have seen only the glow of fires,
    massacres,

Only injustice, humiliation, and the laughable shame of braggarts.
To me is given the hope of revenge on others and on myself,
For I was he who knew
And took from it no profit for myself.

Warsaw, 1944

Café

Of those at the table in the café
where on winter noons a garden of frost glittered on windowpanes
I alone survived.
I could go in there if I wanted to
and drumming my fingers in a chilly void
convoke shadows.

With disbelief I touch the cold marble,
with disbelief I touch my own hand.
It—is, and I—am in ever novel becoming,
while they are locked forever and ever
in their last word, their last glance,
and as remote as Emperor Valentinian
or the chiefs of the Massagetes, about whom I know nothing,
though hardly one year has passed, or two or three.

I may still cut trees in the woods of the far north,
I may speak from a platform or shoot a film
using techniques they never heard of.
I may learn the taste of fruits from ocean islands
and be photographed in attire from the second half of the century.
But they are forever like busts in frock coats and jabots
in some monstrous encyclopedia.

Sometimes when the evening aurora paints the roofs in a poor street
and I contemplate the sky, I see in the white clouds
a table wobbling. The waiter whirls with his tray

and they look at me with a burst of laughter
for I still don't know what it is to die at the hand of man,
they know—they know it well.

Warsaw, 1944

A Poor Christian Looks at the Ghetto

Bees build around red liver,
Ants build around black bone.
It has begun: the tearing, the trampling on silks,
It has begun: the breaking of glass, wood, copper, nickel, silver, foam
Of gypsum, iron sheets, violin strings, trumpets, leaves, balls, crystals.
Poof! Phosphorescent fire from yellow walls
Engulfs animal and human hair.

Bees build around the honeycomb of lungs,
Ants build around white bone.
Torn is paper, rubber, linen, leather, flax,
Fiber, fabrics, cellulose, snakeskin, wire.
The roof and the wall collapse in flame and heat seizes the
     foundations.
Now there is only the earth, sandy, trodden down,
With one leafless tree.

Slowly, boring a tunnel, a guardian mole makes his way,
With a small red lamp fastened to his forehead.
He touches buried bodies, counts them, pushes on,
He distinguishes human ashes by their luminous vapor,
The ashes of each man by a different part of the spectrum.
Bees build around a red trace.
Ants build around the place left by my body.

I am afraid, so afraid of the guardian mole.
He has swollen eyelids, like a Patriarch
Who has sat much in the light of candles
Reading the great book of the species.

What will I tell him, I, a Jew of the New Testament,
Waiting two thousand years for the second coming of Jesus?
My broken body will deliver me to his sight
And he will count me among the helpers of death:
The uncircumcised.

Warsaw, 1943

Outskirts

A hand with cards drops down
on the hot sand.
The sun turned white drops down
on the hot sand.
Ted holds the bank. Now Ted is dealing.
The glare stabs through the sticky pack
into hot sand.

A broken shadow of a chimney. Thin grass.
Farther on, the city torn into red brick.
Brown heaps, barbed wire tangled at stations.
Dry rib of a rusty automobile.
A claypit glitters.

An empty bottle buried
in the hot sand.
A drop of rain raised dust
off the hot sand.
Frank holds the bank. Now Frank is dealing.
We play, Julys and Mays go by.
We play one year, we play a fourth.
The glare pours through our blackened cards
into hot sand.

Farther on, the city torn into red brick.
A lone pine tree behind a Jewish house.
Loose footprints and the plain up to the horizon.
The dust of quicklime, wagons rolling,
and in the wagons a whining lament.

Take a mandolin, on the mandolin
you'll play it all.
Heigh-ho. Fingers, strings.
So nice a song.
A barren field.
The glass tossed off.
No more is needed.

Look, there she goes, a pretty girl.
Cork-soled slippers and curly hair.
Hello sweetheart, let's have a good time.
A barren field.
The sun is setting.

Warsaw, 1944

SONGS OF ADRIAN ZIELIŃSKI

1

The fifth spring of war is beginning.
A young girl is weeping for her lover.
Snow is melting in the Warsaw streets.

I thought my youth would last forever,
That I would always be the same.
And what remains? Fear in the early hours,
I peer at myself as at a plaque of blank, gray stone,
Looking for something I have known.

A carousel drones in the little square.
Somebody is shooting at somebody out there.
A light squall blows from the torpid river.

But what is all that to me?
I am like a child unable to tell a yellow dandelion
From a star. This isn't the wisdom
That I bargained for. What are centuries,
What is history? I hack out each day
And it's a century to me.

O Lord, throw me a tiny plume of your pity.

2

When I go to the fields, to the stunted forest,
To any stretch of wasted land
And observe how the first spring flowers
Are pushed up by a subterranean hand,
I want to bore a tunnel to the center of the earth
So that I can see Hell.
I want to pierce, for what it's worth,

That blue lake of the sun's rays
And have a look at Heaven.

And the heart of the earth, heavy with liquid gold,
And the cold void of whirling spheres
Would be all I'd find. There are no abysses.
Without end or beginning, Nature breeds
Nothing, except this: there is life, there is death,
It's over. There are no abysses.

If only the poorest of devils, Hell's bellhop,
Showed his horns from under the primrose leaf,
If only the angel in Heaven who chops wood
By beating his little wings waved down from a cloud.

Please, understand how hard it is when man alone
Must invent a new Heaven and Hell on earth.

3
First, people and trees: very big.
Then, people and trees: not so big.
Until the whole earth, fields and houses,
People, plants, animals, birds,
Have shrunk to the size of a May leaf,
Like wet clay squeezed in the hand.

You cannot even see yourself
Or your crooked path through the world.
Even the dead cannot be found.
They lie like cramped, black ants
In the sandy, amber-colored ground,
And no eye can pick them out.

Everything is so small that a real dog
Or a real bush of wild roses
Would be as immense as the pyramids,
The city gates to a boy just come
From a distant backwoods village.

I will not find a real rose,
Real moth, real stone, round and shiny.
For me, always, there will be this earth: tiny.

4
Somewhere there are happy cities.
Somewhere there are, but not for certain.
Where, between the market and the sea,
In a spray of sea mist,
June pours wet vegetables from baskets
And ice is carried to a café terrace
Sprinkled with sunlight, and flowers
Drop onto women's hair.

The ink of newspapers new every hour,
Disputes about what is good for the republic.
The teeming cinemas smell of orange peels
And a mandolin hums long into the night.
A bird flicking the dew of song before sunrise.

Somewhere there are happy cities,
But they are of no use to me.
I look into life and death as into an empty winecup.
Glittering buildings or the route of ruins.
Let me go away in peace.
There is a whisper of night that breathes in me.

They are dragging a guy by his stupid legs,
The calves in silk socks,
The head trailing behind.
And a stain in the sand a month of rain won't wash away.
Children with toy automatic pistols
Take a look, resume their play.

To see this or to enter an almond orchard
Or to stand with guitar at a sculpted gate.
Let me go away in peace.
This is not the same; possibly, it is the same.

5

The round ass of a girl passing by
Is a planet carved by sunlight's hand
For poor astronomers who watch the sky
As they sit with their bottle on the sand.

When they glimpse how the deep blue spreads
Across the sky, they are terrified.
Under that vastness, they hang their heads,
To them, the whole thing feels too wide.

They see the ass as it sways away:
Venus in their telescopes, warm as blood.
And spring's green shimmers like waves that play
Under bright Venus after the flood.

6

There is a whisper of night that breathes in me,
Little voices like cats lapping at my days,
And my profound subjugated storms
Erupt in a song of gratitude and praise.

What a wise man you are, Adrian.
You could be a Chinese poet,
You needn't care what century you're in.
You look at a flower
And smile at what you see.

How wise you are, how undeluded
By folly of history or passions of the race.
You walk serenely, the light, occluded,
Eternal, softening your face.

Peace to the house of the sage.
Peace to his prudent wonder.
————————————————
O black treason, black treason—
Thunder.

Warsaw, 1943–1944

FAREWELL

I speak to you, my son,
after years of silence. Verona is no more.
I crumbled its brickdust in my fingers. That is what remains
of the great love of native cities.

I hear your laughter in the garden. And the mad spring's
scent comes toward me across the wet leaves.
Toward me, who, not believing in any saving power,
outlived the others and myself as well.

Do you know how it is when one wakes
at night suddenly and asks,
listening to the pounding heart: what more do you want,
insatiable? Spring, a nightingale is singing.

Children's laughter in the garden. A first clear star
above a foam of buds on the hills
and a light song returns to my lips
and I am young again, as before, in Verona.

To reject. To reject everything. That is not it.
I will neither resurrect the past nor return.
Sleep, Romeo, Juliet, on your headrest of stone feathers.
I won't raise your bound hands from the ashes.
Let the cat visit the deserted cathedrals,
its pupil flashing on the altars. Let an owl
nest on the dead ogive.

In the white noon among the rubble, let the snake
warm itself on leaves of coltsfoot and in the silence
let him coil in lustrous circles around useless gold.
I won't return. I want to know what's left
after rejecting youth and spring,

after rejecting those red lips
from which heat seemed to flow
on sultry nights.

After songs and the scent of wine,
oaths and laments, diamond nights,
and the cry of gulls with the black sun
glaring behind them.

From life, from the apple cut by the flaming knife,
what grain will be saved?

My son, believe me, nothing remains.
Only adult toil,
the furrow of fate in the palm.
Only toil,
Nothing more.

Kraków, 1945

FLIGHT

When we were fleeing the burning city
And looked back from the first field path,
I said: "Let the grass grow over our footprints,
Let the harsh prophets fall silent in the fire,
Let the dead explain to the dead what happened.
We are fated to beget a new and violent tribe
Free from the evil and the happiness that drowsed there.
Let us go"—and the earth was opened for us by a sword of flames.

Goszyce, 1944

IN WARSAW

What are you doing here, poet, on the ruins
Of St. John's Cathedral this sunny
Day in spring?

What are you thinking here, where the wind
Blowing from the Vistula scatters
The red dust of the rubble?

You swore never to be
A ritual mourner.
You swore never to touch
The deep wounds of your nation
So you would not make them holy
With the accursed holiness that pursues
Descendants for many centuries.

But the lament of Antigone
Searching for her brother
Is indeed beyond the power
Of endurance. And the heart
Is a stone in which is enclosed,
Like an insect, the dark love
Of a most unhappy land.

I did not want to love so.
That was not my design.
I did not want to pity so.
That was not my design.
My pen is lighter
Than a hummingbird's feather. This burden
Is too much for it to bear.
How can I live in this country
Where the foot knocks against

The unburied bones of kin?
I hear voices, see smiles. I cannot
Write anything; five hands
Seize my pen and order me to write
The story of their lives and deaths.
Was I born to become
a ritual mourner?
I want to sing of festivities,
The greenwood into which Shakespeare
Often took me. Leave
To poets a moment of happiness,
Otherwise your world will perish.

It's madness to live without joy
And to repeat to the dead
Whose part was to be gladness
Of action in thought and in the flesh, singing, feasts,
Only the two salvaged words:
Truth and justice.

Warsaw, 1945

DEDICATION

You whom I could not save
Listen to me.
Try to understand this simple speech as I would be ashamed of
    another.
I swear, there is in me no wizardry of words.
I speak to you with silence like a cloud or a tree.

What strengthened me, for you was lethal.
You mixed up farewell to an epoch with the beginning of a new one,
Inspiration of hatred with lyrical beauty,
Blind force with accomplished shape.

Here is the valley of shallow Polish rivers. And an immense bridge
Going into white fog. Here is a broken city,
And the wind throws the screams of gulls on your grave
When I am talking with you.

What is poetry which does not save
Nations or people?
A connivance with official lies,
A song of drunkards whose throats will be cut in a moment,
Readings for sophomore girls.

That I wanted good poetry without knowing it,
That I discovered, late, its salutary aim,
In this and only this I find salvation.

They used to pour millet on graves or poppy seeds
To feed the dead who would come disguised as birds.
I put this book here for you, who once lived
So that you should visit us no more.

Warsaw, 1945

DAYLIGHT

(Światło dzienne)

1953

SONG ON PORCELAIN

Rose-colored cup and saucer,
Flowery demitasses:
You lie beside the river
Where an armored column passes.
Winds from across the meadow
Sprinkle the banks with down;
A torn apple tree's shadow
Falls on the muddy path;
The ground everywhere is strewn
With bits of brittle froth—
Of all things broken and lost
Porcelain troubles me most.

Before the first red tones
Begin to warm the sky
The earth wakes up, and moans.
It is the small sad cry
Of cups and saucers cracking,
The masters' precious dream
Of roses, of mowers raking,
And shepherds on the lawn.
The black underground stream
Swallows the frozen swan.
This morning, as I walked past,
The porcelain troubled me most.

The blackened plain spreads out
To where the horizon blurs
In a litter of handle and spout,
A lively pulp that stirs
And crunches under my feet.
Pretty, useless foam:
Your stained colors are sweet,

Spattered in dirty waves
Flecking the fresh black loam
In the mounds of these new graves.
In sorrow and pain and cost,
Sir, porcelain troubles me most.

Washington, D.C., 1947

CHILD OF EUROPE

1

We, whose lungs fill with the sweetness of day,
Who in May admire trees flowering,
Are better than those who perished.

We, who taste of exotic dishes,
And enjoy fully the delights of love,
Are better than those who were buried.

We, from the fiery furnaces, from behind barbed wires
On which the winds of endless autumns howled,
We, who remember battles where the wounded air roared in
    paroxysms of pain,
We, saved by our own cunning and knowledge.

By sending others to the more exposed positions,
Urging them loudly to fight on,
Ourselves withdrawing in certainty of the cause lost.

Having the choice of our own death and that of a friend,
We chose his, coldly thinking: let it be done quickly.

We sealed gas chamber doors, stole bread,
Knowing the next day would be harder to bear than the
    day before.

As befits human beings, we explored good and evil.
Our malignant wisdom has no like on this planet.

Accept it as proven that we are better than they,
The gullible, hot-blooded weaklings, careless with
    their lives.

2

Treasure your legacy of skills, child of Europe,
Inheritor of Gothic cathedrals, of baroque churches,
Of synagogues filled with the wailing of a wronged people.
Successor of Descartes, Spinoza, inheritor of the word
      "honor,"
Posthumous child of Leonidas,
Treasure the skills acquired in the hour of terror.

You have a clever mind which sees instantly
The good and bad of any situation.
You have an elegant, skeptical mind which enjoys pleasures
Quite unknown to primitive races.

Guided by this mind you cannot fail to see
The soundness of the advice we give you:
Let the sweetness of day fill your lungs.
For this we have strict but wise rules.

3

There can be no question of force triumphant.
We live in the age of victorious justice.

Do not mention force, or you will be accused
Of upholding fallen doctrines in secret.

He who has power, has it by historical logic.
Respectfully bow to that logic.

Let your lips, proposing a hypothesis,
Not know about the hand faking the experiment.

Let your hand, faking the experiment,
Not know about the lips proposing a hypothesis.

Learn to predict a fire with unerring precision.
Then burn the house down to fulfill the prediction.

4
Grow your tree of falsehood from a small grain of truth.
Do not follow those who lie in contempt of reality.

Let your lie be even more logical than the truth itself,
So the weary travelers may find repose in the lie.

After the Day of the Lie gather in select circles,
Shaking with laughter when our real deeds are mentioned.

Dispensing flattery called: perspicacious thinking.
Dispensing flattery called: a great talent.

We, the last who can still draw joy from cynicism.
We, whose cunning is not unlike despair.

A new, humorless generation is now arising,
It takes in deadly earnest all we received with laughter.

5
Let your words speak not through their meanings,
But through them against whom they are used.

Fashion your weapon from ambiguous words.
Consign clear words to lexical limbo.

Judge no words before the clerks have checked
In their card index by whom they were spoken.

The voice of passion is better than the voice of reason.
The passionless cannot change history.

6
Love no country: countries soon disappear.
Love no city: cities are soon rubble.

Throw away keepsakes, or from your desk
A choking, poisonous fume will exude.

Do not love people: people soon perish.
Or they are wronged and call for your help.

Do not gaze into the pools of the past.
Their corroded surface will mirror
A face different from the one you expected.

7
He who invokes history is always secure.
The dead will not rise to witness against him.

You can accuse them of any deeds you like.
Their reply will always be silence.

Their empty faces swim out of the deep dark.
You can fill them with any features desired.

Proud of dominion over people long vanished,
Change the past into your own, better likeness.

8

The laughter born of the love of truth
Is now the laughter of the enemies of the people.

Gone is the age of satire. We no longer need mock
The senile monarch with false courtly phrases.

Stern as befits the servants of a cause,
We will permit ourselves only sycophantic humor.

Tight-lipped, guided by reasons only,
Cautiously let us step into the era of the unchained fire.

New York, 1946

MID-TWENTIETH-CENTURY
PORTRAIT

Hidden behind his smile of brotherly regard,
He despises the newspaper reader, the victim of the dialectic of power.
Says: "Democracy," with a wink.
Hates the physiological pleasures of mankind,
Full of memories of those who also ate, drank, copulated,
But in a moment had their throats cut.
Recommends dances and garden parties to defuse public anger.

Shouts: "Culture!" and "Art!" but means circus games really.

Utterly spent.
Mumbles in sleep or anaesthesia: "God, oh God!"
Compares himself to a Roman in whom the Mithras cult has mixed
    with the cult of Jesus.
Still clings to old superstitions, sometimes believes himself to be
    possessed by demons.
Attacks the past, but fears that, having destroyed it,
He will have nothing on which to lay his head.
Likes most to play cards, or chess, the better to keep his own counsel.

Keeping one hand on Marx's writings, he reads the Bible in private.
His mocking eye on processions leaving burned-out churches.
His backdrop: a horseflesh-colored city in ruins.
In his hand: a memento of a boy "fascist" killed in the Uprising.

Kraków, 1945

A NATION

The purest of nations on earth when it's judged by a flash of lightning,
But thoughtless and sly in everyday toil.

Pitiless to its widows and orphans, pitiless to its old people,
Stealing a crust of bread from a child's hand.

Ready to offer their lives to draw Heaven's wrath on their foes,
Smiting their enemy with the screams of orphans and women.

Entrusting power to men with the eyes of traders in gold,
Elevating men with the conscience of brothel-keepers.

The best of its sons remain unknown,
They appear once only, to die on the barricades.

Bitter tears of that people cut a song off in the middle,
And when the song dies away, noisy voices tell jokes.

A shadow stands in a corner, pointing to his heart,
Outside a dog howls to the invisible planet.

Great nation, invincible nation, ironic nation.
They know how to distinguish truth and yet to keep silent.

They camp on marketplaces, conversing in wisecracks,
They deal in old door handles stolen from ruins.

A nation in crumpled caps, carrying all they own,
They go west and south searching for a place to live.

It has no cities, no monuments, no painting or sculpture,
Only the word passed from mouth to mouth and prophecy of poets.

A man of that nation, standing by his son's cradle,
Repeats words of hope, always, till now, in vain.

Kraków, 1945

BIRTH

For the first time he sees light.
The world is garish light.
He doesn't know these are shrieks
Of garish birds.
Their hearts beat quickly
Under enormous leaves.
He doesn't know birds live
In another time than man.
He doesn't know a tree lives
In another time than birds
And will grow slowly
Upward in a gray column
Thinking with its roots
Of the silver of underworld kingdoms.

The last of the tribe, he comes
After great magic dances.
After the dance of the Antelope,
After the dance of the Winged Snakes
Under an eternally blue sky
In a valley of brick-red mountains.

He comes after spotted thongs
On a shield with a monster's face,
After deities who send down
Dreams by their painted eyelid,
After the rust of carved ships
Which the wind has forgotten.

He comes, after grating of swords
And voice of battle horns,
After the weird mass shriek
In the dust of shattered brick

After the flutter of fans
Over a joke of warm teacups,
After swan lake dances,
And after a steam engine.

Wherever he steps, there always
Endures traced in sand
A large-toed footprint
Which clamors to be tried out
By his childish foot arriving
Out of the virgin forests.

Wherever he goes, he always
Will find on things of the earth
A warm luster furbished
By a human hand.
This will never leave him,
It will stay with him always,
A presence close as breath,
His only wealth.

Washington, D.C., 1947

A FAMILY

On a sultry morning, Mother
Wears only her light-brown breast,
Father is soaping his cheeks
Under an iridescent light.
Is it not strange, they say,
That the currents of our bodies
Are unable to impart
Any of the things we have seen?
Memory resides in us only,
Our dreams have their anchor
In the burning ember, deep,
By the chambers of the sea.
For the child our tale is alien
As the words of Josephus Flavius,
Or Gibbon's *Decline and Fall*
Of the Roman Empire.

Yet already we see him walking
Between the broken columns
And dressing building-stones
For his one-room house.
The vineyard has grown wild,
Water-hens are calling
And books with gilded backs
Serve as stands for milk.
Oh, could but our hearts
Construct a star
Stationed above his house
When he will sit on the threshold
And, from under the burdocks
Tall as if they were pines,

Through thick green rafters,
Will glance at the inhabited
Classical sky.

Washington, D.C., 1947

OCEAN

A gentle tongue lapping
Small chubby knees,
Envoys bringing salt
From a billion-year-old abyss.
Here are violet thistles,
Peached suns of jellyfish,
Here with airplane fins
And skin of graters, sharks
Visit the museum of death
Under water-towers of crystal.
A dolphin shows from a wave
The face of a black boy,
In the liquid cities of the desert
Graze leviathans.

Washington, D.C., 1947

THE JOURNEY

In pink fingers of magnolia,
In the downy softness of May,
In the leap from branch to branch
Of a bird, pure-colored, a cardinal,
Between breasts of calm rivers
Lies this city
Into which I ride with a bouquet of stiff roses
On my knees, like the jack of hearts,
Shouting for joy of spring
And the shortness of life.

Waves of scent, a song,
Wet armfuls of purple flowers
Shaken off by a black hand,
Tunnels of neon lights,
The green, and a song again,
Bridges over the birds' realms,
Streetlights—teddy bears' eyes
Made of rubies.

Afternoon whiskers,
Thorny braids of black girls,
Cool drinks, shadowy glasses
At lips painted in the shape of a heart,
Mannequins with thighs in silk,
Constantly combed cemeteries
Recede into night, rocket-like,
Into a bursting night
Tralala
Tralali
Into oblivion.

Washington, D.C., 1948

THE SPIRIT OF THE LAWS

From the cry of children on the floors of stations beyond time,
From the sadness of the engineer of prison trains,
From the red scars of two wars on the forehead,
I awoke under the bronze of winged monuments,
Under the griffins of a Masonic temple
With the dying ash of a cigar.

It was a summer of plane trees in colonnades and pearls of birds
        poured from the dawn,
A summer of joined hands, of black, of violet,
A summer of blue bees, of whistles, of flames
And the tiny propellers of a hummingbird.

And I, with my pine anchor on a sandy plain,
With the silenced memory of dead friends
And the silenced memory of towns and rivers,
I was ready to tear out the heart of the earth with a knife
And put there a glowing diamond of shouts and complaints,
I was ready to smear the bottom of roots with blood
To invoke the names on their leaves,
To cover the malachite of monuments with the skin of night
And write down with phosphorus Mene Tekel Upharsin,
Shining with the traces of melting eyelids.

I could go to the riverside where lovers
Look at the remnants of games floating to the sea,
I could enter parking lots, iridescent soap bubbles
And listen to the laboring
Of the eternal humanity of muted notes,
Of industrious, agile male muscles
Over a hot butterfly of carmine.

Gardens hopping down to the bottom of ravines,
The national dances of gray squirrels
And the white laboratories of winged infants
Always growing up in a different epoch,
The shine, the juice, the rouge of the day
All of it
Seemed to be the beginning of the sun on yellow plains
Where in railway stations at a wobbling table,
Sitting over an empty glass, their faces in their hands,
Are the sad engineers of prison trains.

Washington, D.C., 1947

A LEGEND

Nobody knows the beginning of the city.
Slushy ruts, a call at the ferry,
Resin torches, a fisherman leaning on a spear,
And fish pots and the mists of the shallows.
Then the riders with lances lead in
Half-naked prisoners and pine after pine
Falls down and with huge timbers
A castle is erected above the swift river.
Dark rafters. The whirling of dogs
Crunching bones in the gleam of shields and swords,
Shaky rush-lights and whiskered shadows
Bent over pewter goblets, raucous songs.
In bedchambers, amid spearshafts and leather bands,
Giggling of old gods. In the thicket at night
Their wild stomping and whistling. And yet already a bell
Trickled its tiny voice through the wilderness,
And the monks, raised on their stirrups,
Were turning toward the people below
Who, uncertain, faltered between their rite
And the force of the new imperious laws.

Who knows the beginning? We lived in this city
Without caring about its past. Its walls
Seemed to us eternal. Those who lived there before us
Were just a legend, undeciphered.
Our age is better, we would say. No plague, no sword
To pursue us, so why should we look back?
Let the centuries of terror sleep in the hard earth.
We tuned our instruments, evenings
In a circle of friends would bring us gladness,
Under the colorful lanterns and the green of chestnuts

Feasts were celebrated. The slenderness of our women
Pleased our eyes. Our painters used to choose
Joyous colors. Till that day arrived.

The makeup streamed down women's cheeks. Their rings
Rattled against the pavement. Eyes
Turned to the indifferent abysses of heavens
And accepted death. Foundations of ornate buildings
Burst, the dust of crushed brick
Rose with smoke to the sun, pigeons
Were falling from the sky. We propped our street fortresses
Against the rubble of our homes, till they fell,
Our fortresses, and hands, and arms. The smell of defeat,
Cadaverous, nauseating, atrocious silence
After the din of battle descended on smoldering cinders,
The autumn rain beat down and the survivors
Received upon their brows the stigma of the slave.
The enemy debased memory, ascribing to himself
Both ancient and future glory.

And then, sitting where once it had stood,
That beautiful city, sifting through our fingers
The sand of the barrens, we discovered
The sweet name of our country. It was no more
Than the sand and the rustle of the wind in wormwood.
For a country without a past is nothing, a word
That, hardly spoken, loses its meaning,
A perishable wall destroyed by flame,
An echo of animal emotions. In the sand we saw
The ashes of centuries mixed with fresh blood.

Pride then left us and we rendered homage
To men and women who once lived and ever since
We have had our home founded in history.

Washington, D.C., 1949

EARTH

My sweet European homeland,

A butterfly lighting on your flowers stains its wings with blood,
Blood gathers in the mouths of tulips,
Shines, star-like, inside a morning glory
And washes the grains of wheat.

Your people warm their hands
At the funeral candle of a primrose
And hear on the fields the wind howling
In the cannons ready to be fired.

You are a land where it's no shame to suffer
For one is served here a glass of bitter liquor
With lees, the poison of centuries.

On your broken evening of wet leaves,
By the waters that carry the rust
Of centurions' sunken armor,
At the foot of blasted towers,
In the shadow of their spans like aqueducts,
Under the quiet canopy of an owl's wings,

A red poppy, touched by the ice of tears.

Washington, D.C., 1949

YOU WHO WRONGED

You who wronged a simple man
Bursting into laughter at the crime,
And kept a pack of fools around you
To mix good and evil, to blur the line,

Though everyone bowed down before you,
Saying virtue and wisdom lit your way,
Striking gold medals in your honor,
Glad to have survived another day,

Do not feel safe. The poet remembers.
You can kill one, but another is born.
The words are written down, the deed, the date.

And you'd have done better with a winter dawn,
A rope, and a branch bowed beneath your weight.

Washington, D.C., 1950

MITTELBERGHEIM

Wine sleeps in casks of Rhine oak.
I am wakened by the bell of a chapel in the vineyards
Of Mittelbergheim. I hear a small spring
Trickling into a well in the yard, a clatter
Of sabots in the street. Tobacco drying
Under the eaves, and ploughs and wooden wheels
And mountain slopes and autumn are with me.

I keep my eyes closed. Do not rush me,
You, fire, power, might, for it is too early.
I have lived through many years and, as in this half-dream,
I felt I was attaining the moving frontier
Beyond which color and sound come true
And the things of this earth are united.
Do not yet force me to open my lips.
Let me trust and believe I will attain.
Let me linger here in Mittelbergheim.

I know I should. They are with me,
Autumn and wooden wheels and tobacco hung
Under the eaves. Here and everywhere
Is my homeland, wherever I turn
And in whatever language I would hear
The song of a child, the conversation of lovers.
Happier than anyone, I am to receive
A glance, a smile, a star, silk creased
At the knee. Serene, beholding,
I am to walk on hills in the soft glow of day
Over waters, cities, roads, human customs.

Fire, power, might, you who hold me
In the palm of your hand whose furrows
Are like immense gorges combed

By southern wind. You who grant certainty
In the hour of fear, in the week of doubt,
It is too early, let the wine mature,
Let the travelers sleep in Mittelbergheim.

Alsace, 1951

A TREATISE
ON POETRY

(Traktat poetycki)

✦

1957

PREFACE

First, plain speech in the mother tongue.
Hearing it you should be able to see,
As if in a flash of summer lightning,
Apple trees, a river, the bend of a road.

And it should contain more than images.
Singsong lured it into being,
Melody, a daydream. Defenseless,
It was bypassed by the dry, sharp world.

You often ask yourself why you feel shame
Whenever you look through a book of poems.
As if the author, for reasons unclear to you,
Addressed the worst side of your nature,
Pushing thought aside, cheating thought.

Poetry, seasoned with satire, clowning,
Jokes, still knows how to please.
Then its excellence is much admired.
But serious combat, where life is at stake,
Is fought in prose. It was not always so.

And our regret has remained unconfessed.
Novels and essays serve but will not last.
One clear stanza can take more weight
Than a whole wagon of elaborate prose.

I. BEAUTIFUL TIMES

Kraków 1900–1914

Cabbies were dozing by St. Mary's tower.
Kraków was tiny as a painted egg
Just taken from a pot of dye on Easter.
In their black capes poets strolled the streets.
Nobody remembers their names today,
And yet their hands were real once,
And their cufflinks gleamed above a table.
An *Ober* brings the paper on a stick
And coffee, then passes away like them
Without a name. Muses, Rachels in trailing shawls,
Put tongues to lips while pinning up their braids.
The pin lies with their daughters' ashes now,
Or in a glass case next to mute seashells
And a glass lily. Angels of Art Nouveau
In the dark WC's of their parents' homes,
Meditating on the link between sex and the soul,
Went to Vienna for migraines and the blues
(Dr. Freud, I hear, is also from Galicia),
And Anna Csilag grew her long, long hair.
The hussars' tunics were trimmed out with braid.
News of the emperor spread through mountain villages.
Someone had seen his carriage in the valley.

This is our beginning. Useless to deny it.
Useless to recall a distant golden age.
We have to accept and take as our own
The mustache with pomade, the bowler hat acock.
Also the jingle of a tombac watch chain.
It's ours, the worker's song, the mug of beer
In factory towns black as heavy cloth.
The match struck at dawn and the twelve hours
Labor to make wealth and progress out of smoke.

Lament, Europe! And wait for a *Schiffskarte*.
On a December evening in the port at Rotterdam
A ship full of immigrants stands silent
Under the frozen masts like snow-clad firs.
A chorus, or litany, breaks from below deck
In some peasant, Slovenian or Polish, dialect.
A pianola, hit by a bullet, begins to play.
A quadrille in a saloon drives the wild couples,
And she, fat, red-haired, snapping her garter,
In fluffy slippers, her thighs sprawling
Waits on a throne, she, mystery,
For traveling salesmen of Salvarsan and condoms.

This is our beginning. A cinematograph:
Max Linder leads a cow and falls down flat.
In open-air cafés lamps shine through the leaves.
A women's orchestra blows into trombones.

Till from hands, jeweled rings, lilac corsets,
From the ashes of cigars, it all unwinds, meanders
Through forests, lowlands, mountains, plains—
The command *"Vorwarts!" "En avant!" "Allez!"*

There are our hearts, sprinkled with quicklime
On empty fields that have been licked by flame.
And nobody knew why it suddenly ended,
—A pianola played—progress and wealth.

Our style, unpleasant to say it, was born there.
The sound of a lyre from a garret window
Hums in the dawn above a *Tingeltangel*,
The song as ethereal as the creaking stars,
Not needed by tradesmen and their wives, not needed

By the peasant farmers in a mountain village,
A pure thing, against the sad affairs of earth.
Pure, forbidden the use of certain words:
Toilet, telephone, ticket, ass, money.

A muse with long hair learns to read
In the dark toilet of her parents' home
And knows already what is not poetry,
Which is only a mood and a breeze. It dwells
In three dots, followed by a comma.

It flows and waves, ineffable. A stand-in
For religion, and such it will remain.
The breath of normal syntax will be banned:
"Eh, journalism. Let them write in prose."
Then, in the schools of a new avant-garde,
They will call this old injunction a discovery.
Not all poets vanished without a trace.
Kasprowicz roared, tore at the silken tethers
Yet could not break them: they were invisible.
And not tethers, they were more like bats
Sucking the blood out of speech on the fly.
Leopold Staff was the color of honey.
He praised witches, gnomes, and the rains of spring.
His praise was as if in a world of as if.
As to Leśmian, he drew his own conclusions:
If it's all a dream, let's dream it to the bottom.

In Kraków, on a narrow little street,
Two boys lived not far from one another.
When one of them walked to St. Anne's school,
He saw the other playing in the sand.
They had different fates, different fames.

For the sailor oceans, vast, incomprehensible,
Islands where naked tribes sounded a conch
Beyond a coral reef. The moment still exists
When, in a deserted street, in humid Brussels,
He walked slowly up the marble stairs
And pushed a bell marked by the letter S,
The Anonymous Society, listened to the silence,
Entered. Two women, knitting, pulled at threads—
They seemed to him Parcae—, then put away
Their skeins and gestured toward a door,
Behind which rose the managing director,
Also anonymous, to shake his hand.
It was in this way that Joseph Conrad
Came to captain a steamer on the Congo,
As was fated. For those who would hear it,
His tale of a jungle river was a warning:
One of the civilizers, a madman named Kurtz,
A gatherer of ivory stained with blood,
Scribbled in the margin of his report
On the Light of Culture: "The horror." And climbed
Into the twentieth century.
                      Meanwhile
In a Krakóvian village, peasant costumes,
Wedding dances until daybreak to the tune
Of a double bass, also a puppet theater,
The same for centuries. Indomitable Wyspiański
Dreamed of a national theater, as in Greece.
He couldn't overcome the contradiction.
His medium deformed his vision and our speech.
It would make us prisoners of history,
Not persons, traces of persons, on a seal
Stamped only with the style of a time.
Wyspiański has not been of help to us.

As heritage we received another monument:
Conceived as a joke, not for any glory,
As much of the language as a street song,
A thumbing of the nose at abstract thought.
A pity it's a trifle: *Little Words* by Boy.
That day fades. Someone has lit the candles.
On Oleandry field the locks of the carbines
Don't click anymore, the plain is empty.
The aesthetes in infantry boots have departed.
Their hair has been swept from the barber's floor.
Fog and a smell of smoke hang about the place.

And she, she wears a lilac-colored veil.
By candlelight she puts her fingers to the keys
And while the doctor fills glasses with liqueur
She sings an air that seems to come from nowhere:

The laughter in cafés
Echoes about a hero's grave.

II. THE CAPITAL

Warsaw, 1918–1939

You, alien city on a dusty plain,
Under the cupola of the Orthodox cathedral,
Your music was the fifes of regiments,
The Cavalry Guard was your soldier of soldiers,
From a droshky rings a lewd Caucasian ditty.
Thus one should begin an ode to you, Warsaw,
To your grief and debauchery and misery.
A street vendor, hands clumsy with cold,
Measures out a peck of sunflower seeds.
An ensign elopes with a railwayman's daughter.
He will make her a princess in Elisavetgrad.

At Czerniakowski Street, at Górna and Wola,
Black Mary carouses in the humming dives.
Upstairs she lifts a muslin skirt with frills.

And you are ruled, City, from a citadel.
Cossack horses prick their ears at the echo
Of a song: "Red banners wave above the thrones."

You have enough administering a province.
You, an amusement park on the Vistula,
How could you become the capital of a state
Crowded with refugees from the Ukraine
Peddling jewels from their manors near Odessa?
A saber, rifles from French army surplus,
These will have to serve you in your battles.
They are striking against you—ridiculous—
On the London docks and in enlightened
    Prague.

And so volunteers in the propaganda offices
Write articles about the onslaught from the East.
They don't know that, one day, harsh brasses will play
The "Internationale" above their graves.

Yet you exist. With your blackened ghetto,
The somnolent anger of your unemployed,
Your women's tears and their prewar shawls.

For years Piłsudski paced in the Belvedere.
He could never believe in permanence.
And would say again: "They will attack us."
Who? He pointed to the East, the West.
"I've stopped the wheel of history a moment."

Morning glories will sprout from spots of blood.
Where wheat is kneeling, boulevards will rise.
And a generation will ask how that moment felt.

Till not one stone, O city, remains
Upon a stone, and you too will pass away.
Flame will consume the painted history.
Your memory will become a dug-up coin.
And for your disasters this is your reward:
As a sign that language only is your home,
Your ramparts will be built by poets.

A poet needs, first, to issue from good stock,
To have a saintly tzaddic in his lineage.
His parents, of course, would have read Lassalle,
Believed in progress and lieder from Berlin.

Refinement distills itself slowly. Some
Came from much less fancy folk, from gentry
Or burghers, even from a German in a nightcap.

Noisy at the Picadore they did not guess
That laurels sometimes have a bitter taste.
Tuwim dilated his nostrils when reciting,
Shouted "*Ça ira!*" in Grodno or Tykocin,
And set the crowd of native youth trembling
At a sound belated by a hundred years.
He would meet his admirers who survived
Years later at a ball for the Security Police,
Which brought a fiery circle to its close:
The ball at the Senator goes on and on.
Lechoń-Herostrates trampled on the past.
He wanted to see green spring, not Poland.
Yet he was to meditate all his life
On Old Poland's dress and antique manners,
Or on religion, Polish, not Catholic,
And made of poor Or-Ot its priest.

What of Słonimski, sad and noble-minded?
Who thought the time of reason was at hand,
Giving himself to the future, proclaiming it
In the manner of Wells, or some other manner.
When the sky of Reason had grown bloodred,
He gave his waning years to Aeschylus,
Promised grandchildren the sight of Prometheus
Coming down a mountain in the Caucasus.

Iwaszkiewicz built his house of brilliant stones,
Indifferent to the call of public virtue.

Later on, an orator and citizen
Under the pressure of harsh necessity.
To recognize that everything is relative—
For a simple reason, because it passes—
He praised Slavic virtues to the folk,
Accompanied by a lively peasant band.
It was, all in all, a melancholy fate.

Not morally superior, just more proud,
That solitude among American winters.
The trace of a bird in snow, as always.
Time doesn't hurt anymore, nor help much.
A blue jay, kin to the Carpathian one,
Would peer into Wierzyński's window.
Oh, in the end there is a price exacted
For a young man's joy, for spring and wine.

There had never been such a Pléiade!
Yet something in their speech was flawed,
A flaw of harmony, as in their masters.
The transformed choir did not much resemble
The disorderly choir of ordinary things.

It was there everything sprouted, fermented,
Deeper than a rounded word can reach.
Tuwim lived in awe, twisted his fingers,
His face broke out in reddish, hectic spots.
One could say that he fooled the officials,
Just as he later cheated earnest Communists.
It choked him. Inside his scream was another:
That human life was chaos and a marvel,

That we walk, eat, talk, and at the same time
The light of eternity shines on our souls.

There are those who see a pretty, smiling girl
And imagine a skeleton with rings on the bones.
Such was Tuwim. He aspired to long poems.
But his thought was conventional, used
As easily as he used assonance and rhyme,
To cover his visions, of which he grew ashamed.

Whoever, in this century, forms letters
In ordered lines on a sheet of paper
Hears knockings, the voices of poor spirits
Imprisoned in a table, a wall, a vase
Of flowers. They seem to want to remind us
Whose hands brought all these objects into being.
Hours of labor, boredom, hopelessness
Live inside things and will not disappear.
The one who holds the pen, to whom this world
Of things is given, feels uneasy, is afraid.
He tries to achieve a childish innocence,
But the magic had fled from magic spells.

That's why it was that the new generation
Liked these poets only moderately,
Paid them tribute, but with a certain anger.
It wanted to stutter programmatically,
For a stutterer at least expressed a sense.
Nor did Broniewski win their admiration,
Though he took something strong from underground
Worked up as stanzas for the working class.
The Spring of Nations, for the second time,
Turned out to be melodious bel canto.

What they really wanted was a new Whitman
Who, amidst the wagoners and lumbermen,
Would make everyday life shine out like the sun.
Who would see in tongs, hammers, planes and chisels
Brilliant man running through the cosmos.

In the swarm of the Kraków avant-garde
Only Przyboś merits our surprise.
Nations and countries crumbled to dust,
To ashes, and Przyboś remained Przyboś.
No madness ate at his heart, which is human,
And thus intelligible. What was his secret?
In Shakespeare's time they called it euphuism.
A style composed of metaphor entirely.
Przyboś was a rationalist deep down.
He felt what a reasonable social person
Was supposed to feel, thought what they thought.
He wanted to put motion into static images.

And the avant-garde made the usual mistake.
They renovated an old Krakóvian rite:
Ascribing to language more importance
Than it could, without ridicule, sustain.
They must have known that from clenched jaws
Their voice issued in a strange falsetto
And that their dream of a folkish strength
Was the subterfuge of a frightened art.

Let us reach deeper. This was a time of schism.
"God and country" had ceased to be a lure.
A poet despised a cavalry officer more
Than bohemians had once despised a banker.
He mocked national banners and a show of flag,

Would spit when a crowd of screaming youths
Marched, wielding canes, against a Jewish merchant.

The end was prepared in advance. It was not
For lack of armor and cannon that the Republic fell.
In Poland a poet is a barometer,
Even if he published in *Linia* or *Kwadryga*.
A skein of common values came undone.
No common faith bound our minds together.
Those who saw took refuge in irony
And lived in the crowd as on a desert island.
One of those who understood pretended
To worship the gods the nation worshipped.

Gałczyński wanted to fall on his knees.
His story contains an elemental truth,
Namely, that a poet without community
Rustles in the wind like dry grass in December.
It's not up to him to put custom in doubt
Unless he's ready to be ostracized.
Let it be stated here clearly: the Party
Descends directly from the fascist Right.
Outside of them there was never anything
But rebels whose posturing merited scorn.
Who resurrected the sword of Bolesław the Brave?
Who drove pillars into the bottom of the Oder?
And who recognized that the way to power
Was to blow on the coals of national passions?

Gałczyński tied these elements together:
Jeering at the middle class, evoking Scythian

Virtues, penning a Polish Horst Wessel lied.
His fame has burgeoned through two epochs.

Czechowicz, the bucolic, was quite different.
Thatched huts, a patch of cumin and carrots,
A clear, lustrous morning by the river,
Which carries the echo of a Kuyavian dance
Sung by women washing linen in a stream.
He loved everything small. He made the idyll
Of a land with no politics and no defenses.
Be good to him, you birds and trees. Guard him,
From ravaging time protect his grave in Lublin.

Not one nation but a hundred nations
Appealed to Szenwald. And though a Stalinist
He knew how to profit from Marx and the Greeks.
A scene by a brook: a school excursion encounters
Barefoot peasant children stealing wood for fuel.
Or the tale of a little worker's child for whom
A bicycle is miracle and inspiration.
Poetry has nothing to do with morals,
As Szenwald, a Red Army lieutenant, proved.
At a time when, in the gulags of the north,
The corpses of a hundred nations whitened,
He was writing an ode to Mother Siberia,
One of the finer Polish-language poems.

On a steep street somewhere a schoolboy
Comes home from the library, carrying a book.
The book has a title: *Afloat in the Forest*.
Stained by the fingers of diligent Indians.
A ray of sunlight on Amazon lianas,

Leaves spreading on the green water in mats
So thick a man can walk across them.
The dreamer wanders from one bank to the other,
The monkeys, brown and hairy as a nut,
Make hanging bridges in trees above his head.

He is the future reader of our poets.
Impervious to crooked fences, the calling of crows
In cloudy skies, he lives among his marvels,
And, if he survives destruction, it is he
Who will preserve with tenderness his guides,
Iwaszkiewicz, Lechoń, and Słonimski.
Wierzyński and Tuwim will live forever
As they lived in his young and ardent mind.
He won't ask who is greater, who is less,
Finding in each of them a different nuance,
While a pirogue takes him up some Amazon.

For him Wittlin puts a spoonful of soup
Into the grizzled mouth of human hunger,
Baliński hears bells of a meandering caravan
In the rosy gray dusks of dusty Isfahan.
Wazyk eyes the ship model in a window
And a wave sparkles in the poems of Apollinaire.
And there was, to be heard, the exquisite lament
of a Polish Sappho, Ursula's, renewed
After four hundred years. Life fades quickly
And the turning disk preserves, longer even
Than the velvet of Caruso, that complaint
Of Maria Pawlikowska: "*Perchè? Perchè?*"
Perhaps it was not for nothing, the soldier's blood
Darkening into small stars beneath a birch.

Piłsudski should not shoulder all the blame—
Though he cared only for a secure border.
He bought us twenty years, he wore a cloak
Of injury and guilt, so that beauty
Had a little space to grow, though beauty is,
It's often said, a matter of no importance.

Young reader, you won't live inside a rose.
That country has its planets, its rivers,
But it is as frail as the edge of the morning.
It's we who create it every day anew,
By respecting as real many more things
Than are frozen between a noun and its sound.
We wrest them into the world by force.
If got too easily, they don't exist at all.
So, farewell, things gone. Your echo calls us,
But we need to speak gracelessly and roughly.

The last poem of the epoch went to print.
Its author, Władysław Sebyła,
Liked to take his violin from the wardrobe,
Putting its case by the volumes of Norwid.
He kept the collar of his blue uniform
Unbuttoned (He worked for the railway at Praga).
In that poem, as if it were his last will,
Poland is the ancient, two-faced god
Swiatowid, listening as the drums beat closer
On plains to the east, plains to the west,
While in its sleep the country dreams of bees
Buzzing through noons in Hesperidian groves.
Was it for this they shot him in the head
And buried his body in a Smolensk forest?

A beautiful night. A huge, lambent moon
Pours down a light that only happens
In September. In the hours before dawn
The air above Warsaw is utterly silent.
Barrage balloons hang like ripened fruit
In a sky just grown silvery with dawn.

On Tamka Street a girl's heels click.
She calls in a half whisper. They go together
To an empty lot overgrown with weeds.
A watchman on duty, hidden in the shadows,
Hears their soft voices in the bedding dark.
I do not know how to bear my pity.

Or how to find words for our common plight.
A little whore and a worker from Tamka.
Before them, the terror of the rising sun.
Later I would ask myself more than once
What became of them in the coming years and ages.

III. THE SPIRIT OF HISTORY

Warsaw, 1939–1945

When gold paint flakes from the arms of sculptures,
When the letter falls out of the book of laws,
Then consciousness is naked as an eye.

When the pages of books fall in fiery scraps
Onto smashed leaves and twisted metal,
The tree of good and evil is stripped bare.

When a wing made of canvas is extinguished
In a potato patch, when steel disintegrates,
Nothing is left but straw huts and cow dung.

In Masovian forests, on needle-covered paths,
Between the Reich and the General Government,
The flat feet of a peasant woman in the sand.
She stops, backs her burden against a pine
And pulls a thorn from her dust-covered foot.
A slab of butter in a wet rag is molded
To the shape of her archaic shoulder bones.
There's a shuffle for places at the ferry.

Chickens cackle. Geese stretch their necks from baskets.
In the town, a bullet is carving a dry trace
In the sidewalk near bags of homegrown tobacco.
All night long, on the outskirts of the city,
An old Jew, tossed in a clay pit, has been dying.
His moans subside only when the sun comes up.
The Vistula is gray, it washes through osiers
And fashions fans of gravel in the shallows.
An overburdened steamer, with its smugglers' load,
Churns up white froth with its paddle wheel.

Stanisław, or Henryk, sounds the bottom with a pole.
"Meter." Chlup. "Meter." Chlup. "Meter Twenty."

Where wind carries the smell of the crematorium
And a bell in the village tolls the Angelus,
The Spirit of History is out walking.
He whistles, he likes these countries washed
By a deluge, deprived of shape and now ready.
A worm-fence, a homespun skirt is pleasant to him,
The same in Poland, in India, Arabia.

He stretches his thick fingers toward the sky.
Under his palm, a rider on a bicycle:
The organizer of a security network,
A delegate of the military faction in London.
Poplars, as tiny as rye plants in a gully,
Conduct the eye to the roof of a manor
From the forest, and there, in the dining room,
Tired boys are lounging in officers' boots.
A poet has already recognized the walker,
An inferior god to whom time and the fate
Of one-day-long kingdoms is submitted.
His face is the size of ten moons. He wears
About his neck a chain of severed heads.
Who does not acknowledge him begins to
    mumble.
Whoever bows to him attracts his scorn.

Lutes, arcadian groves, and leaves of laurel,
Bright ladies, princes with consorts, where are you?
You could be courted with a well-turned phrase,
A graceful leap to catch a bag of gold.
He asks for more. He asks for flesh and blood.

Who are you, Powerful One? The nights are long.
Do we know you as the Spirit of the Earth,
Shaking down caterpillars from an apple tree
So that the thrushes have an easy gleaning?
Who gathers beetles' legs for a fecund humus
From which in time the hyacinth flowers?

Are you and he the same, O Destroyer?
He, inseparable, our faithful companion,
How many times has he guided our hand
Along the shoulder and neck of a girl,
When couples walked in the dusks of July
Through a meadow, in the scent of pines,
While a harmonium plays a melody, unreal,
About lemon trees and an island of lovers
So utterly lost it is painful to think of?
How many times has he, beauty and glory,
Splendor and the mating cries of grouse,
Curled our lips into an ironic smile
By whispering in our ears that spring,
the nightingale's trill, our own inspiration,
Are his prodigal lures, so that the law
Of the species is fulfilled. It will cool,
our blood, and we, touched by rust, dressed
In our cloaks of fading purple, will fall
Down into the dust of a million years, mingled
At last with our cousin pithecanthropus
Who's been waiting. And you, is it just that you,
in a reasonable frock like Hegel's,
Have chosen for yourself a different name?

Clandestine bulletins in a green bag.
The poet who reads them hears him laughing.

"For punishment I took away their reason.
No one will think to step outside my will."

With what word to reach into the future,
With what word to defend human happiness—
It has the smell of freshly baked bread—
If the language of poets cannot search out
Standards of use to later generations?
We have not been taught. We do not know at all
How to unite Freedom and Necessity.

In a dream the mind visits two sharp edges.
Woe to the unearthly, the radiant ones.
While storming heaven, they neglect the Earth
With its joy and warmth and animal strength.
Woe to the reasonable, the heavy-minded.
Their lies will extinguish the morning star,
A gift more durable than Nature is, or Death.

Clandestine bulletins in a green bag.
The poem of propaganda will not last.
It's false because it knows less than we know.
Poetry feels too much. Therefore its silence.
Still it responds to a distant call,
Not ready to bear the weight of something new.

The twenty-year-old poets of Warsaw
Did not want to know that something in this century
Submits to thought, not to Davids with their slings.
They were like a man in a hospital room
Who, indifferent to pacts with the future,
Wants to be faithful only to the moment,
Wants to possess the laughter of children,

The aerial games of the birds, at least once,
For the last time, before the stone gate closes.
The makeshift barricade was not adorned
With mankind's auroras, bards' promises.
Over a yellow field and a ring of the dead
In combat, Madonna stood, wounded by a sword.

The young, amazed by every morning, touched
A table or a chair, as if they had found
An entire puffball gleaming in the rain,
Intact. Objects for them were rainbows,
Misty as their years sent out before them.
They had to let go of fame, peace, wisdom.
Their poems were a prayer for manfulness.
"When they chase us from life as from a city,
Oh you, our golden home, secure us a bed
Of malachite, only for the night, though it's
        eternal."
No ancient Greek hero entered into combat
So deprived of hope, in their heads the image
Of a white skull kicked by feet in passing.

Copernicus: the statue of a German or a Pole?
Leaving a spray of flowers, Bojarski perished:
A sacrifice should be pure, unreasoned.
Trzebiński, the new Polish Nietzsche,
Had his mouth plastered shut before he died.
He took with him the view of a wall, low clouds
His black eyes had just a moment to absorb.
Baczyński's head fell against his rifle.
The uprising scared up flocks of pigeons.
Gajcy, Stroiński were raised to the sky,
A red sky, on the shield of an explosion.

Under a linden tree, as before, daylight
Quivered on a goose quill dipped in ink.
Books were still governed by the old rule,
Born of a belief that visible beauty
Is a little mirror for the beauty of being.
The survivors ran through fields, escaping
From themselves, knowing they wouldn't return
For a hundred years. Before them were spread
Those quicksands where a tree changes into nothing,
Into an anti-tree, where no borderline
Separates a shape from a shape, and where,
Amid thunder, the golden house of *is*
Collapses, and the word *becoming* ascends.

Till the end of their days all of them
Carried the memory of their cowardice,
For they didn't want to die without a reason.
Now He, expected, for a long time awaited,
Raised up the smoke of a thousand censers.
They crawled on slippery paths to his feet.

—"King of the centuries, ungraspable Movement,
You who fill the grottoes of the ocean
With a roiling silence, who dwell in the blood
Of the gored shark devoured by other sharks,
In the whistle of a half-bird, half-fish,
In the thundering sea, in the iron gurgling
Of the rocks when archipelagoes surge up.

"The churning of your surf casts up bracelets,
Pearls not eyes, bones from which the salt
Has eaten crowns and dresses of brocade.

You without beginning, you always between
A form and a form, O stream, bright spark,
Antithesis that ripens toward a thesis,
Now we have become equal to the gods,
Knowing, in you, that we do not exist.

"You, in whom cause is married to effect,
Drew us from the depth as you draw a wave,
For one instant, limitless, of transformation.
You have shown us the agony of this age
So that we could ascend to those heights
Where your hand commands the instruments.
Spare us, do not punish us. Our offense
Was grave: we forgot the power of your law.
Save us from ignorance. Accept now our
     devotion."

So they forswore. But every one of them
Kept hidden a hope that the possessions of time
Were assigned a limit. That they would one day
Be able to look at a cherry tree in blossom,
For a moment, unique among the moments,
Put the ocean to sleep, close the hourglass,
And listen to how the clocks stop ticking.

When they put a rope around my neck,
When they choke off my breath with a rope,
I'll turn around once, and what will I be?

When they give me an injection of phenol,
When I walk half a step with phenol in my veins,
What wisdom of the prophets will enlighten me?

When they tear us from this one embrace,
When they destroy forever the shaft of tender light,
What Heaven will see us reunited?

A singer cursed white clouds above the ghetto.
I used to give pennies to the blind poet.
Let his songs stay with me to the end.

On the wall of my cell for a whole night I carved
A word of love, so that syllables survive,
And roll with this prison around the sun.

I was beating the rhythm on an empty can,
I who am not, who only was once,
There where the road led to the camp gate.

My trace, a diary hidden between bricks.
Perhaps someday it will be unearthed,
A day of forgiveness or a day of penance.

Soil of annihilation, soil of hate,
No word will purify it ever.
No such poet will be born.

For even if one had been called, he walked
Beside us to the last gate, for only
A child of the ghetto could utter the words.

The awkward speech of Slavic peasants
Was busy for centuries with rustling rhymes:
It produced at last an anonymous song
Still audible in the trembling of the air,

There where white foam hisses under palm trees
And where an osprey in the Labrador currents
Plunges to the sea, a plough of brightness
Beneath the firs of Maine. A madrigal
Humming on the strings of a viola, simple,
A song for ladies in a pretty season
Whose meaning time just happened to reverse.

Winter will end

Marching girls, Jewish,
Expressed their only joy, of vengeance.
Yes, soon at night the voice of flying cranes.
Soon the dry snow will numb no worker's hand.
Yes, in a stream a pebble as rosy as lips
Will crunch in the streambed under a passing foot.

Spring will arrive

Yes, juices will surge in the tulip
And a May beetle, humming, tap at a window.
Yes, a bridegroom will pick young leaves of
    the oak
To plait a wreath for his bride.

Above our bodies

Our bodies are one body now.
Bone, muscle, nerves not mine but ours.
The names of Miriam, Sonia, Rachel
Darken and cool in the slow air.

Grass will thrive.

Grass, defeated by the irony of a song.

Pickled cucumbers in a sweating jar.
A sprig of dill. Cucumbers are eternal.
Early morning twigs crackle on the hearth.
In a clay bowl wooden spoons and gruel.
At the door baskets and hoes where hens roost.
And the dead-straight farm track, fields without limit.
Plains, empty and misty, to Skierniewice.
Plains, empty and misty, to the Ural Mountains.
Hey, don't rest yet. Noon is a long way off.

Light Nanking silk our shoulders adorn,
In a circle of well-born youth we sit.
We pass in dressing the hours of the morn
And evenings we sharpen our wit.

Above potato fields and the autumn earth,
A spark like a snowflake: an aeroplane
Rolling and turning, high up, beyond the clouds.

Say what you desire
Tell us your hungers and your thirsts.

No need for the bitterness of mustard seed.
Poetry is well served by warm porcelains,
By the company of a clutch of charming Graces,
By essences distilled from classical herbs.
Puffing his pipe, dressed in Nanking fabric,
Let the poet pursue his wayward dreams.
A wooden house, of course, but well-made, plumb.

The *Phaedo* at arm's length, also Cato's *Life*.
On Friday evenings the family would light
A row of candles in bright chandeliers.
From the rhythms of Daniel, rhythms of Isaiah,
A young man received more than enough instruction
In how to keep silent, how to compose a verse.

A castle sits on the Nowogródek hill.

What we do need are forests, clear waters.
For there's nothing here to defend a man.
When he studies the void of the horizon
The idea of a center slowly fades.
His only counsel is his moving shadow.

The man not born to these level plains
Will sail the seas, wander the country
On the banks of the Vezere under apple trees
Or chase the reflection of his homeland
In the pines and black-green rivers of Maine
As one scans the faces in a crowd of strangers
For that one face, uniquely and ardently loved.

Mickiewicz is too difficult for us.
Ours is not a lordly or a Jewish knowledge.
We worked with a plough, with a harrow.
On feast days we heard another music.

Ho la ho la
Lambs bleat baa baa
Shepherds run to see

Come to the stable
As soon as you're able
Ho la ho la
Even Jack with his stutter
Sings to the Mother
The Holy Mother
Ho la

The double bass with its huge belly buzzes.

Hu du hu du
We are playing too
We sing to Christ the Lord
Not for a reward
Hu du

The violin, made from linden, thinly wails.

Ti ri ti ri
We play a joyous trill
Wa li wa li
From dawn to evening still
Wa li

Old Gregor blows and squeezes on the pipe:

Me-e lee me-e lay
To the child we play

And the clarinet is not far behind:

mu-la mu-la
To the mother and the child

And the double bass repeats:

Hu du hu du
We are playing too
We play for Christ the Lord

So many things have passed, so many things.
And while no work accomplished helps us,
Tytus Czyzewski returns with his Christmas carol.
The double bass used to boom, so he booms.

I rolled a cigarette and licked the paper.
Then a match in the little house of my hand.
And why not a tinderbox with flint?
The wind was blowing. I sat on the road at noon,
Thinking and thinking. Beside me, potatoes.

IV. NATURA

Pennsylvania, 1948–1949

The garden of Nature opens.
The grass at the threshold is green.
And an almond tree begins to bloom.

Sunt mihi Dei Acherontis propitii!
Valeat numen triplex Jehovae!
Ignis, aeris, aquae, terrae spiritus,
Salvete!—says the entering guest.

Ariel lives in the palace of an apple tree,
But will not appear, vibrating like a wasp's wing,
And Mephistopheles, disguised as an abbot
Of the Dominicans or the Franciscans,
Will not descend from a mulberry bush
Onto a pentagram drawn in the black loam of the path.

But a rhododendron walks among the rocks
Shod in leathery leaves and ringing a pink bell.
A hummingbird, a child's top in the air,
Hovers in one spot, the beating heart of motion.
Impaled on the nail of a black thorn, a grasshopper
Leaks brown fluid from its twitching snout.
And what can he do, the phantom-in-chief,
As he's been called, more than a magician,
The *Socrates of snails*, as he's been called,
Musician of pears, arbiter of orioles, man?
In sculptures and canvases our individuality
Manages to survive. In Nature it perishes.
Let him accompany the coffin of the woodsman
Pushed from a cliff by a mountain demon,
The he-goat with its jutting curl of horn.
Let him visit the graveyard of the whalers

Who drove spears into the flesh of leviathan
And looked for the secret in guts and blubber.
The thrashing subsided, quieted to waves.
Let him unroll the textbooks of alchemists
Who almost found the cipher, thus the scepter.
Then passed away without hands, eyes, or elixir.

Here there is sun. And whoever, as a child,
Believed he could break the repeatable pattern
Of things, if only he understood the pattern,
Is cast down, rots in the skin of others,
Looks with wonder at the colors of the butterfly,
Inexpressible wonder, formless, hostile to art.

To keep the oars from squeaking in their locks,
He binds them with a handkerchief. The dark
Had rushed east from the Rocky Mountains
And settled in the forests of the continent:
Sky full of embers reflected in a cloud,
Flights of herons, trees above a marsh,
The dry stalks in water, livid, black. My boat
Divides the aerial utopias of the mosquitoes
Which rebuild their glowing castles instantly.
A water lily sinks, fizzing, under the boat's bow.

Now it is night only. The water is ash-gray.
Play, music, but inaudibly! I wait an hour
In the silence, senses tuned to a beaver's lodge.
Then suddenly, a crease in the water, a beast's
black moon, rounded, ploughing up quickly
from the pond-dark, from the bubbling methanes.
I am not immaterial and never will be.
My scent in the air, my animal smell,

Spreads, rainbow-like, scares the beaver:
A sudden *splat*.
                              I remained where I was
In the high, soft coffer of the night's velvet,
Mastering what had come to my senses:
How the four-toed paws worked, how the hair
Shook off water in the muddy tunnel.
It does not know time, hasn't heard of death,
Is submitted to me because I know I'll die.

I remember everything. That wedding in Basel,
A touch to the strings of a viola and fruit
In silver bowls. As was the custom in Savoy,
An overturned cup for three pair of lips,
And the wine spilled. The flames of the candles
Wavery and frail in a breeze from the Rhine.
Her fingers, bones shining through the skin,
Felt out the hooks and clasps of the silk
And the dress opened like a nutshell,
Fell from the turned graininess of the belly.
A chain for the neck rustled without epoch,
In pits where the arms of various creeds
Mingle with bird cries and the red hair of caesars.

Perhaps this is only my own love speaking
Beyond the seventh river. Grit of subjectivity,
Obsession, bar the way to it.
Until a window shutter, dogs in the cold garden,
The whistle of a train, an owl in the firs
Are spared the distortions of memory.
And the grass says: how it was I don't know.

Splash of a beaver in the American night.
The memory grows larger than my life.
A tin plate, dropped on the irregular red bricks
Of a floor, rattles tinnily forever.
Belinda of the big foot, Julia, Thaïs,
The tufts of their sex shadowed by ribbon.

Peace to the princesses under the tamarisks.
Desert winds beat against their painted eyelids.
Before the body was wrapped in bandelettes,
Before wheat fell asleep in the tomb,
Before stone fell silent, and there was only pity.

Yesterday a snake crossed the road at dusk.
Crushed by a tire, it writhed on the asphalt.
We are both the snake and the wheel.
There are two dimensions. Here is the unattainable
Truth of being, here, at the edge of lasting
and not lasting. Where the parallel lines intersect,
Time lifted above time by time.

Before the butterfly and its color, he, numb,
Formless, feels his fear, he, unattainable.
For what is a butterfly without Julia and Thaïs?
And what is Julia without a butterfly's down
In her eyes, her hair, the smooth grain of her belly?
The kingdom, you say. We do not belong to it,
And still, in the same instant, we belong.
For how long will a nonsensical Poland
Where poets write of their emotions as if
They had a contract of limited liability

Suffice? I want not poetry, but a new diction,
Because only it might allow us to express
A new tenderness and save us from a law
That is not our law, from necessity
Which is not ours, even if we take its name.

From broken armor, from eyes stricken
By the command of time and taken back
Into the jurisdiction of mold and fermentation,
We draw our hope. Yes, to gather in an image
The furriness of the beaver, the smell of rushes,
And the wrinkles of a hand holding a pitcher
From which wine trickles. Why cry out
That a sense of history destroys our substance
If it, precisely, is offered to our powers,
A muse of our gray-haired father, Herodotus,
As our arm and our instrument, though
It is not easy to use it, to strengthen it
So that, like a plumb with a pure gold center,
It will serve again to rescue human beings.

With such reflections I pushed a rowboat,
In the middle of the continent, through tangled stalks,
In my mind an image of the waves of two oceans
And the slow rocking of a guard-ship's lantern.
Aware that at this moment I—and not only I—
Keep, as in a seed, the unnamed future.
And then a rhythmic appeal composed itself,
Alien to the moth with its whirring of silk:

O City, O Society, O Capital,
We have seen your steaming entrails.

You will no longer be what you have been.
Your songs no longer gratify our hearts.

Steel, cement, lime, law, ordinance,
We have worshipped you too long,
You were for us a goal and a defense,
Ours was your glory and your shame.

And where was the covenant broken?
Was it in the fires of war, the incandescent sky?
Or at twilight, as the towers fly past, when one looked
From the train across a desert of tracks

To a window out past the maneuvering locomotives
Where a girl examines her narrow, moody face
In a mirror and ties a ribbon to her hair
Pierced by the sparks of curling papers?

Those walls of yours are shadows of walls,
And your light disappeared forever.
Not the world's monument anymore, an oeuvre of our own
Stands beneath the sun in an altered space.

From stucco and mirrors, glass and paintings,
Tearing aside curtains of silver and cotton,
Comes man, naked and mortal,
Ready for truth, for speech, for wings.

Lament, Republic! Fall to your knees!
The loudspeaker's spell is discontinued.
Listen! You can hear the clocks ticking.
Your death approaches by his hand.

An oar over my shoulder, I walked from the woods.
A porcupine scolded from the fork of a tree,
A horned owl, not changed by the century,
Not changed by place or time, looked down.
Bubo maximus, from the work of Linnaeus.

America for me has the pelt of a raccoon,
Its eyes are a raccoon's black binoculars.
A chipmunk flickers in a litter of dry bark
Where ivy and vines tangle in the red soil
At the roots of an arcade of tulip trees.
America's wings are the color of a cardinal,
Its beak is half-open and a mockingbird trills
From a leafy bush in the sweat-bath of the air.
Its line is the wavy body of a water moccasin
Crossing a river with a grass-like motion,
A rattlesnake, a rubble of dots and speckles,
Coiling under the bloom of a yucca plant.

America is for me the illustrated version
Of childhood tales about the heart of tanglewood,
Told in the evening to the spinning wheel's hum.
And a violin, shivvying up a square dance,
Plays the fiddles of Lithuania or Flanders.
My dancing partner's name is Birute Swenson.
She married a Swede, but was born in Kaunas.
Then from the night window a moth flies in
As big as the joined palms of the hands,
With a hue like the transparency of emeralds.

Why not establish a home in the neon heat
Of Nature? Is it not enough, the labor of autumn,
Of winter and spring and withering summer?

You will hear not one word spoken of the court
of Sigismund Augustus on the banks of the Delaware River.
The Dismissal of the Greek Envoys is not needed.
Herodotus will repose on his shelf, uncut.
And the rose only, a sexual symbol,
Symbol of love and superterrestrial beauty,
Will open a chasm deeper than your knowledge.
About it we find a song in a dream:

Inside the rose
Are houses of gold,
black isobars, streams of cold.
Dawn touches her finger to the edge of the Alps
And evening streams down to the bays of the sea.

If anyone dies inside the rose,
They carry him down the purple-red road
In a procession of clocks all wrapped in folds.
They light up the petals of grottoes with torches.
They bury him there where color begins,
At the source of the sighing,
Inside the rose.

Let names of months mean only what they mean.
Let the *Aurora's* cannons be heard in none
Of them, or the tread of young rebels marching.
We might, at best, keep some kind of souvenir,
Preserved like a fan in a garret. Why not
Sit down at a rough country table and compose
An ode in the old manner, as in the old times
Chasing a beetle with the nib of our pen?

ODE

O October
You are my true delight,
Month of the cranberry and the red of the maple,
Of Hudson Bay geese a-wing in the transparent air,
Dry vines and withering grasses and smoky light,
Oh October

O October
The silence of roads in a carpet of pine needles,
A birdcall fashioned from an owl's wing,
The wailing of dogs on the scent of a buck,
And the startled peal of a bird in the spruces,
Oh October

O October
Shine of frost on the blade of a sword
When a Polish engineer glimpses near West Point
In the vivid woods the maple-red coats of British soldiers
Moving soundlessly up the Appalachian trail,
Oh October

O October
Cold is your crystal wine,
Tart is the taste of your lips above a necklace of rowanberries,
Your panting sides are the color
Of the fallow hair of a mountain deer,
Oh October

O October
Pouring dew on the rusty traces,
Blowing a buffalo horn above the rebel camp,
Burning bare feet on the sloping hill paths

When the smokes of autumn and of cannons drift past,
Oh October

O October
Season of poetry, of the total daring
Of starting one's life at every moment anew,
You gave me the magic ring which, when turned,
Sends down a gleam from your jewel of freedom,
Oh October

There is much with which to reproach us.
Given the choice, we rejected peaceful silence
And long meditation on the structure of the world
Which deserves respect. Neither the eternal moment
Attracted us as it should, nor purity of style.
We wanted, instead, to move as words move,
Raising the dust of names and of events.
We didn't care enough that they disappear
In a thousand sparks and we with them. Even
The disrepute we have taken on ourselves
Was not completely far from our designs,
And so, though unwillingly, we pay the price.

Many a man will concede, if he knows himself,
That he was like one who hears a chorus
Of voices and doesn't know what they mean.
Thence, fury. A foot to the accelerator, as if
Speed could save us from voices and phantoms.
We trailed everywhere an invisible rope
And felt its hook inside us every moment.

And yet the accusers were mistaken, if,
Shedding tears over the evils of this age,

They saw us as angels, hurled into an abyss,
Shaking our fists at the works of God.
There is no doubt that many perished, infamously,
Because, like an illiterate discovering chemistry,
They suddenly discovered relativity and time.
For others the very roundness of a stone
Picked up on the bank of a river provided
The lesson. Or the bleeding gills of a perch,
Or—the moon rising over banks of clouds—
A beaver ploughing the slumbering softness of water.

For contemplation fades without resistance.
For its own sake, it should be forbidden.
And we, certainly, were happier than those
Who drank sadness from the books of Schopenhauer,
While they listened from their garrets to the din
Of music from the tavern down below.
At least poetry, philosophy, action were not,
For us, separated, as they were for them,
But joined in one will: we needed to be of use.
And that is the—sometimes burdensome—recompense.

If we, thought our faults were merely historical,
Will not receive the laurel of long fame,
So what, after all? Some are given monuments
And mausoleums, yet in a soft May rain,
Covered by a single overcoat, a boy and girl
Rush by, entirely indifferent to that perfection.
And some word of us may remain in any case,
Some remembrance of our half-opened lips:
They did not have time to say what they wanted.

Spirits of the air, of fire, of water,
Keep close to us, but not too close.
The ship's propeller drives us from you.
It's not fulfilled: the old hope that Neptune
Will show his beard, trailing a retinue of nymphs.
Nothing but ocean which boils and repeats:
In vain, in vain. Nothingness is so strong
We try to master it by thinking of the bones
Of pirates, the silky eyebrows of governors
On which the crabs feast. And our hands grip
Harder at the cool metal of the railing.
Look for help in the smell of paint and soap.
The ship's body, creaking, carries the freight
of our foolishness, vagueness, and hidden faith,
The dirt of our subjectivity, and the homeless
White faces of the ones who were killed in combat.
Carries it where? To the isles of bliss? No,
In us storm winds drowned that stanza of Horace
A penknife worked into a wooden bench at school.
It will not find us in this salt and void:

Iam Cytherea choros ducit Venus imminente luna

Brie-Comte-Robert, 1956

KING POPIEL

AND

OTHER

POEMS

(Król Popiel i inne wiersze)

1 9 6 2

KING POPIEL

*Popiel, a legendary king of Polish prehistory, is said to have been eaten by
mice on his island in the middle of a big lake.*

Those were not, it is certain, crimes just like ours.
It was all about dugouts carved out of linden trunks
And some beavers' pelts. He ruled over marshes
Where the moose echoes in a moon of acid frosts
And lynxes walk in springtime onto the drying holms.

His palisade, his timber fort, and the tower
Built by the fins of the gods of night
Could be seen beyond the water by the hidden hunter
Who dared not push aside the branches with his bow.
Until one of them returned with the news. Over the deep into the
    rushes
The wind chased the largest boat, and it was empty.

Mice have eaten Popiel. The diamond-studded crown
He got later. And to him, who vanished forever,
Who kept in his treasury three Gothic coins
And bars of bronze, to him who went away,
No one knows where, with his children and women,
To him lands and seas were left by Galileo,
Newton, and Einstein. So that for long centuries
He might smooth, on his throne, his javelin with a knife.

Montgeron, 1958

MAGPIETY

The same and not quite the same, I walked through oak forests
Amazed that my Muse, Mnemosyne,
Has in no way diminished my amazement.
A magpie was screeching and I said: Magpiety?
What is magpiety? I shall never achieve
A magpie heart, a hairy nostril over the beak, a flight
That always renews just when coming down,
And so I shall never comprehend magpiety.
If however magpiety does not exist
My nature does not exist either.
Who would have guessed that, centuries later,
I would invent the question of universals?

Montgeron, 1958

LESSONS

Since that moment when in a house with low eaves
A doctor from the town cut the navel-string
And pears dotted with white mildew
Reposed in their nests of luxuriant weeds,
I have been in the hands of humans. They could have strangled
My first scream, squeezed with a giant hand
The defenseless throat that aroused their tenderness.

From them I received the names of plants and birds,
I lived in their country that was not too barren,
Not too cultivated, with a field, a meadow,
And water in a boat moored behind a shed.

Their lessons met, it is true, with a barrier
Deep in myself and my will was dark,
Not very compliant with their intents or mine.
Others, whom I did not know or knew only by name,
Were pacing in me and I, terrified,
Heard, in myself, locked creaky rooms
That one should not peep into through a keyhole.
They did not mean much to me—Kazimir, Hrehory
Or Emilia or Margareta.
But I had to reenact all by myself
Every flaw and sin of theirs. This humiliated me.
So that I wanted to shout: you are to blame
For my not being what I want and being what I am.

Sunlight would fall in my book upon Original Sin.
And more than once, when noon was humming in the grass
I would imagine the two of them, with my guilt,
Trampling a wasp beneath the apple tree in Eden.

Montgeron, 1957

NO MORE

I should relate sometime how I changed
My views on poetry, and how it came to be
That I consider myself today one of the many
Merchants and artisans of Old Japan,
Who arranged verses about cherry blossoms,
Chrysanthemums and the full moon.

If only I could describe the courtesans of Venice
As in a loggia they teased a peacock with a twig,
And out of brocade, the pearls of their belt,
Set free heavy breasts and the reddish weal
Where the buttoned dress marked the belly,
As vividly as seen by the skipper of galleons
Who landed that morning with a cargo of gold;
And if I could find for their miserable bones
In a graveyard whose gates are licked by greasy water
A word more enduring than their last-used comb
That in the rot under tombstones, alone, awaits the light,

Then I wouldn't doubt. Out of reluctant matter
What can be gathered? Nothing, beauty at best.
And so, cherry blossoms must suffice for us
And chrysanthemums and the full moon.

Montgeron, 1957

ODE TO A BIRD

O composite,

O unconscious,

Holding your feathery palms behind you,
Propped on your gray lizard legs,
On cybernetic gloves
That grasp at whatever they touch.

O incommensurate.
Larger than the precipice
In a lily-of-the-valley
Or the eye of a scarab in the grass,
Reddish, turned violet-green by the sun.

More vast than a galleried night
With the headlights of an ant—
And a galaxy in its body
Indeed, equal to any.

Beyond will, without will
You sway on a branch above lakes of air
And their submerged palaces, towers of leaves,
Terraces where you can land in a harp of shadow.
You lean forward, summoned, and I contemplate the instant
When your foot loosens its hold, your arm extends.
The place you have left is rocking, into the lines of crystal
You take your warm palpitating heart.
O not similar to anything, indifferent
To the sound *pta, pteron, fvgls, brd*.
Beyond name, without name,
An impeccable motion in an expanse of amber.
So that I comprehend, while your wings beat,

What divides me from things I name every day,
And from my vertical figure
Though it extends itself upward to the zenith.

But your half-opened beak is with me always.
Its inside is so fleshy and amorous
That a shiver makes my hair stand up
In kinship with your ecstasy.
Then one afternoon I wait in a front hall,
Beside bronze lions I see lips
And I touch a naked arm
In the scent of springwater and of bells.

Montgeron, 1959

HAPPINESS

How warm the light! From the glowing bay
The masts like spruce, repose of the ropes
In the morning mist. Where a stream trickles
Into the sea, by a small bridge—a flute.
Farther, under the arch of ancient ruins
You see a few tiny walking figures.
One wears a red kerchief. There are trees,
Ramparts, and mountains at an early hour.

Washington, D.C., 1948

WHAT ONCE WAS GREAT

To A. and O. Wat

What once was great, now appeared small.
Kingdoms were fading like snow-covered bronze.

What once could smite, now smites no more.
Celestial earths roll on and shine.

Stretched on the grass by the bank of a river,
As long, long ago, I launch my boats of bark.

Montgeron, 1959

SHOULD, SHOULD NOT

A man should not love the moon.
An ax should not lose weight in his hand.
His garden should smell of rotting apples
And grow a fair amount of nettles.
A man when he talks should not use words that are dear to him,
Or split open a seed to find out what is inside it.
He should not drop a crumb of bread, or spit in the fire
(So at least I was taught in Lithuania).
When he steps on marble stairs,
He may, that boor, try to chip them with his boot
As a reminder that the stairs will not last forever.

Berkeley, 1961

WHAT DOES IT MEAN

It does not know it glitters
It does not know it flies
It does not know it is this not that.

And, more and more often, agape,
With my Gauloise dying out,
Over a glass of red wine,
I muse on the meaning of being this not that.

Just as long ago, when I was twenty,
But then there was a hope I would be everything,
Perhaps even a butterfly or a thrush, by magic.
Now I see dusty district roads
And a town where the postmaster gets drunk every day
Melancholy with remaining identical to himself.

If only the stars contained me.
If only everything kept happening in such a way
That the so-called world opposed the so-called flesh.
Were I at least not contradictory. Alas.

Montgeron, 1960

HERACLITUS

He pitied them, himself deserving pity.
Because this is beyond the means of any language.
Even his syntax, obscure—as went the reproach—
Words so combined they had triple meaning
Encompassed nothing. Those toes in a sandal,
A girl's breast so fragile under Artemis's hand,
Sweat, oil on the face of a man from the fleet
Participate in the universal, existing separately.
Our own when we are asleep, devoted but to ourselves,
In love with the scent of perishable flesh,
With the central warmth under the pubic hair,
Our knees under our chin, we know there is the All
And we long in vain. An animal's: that is, our own.
Particular existence keeps us from the light
(That sentence can be read in reverse as well).
"Nobody was so proud and scornful as he."
For he tortured himself, unable to forgive
That a moment of consciousness never will change us.
Pity turned into anger. So he fled from Ephesus.
Didn't want to see a human face. Lived in the mountains.
Ate grass and leaves, as reports Laertius.
The sea lay down waves beneath the steep shore of Asia
(From above the waves are not seen, you look just at the sea).
And there, is it an echo of bells tinkling at a monstrance?
Or Orlando Furioso's golden clothes afloat?
Or is it a fish's mouth nibbling lipstick
From the lips of a radio-girl drowned in a submarine?

Montgeron, 1960

165]

GREEK PORTRAIT

My beard is thick, my eyelids half cover
My eyes, as with those who know the value
Of visible things. I keep quiet as is proper
For a man who has learned that the human heart
Holds more than speech does. I have left behind
My native land, home, and public office.
Not that I looked for profit or adventure.
I am no foreigner on board a ship.
My plain face, the face of a tax-collector,
Merchant, or soldier, makes me one of the crowd.
Nor do I refuse to pay due homage
To local gods. And I eat what others eat.
About myself, this much will suffice.

Washington, D.C., 1948

THE MASTER

They say that my music is angelic.
That when the Prince listens to it
His face, hidden from sight, turns gentle.
With a beggar he would share power.
A fan of a lady-in-waiting is immobile,
Silk by its touch does not induce pleasant immodest thoughts
And under a pleat her knees, far off in a chasm, grow numb.

Everyone has heard in the cathedral my Missa Solemnis.
I changed the throats of girls from the Saint Cecilia choir
Into an instrument which raises us
Above what we are. I know how to free
Men and women from remembrances of their long lives
So that they stand in the smoke of the nave
Restored to the mornings of childhood
When a drop of dew and a shout on the mountains
Were the truth of the world.

Leaning on a cane at sunset
I may resemble a gardener
Who has planted and reared a tall tree.

I was not wasting the years of frail youthful hope.
I measure what is done. Over there a swallow
Will pass away and return, changed in its slanting flight.
Steps will be heard at the well but of other people.
The ploughs will erase a forest. The flute and the violin
Will always work as I have ordered them.

No one knows how I was paying. Ridiculous, they believe
It may be got for nothing. We are pierced by a ray.
They want a ray because this helps them to admire.
Or they accept a folktale: once, under an alder

A demon appeared to us, as black as a pond,
He drew two drops of blood with a sting of a gnat
And impressed in the wax his amethyst ring.

The celestial spheres endlessly resound.
But an instant is invincible in memory.
It comes back in the middle of the night. Who are those holding
    torches,
So that what is long past occurs in full light?

Regret, to no end, in every hour
Of a long life. What beautiful work
Will redeem the heartbeats of a living creature
And what use to confess deeds that last forever?

When old and white-haired under their laced shawls
They dip their fingers in a basin at the entrance
It seems to me she might have been one of them. The same firs
Rustle and with a shallow wave sheens the lake.

And yet I loved my destiny.
Could I move back time, I am unable to guess
Whether I would have chosen virtue. My line of fate does not tell.
Does God really want us to lose our soul
For only then He may receive a gift without blemish?

A language of angels! Before you mention Grace
Mind that you do not deceive yourself and others.
What comes from my evil—that only is true.

Montgeron, 1959

A FRIVOLOUS CONVERSATION

—My past is a stupid butterfly's overseas voyage.
My future is a garden where a cook cuts the throat of a rooster.
What do I have, with all my pain and rebellion?

—Take a moment, just one, and when its fine shell,
Two joined palms, slowly opens
What do you see?

    —A pearl, a second.

—Inside a second, a pearl, in that star saved from time,
What do you see when the wind of mutability ceases?

—The earth, the sky, and the sea, richly cargoed ships,
Spring mornings full of dew and faraway princedoms.
At marvels displayed in tranquil glory
I look and do not desire for I am content.

Goszyce, 1944

IN MILAN

How far off are those years, mine and not mine,
When one wrote poems on Italy
Telling about evenings in the fields of Siena
Or about cicadas in Sicilian ruins.

Long into the night we were walking on the Piazza del Duomo.
He: That I was too politicized.
And I answered him more or less as follows:

If you have a nail in your shoe, what then?
Do you love that nail? Same with me.
I am for the moon amid the vineyards
When you see high up the snow on the Alps.
I am for the cypresses at dawn
And for the bluish air in the valleys.
I could compose, right now, a song
On the taste of peaches, on September in Europe.
No one can accuse me of being without joy
Or of not noticing girls who pass by.
I do not deny that I would like to gobble up
All existing flowers, to eat all the colors.
I have been devouring this world in vain
For forty years, a thousand would not be enough.
Yes, I would like to be a poet of the five senses,
That's why I don't allow myself to become one.
Yes, thought has less weight than the word *lemon*
That's why in my words I do not reach for fruit.

Brie-Comte-Robert, 1955

FROM THE CHRONICLES
OF THE TOWN OF PORNIC

Bluebeard's Castle

The castle on the rock briny from surf
Was built in the tenth century. The arrow of a crossbow
Could reach the mast of any ship entering the port at high tide.
The ebb uncovers a thin line of reefs.
As for Gilles de Laval, Baron de Retz,
He was, I think, a hooligan or a teddy boy or a *Halbstarke*.
His father perished when hunting in the year 1415
Because his cutlass missed the tough heart of a boar.
And perhaps Gilles was given too much freedom
Though they taught him how to read and write in Latin
As well as how to appreciate the liberal arts.
In the bad company of his courtly Falstaffs
This pup was the terror of the region.
He was sixteen when he married Catherine de Thouars.
And he was one of the first to come to the aid of Jeanne d'Arc.
Fearless, the right hand of Jeanne,
It was he who supported her, wounded, at the battle of Tournelles.
He grew bored, so he paid poets and actors
And "violated all divine and human rights," says the Chronicle,
Leading a life of debauchery, here, in the castle of Pornic.
He was condemned in Nantes by lay and ecclesiastical courts.
The executioner strangled him but his body did not fall into the flames
Because six women gathered it up to bury it in consecrated ground.
They say that his family, the archbishop, and the prince
Put him to death out of greed for his land.

The Owners

La Marquise Brie-Serrant and her daughter Anne
Were arrested for harboring the vicar Galipaud.
They did not lower their eyes when getting into the coach
Because their duty had been done.
On the way to Nantes, more exactly, in Moutiers,
Drunk men punished them for their pride.
A revolutionary tribunal pronounced the verdict
And they did not cry in the death cell.
When they were being led to the place of execution
Bearded strongmen knocked over the sentries.
They were sailors from the corvette *Alcyon*
Anchored in the estuary of the Loire.
Anne, reflecting on the fierceness of the world
Which takes from us the virginity of memory and flesh,
Entered a convent after the death of her mother.
Le Marquis was beheaded in Paris for his part in a plot.
He planned to snatch the King away from the guillotine.
The castle stood empty. Until the poorest of the citizens,
A blacksmith called Misery, settled in it.
Monsieur Lebreton, a merchant, gave him two hundred francs
To get out, and with another twelve hundred
Bought off the debt of fifty thousand left by the previous owners.
The castle was then inherited by Joubert, manufacturer of cloth.

Vandeans

O thoughtless Vandeans! That you, regarded as bandits,
Wanted revenge after taking Pornic, is understandable.
And so you shot Viau the tailor, the notary Bonamy, Libau the
    blacksmith,
Merchants Martin and Tardiff, the forester Poisson, two shipwrights,
And even old man Naud who was eighty.
But to celebrate the evening of triumph with wine
And to get dead drunk as peasants can
Without even posting some guards?
A detachment led by a priest-patriot is already on its way in the
    darkness
And you will be slain or taken prisoner.
At dawn holes were dug in the sand on the beach
(Which means that it happened at low tide).
And two hundred fifteen of you were given to the crabs
While two hundred fifty stood there, reeling,
Their mouths dripping with the saliva of terror.
Until recently the testimony of a very old woman
Was repeated here: then, as a child of four,
She was running, basket in hand, along a path near the castle.
Armed men ordered her to leave
Because when prisoners are shot, witnesses are unwelcome.

Our Lady of Recovery

Once there were harsh winters when frost destroyed the vineyards.
Wolves roamed the streets in the darkness.
There were evenings when women arrayed in their finest
Would gather in vain on a cliff to cast spells on the birds.
What the bird sees below is the dark, dark sea.
A rust-colored sail dragged in the furrow of a wave
Looks like algae, the faces of the drowning
Are not those of husbands and lovers.
But century after century Our Lady of Recovery
Extended her arms in a granite chapel.
Indeed, the ocean shows us what we really are:
Children who for a moment feign the wisdom of captains
And humanity is then a beloved family
And a thousand years are counted as one day.
O Holy Mother, save me, my life is so sinful.
Return me to the dear earth, allow me another day.
O Holy Mother, I am not deserving but I will begin anew,
You didn't live far away because You are near me.
And in their dripping hoods, barefoot, with bowed heads
Thinking: why was it me that she saved?
They went to light the promised candle at her altar.
Later they drank, grew boisterous, their women conceived.
Her smile meant that it was all according to her will.

Pornic–Montgeron, 1960

ALBUM OF DREAMS

May 10
Did I mistake the house or the street
or perhaps the staircase, though once I was there every day?
I looked through the keyhole. The kitchen: the same and not the
    same.
And I carried, wound on a reel,
a plastic tape, narrow as a shoelace,
that was everything I had written over the long years.
I rang, uncertain whether I would hear that name.
She stood before me in her saffron dress,
unchanged, greeting me with a smile without one tear of time.
And in the morning chickadees were singing in the cedar.

June 17
And that snow will remain forever,
unredeemed, not spoken of to anyone.
On it their track freezes at sunset
in an hour, in a year, in a district, in a country.

And that face will remain forever
beaten for ages by drops of rain.
One drop is running from eyelid to lip
on an empty square, in an unnamed city.

August 14
They ordered us to pack our things, as the house was to be burned.
There was time to write a letter, but that letter was with me.
We laid down our bundles and sat against the wall.
They looked when we placed a violin on the bundles.
My little sons did not cry. Gravity and curiosity.
One of the soldiers brought a can of gasoline. Others were tearing
    down curtains.

November 18

He showed us a road which led down.
We would not get lost, he said, there were many lights.
Through abandoned orchards, vineyards and embankments
overgrown with brambles we took a shortcut,
and the lights were, as you will—the lanterns
of gigantic glowworms, or small planets
descending in uncertain flight.
Once, when we tried to make a turn up
everything went out. And in total darkness
I understood we must march on into the gorge
since only then the lights would lead us again.
I held her hand, we were united
by bodily memory
of journeying together on a lovers' bed,
that is to say, one time in the wheat or a dense forest.
Below a torrent roared, there were frozen rockslides
the atrocious color of lunar sulphur.

November 23

A long train is standing in the station and the platform is empty.
Winter, night, the frozen sky is flooded with red.
Only a woman's weeping is heard. She is pleading for something
from an officer in a stone coat.

December 1

The halls of the infernal station, drafty and cold.
A knock at the door, the door opens
and my dead father appears in the doorway
but he is young, handsome, beloved.
He offers me his hand. I run away from him
down a spiral staircase, never-ending.

December 3
With a broad white beard and dressed in velvet,
Walt Whitman was leading dances in a country manor
owned by Swedenborg, Emanuel.
And I was there as well, drinking mead and wine.
At first we circled hand in hand
and resembled stones overgrown with mold,
set into motion. Then the invisible
orchestras played more quickly, and we were seized
by the madness of the dance, in elation.
And that dance, of harmony, of concord
was a dance of happy Hassidim.

December 14
I moved my strong wings, below were gliding
bluish meadows, willows, a winding river.
Here is the castle with its moat, and nearby, the gardens
where my beloved takes a walk.
But as I returned, I had to take care
not to lose the magic book
stuck in my belt. I could never manage
to soar very high, and there were mountains.
I struggled painfully to the ridge above the forest
rusty from the leaves of oaks and chestnuts.
There, at birds carved on a dry branch,
an invisible hand was throwing boughs
to draw me down by magic means.
I fell. She kept me on her glove,
now a hawk with bloodstained plume,
the Witch of the Desert. In the castle she had
    found out
the incantations printed in my book.

March 16
The unsummoned face. How he died no one knows.
I repeated my question until he took flesh.
And he, a boxer, hits the guard in the jaw,
for which boots trample him. I look at the guard
with dog's eyes and have one desire:
to carry out every order, so he will praise me.
And even when he sent me to the city,
a city of arcades, of passages, of marble squares
(it seems to be Venice), stepping on the slabs,
in funny rags, barefoot, with an oversize cap,
I think of fulfilling only what he assigned me,
I show my permits and carry for him
a Japanese doll (the vendor didn't know its value).

March 24
It is a country on the edge of the Rudnicka Wilderness,
for example, beside the sawmill at Jashuny, between the fir-forest of
     Kiejdzie
and the villages of Czernica, Mariampol, Halina.
Perhaps the river Yerres runs there
between banks of anemones on marshy meadows.
The inseminator-pines, footbridges, tall ferns.
How the earth heaves! Not in order to burst,
but it tells with a movement of its skin
that it can make trees bow to one another and tumble down.
For that reason joy. Such as people never
have known before. Rejoice! Rejoice!
in a path, in a shack, in a protruding stone.
And water! But in that water whatever you shoot sinks.
Joseph, smelling of cheap tobacco, stands on the bank.
—I shot a bear, but it fell in.—When?

—This afternoon.—Stupid, look, see that keg?
There's your bear, floating in it. Where's the bear? Shame.
It's only a wounded bear cub breathing.

March 26
Through the meadow fields at night,
through the meadow fields of civilization
we ran shouting, singing, in a tongue not our own
but one which terrified others.
They ran before us, we took two-yard,
three-yard strides,
limitlessly powerful, happy.
Turning out its lights, a car stopped: a different one,
a car from there. We heard voices
speaking near us in a tongue we had used only for amusement.
Now we, the pretenders, were seized by fear
so great that over fences and palisades
in fourteen-yard leaps we ran into the depths of the forest.
And behind us the hue and cry
in a Scythian or Lombard dialect.

April 3
Our expedition rode into a land of dry lava.
Perhaps under us were armor and crowns
but here there was not a tree,
or even lichens growing on the rocks,
and in the birdless sky, racing through filmy clouds
the sun went down between black concretions.

When slowly, in that complete stillness
in which not a lizard was rustling
gravel began to crunch under the wheels of the trucks

suddenly we saw, standing on a hill,
a pink corset with ribbon floating.
Further a second and a third. So, baring our heads,
we walked toward them, temples in ruins.

Montgeron, 1955

FAR WEST

"Gently, my lambs, move gently"
Through bays, many, of darkening time.
Sea lions with scepters on rocky thrones.
Far, far from everything, throw behind you a comb, a forest will grow,
Throw behind you a mirror, an ocean will ripen.

All reputation at last overthrown.
No years, no clocks, no memory of how, kneeling, we panned gold.
The saddles creaked and in the bison grass statues fell apart.
Till there was what was fated. Only the earth and the sea.

Salt, yellow mountains, a dwarf oak and foam.
Would they whisper of their merits to the albatrosses?
We know better. Nothing witnesses here.
Gently, my lambs, move gently.

Berkeley, 1962

THROUGHOUT OUR LANDS

1

When I pass'd through a populous city
(as Walt Whitman says, in the Polish version)
When I pass'd through a populous city,
for instance near San Francisco harbor, counting gulls,
I thought that between men, women, and children there is
something, neither happiness nor unhappiness.

2

At noon white rubble of cemeteries on the hillsides:
a city of eye-dazzling cements
glued together with the slime of winged insects
spins with the sky about the spiraled freeways.

3

If I had to tell what the world is for me
I would take a hamster or a hedgehog or a mole
and place him in a theater seat one evening
and, bringing my ear close to his humid snout,
would listen to what he says about the spotlights,
sounds of the music, and movements of the dance.

4

Was I breaking the sound barrier?
And then clouds with cathedrals,
ecstatic greens beyond wrought-iron gates
and silence, surprisingly, different from what I'd known.
Here I am where the fist of an old woman is wrapped
        with a rosary,
a cane taps on flagstones between dappled shadows.
Is it a shame or not
that this is my portion?

5

Waking before dawn, I saw the gray lake
and, as usual, two men trolling in a motorboat, which sputtered
    slowly.
Next, I was awakened by the sun shining straight into my eyes
as it stood above the pass on the Nevada side.
Between the moment and the moment I lived through much in my
    sleep
so distinctly that I felt time dissolve
and knew that what was past still is, not was.
And I hope this will be counted somehow in my defense:
my regret and great longing once to express
one life, not for my glory, for a different splendor.
Later on a slight wind creased the iridescent water.
I was forgetting. Snow glittered on the mountains.

6

And the word revealed out of darkness was: *pear*.
I hovered around it hopping or trying my wings.
But whenever I was just about to drink its sweetness, it withdrew.
So I tried Anjou—then a garden's corner,
scaling white paint of wooden shutters,
a dogwood bush and rustling of departed people.
So I tried Comice—then right away fields
beyond this (not another) palisade, a brook, countryside.
So I tried Jargonelle, Bosc, and Bergamot.
No good. Between me and pear, equipages, countries.
And so I have to live, with this spell on me.

7

With their chins high, girls come back from the tennis courts.
The spray rainbows over the sloping lawns.

With short jerks a robin runs up, stands motionless.
The eucalyptus tree trunks glow in the light.
The oaks perfect the shadow of May leaves.
Only this is worthy of praise. Only this: the day.

But beneath it elemental powers are turning somersaults;
and devils, mocking the naive who believe in them,
play catch with hunks of bloody meat,
whistle songs about matter without beginning or end,
and about the moment of our death
when everything we have cherished will appear
an artifice of cunning self-love.

8
And what if Pascal had not been saved
and if those narrow hands in which we laid a cross
are all he is, entire, like a lifeless swallow
in the dust, under the buzz of the poisonous-blue flies?

And if they all, kneeling with poised palms,
millions, billions of them, ended together with their illusion?
I shall never agree. I will give them the crown.
The human mind is splendid; lips powerful,
and the summons so great it must open Paradise.

9
They are so persistent, that give them a few stones
and edible roots, and they will build the world.

10
Over his grave they were playing Mozart,
Since they had nothing to keep themselves distinct

From the yellow dirt, clouds, wilted dahlias,
And under a sky too big, there was too much silence.

And just as at the tea party of a princess
When a stalactite of wax drips out the measure,
And a wick sizzles, and shoulders in frock coats
Gleam in their rows of high gold-braided collars,

Mozart has sounded, unwrapped from the powder of wigs,
And suspended on trails of late-summer gossamer,
Vanishing overhead, in that void where
A jet has gone, leaving a thin white seam.

While he, a contemporary of no one,
Black as a grub beneath the winter bark,
Was at work already, calling in rust and mold
So as to vanish, before they took the faded wreaths.

11
Paulina, her room behind the servants' quarters, with one window
    on the orchard
where I gather the best apples near the pigsty
squishing with my big toe the warm muck of the dunghill,
and the other window on the well (I love to drop the
    bucket down
and scare its inhabitants, the green frogs).
Paulina, a geranium, the chill of a dirt floor,
a hard bed with three pillows,
an iron crucifix and images of the saints,
decorated with palms and paper roses.
Paulina died long ago, but is.
And, I am somehow convinced, not just in my consciousness.

Above her rough Lithuanian peasant face
hovers a spindle of hummingbirds, and her flat calloused feet
are sprinkled by sapphire water in which dolphins
with their backs arching
frolic.

12
Wherever you are, colors of the sky envelop you
just as here, shrill oranges and violets,
the smell of a leaf pulped in your fingers accompanies you
even in your dream, birds are named
in the language of that place: a *towhee* came to the kitchen,
scatter some bread on the lawn, *juncos* have arrived.
Wherever you are, you touch the bark of trees
testing its roughness different yet familiar.
Grateful for a rising and a setting sun
Wherever you are, you could never be an alien.

Was Father Junipero an alien, when on mule-back
he came here, wandering through the deserts of the south.
He found redskin brothers. Their reason and memory
were dimmed. They had been roaming very far
from the Euphrates, the Pamirs, and the heights of Cathay,
slowly, as far as any generation can
pursuing its goal: good hunting grounds.
And there, where later the land sank into the cold
shallow sea, they had lived thousands of years,
until they had almost completely forgotten the Garden of Eden
and had not yet learned the reckoning of time.
Father Junipero, born on the Mediterranean,
brought them news about their first parents,
about the signs, the promise, and the expectation.
He told them, exiles, that there, in their native land,

their guilt had been washed away, just as dust is washed
from their foreheads, sprinkled with water.
It was like something they had heard of long ago.
But, poor people, they had lost the gift of concentration
and a preacher had to hang from his neck a roasted flank
     of deer
in order to attract their greedy eyes.
But then they slobbered, so loudly, he could not speak.

Nonetheless it was they who in my place took possession
of rocks on which only mute dragons
were basking from the beginning, crawling out of the sea.
They sewed a clock from the plumage of flickers, hummingbirds,
     and tanagers,
and a brown arm, throwing back the mantle, would point to: this.
And the land was henceforth conquered: seen.

13
Whiskers of rabbits and downy necks
of yellow-black ducklings, the flowing fire
of a fox in the green, touch the heart
of master and slave. And also musics
starting under the trees. A snare drum, a flute
or a concertina or from a gramophone
the voices of djinns bleating jazz.
A swing goes up to the clouds, and those looking from below
have their breath taken away by the darkness under a skirt.
Who has not dreamt of the Marquis de Sade's châteaux?
When one ("ah-h-h!") rubs his hands
and to the job: to gouge with a spur
young girls drawn up in line for footrace
or to order naked nuns in black net stockings
to lash us with a whip as we bite the bedsheets.

14

Cabeza, if anyone knew all about civilization, it was you.
A bookkeeper from Castile, what a fix you were in
to have to wander about, where no notion,
no cipher, no stroke of a pen dipped in sepia,
only a boat thrown up on the sand by surf,
crawling naked on all fours, under the eye of immobile Indians,
and suddenly their wail in the void of sky and sea,
their lament: that even the gods are unhappy.
For seven years you were their predicted god,
bearded, white-skinned, beaten if you couldn't work a miracle.
Seven years' march from the Mexican Gulf to California,
the hu-hu-hu of tribes, hot bramble of the continent.
But afterward? Who am I, the lace of cuffs
not mine, the table carved with lions not mine, Doña Clara's
fan, the slipper from under her gown—hell, no.
On all fours! On all fours!
Smear our thighs with war paint.
Lick the ground. Wha wha, hu hu.

Berkeley, 1961

BOBO'S

METAMORPHOSIS

(Gucio zaczarowany)

1 9 6 5

IT WAS WINTER

Winter came as it does in this valley.
After eight dry months rain fell
And the mountains, straw-colored, turned green for a while.
In the canyons where gray laurels
Graft their stony roots to granite,
Streams must have filled the dried-up creek beds.
Ocean winds churned the eucalyptus trees,
And under clouds torn by a crystal of towers
Prickly lights were glowing on the docks.

This is not a place where you sit under a café awning
On a marble piazza, watching the crowd,
Or play the flute at a window over a narrow street
While children's sandals clatter in the vaulted entryway.

They heard of a land, empty and vast,
Bordered by mountains. So they went, leaving behind crosses
Of thorny wood and traces of campfires.
As it happened, they spent winter in the snow of a mountain pass,
And drew lots and boiled the bones of their companions;
And so afterward a hot valley where indigo could be grown
Seemed beautiful to them. And beyond, where fog
Heaved into shoreline coves, the ocean labored.

Sleep: rocks and capes will lie down inside you,
War councils of motionless animals in a barren place,
Basilicas of reptiles, a frothy whiteness.
Sleep on your coat, while your horse nibbles grass
And an eagle gauges a precipice.

When you wake up, you will have the parts of the world.
West, an empty conch of water and air.
East, always behind you, the voided memory of snow-covered fir.

And extending from your outspread arms
Nothing but bronze grasses, north and south.

We are poor people, much afflicted.
We camped under various stars,
Where you dip water with a cup from a muddy river
And slice your bread with a pocketknife.
This is the place; accepted, not chosen.
We remembered that there were streets and houses where we came
    from,
So there had to be houses here, a saddler's signboard,
A small veranda with a chair. But empty, a country where
The thunder beneath the rippled skin of the earth,
The breaking waves, a patrol of pelicans, nullified us.
As if our vases, brought here from another shore,
Were the dug-up spearheads of some lost tribe
Who fed on lizards and acorn flour.

And here I am walking the eternal earth.
Tiny, leaning on a stick.
I pass a volcanic park, lie down at a spring,
Not knowing how to express what is always and everywhere:
The earth I cling to is so solid
Under my breast and belly that I feel grateful
For every pebble, and I don't know whether
It is my pulse or the earth's that I hear,
When the hems of invisible silk vestments pass over me,
Hands, wherever they have been, touch my arm,
Or small laughter, once, long ago over wine,
With lanterns in the magnolias, for my house is huge.

Berkeley, 1964

BOBO'S METAMORPHOSIS

The distance between being and nothingness is infinite.
      —Entertainments Pleasant and Useful
      (Zabawy przyjemne i pożyteczne, 1776)

I
Fields sloping down and a trumpet.

    ÷

Dusk and a bird flies low and waters flare.

    ÷

Sails unfurled to the daybreak beyond the straits.

    ÷

I was entering the interior of a lily by a bridge of brocade.

    ÷

Life was given but unattainable.

    ÷

From childhood till old age ecstasy at sunrise.

II
As life goes, many of these mornings.
My eyes closed, I was grown up and small.
I was wearing plumes, silks, ruffles and armor,
Women's dresses, I was licking the rouge.
I was hovering at each flower from the day of creation,
I knocked on the closed doors of the beaver's halls and the mole's.
It's incredible that there were so many unrecorded voices
Between a toothpaste and a rusted blade,
Just over my table in Wilno, Warsaw, Brie, Montgeron, California.
It's incredible that I die before I attain.

III

From the taste and scent of bird-cherry trees above rivers
Consciousness hikes through bay and hibiscus thickets
Gathering specimens of the Earth into a green box.
Above it, the red bark of *Sequoia sempervirens*
And jays, different from those beyond the Bering Strait,
Open their wings of indigo color.
Consciousness alone, without friends and foes,
Embraces forest slopes, an eagle's nest.
Incomprehensible as it is to a snake with a yellow stripe,
Itself unable to grasp the principle of the snake and tree.

IV

Stars of Philemon, stars of Baucis,
Above their house entangled by the roots of an oak.
And a wandering god, soundly asleep on a thong-strung bed,
His fist for a pillow.
An advancing weevil encounters his sandal
And pushes on painfully through a foot-polished mesa.

I hear also sounds of a pianoforte.
I steal through humid blackness under the jungle of spirea
Where are scattered clay flasks from Dutch aquavit.
She appears, a young lady with a curl on her ear.
But I grew a beard when walking on all fours
And my Indian bow rotted from snow and rain.
She plays music and simultaneously grows small, sits down on her
     chamberpot,
At a swing she pulls up her skirt
To do indecent things with me or her cousin.
And all of a sudden she walks grayhaired in a scraggy suburb,
Then departs without delay where all the maidens go.

Let there be an island—and an island crops out of the deep.
The pale rose of its cliffs is tinged with violet.
Seeds sprout, on the hills, presto, chestnuts and cedars,
A spring waves a fern just above the harbor.

On flat rocks over fir-green water of the cove
Spirits lounge, similar to skin divers with their oxygen tanks.
The only daughter of a sorcerer, Miranda,
Rides a donkey in the direction of the grotto
By a path strewn with creaking leaves.
She sees a tripod, a kettle, and bundles of dry twigs.
Vanish, island! Or stronger: go away!

V
I liked him as he did not look for an ideal object.
When he heard: "Only the object which does not exist
Is perfect and pure," he blushed and turned away.

In every pocket he carried pencils, pads of paper
Together with crumbs of bread, the accidents of life.

Year after year he circled a thick tree
Shading his eyes with his hand and muttering in amazement.

How much he envied those who draw a tree with one line!
But metaphor seemed to him something indecent.

He would leave symbols to the proud busy with their cause.
By looking he wanted to draw the name from the very thing.

When he was old, he tugged at his tobacco-stained beard:
"I prefer to lose thus than to win as they do."

Like Peter Breughel the father he fell suddenly
While attempting to look back between his spread-apart legs.

And still the tree stood there, unattainable.
Veritable, true to the very core.

VI
They reproached him with marrying one woman and living with
    another.
Have no time—he answered—for nonsense, a divorce and so on.
A man gets up, a few strokes of a brush and then already it's evening.

VII
Bobo, a nasty boy, was changed into a fly.
In accordance with the rite of the flies he washed himself by a rock
    of sugar
And ran vertically in caves of cheese.
He flew through a window into the bright garden.
There, indomitable ferryboats of leaves
Carried a drop taut with the excess of its rainbow,
Mossy parks grew by ponds of light in the mountains of bark,
An acrid dust was falling from flexible columns inside cinnabar
    flowers.
And though it did not last longer than from teatime till supper,
Later on, when he had pressed trousers and a trimmed
    moustache,
He always thought, holding a glass of liquor, that he was cheating
    them
For a fly should not discuss the nation and productivity.
A woman facing him was a volcanic peak
Where there were ravines, craters and in hollows of lava
The movement of earth was tilting crooked trunks of pines.

VIII

Between her and me there was a table, on the table a glass.
The chapped skin of her elbows touched the shining surface
In which the contour of shade under her armpit was reflected.
A drop of sweat thickened over her wavy lip.
And the space between her and me fractionized itself infinitely
Buzzing with pennate Eleatic arrows.
Not a year, not a hundred years of journey would exhaust it.
Had I overturned the table what would we have accomplished.
That act, a non-act, always no more than potential
Like the attempt to penetrate water, wood, minerals.
But she, too, looked at me as if I were a ring of Saturn
And knew I was aware that no one attains.
Thus were affirmed humanness, tenderness.

Berkeley, 1962

RIVERS GROW SMALL

Rivers grow small. Cities grow small. And splendid gardens
show what we did not see there before: crippled leaves and dust.
When for the first time I swam across the lake
it seemed immense, had I gone there these days
it would have been a shaving bowl
between post-glacial rocks and junipers.
The forest near the village of Halina once was for me primeval,
smelling of the last but recently killed bear,
though a ploughed field was visible through the pines.
What was individual becomes a variety of a general pattern.
Consciousness even in my sleep changes primary colors.
The features of my face melt like a wax doll in the fire.
And who can consent to see in the mirror the mere face of man?

Berkeley, 1963

THEY WILL PLACE THERE
TELESCREENS

They will place telescreens there and our life
will be appearing from end to end
with everything we have managed to forget, as it seemed, forever,
and with dresses of our time, which would be laughable and piteous
had we not been wearing them because we knew nothing better.
Armageddon of men and women. It is no use to cry: I loved them,
every one seemed to me a child, greedy and in need of caresses.
I liked beaches, swimming pools, and clinics
for there they were the bone of my bone, the flesh of my flesh.
I pitied them and myself, but this will not protect me.
The word and the thought are over, a shifting of a glass,
an averting of one's eyes, fingers unbuttoning a blouse, foolishness,
a cheating gesture, contemplation of clouds,
a convenient dispatch: only that.
And what if they march out, tinkling bells
at their ankles, if slowly they enter the flame
which has taken them as well as me? Bite your (if you have any)
    fingers
and again look at everything from end to end.

Berkeley, 1964

ON THE OTHER SIDE

Falling, I caught the curtain,
Its velvet was the last thing I could feel on earth
As I slid to the floor, howling: aah! aaah!

To the very end I could not believe that I too must . . .
Like everyone.

Then I trod in wheel-ruts
On an ill-paved road. Wooden shacks,
A lame tenement house in a field of weeds.
Potato patches fenced in with barbed wire.
They played as-if-cards, I smelled as-if-cabbage,
There was as-if-vodka, as-if-dirt, as-if-time.
I said: "See here . . . ," but they shrugged their shoulders,
Or averted their eyes. This land knew nothing of surprise.
Nor of flowers. Dry geraniums in tin cans,
A deception of greenery coated with sticky dust.
Nor of the future. Gramophones played,
Repeating endlessly things which had never been.
Conversations repeated things which had never been.
So that no one should guess where he was, or why.
I saw hungry dogs lengthening and shortening their muzzles,
And changing from mongrels, to greyhounds, then dachshunds,
As if to signify they were perhaps not quite dogs.
Huge flocks of crows, freezing in midair,
Exploded under the clouds . . .

Berkeley, 1964

AND THE CITY STOOD
IN ITS BRIGHTNESS

And the city stood in its brightness when years later I returned.
And life was running out, Ruteboeuf's or Villon's.
Descendants, already born, were dancing their dances.
Women looked in their mirrors made from a new metal.
What was it all for if I cannot speak.
She stood above me, heavy, like the earth on its axis.
My ashes were laid in a can under the bistro counter.

And the city stood in its brightness when years later I returned
To my home in the display case of a granite museum,
Beside eyelash mascara, alabaster vials,
And menstruation girdles of an Egyptian princess.
There was only a sun forged out of gold plate,
On darkening parquetry the creak of unhurried steps.

And the city stood in its brightness when years later I returned,
My face covered with a coat though now no one was left
Of those who could have remembered my debts never paid,
My shames not forever, base deeds to be forgiven.
And the city stood in its brightness when years later I returned.

Paris–Berkeley, 1963

THOSE CORRIDORS

I walk those corridors by torchlight
Hearing water trickle down onto broken slabs.
Deep into the mountain. In niches, busts of my friends,
Their eyes are of marble. Only the light and shadow
Throw over their faces a brief sour grimace of life.
So, farther into the labyrinth leading to the dark interior,
Where there are no kobolds, only the echo of my steps,
Until the torch gutters out, and on the unknown bend
Where it is fated, I will turn to stone.
But at the entrance, blocked by a landslide and soon forgotten,
In a fir forest by a stream falling from a glacier,
A doe will give birth to her freckled fawn and the air
Will unfurl intricate leafy spirals to other eyes, as once to mine.
And every joy of morning will be discovered again,
Each savoring of an apple picked in the tall orchard.
So I can leave peacefully everything I loved.
The earth will carry aqueducts, amphoras, brass chandeliers.
And when some day dogs chasing a bear
Burst into a crevasse and people of far-off generations
Decipher our angular letters on the walls—
They will be amazed that we knew so many of their own joys,
Though our futile palace has come to mean so little.

Oregon–Berkeley, 1964

THREE TALKS ON CIVILIZATION

1

The dark blush of anger
the impolite reply
the loathing of foreigners
uphold the State.

Roars at a touchdown
slums near the harbors
liquor for the poor
uphold the State.

Hermance, if at a twist of my ring
those quarters vanished through which my retinue
rushes forward not to see eyes fixed on nothing,

if people (instead of everyday necessity and the, so to speak,
hairy pleasures proper to the flesh),
spick-and-span, pretending they do not stink at all,

nibbled chocolates in a theater,
if they were moved by the loves of Amyntas,
and in the daytime read the *Summa*, luckily too difficult,

none would be fit for the barracks. The State would fall.

2

Yes, it is true that the landscape changed a little.
Where there were forests, now there are pears of factories, gas tanks.
Approaching the mouth of the river we hold our noses.
Its current carries oil and chlorine and methyl compounds,
Not to mention the by-products of the Books of Abstraction:
Excrement, urine, and dead sperm.
A huge stain of artificial color poisons fish in the sea.

Where the shore of the bay was overgrown with rushes
Now it is rusted with smashed machines, ashes, and bricks.
We used to read in old poets about the scent of earth
And grasshoppers. Now we bypass the fields:
Ride as fast as you can through the chemical zone of the farmers.
The insect and the bird are extinguished. Far away a bored man
Drags the dust with his tractor, an umbrella against the sun.
What do we regret?—I ask. A tiger? A shark?
We created a second Nature in the image of the first
So as not to believe that we live in Paradise.
It is possible that when Adam woke in the garden
The beasts licked the air and yawned, friendly,
While their fangs and their tails, lashing their backs,
Were figurative and the red-backed shrike,
Later, much later, named *Lanius collurio*,
Did not impale caterpillars on spikes of the blackthorn.
However, other than that moment, what we know of Nature
Does not speak in its favor. Ours is no worse.
So I beg you, no more of those lamentations.

3
If I only knew one thing, this one thing:
Can contrition be just wounded pride?

Wood-paneled corridors open.
A satin slipper patters down a sloping floor.
Dear neck, its scent lingers forever.
Already henchmen come running with proofs of my crime:
Bloodstains in a suburb, the forgotten knife.

And when they chase me on the stairs till dawn,
I cannot tell, stumbling, grasping at curtains,
Whether my terror is perfect remorse,

Or shame of dying without dignity.
Later I stare in the mirror at my swollen eyelids.

Therefore, I think, I wrote to Alexander,
Advising him to curb the youth societies,
(You will find this, Hermantia, dated eighteen twenty).
I detested these pups of foolish Jean-Jacques,
And envied them their belief in their own noble nature.

Berkeley, 1963

SENTENCES

What constitutes the training of the hand?
I shall tell what constitutes the training of the hand.
One suspects something is wrong with transcribing signs
But the hand transcribes only the signs it has learned.
Then it is sent to the school of blots and scrawls
Till it forgets what is graceful. For even the sign of a butterfly
Is a well with coiled poisonous smoke inside.

÷

Perhaps we should have represented him otherwise
Than in the form of dove. As fire, yes, but that is beyond us.
For even when it consumes logs on a hearth
We search in it for eyes and hands. Let him then be green,
All blades of calamus, running on footbridges
Over meadows, with a thump of his bare feet. Or in the air
Blowing a birchbark trumpet so strongly that farther down
There tumbles from its blast a crowd of petty officials,
Their uniforms unbuttoned and their women's combs
Flying like chips when the ax strikes.

÷

Still it's just too great a responsibility to lure the souls
From where they lived attentive to the idea of the hummingbird,
      the chair, and the star.
To imprison them within either-or: male sex, female sex,
So that they wake up in the blood of childbirth, crying.

Berkeley, 1963–1965

I SLEEP A LOT

I sleep a lot and read St. Thomas Aquinas
or *The Death of God* (that's a Protestant book).
To the right the bay as if molten tin,
beyond the bay, city, beyond the city, ocean,
beyond the ocean, ocean, till Japan.
To the left dry hills with white grass,
beyond the hills an irrigated valley where rice is grown,
beyond the valley, mountains and Ponderosa pines,
beyond the mountains, desert and sheep.

When I couldn't do without alcohol, I drove myself on alcohol,
When I couldn't do without cigarettes and coffee, I drove myself
    on cigarettes and coffee.
I was courageous. Industrious. Nearly a model of virtue.
But that is good for nothing.

Please, Doctor, I feel a pain.
Not here. No, not here. Even I don't know.
Maybe it's too many islands and continents,
unpronounced words, bazaars, wooden flutes,
or too much drinking to the mirror, without beauty,
though one was to be a kind of archangel
or a Saint George, over there, on St. George Street.

Please, Medicine Man, I feel a pain.
I always believed in spells and incantations.
Sure, women have only one, Catholic, soul,
but we have two. When you start to dance
you visit remote pueblos in your sleep
and even lands you have never seen.
Put on, I beg you, charms made of feathers,
now it's time to help one of your own.
I have read many books but I don't believe them.

When it hurts we return to the banks of certain rivers.
I remember those crosses with chiseled suns and moons
and wizards, how they worked during an outbreak of typhus.
Send your second soul beyond the mountains, beyond time.
Tell me what you saw, I will wait.

Berkeley, 1962

DITHYRAMB

We have seen so much on earth and yet malachite mountains at sunset
    are greeted as always with a song and a low bow.
The same spring dance summons when under the rubble of basalt cliffs
    flocks of birds plunge in translucent waters of coves.
And a finny hand of a sea otter glimmers as it wallows in the foam at
    Point Lobos.
While in the fog the red of azaleas glows from the bottom of steamy
    ravines.
Nothing has been added, nothing has been taken away, o
    imperturbable, perfect, inviolable world.
No memory is preserved about anything that would be ours for
    certain.
A melody of a mouth organ from afar, from indefinite years or a path
    on which we fell united by a kiss.
Flax asleep on spinning wheels, apples and grain in barn bays, brown
    circles on the breasts of cousin Tonia.
Submachine gun bursts on a plain burrowed with anti-tank trenches,
    under the torn curtain of a cloudy dawn.
Who will affirm, who will call "mine" a fruitless, fruitless, painfully
    called-back dream?
With rustling of Renaissance dresses our dead women pass by, turn
    about and put a finger to their lips.
Armored companions sat down at a chessboard, setting aside their
    visored helmets.
And love's dominion, a live gold in blood, annihilates forever our
    empty name.

Berkeley, 1965

CITY
WITHOUT
A NAME

(Miasto bez imienia)

1969

THE YEAR

I looked around in the unknown year, aware that few are those who
    come from so far, I was saturated with sunlight as a plant with
    water.
That was a high year, fox-colored, like a crosscut redwood stump or
    vine leaves on the hills in November.
In its groves and chambers the pulse of music was beating strongly,
    running down from dark mountains, tributaries entangled.
A generation clad in patterned robes trimmed with little bells greeted
    me with the banging of conga drums.
I repeated their guttural songs of ecstatic despair walking by the sea
    when it bore in boys on surfboards and washed my footprints
    away.
At the very border of inhabited time the same lessons were being
    learned, how to walk on two legs and to pronounce the signs
    traced in the always childish book of our species.
I would have related, had I known how, everything which a single
    memory can gather for the praise of men.
O sun, o stars, I was saying, holy, holy, holy is our being beneath
    heaven and the day and our endless communion.

Berkeley, 1965

CITY WITHOUT A NAME

1

Who will honor the city without a name
If so many are dead and others pan gold
Or sell arms in faraway countries?

What shepherd's horn swathed in the bark of birch
Will sound in the Ponary Hills the memory of the absent—
Vagabonds, Pathfinders, brethren of a dissolved lodge?

This spring, in a desert, beyond a campsite flagpole,
—In silence that stretched to the solid rock of yellow and red
    mountains—
I heard in a gray bush the buzzing of wild bees.

The current carried an echo and the timber of rafts.
A man in a visored cap and a woman in a kerchief
Pushed hard with their four hands at a heavy steering oar.

In the library, below a tower painted with the signs of the zodiac,
Kontrym would take a whiff from his snuffbox and smile
For despite Metternich all was not yet lost.

And on crooked lanes down the middle of a sandy highway
Jewish carts went their way while a black grouse hooted
Standing on a cuirassier's helmet, a relict of La Grande Armée.

2

In Death Valley I thought about styles of hairdo,
About a hand that shifted spotlights at the Students' Ball
In the city from which no voice could reach me.
Minerals did not sound the last trumpet.
There was only the rustle of a loosened grain of lava.

In Death Valley salt gleams from a dried-up lake bed.
Defend, defend yourself, says the tick-tock of the blood.
From the futility of solid rock, no wisdom.

In Death Valley no hawk or eagle against the sky.
The prediction of a Gypsy woman has come true.
In a lane under an arcade, then, I was reading a poem
Of someone who had lived next door, entitled "An Hour of
    Thought."

I looked long at the rearview mirror: there, the one man
Within three hundred miles, an Indian, was walking a bicycle uphill.

3
With flutes, with torches
And a drum, boom, boom,
Look, the one who died in Istanbul, there, in the first row.
He walks arm in arm with his young lady,
And over them swallows fly.

They carry oars or staffs garlanded with leaves
And bunches of flowers from the shores of the Green Lakes,
As they come closer and closer, down Castle Street.
And then suddenly nothing, only a white puff of cloud
Over the Humanities Students Club,
Division of Creative Writing.

4
Books, we have written a whole library of them.
Lands, we have visited a great many of them.
Battles, we have lost a number of them.
Till we are no more, we and our Maryla.

5

Understanding and pity,
We value them highly.
What else?

Beauty and kisses,
Fame and its prizes,
Who cares?

Doctors and lawyers,
Well-turned-out majors,
Six feet of earth.

Rings, furs, and lashes,
Glances at Masses,
Rest in peace.

Sweet twin breasts, good night.
Sleep through to the light,
Without spiders.

6

The sun goes down above the Zealous Lithuanian Lodge
And kindles fire on landscapes "made from nature":
The Wilia winding among pines; black honey of the Żejmiana;
The Mereczanka washes berries near the Żegaryno village.
The valets had already brought in Theban candelabra
And pulled curtains, one after the other, slowly,
While, thinking I entered first, taking off my gloves,
I saw that all the eyes were fixed on me.

7

When I got rid of grieving
And the glory I was seeking,
Which I had no business doing,

I was carried by dragons
Over countries, bays, and mountains,
By fate, or by what happens.

Oh yes, I wanted to be me.
I toasted mirrors weepily
And learned my own stupidity.

From nails, mucous membrane,
Lungs, liver, bowels, and spleen
Whose house is made? Mine.

So what else is new?
I am not my own friend.
Time cuts me in two.

Monuments covered with snow,
Accept my gift. I wandered;
And where, I don't know.

8

Absent, burning, acrid, salty, sharp.
Thus the feast of Insubstantiality.
Under a gathering of clouds anywhere.
In a bay, on a plateau, in a dry arroyo.
No density. No hardness of stone.
Even the *Summa* thins into straw and smoke.

And the angelic choirs fly over in a pomegranate seed
Sounding every few instants, not for us, their trumpets.

9
Light, universal, and yet it keeps changing.
For I love the light too, perhaps the light only.
Yet what is too dazzling and too high is not for me.
So when the clouds turn rosy, I think of light that is level
In the lands of birch and pine coated with crispy lichen,
Late in autumn, under the hoarfrost when the last milk caps
Rot under the firs and the hounds' barking echoes,
And jackdaws wheel over the tower of a Basilian church.

10
Unexpressed, untold.
But how?
The shortness of life,
the years quicker and quicker,
not remembering whether it happened in this or that autumn.
Retinues of homespun velveteen skirts,
giggles above a railing, pigtails askew,
sittings on chamberpots upstairs
when the sledge jingles under the columns of the porch
just before the moustachioed ones in wolf fur enter.
Female humanity,
children's snot, legs spread apart,
snarled hair, the milk boiling over,
stench, shit frozen into clods.
And those centuries,
conceiving in the herring smell of the middle of the night
instead of playing something like a game of chess
or dancing an intellectual ballet.
And palisades,

and pregnant sheep,
and pigs, fast eaters and poor eaters,
and cows cured by incantations.

11

Not the Last Judgment, just a kermess by a river.
Small whistles, clay chickens, candied hearts.
So we trudged through the slush of melting snow
To buy bagels from the district of Smorgonie.

A fortune-teller hawking: "Your destiny, your planets."
And a toy devil bobbing in a tube of crimson brine.
Another, a rubber one, expired in the air squeaking,
By the stand where you bought stories of King Otto and Melusine.

12

Why should that city, defenseless and pure as the wedding necklace of a
forgotten tribe, keep offering itself to me?

Like blue and red-brown seeds beaded in Tuzigoot in the copper desert
seven centuries ago.

Where ocher rubbed into stone still waits for the brow and cheekbone
it would adorn, though for all that time there has been no one.

What evil in me, what pity has made me deserve this offering?

It stands before me, ready, not even the smoke from one chimney is
lacking, not one echo, when I step across the rivers that separate us.

Perhaps Anna and Dora Drużyno have called to me, three hundred
miles inside Arizona, because except for me no one else knows that they
ever lived.

They trot before me on Embankment Street, two gently born parakeets from Samogitia, and at night they unravel for me their spinster tresses of gray hair.

Here there is no earlier and no later; the seasons of the year and of the day are simultaneous.

At dawn shit-wagons leave town in long rows and municipal employees at the gate collect the turnpike toll in leather bags.

Rattling their wheels, "Courier" and "Speedy" move against the current to Werki, and an oarsman shot down over England skiffs past, spread-eagled by his oars.

At St. Peter and Paul's the angels lower their thick eyelids in a smile over a nun who has indecent thoughts.

Bearded, in a wig, Mrs. Sora Klok sits at the counter, instructing her twelve shopgirls.

And all of German Street tosses into the air unfurled bolts of fabric, preparing itself for death and the conquest of Jerusalem.

Black and princely, an underground river knocks at cellars of the cathedral under the tomb of St. Casimir the Young and under the half-charred oak logs in the hearth.

Carrying her servant's-basket on her shoulder, Barbara, dressed in mourning, returns from the Lithuanian Mass at St. Nicholas to the Romers' house on Bakszta Street.

How it glitters! the snow on Three Crosses Hill and Bekiesz Hill, not to be melted by the breath of these brief lives.

And what do I know now, when I turn into Arsenal Street and open my eyes once more on a useless end of the world?

I was running, as the silks rustled, through room after room without stopping, for I believed in the existence of a last door.

But the shape of lips and an apple and a flower pinned to a dress were all that one was permitted to know and take away.

The Earth, neither compassionate nor evil, neither beautiful nor atrocious, persisted, innocent, open to pain and desire.

And the gift was useless, if, later on, in the flarings of distant nights, there was not less bitterness but more.

If I cannot so exhaust my life and their life that the bygone crying is transformed, at last, into a harmony.

Like a *Noble Jan Dęboróg* in the Straszun's secondhand-book shop, I am put to rest forever between two familiar names.

The castle tower above the leafy tumulus grows small and there is still a hardly audible—is it Mozart's *Requiem?*—music.

In the immobile light I move my lips and perhaps I am even glad not to find the desired word.

Berkeley, 1968

WHEN THE MOON

When the moon rises and women in flowery dresses are strolling,
I am struck by their eyes, eyelashes, and the whole arrangement of
    the world.
It seems to me that from such a strong mutual attraction
The ultimate truth should issue at last.

Berkeley, 1966

VENI CREATOR

Come, Holy Spirit,
bending or not bending the grasses,
appearing or not above our heads in a tongue of flame,
at hay harvest or when they plough in the orchards or when snow
covers crippled firs in the Sierra Nevada.
I am only a man: I need visible signs.
I tire easily, building the stairway of abstraction.
Many a time I asked, you know it well, that the statue in church
lift its hand, only once, just once, for me.
But I understand that signs must be human,
therefore call one man, anywhere on earth,
not me—after all I have some decency—
and allow me, when I look at him, to marvel at you.

Berkeley, 1961

WINDOW

I looked out the window at dawn and saw a young apple tree translucent in brightness.

And when I looked out at dawn once again, an apple tree laden with fruit stood there.

Many years had probably gone by but I remember nothing of what happened in my sleep.

Berkeley, 1965

WITH TRUMPETS AND ZITHERS

1

The gift was never named. We lived and a hot light created stood in
 its sphere.

Castles on rocky spurs, herbs in river valleys, descents into the bays
 under ash trees.

All past wars in the flesh, all loves, conch shells of the Celts, Norman
 boats by the cliffs.

Breathing in, breathing out, o Elysium, we would kneel and kiss the
 earth.

A naked girl crossed a town overgrown with green moss and bees
 returned heavy for their evening milking.

Labyrinths of species at our headrest up to the thick of phosphorous
 woods at the entrance of limestone caves.

And in a summer rainstorm putting out paper lanterns on the dark
 village square, couples laughing in flight.

Water steamed at dawn by Calypso's island where an oriole flutters in
 the white crown of a poplar.

I looked at fishermen's dinghies stopped at the other shore and the
 year once again turned over, the vintage season began.

2

I address you, my consciousness, when in a sultry night shot with
 lightnings the plane is landing at Beauvais or Kalamazoo.

And a stewardess moves about quietly so not to wake anyone while
 the cellular wax of cities glimmers beneath.

I believed I would understand but it is late and I know nothing except
 laughter and weeping.

The wet grasses of fertile deltas cleansed me from time and changed all
 into a present without beginning or end.

I disappear in architectural spirals, in lines of a crystal, in the sound of
 instruments playing in forests.

Once again I return to excessive orchards and only the echo seeks me
 in that house on the hill under a hundred-year-old hazel tree.

Then how can you overtake me, you, weighing blame and merit, now
  when I do not remember who I am and who I was?
On many shores at once I am lying cheek on the sand and the same
  ocean runs in, beating its ecstatic drums.

3

And throughout the afternoon the endless talk of cicadas while on the
  slope they are drinking wine from a traveler's goblet.
Fingers ripping at meat, juice trickles on graying beards, a ring
  perhaps or glitter of a gold chain round the neck.
A beauty arrives from canopied beds, from cradles on rockers, washed
  and combed by her mother's hand so that undoing her hair we
  remove a tortoiseshell comb.
Skin scented with oils, arch-browed on city squares, her breasts for
  our cupped hands in the Tigris and Euphrates gardens.
Then they beat on the strings and shout on the heights and below at
  the bend of a river the campground's orange tents slowly
  surrender to shadows.

4

Nothing but laughter and weeping. Terror and no defense and arm in
  arm they drag me to a pit of tangled bones.
Soon I will join their dance, with bailiffs, wenches, and kings, such as
  they used to paint on the tablecloth at our revels.
With a train of my clock carried by the Great Jester, not I, just the
  Sinner to whom a honey-sweet age was brought by winged
  Fortune.
To whom three masked Slavic devils, Duliban, Kostruban, Mendrela,
  squealing and farting, would offer huge smoking plates.
Fingers grabbing at fingers, tongues fornicating with tongues, but not
  mine was the sense of touch, not mine was the knowledge.
Beyond seven rocky mountains I searched for my Teacher and yet I
  am here, not myself, at a pit of tangled bones.

I am standing on a theatrum, astonished by the last things, the puppet
   Death has black ribs and still I cannot believe.

5

The scent of freshly mown clover redeemed the perished armies and
   the meadows glittered in headlights forever.
An immense night of July filled my mouth with a taste of rain and
   near Puybrun by the bridges my childhood was given back.
The warm encampments of crickets chirped under a low cloud just as
   in our lost homelands where a wooden cart goes creaking.
Borne by an inscrutable power, one century gone, I heard, beating in
   darkness, the heart of the dead and the living.

6

What separates, falls. Yet my scream "no!" is still heard though it
   burned out in the wind.
Only what separates does not fall. All the rest is beyond persistence.
I wanted to describe this, not that, basket of vegetables with a
   redheaded doll of a leek laid across it.
And a stocking on the arm of a chair, a dress crumpled as it was, this
   way, no other.
I wanted to describe her, no one else, asleep on her belly, made secure
   by the warmth of his leg.
Also a cat in the unique tower as purring he composes his memorable
   book.
Not ships but one ship with a blue patch in the corner of its sail.
Not streets, for once there was a street with a shop sign:
   "Schuhmacher Pupke."
In vain I tried because what remains is the ever-recurring basket.
And not she whose skin perhaps I, of all men, loved, but a
   grammatical form.
No one cares that precisely this cat wrote *The Adventures of Telemachus*.
And the street will always be only one of many streets without name.

7

From a limbo for unbaptized infants and for animal souls let a dead fox
  step out to testify against the language.
Standing for a second in an ant-wing light of pine needles before a
  boy summoned to speak of him forty years later.
Not a general one, a plenipotentiary of the idea of the fox, in his cloak
  lined with the universals.
But he, from a coniferous forest near the village Żegary.
I bring him before the high tribunal in my defense, for what remains
  after desires are doubt and much regret.
And one runs and sails through archipelagoes in the hope of finding a
  place of immutable possession.
Till chandeliers in the rooms of Heloise or Annalena die out and
  angels blow trumpets on the steps of a sculptured bed.
A cheerless dawn advances beyond a palm-lined alley, loudly
  proclaimed by the rattling surf.
And whatever once entered a bolted house of the five senses now is
  set in the brocade of a style.
Which, your honor, does not distinguish particular cases.

8

At dawn the expanse takes its rise, a high horizontal whiteness up to
  the slopes of Tamalpais.
It is torn apart and in the wool of vapor a herd of islands and
  promontories on their watery pastures.
Knife-blue in twilight, a rose-tinted tin, liquid copper, izumrud,
  smaragdos.
Quiverfuls of buildings touched by a ray: Oakland, San Francisco,
  before the mica in motion lights up below: Berkeley, El Cerrito.
In the oceanic wind eucalyptus husks clashing and disentangling.
Height, length, and width take in their arms a sleeping caterpillar of a
  rolled body.

And carry it over a frozen waste of the Sierras to the most distant
    province of the continent.
Layers of Christmas tinsels wheel round, cities on the bay, buckled by
    luminous ropes of three bridges.
In the hour of ending night it amazes—this place, this time, assigned
    for an awakening of this particular body.

9
I asked what was the day. It was St. Andrew's Eve.
She and her smashed little mirrors under the weeds and snows where
    also the States and banners molder.
Outlandish districts in mud up to the axle-tree, names I alone
    remember: Gineitai, Apýtalaukis.
In the silence of stopped spinning-wheels, fear by the flame of two
    candles, a mouse scratching, a nuptial of phantoms.
In electronic music I heard lugubrious sirens, people's panicky calls
    crushed into flutters and rustles.
I was sitting before a mirror but no hand reached out of darkness to
    touch me on the shoulder.
There, behind me, flash after flash, flocks of birds were taking off from
    the banks of spring ice.
Fanning with their four wings storks stood on their nest in a majestic
    copulation.
My dishonest memory did not preserve anything, save the triumph of
    nameless births.
When I would hear a voice, it seemed to me I distinguished in it
    words of forgiveness.

10
The dream shared at night by all people has inhabitants, hairy animals.
It is a huge and snug forest and everyone entering it walks on all fours
    till dawn through the very thick of the tangle.

Through the wilderness inaccessible to metal objects, all-embracing
     like a warm and deep river.
In satin tunnels the touch distinguishes apples and their color that does
     not recall anything real.
All are quadrupeds, their thighs rejoice at the badger-bear softness,
     their rosy tongues lick each other's fur.
The "I" is felt with amazement in the heartbeat, but so large it cannot
     be filled by the whole Earth with her seasons.
Nor would the skin guarding a different essence trace any boundary.
Later on, in crude light, separated into you and me, they try with a
     bare foot pebbles of the floor.
The two-legged, some to the left, some to the right, put on their
     belts, garters, slacks, and sandals.
And they move on their stilts, longing after a forest home, after low
     tunnels, after an assigned return to It.

11

A coelentera, all pulsating flesh, animal-flower,
All fire, made up of falling bodies joined by the black pin of sex.
It breathes in the center of a galaxy, drawing to itself star after star.
And I, an instant of its duration, on multilaned roads which penetrate
     half-opened mountains.
Bare mountains overgrown with an ageless grass, opened and frozen at
     a sunset before the generations.
Where at large curves one sees nests of cisterns or transparent towers,
     perhaps of missiles.
Along brown leaks by the seashore, rusty stones and butcheries where
     quartered whales are ground to powder.
I wanted to be a judge but those whom I called "they" have changed
     into myself.
I was getting rid of my faith so as not to be better than men and
     women who are certain only of their unknowing.

And on the roads of my terrestrial homeland turning round with the
    music of the spheres
I thought that all I could do would be done better one day.

Berkeley, 1965

HOW IT WAS

Stalking a deer I wandered deep into the mountains and from there I saw.

Or perhaps it was for some other reason that I rose above the setting sun.

Above the hills of blackwood and a slab of ocean and the steps of a glacier, carmine-colored in the dusk.

I saw absence; the mighty power of counter-fulfillment; the penalty of a promise lost forever.

If, in tepees of plywood, tire shreds, and grimy sheet iron, ancient inhabitants of this land shook their rattles, it was all in vain.

No eagle-creator circled in the air from which the thunderbolt of its glory had been cast out.

Protective spirits hid themselves in subterranean beds of bubbling ore, jolting the surface from time to time so that the fabric of freeways was bursting asunder.

God the Father didn't walk about any longer tending the new shoots of a cedar, no longer did man hear his rushing spirit.

His son did not know his sonship and turned his eyes away when passing by a neon cross flat as a movie screen showing a striptease.

This time it was really the end of the Old and the New Testament.

No one implored, everyone picked up a nodule of agate or diorite to whisper in loneliness: I cannot live any longer.

Bearded messengers in bead necklaces founded clandestine communes in imperial cities and in ports overseas.

But none of them announced the birth of a child-savior.

Soldiers from expeditions sent to punish nations would go disguised and masked to take part in forbidden rites, not looking for any hope.

They inhaled smoke soothing all memory and, rocking from side to side, shared with each other a word of nameless union.

Carved in black wood the Wheel of Eternal Return stood before the tents of wandering monastic orders.

And those who longed for the Kingdom took refuge like me in the mountains to become the last heirs of a dishonored myth.

Berkeley, 1968

ON THE ROAD

To what summoned? And to whom? blindly, God almighty, through horizons of woolly haze,

Fata morganas of coppery scales on the fortresses of maritime provinces,

Through a smoke of vines burning over creek beds or through the blue myrrh of dimmed churches,

To the unattainable, small valley, shaded forever by words, where the two of us, naked and kneeling, are cleansed by an unreal spring.

Without the apple of knowledge, on long loops from earth to sky, from sky to the dried blood of potter's soil.

Disinherited of prophecies, eating bread at noon under a tall pine stronger than any hope.

St.-Paul-de-Vence, 1967

WHITENESS

O white, white, white. White city where women carry bread and
    vegetables, women born under the signs of the ever-gyrating
    zodiacs.
The jaws of fountains spout water in the green sun as in the days past
    of nuptials, of strolls in the cold aurora from one outskirt to
    another.
Buckles from schoolboys' belts somewhere in the dense earth, bunkers
    and sarcophagi bound with blackberry ropes.
Revelations of touch, again and again new beginnings, no knowledge,
    no memory ever accepted.
A faltering passerby, I walk through a street market after the loss of
    speech.
The candlesticks in the conquerors' tents overflow with wax, anger has
    left me and on my tongue the sourness of winter apples.
Two Gypsy women rising from the ashes beat a little drum and dance
    for immortal men.
In a sky inhabited or empty (no one cares) just pigeons and echoes.
Loud is my lament, for I believed despair could last and love could
    last.
In the white city which does not demand, does not know, does not
    name, but which was and which will be.

Paris, 1966

THESIS AND COUNTER-THESIS

—Love of God is love of self.
The stars and the seas are filled by precious *I*
Sweet as a pillow and a sucked thumb.

—It would be most unflattering for adoring men
If the grasshopper chirping in the warm grass
Could glorify that attribute called *Being*
In a general manner, without referring it to his own persona.

Berkeley, 1962

COUNSELS

If I were in the place of young poets
(quite a place, whatever the generation might think)
I would prefer not to say that the earth is a madman's dream,
a stupid tale full of sound and fury.

It's true, I did not happen to see the triumph of justice.
The lips of the innocent make no claims.
And who knows whether a fool in a crown,
a winecup in his hand, roaring that God favors him
because he poisoned, slew, and blinded so many,
would not move the onlookers to tears: he was so gentle.

God does not multiply sheep and camels for the virtuous
and takes nothing away for murder and perjury.
He has been hiding so long that it has been forgotten
how he revealed himself in the burning bush
and in the breast of a young Jew
ready to suffer for all who were and will be.

It is not certain if Ananke awaits her hour
to pay back what is due for the lack of measure and for pride.

Man has been given to understand
that he lives only by the grace of those in power.
Let him therefore busy himself sipping coffee, catching butterflies.
He who cares for the Republic will have his right hand cut off.

And yet, the Earth merits a bit, a tiny bit, of affection.
Not that I take too seriously consolations of nature,
and baroque ornaments, the moon, chubby clouds
(although it's beautiful when bird-cherries blossom on the banks of the
    Wilia).
No, I would even advise to keep further from Nature,

from persistent images of infinite space,
of infinite time, from snails poisoned
on a path in a garden, just like our armies.

There is so much death, and that is why affection
for pigtails, bright-colored skirts in the wind,
for paper boats no more durable than we are . . .

Montgeron, 1959

INCANTATION

Human reason is beautiful and invincible.
No bars, no barbed wire, no pulping of books,
No sentence of banishment can prevail against it.
It establishes the universal ideas in language,
And guides our hand so we write Truth and Justice
With capital letters, lie and oppression with small.
It puts what should be above things as they are,
Is an enemy of despair and a friend of hope.
It does not know Jew from Greek or slave from master,
Giving us the estate of the world to manage.
It saves austere and transparent phrases
From the filthy discord of tortured words.
It says that everything is new under the sun,
Opens the congealed fist of the past.
Beautiful and very young are Philo-Sophia
And poetry, her ally in the service of the good.
As late as yesterday Nature celebrated their birth,
The news was brought to the mountains by a unicorn and an echo.
Their friendship will be glorious, their time has no limit.
Their enemies have delivered themselves to destruction.

Berkeley, 1968

ARS POETICA?

I have always aspired to a more spacious form
that would be free from the claims of poetry or prose
and would let us understand each other without exposing
the author or reader to sublime agonies.

In the very essence of poetry there is something indecent:
a thing is brought forth which we didn't know we had in us,
so we blink our eyes, as if a tiger had sprung out
and stood in the light, lashing his tail.

That's why poetry is rightly said to be dictated by a daimonion,
though it's an exaggeration to maintain that he must be an angel.
It's hard to guess where that pride of poets comes from,
when so often they're put to shame by the disclosure of their frailty.

What reasonable man would like to be a city of demons,
who behave as if they were at home, speak in many tongues,
and who, not satisfied with stealing his lips or hand,
work at changing his destiny for their convenience?

It's true that what is morbid is highly valued today,
and so you may think that I am only joking
or that I've devised just one more means
of praising Art with the help of irony.

There was a time when only wise books were read,
helping us to bear our pain and misery.
This, after all, is not quite the same
as leafing through a thousand works fresh from psychiatric clinics.

And yet the world is different from what it seems to be
and we are other than how we see ourselves in our ravings.

People therefore preserve silent integrity,
thus earning the respect of their relatives and neighbors.

The purpose of poetry is to remind us
how difficult it is to remain just one person,
for our house is open, there are no keys in the doors,
and invisible guests come in and out at will.

What I'm saying here is not, I agree, poetry,
as poems should be written rarely and reluctantly,
under unbearable duress and only with the hope
that good spirits, not evil ones, choose us for their instrument.

Berkeley, 1968

HIGHER ARGUMENTS
IN FAVOR OF DISCIPLINE
DERIVED FROM THE SPEECH
BEFORE THE COUNCIL OF THE
UNIVERSAL STATE IN 2068

We call for discipline not expecting applause.
Because we do not need their cheers.
Loyal citizens can enjoy our protection
And we demand nothing in exchange, except obedience.
Nevertheless, much evidence inclines us
To express the hope that people correctly assess
How much the rightness of the line we take
Differs from their irrational suppositions and desires.
We can say boldly that we, and no one else,
Rescued them from a waste of contradictory opinions,
Where what is true does not have full weight
For equal weight is given to untruth.
We led them from that place, from that wasteland
Where each of them, alone in his own ignorance,
Meditated on the sense and nonsense of the world.
Freedom for them meant nakedness of women,
And their bread had no taste: the bakeries were full of it.
Under the name of Art they favored the antics of their boredom
And a daily terror of passing time.
We, and no one else, discovered the Law of Blackout,
Being aware that a mind left to itself
Reached out for the ultimate, not on its scale.
We, and no one else, discovered the Law of Diminished Goals
For a necessary condition of happiness is poverty and rancor.
And when today, foolish, they curse prohibitions
They already fear that we may lift prohibitions.
Thanks to repression they imagine they are bigger than nature,
Giants, angels maybe, stopped by force in their flight.
Their truth, they know, is true only when opposed to ours

Or opposed to our lies, which we take with humor.
The land of Cockaigne allures them and repels;
They would find there nothingness, i.e., themselves.
Let it be stated explicitly and clearly:
Though tough, we do not rule without consent.
According to new data most of them in their sleep whisper:
Blessed be censorship, blessed be scarcity.

Berkeley, 1968

ISLAND

Think however you like about this island, its ocean whiteness, grottoes overgrown with vines, under violets, springs.

I'm frightened, for I can hardly remember myself there, in one of those medi-terranean civilizations from which one must sail far, through the gloom and rustle of icebergs.

Here a finger points at fields in rows, pear trees, a bridle, the yoke of a water carrier, everything enclosed in crystal, and then I believe that, yes, I once lived there, instructed in those customs and manners.

I pull my coat around me listening to the incoming tide, I rock and lament my foolish ways, but even if I had been wise I would have failed to change my fate.

Lament my foolishness then and later and now, for which I would like so much to be forgiven.

Berkeley, 1968

MY FAITHFUL MOTHER TONGUE

Faithful mother tongue,
I have been serving you.
Every night, I used to set before you little bowls of colors
so you could have your birch, your cricket, your finch
as preserved in my memory.

This lasted many years.
You were my native land; I lacked any other.
I believed that you would also be a messenger
between me and some good people
even if they were few, twenty, ten
or not born, as yet.

Now, I confess my doubt.
There are moments when it seems to me I have squandered my life.
For you are a tongue of the debased,
of the unreasonable, hating themselves
even more than they hate other nations,
a tongue of informers,
a tongue of the confused,
ill with their own innocence.

But without you, who am I?
Only a scholar in a distant country,
a success, without fears and humiliations.
Yes, who am I without you?
Just a philosopher, like everyone else.

I understand, this is meant as my education:
the glory of individuality is taken away,
Fortune spreads a red carpet

before the sinner in a morality play
while on the linen backdrop a magic lantern throws
images of human and divine torture.

Faithful mother tongue,
perhaps after all it's I who must try to save you.
So I will continue to set before you little bowls of colors
bright and pure if possible,
for what is needed in misfortune is a little order and beauty.

Berkeley, 1968

UNCOLLECTED
POEMS

✦

1954–1969

I looked at that face, dumbfounded. The lights of *métro* stations flew by; I didn't notice them. What can be done, if our sight lacks absolute power to devour objects ecstatically, in an instant, leaving nothing more than the void of an ideal form, a sign like a hieroglyph simplified from the drawing of an animal or bird? A slightly snub nose, a high brow with sleekly brushed-back hair, the line of the chin—but why isn't the power of sight absolute?—and in a whiteness tinged with pink two sculpted holes, containing a dark, lustrous lava. To absorb that face but to have it simultaneously against the background of all spring boughs, walls, waves, in its weeping, its laughter, moving it back fifteen years, or ahead thirty. To have. It is not even a desire. Like a butterfly, a fish, the stem of a plant, only more mysterious. And so it befell me that after so many attempts at naming the world, I am able only to repeat, harping on one string, the highest, the unique avowal beyond which no power can attain: *I am, she is.* Shout, blow the trumpets, make thousands-strong marches, leap, rend your clothing, repeating only: *is!*

She got out at Raspail. I was left behind with the immensity of existing things. A sponge, suffering because it cannot saturate itself; a river, suffering because reflections of clouds and trees are not clouds and trees.

Brie-Comte-Robert, 1954

A MISTAKE

I thought: all this is only preparation
For learning, at last, how to die.
Mornings and dusks, in the grass under a maple
Laura sleeping without pants, on a headrest of raspberries,
While Filon, happy, washes himself in the stream.
Mornings and years. Every glass of wine,
Laura, and the sea, land, and archipelago
Bring us nearer, I believed, to one aim
And should be used with a thought to that aim.

But a paraplegic in my street
Whom they move together with his chair
From shade into sunlight, sunlight into shade,
Looks at a cat, a leaf, the chrome steel on an auto,
And mumbles to himself, *"Beau temps, beau temps."*

It is true. We have a beautiful time
As long as time is time at all.

Montgeron, 1957

HOW UGLY

How ugly, those elderly specimens
With hair in the pit between breast and belly,
With their melancholy of bad teeth, reek of tobacco,
And their fat, experienced smiles.

They shuffle cards, whistle tangos
Popular in their youth, and reminisce
About ball games and terraces and adventures in the bushes.

One should probably pity
The women who associate with them, forced
Undoubtedly by some urgent need.

But they should be pitied as well,
Because they associate with the women,
Beautifully fetid lilies,
Rattles of throaty laughter if you shake them,
Stuffed with loose calculations.
Afterward they comb their hair a long time before the mirror.

Montgeron, 1959

TO ROBINSON JEFFERS

If you have not read the Slavic poets
so much the better. There's nothing there
for a Scotch-Irish wanderer to seek. They lived in a childhood
prolonged from age to age. For them, the sun
was a farmer's ruddy face, the moon peeped through a cloud
and the Milky Way gladdened them like a birch-lined road.
They longed for the Kingdom which is always near,
always right at hand. Then, under apple trees
angels in homespun linen will come parting the boughs
and at the white kolkhoz tablecloth
cordiality and affection will feast (falling to the ground at times).

And you are from surf-rattled skerries. From the heaths
where burying a warrior they broke his bones
so he could not haunt the living. From the sea night
which your forefathers pulled over themselves, without a word.
Above your head no face, neither the sun's nor the moon's,
only the throbbing of galaxies, the immutable
violence of new beginnings, of new destruction.

All your life listening to the ocean. Black dinosaurs
wade where a purple zone of phosphorescent weeds
rises and falls on the waves as in a dream. And Agamemnon
sails the boiling deep to the steps of the palace
to have his blood gush onto marble. Till mankind passes
and the pure and stony earth is pounded by the ocean.

Thin-lipped, blue-eyed, witout grace or hope,
before God the Terrible, body of the world.
Prayers are not heard. Basalt and granite.
Above them, a bird of prey. The only beauty.

What have I to do with you? From footpaths in the orchards,
from an untaught choir and shimmers of a monstrance,
from flower beds of rue, hills by the rivers, books
in which a zealous Lithuanian announced brotherhood, I come.
Oh, consolations of mortals, futile creeds.

And yet you did not know what I know. The earth teaches
More than does the nakedness of elements. No one with impunity
gives to himself the eyes of a god. So brave, in a void,
you offered sacrifices to demons: there were Wotan and Thor,
the screech of Erinyes in the air, the terror of dogs
when Hekate with her retinue of the dead draws near.

Better to carve suns and moons on the joints of crosses
as was done in my district. To birches and firs
give feminine names. To implore protection
against the mute and treacherous might
than to proclaim, as you did, an inhuman thing.

Berkeley, 1963

TO RAJA RAO

Raja, I wish I knew
the cause of that malady.

For years I could not accept
the place I was in.
I felt I should be somewhere else.

A city, trees, human voices
lacked the quality of presence.
I would live by the hope of moving on.

Somewhere else there was a city of real presence,
of real trees and voices and friendship and love.

Link, if you wish, my peculiar case
(on the border of schizophrenia)
to the messianic hope
of my civilization.

Ill at ease in the tyranny, ill at ease in the republic,
in the one I longed for freedom, in the other for the end of corruption.

Building in my mind a permanent polis
forever deprived of aimless bustle.

I learned at last to say: this is my home,
here, before the glowing coal of ocean sunsets,
on the shore which faces the shores of your Asia,
in a great republic, moderately corrupt.

Raja, this did not cure me
of my guilt and shame.

A shame of failing to be
what I should have been.

The image of myself
grows gigantic on the wall
and against it
my miserable shadow.

That's how I came to believe
in Original Sin
which is nothing but the first
victory of the ego.

Tormented by my ego, deluded by it
I give you, as you see, a ready argument.

I hear you saying that liberation is possible
and that Socratic wisdom
is identical with your guru's.

No, Raja, I must start from what I am.
I am those monsters which visit my dreams
and reveal to me my hidden essence.

If I am sick, there is no proof whatsoever
that man is a healthy creature.

Greece had to lose, her pure consciousness
had to make our agony only more acute.

We needed God loving us in our weakness
and not in the glory of beatitude.

No help, Raja, my part is agony,
struggle, abjection, self-love, and self-hate,
prayer for the Kingdom
and reading Pascal.

Berkeley, 1969

FROM
THE RISING
OF THE SUN

(Gdzie wschodzi słońce i kędy zapada)

1974

A TASK

In fear and trembling, I think I would fulfill my life
Only if I brought myself to make a public confession
Revealing a sham, my own and of my epoch:
We were permitted to shriek in the tongue of dwarfs and demons
But pure and generous words were forbidden
Under so stiff a penalty that whoever dared to pronounce one
Considered himself as a lost man.

Berkeley, 1970

AN HOUR

Leaves glowing in the sun, zealous hum of bumblebees,
From afar, from somewhere beyond the river, echoes of lingering
    voices
And the unhurried sounds of a hammer gave joy not only to me.
Before the five senses were opened, and earlier than any beginning
They waited, ready, for all those who would call themselves mortals,
So that they might praise, as I do, life, that is, happiness.

Berkeley, 1972

A STORY

Now I will tell Meader's story; I have a moral in view.
He was pestered by a grizzly so bold and malicious
That he used to snatch caribou meat from the eaves of the cabin.
Not only that. He ignored men and was unafraid of fire.
One night he started battering the door
And broke the window with his paw, so they curled up
With their shotguns beside them, and waited for the dawn.
He came back in the evening, and Meader shot him at close range,
Under the left shoulder blade. Then it was jump and run,
A real storm of a run: a grizzly, Meader says,
Even when he's been hit in the heart, will keep running
Until he falls down. Later, Meader found him
By following the trail—and then he understood
What lay behind the bear's odd behavior:
Half of the beast's jaw was eaten away by an abscess, and caries.
Toothache, for years. An ache without comprehensible reason,
Which often drives us to senseless action
And gives us blind courage. We have nothing to lose,
We come out of the forest, and not always with the hope
That we will be cured by some dentist from heaven.

Berkeley, 1969

READINGS

You asked me what is the good of reading the Gospels in Greek.
I answer that it is proper that we move our finger
Along letters more enduring than those carved in stone,
And that, slowly pronouncing each syllable,
We discover the true dignity of speech.
Compelled to be attentive we shall think of that epoch
No more distant than yesterday, though the heads of caesars
On coins are different today. Yet still it is the same eon.
Fear and desire are the same, oil and wine
And bread mean the same. So does the fickleness of the throng
Avid for miracles as in the past. Even mores,
Wedding festivities, drugs, laments for the dead
Only seem to differ. Then, too, for example,
There were plenty of persons whom the text calls
Daimonizomenoi, that is, the demonized
Or, if you prefer, the bedeviled (as for "the possessed"
It's no more than the whim of a dictionary).
Convulsions, foam at the mouth, the gnashing of teeth
Were not considered signs of talent.
The demonized had no access to print and screens,
Rarely engaging in arts and literature.
But the Gospel parable remains in force:
That the spirit mastering them may enter swine,
Which, exasperated by such a sudden clash
Between two natures, theirs and the Luciferic,
Jump into water and drown (which occurs repeatedly).
And thus on every page a persistent reader
Sees twenty centuries as twenty days
In a world which one day will come to its end.

Berkeley, 1969

OECONOMIA DIVINA

I did not expect to live in such an unusual moment.
When the God of thunders and of rocky heights,
the Lord of hosts, Kyrios Sabaoth,
would humble people to the quick,
allowing them to act whatever way they wished,
leaving to them conclusions, saying nothing.
It was a spectacle that was indeed unlike
the agelong cycle of royal tragedies.
Roads on concrete pillars, cities of glass and cast iron,
airfields larger than tribal dominions
suddenly ran short of their essence and disintegrated.
Not in a dream but really, for, subtracted from themselves,
they could only hold on as do things which should not last.
Out of trees, field stones, even lemons on the table,
materiality escaped and their spectrum
proved to be a void, a haze on a film.
Dispossessed of its objects, space was swarming.
Everywhere was nowhere and nowhere, everywhere.
Letters in books turned silver-pale, wobbled, and faded.
The hand was not able to trace the palm sign, the river sign, or the
    sign of ibis.
A hullabaloo of many tongues proclaimed the mortality of the language.
A complaint was forbidden as it complained to itself.
People, afflicted with an incomprehensible distress,
were throwing off their clothes on the piazzas so that nakedness might
    call for judgment.
But in vain they were longing after horror, pity, and anger.
Neither work nor leisure
was justified,
nor the face, nor the hair nor the loins
nor any existence.

Berkeley, 1973

TIDINGS

Of earthly civilization, what shall we say?

That it was a system of colored spheres cast in smoked glass,
Where a luminescent liquid thread kept winding and unwinding.

Or that it was an array of sunburst palaces
Shooting up from a dome with massive gates
Behind which walked a monstrosity without a face.

That every day lots were cast, and that whoever drew low
Was marched there as sacrifice: old men, children, young boys, and
   young girls.

Or we may say otherwise: that we lived in a golden fleece,
In a rainbow net, in a cloud cocoon
Suspended from the branch of a galactic tree.
And our net was woven from the stuff of signs,
Hieroglyphs for the eye and ear, amorous rings.
A sound reverberated inward, sculpturing our time,
The flicker, flutter, twitter of our language.

For from what could we weave the boundary
Between within and without, light and abyss,
If not from ourselves, our own warm breath,
And lipstick and gauze and muslin,
From the heartbeat whose silence makes the world die?

Or perhaps we'll say nothing of earthly civilization.
For nobody really knows what it was.

Berkeley, 1973

L'ACCÉLÉRATION DE
L'HISTOIRE

It's late for the world.
One after another Kassandras fall silent.

Not with flames, not with the cracking of walls.
It approaches on cat's paws.

Commentary:
Pessimist! Cosmic annihilation, again?
Not at all. I am afraid of "hands fighting for the people
Which the people themselves will cut off."

Berkeley, 1971

ELEGY FOR N. N.

Tell me if it is too far for you.
You could have run over the small waves of the Baltic
and past the fields of Denmark, past a beech wood
could have turned toward the ocean, and there, very soon
Labrador, white at this season.
And if you, who dreamed about a lonely island,
were frightened of cities and of lights flashing along the highway
you had a path straight through the wilderness
over blue-black, melting waters, with tracks of deer and caribou
as far as the Sierras and abandoned gold mines.
The Sacramento River could have led you
between hills overgrown with prickly oaks.
Then just a eucalyptus grove, and you had found me.

True, when the manzanita is in bloom
and the bay is clear on spring mornings
I think reluctantly of the house between the lakes
and of nets drawn in beneath the Lithuanian sky.
The bath cabin where you used to leave your dress
has changed forever into an abstract crystal.
Honey-like darkness is there, near the veranda,
and comic young owls, and the scent of leather.

How could one live at that time, I really can't say.
Styles and dresses flicker, indistinct,
not self-sufficient, tending toward a finale.
Does it matter that we long for things as they are in themselves?
The knowledge of fiery years has scorched the horses standing at the
      forge,
the little columns in the marketplace,
the wooden stairs and the wig of Mama Fliegeltaub.

We learned so much, this you know well:
how, gradually, what could not be taken away
is taken. People, countrysides.
And the heart does not die when one thinks it should,
we smile, there is tea and bread on the table.
And only remorse that we did not love
the poor ashes in Sachsenhausen
with absolute love, beyond human power.

You got used to new, wet winters,
to a villa where the blood of the German owner
was washed from the wall, and he never returned.
I too accepted but what was possible, cities and countries.
One cannot step twice into the same lake
on rotting alder leaves,
breaking a narrow sunstreak.

Guilt, yours and mine? Not a great guilt.
Secrets, yours and mine? Not great secrets.
Not when they bind the jaw with a kerchief, put a little cross
    between the fingers,
and somewhere a dog barks, and the first star flares up.

No, it was not because it was too far
you failed to visit me that day or night.
From year to year it grows in us until it takes hold,
I understood it as you did: indifference.

Berkeley, 1963

AN APPEAL

You, my friends, wherever you are,
Whether you are grieving just now, or full of joy,
To you I lift this cup of pungent wine
As they often do in the land of France.
From a landscape of cranes and canals,
Of tangled railway tracks and winter fog,
In the smoke of black tobacco, I make my way
Toward you and I ask you a question.
Tell me, for once at least laying
Caution aside, and fear and guarded speech,
Tell me, as you would in the middle of the night
When we face only night, the ticking of a watch,
The whistle of an express train, tell me
Whether you really think that this world
Is your home? That your internal planet
That revolves, red-hot, propelled by the current
Of your warm blood, is really in harmony
With what surrounds you? Probably you know very well
The bitter protest, every day, every hour,
The scream that wells up, stifled by a smile,
The feeling of a prisoner who touches a wall
And knows that beyond it valleys spread,
Oaks stand in summer splendor, a jay flies
And a kingfisher changes a river to a marvel.
In you, as in me, there is a hidden certainty
That soon you will rise, in undiminished light,
And be real, strong, free from what restrained you.
That above the mold of broken flagstones,
Above memory and your transformation
Which is like the flight of birds when ice
Crumbles in the traces of hooves—above everything,
It will be given to you to run as celestial fire,
To set sails ablaze with your flame at dawn

When ships trail smoke and archipelagoes
Wake up, shaking copper from their hair.

No, I address you here, from the ashes of winter,
In the simplest words, not to induce doubt
Or to call melancholy, for instance, the sister of fate.
On and on. The heart is still beating.
Nothing is lost. If one day our words
Come so close to the bark of trees in the forest,
And to orange blossoms, that they become one with them,
It will mean that we have always defended a great hope.

How should I defend it? By naming things.
That isn't easy. I say the word "dawn"
And the tongue by itself affixes "rosy-fingered"
As in the childhood of Greece. The sun and the moon
Have the faces of gods. I am not certain
That Poseidon won't emerge suddenly
From the sea bottom (he wears an earring)
Ploughing the waves with his motor, towing a retinue of nymphs.
And when I wander in alpine forests and meadows
Every cleft in the rock seems to me a gate
Through which one enters the underworld. I wait for a guide.

And space, what is it like? Is it mechanical,
Newtonian? A frozen prison?
Or the lofty space of Einstein, the relation
Between movement and movement? No reason to pretend
I know. I don't know, and if I did,
Still my imagination is a thousand years old.

Jump into the water with your clothes on.
Such heaviness (deadweight, as sometimes in our dreams).

It's the same with us. We wear the brocade
Of past centuries or dress in false purple.
Covering our faces with velvet masks,
Classical, playing again what has been played before,
And yet, I affirm, this is the earth of wonder.
It gives us the gift of eternal youth.

To you I lift this cup, here, on the stage,
I, one voice, no more, in the vast theater.
Against closed eyes, bitter lips.
Against silence, which is slavery.

Brie-Comte-Robert, 1954

CALLING TO ORDER

You could scream
Because mankind is mad.
But you, of all people, should not.

Out of what thin sand
And mud and slime
Out of what dogged splinters
Did you fashion your castle against the test of the sea,
And now it is touched by a wave.

What chaos
Received bounds, from here to there.
What abyss
Was seen and passed over in silence.
What fear
Of what you are.

It shows itself
But that is not it.
It is named
Yet remains nameless.
It is coming to be
But has not begun.

Your castle will topple
Into the wine-colored
Funereal sea,
She will assuage your pride.

Yet you knew how
To use next to nothing.

It is not a matter of wisdom
Or virtue.

So how can you condemn
The unreason of others.

Berkeley, 1969

NOT THIS WAY

Forgive me. I was a schemer like many of those who steal by human habitations at night.

I reckoned the positions of guards before I dared approach closed borders.

Knowing more, I pretended that less would suffice, unlike those who give testimony,

Indifferent to gunfire, hue and cry in the brushwood, and mockery.

Let sages and saints, I thought, bring a gift to the whole Earth, not merely to language.

I protect my good name for language is my measure.

A bucolic, childish language that transforms the sublime into the cordial.

And the hymn or psalm of a choirmaster falls apart, only a canticle remains.

My voice always lacked fullness, I would like to render a different thanksgiving,

And generously, without irony which is the glory of slaves.

Beyond the seven borders, under the morning star.

In the language of fire, water, and all the elements.

Berkeley, 1972

SO LITTLE

I said so little.
Days were short.

Short days.
Short nights.
Short years.

I said so little.
I couldn't keep up.

My heart grew weary
From joy,
Despair,
Ardor,
Hope.

The jaws of Leviathan
Were closing upon me.

Naked, I lay on the shores
Of desert islands.

The white whale of the world
Hauled me down to its pit.

And now I don't know
What in all that was real.

Berkeley, 1969

·ON ANGELS

All was taken away from you: white dresses,
wings, even existence.
Yet I believe you,
messengers.

There, where the world is turned inside out,
a heavy fabric embroidered with stars and beasts,
you stroll, inspecting the trustworthy seams.

Short is your stay here:
now and then at a matinal hour, if the sky is clear,
in a melody repeated by a bird,
or in the smell of apples at the close of day
when the light makes the orchards magic.

They say somebody has invented you
but to me this does not sound convincing
for humans invented themselves as well.

The voice—no doubt it is a valid proof,
as it can belong only to radiant creatures,
weightless and winged (after all, why not?),
girdled with the lightning.

I have heard that voice many a time when asleep
and, what is strange, I understood more or less
an order or an appeal in an unearthly tongue:

day draws near
another one
do what you can.

Berkeley, 1969

SEASONS

Transparent tree, full of migrating birds on a blue morning,
Cold because there is still snow in the mountains.

Berkeley, 1971

GIFT

A day so happy.
Fog lifted early, I worked in the garden.
Hummingbirds were stopping over honeysuckle flowers.
There was no thing on earth I wanted to possess.
I knew no one worth my envying him.
Whatever evil I had suffered, I forgot.
To think that once I was the same man did not embarrass me.
In my body I felt no pain.
When straightening up, I saw the blue sea and sails.

Berkeley, 1971

FROM THE RISING OF THE SUN

I. The Unveiling

Whatever I hold in my hand, a stylus, reed, quill or a ballpoint,
Wherever I may be, on the tiles of an atrium, in a cloister cell, in a
    hall before the portrait of a king,
I attend to matters I have been charged with in the provinces.
And I begin, though nobody can explain why and wherefore.
Just as I do now, under a dark-blue cloud with a glint of the red horse.
Retainers are busy, I know, in underground chambers,
Rustling rolls of parchment, preparing colored ink and sealing wax.

This time I am frightened. Odious rhythmic speech
Which grooms itself and, of its own accord, moves on.
Even if I wanted to stop it, weak as I am from fever,
Because of a flu like the last one that brought mournful revelations
When, looking at the futility of my ardent years,
I heard a storm from the Pacific beating against the window.
But no, gird up your loins, pretend to be brave to the end
Because of daylight and the neighing of the red horse.

Vast lands. Flickering of hazy trains.
Children walk by an open field, all is gray beyond an Estonian village.
Royza, captain of the cavalry. Mowczan. Angry gales.
Never again will I kneel in my small country, by a river,
So that what is stone in me could be dissolved,
So that nothing would remain but my tears, tears.

> *Chorus:*
> Hope of old people,
> Never assuaged.
> They wait for their day
> Of power and glory.

For a day of comprehension.
They have so much to accomplish
In a month, in a year,
To the end.

It rolls along, sky-like, in the sun on its islands, in the flow of salty
    breezes.
It flies past and does not, new and the same.
Narrow sculptured boats, a hundred oars, on the stern a dancer
Beats baton against baton, flinging his knees.
Sonorous pagodas, beasts in pearl-studded nets,
Hidden staircases of princesses, floodgates, gardens of lilies.
It rolls along, it flies by, our speech.

    Chorus:
    He whose life was short can easily be forgiven.
    He whose life was long can hardly be forgiven.
    When will that shore appear from which at last we see
    How all this came to pass and for what reason?

Darkly, darkly cities return.
The roads of a twenty-year-old are littered with maple leaves
As he walks along one acrid morning, looking through the fences at
    gardens
And courtyards, where a black dog barks, and someone chops wood.

Now on a bridge he listens to the babble of the river, bells are
    resounding.
Under the pines of sandy bluffs he hears echoes, sees white frost and fog.

How did I come to know the scent of smoke, of late autumn dahlias
On the sloping little streets of a wooden town

Since it was so long ago, in a millennium visited in dreams
Far from here, in a light of which I am uncertain?

Was I there, cuddled like a vegetal baby in a seed,
Called long before the hours, one after another, would touch me?
Does so little remain of our labors lasting till evening
That we have nothing left except our completed fate?

Under the dark-blue cloud with a glint of the red horse
I dimly recognize all that has been.
The clothes of my name fall away and disappear.
The stars in wide waters grow smaller.
Again the other, unnamed one, speaks for me.
And he opens fading dream-like houses
So that I write here in desolation
Beyond the land and sea.

II. Diary of a Naturalist

In search of a four-leaf clover through the meadows at dawn,
In search of a double hazelnut into deep forest.
There we were promised a great, great life
And it waited, though we weren't yet born.

The oak our father, rough was his shoulder.
Sister birch led us with a whisper.
Farther and farther we went on to meet
The living water in which all strength revives.

Until, wandering through a dense black forest
All the long day of a young summer,
We will come at dusk to the edge of bright waters
Where the king of beavers rules over the crossings.

Fare well, Nature.
Fare well, Nature.

We were flying over a range of snowpeaked mountains
And throwing dice for the soul of the condor.
—Should we grant reprieve to the condor?
—No, we won't grant reprieve to the condor.
It didn't eat from the Tree of Knowledge and so it must perish.

In a park by a river a bear blocked our way
And extending his paw begged for assistance.
—Was it this one that frightened lost travelers?
—Let's give him a bottle of beer to cheer him up.
Once he had treefuls of honey on his estates.

He loped gracefully across an asphalt freeway
And once more a wood misty with rain moved past in our lights.
—It looked like a cougar.
—That would make sense.
They should be here according to statistics.

Fare well, Nature.
Fare well, Nature.

I show here how my childish dream was denied:

And now, on my school bench but not present, I slip into a picture on a wall in the classroom, "Animals of North America."

Fraternizing with the raccoon, stroking the wapiti, chasing wild swans over a caribou trail.

The wilderness protects me, there a gray squirrel can walk for weeks on the treetops.

But I will be called to the blackboard, and who can guess when, in what years.

The chalk breaks in my fingers, I turn around and hear a voice, mine, probably mine:

"White as horse skulls in the desert, black as a trail of interplanetary night

Nakedness, nothing more, a cloudless picture of Motion.

It was Eros who plaited garlands of fruit and flowers,

Who poured dense gold from a pitcher into sunrises and sunsets.

He and no one else led us into fragrant landscapes

Of branches hanging low by streams, of gentle hills,

And an echo lured us on and on, a cuckoo promised

A place, deep in a thicket, where there is no longing.

Our eyes were touched: instead of decay, the green,

The cinnabar of a tiger lily, the bitter blue of a gentian,

Furriness of bark in half-shade, a marten flickered,

Yes, only delight, Eros. Should we then trust

The alchemy of blood, marry forever the childish earth of illusion?

Or bear a naked light without color, without speech,

That demands nothing from us and calls us nowhere?"

I covered my face with my hands and those sitting on the benches kept silent.

They were unknown to me, for my age was over and my generation lost.

I tell about my acumen at a time when, guessing a few things in advance, I hit upon an idea, certainly not new, but highly regarded by my betters about whom I knew nothing:

My generation was lost. Cities too. And nations.
But all this a little later. Meanwhile, in the window, a swallow
Performs its rite of the second. That boy, does he already suspect
That beauty is always elsewhere and always delusive?
Now he sees his homeland. At the time of the second mowing.
Roads winding uphill and down. Pine groves. Lakes.
An overcast sky with one slanting ray.
And everywhere men with scythes, in shirts of unbleached linen
And the dark-blue trousers that were common in the province.
He sees what I see even now. Oh but he was clever,
Attentive, as if things were instantly changed by memory.
Riding in a cart, he looked back to retain as much as possible.
Which means he knew what was needed for some ultimate
    moment
When he would compose from fragments a world perfect at last.

Everything would be fine if language did not deceive us by finding different
names for the same thing in different times and places:

    The Alpine shooting star, *Dodecatheon alpinum,*
    Grows in the mountain woods over Rogue River,
    Which river, in southern Oregon,
    Owing to its rocky, hardly accessible banks,
    Is a river of fishermen and hunters. The black bear and the cougar
    Are still relatively common on these slopes.
    The plant was so named for its pink-purple flowers
    Whose slanting tips point to the ground from under the petals,
    And resembles a star from nineteenth-century illustrations
    That falls, pulling along a thin sheaf of lines.
    The name was given to the river by French trappers
    When one of them stumbled into an Indian ambush.
    From that time on they called it La Rivière des Coquins,
    The River of Scoundrels, or Rogue, in translation.

I sat by its loud and foamy current
Tossing in pebbles and thinking that the name
Of that flower in the Indian language will never be known,
No more than the native name of their river.
A word should be contained in every single thing
But it is not. So what then of my vocation?

Nonsensical stanzas intrude, about Anusia and *żalia rutéle*, or green rue, always, it seems, a symbol of life and happiness:

Why did Anusia grow that rue
The evergreen rue in her maiden's garden?
And why did she sing of *żalia rutéle*
So that evening echoes carried over the water?

And where did she go in her wreath of fresh rue?
Did she take the skirt from her coffer when leaving?
And who will know her in the Indian beyond
When her name was Anusia and she is no more?

I give a brief account of what happened to a book which was once my favorite, *Our Forest and Its Inhabitants:*

The lament of a slaughtered hare fills the forest.
It fills the forest and disturbs nothing there.
For the dying of a particular being is its own private business
And everyone has to cope with it in whatever way he can.
Our Forest and Its Inhabitants. Our, of our village,
Fenced in with a wire. Sucking, munching, digesting,
Growing, and being annihilated. A callous mother.
If the wax in our ears could melt, a moth on pine needles,
A beetle half-eaten by a bird, a wounded lizard
Would all lie at the center of the expanding circles

Of their vibrating agony. That piercing sound
Would drown out the loud shots of bursting seeds and buds,
And our child who gathers wild strawberries in a basket.
Would not hear the trilling, nice after all, of the thrush.

I pay homage to Stefan Bagiński who taught me how to operate a microscope
and prepare a slide. Nor am I forgetting about the main contributor to my
pessimism, and even quote from a work about his deeds in the service of science,
published for the use of young people in the year 1890 in Warsaw: Prof. Erazm
Majewski, *Doctor Catchfly; Fantastic Adventures in the World of Insects:*

To the masters of our youth, greetings.
To you, my teacher, Mr. Life Science,
Spleeny Bagiński in checkered knickers,
The ruler of *infusoria* and amoebas.
Wherever your skull with its woolly tuft
Reposes, rocked by the whirling elements,
Whatever fate befell your glasses
In their gold-wire rims,
I offer you these words.

And to you, Doctor Catchfly,
Who are free from destruction, the hero
Of a historic expedition to the land of insects.
You live as always on Miodowa in Warsaw
And your servant Gregory dusts carpets every morning,
While you set off on your old bachelor's walk
Through the park, the place of your victory
Over all things subject to ruin and change.

It happened in the summer of the year 187*:

"The day when our naturalist was to lead his beautiful fiancée to the altar
was calm, sunny and without a breeze. Precisely the kind of day needed

for a specimen-gathering expedition. But Dr. Catchfly, already dressed in his frock-coat, was not thinking of two-winged creatures. Attracted by the fine weather and faithful to his habits, he simply decided to spend his last free hour in the Park of the Royal Baths. While walking, he was meditating on the happiness of their future life together when suddenly something flickered before his dreamy eyes: a tiny little two-winged thing. He glanced and stopped, dumbfounded. Before him was a robber fly, but one that he had never seen before! His heart began pounding. He held his breath and drew closer to the leaf in order to better observe this rare specimen. But the wary insect, allowing him just enough time to make sure it was indeed extraordinary, flew off to another branch. Our naturalist, his eyes fixed on the insect, approached on tiptoe but the robber fly, quite smart, it seems, took its leave in time. This was repeated a few times and the frolicsome fly led him to the other side of the flower bed. The naturalist was losing it from sight and finding it again, while time passed. The hour of the wedding arrived but the robber fly placed itself very high, so high, as a matter of fact, that to keep it in sight, it was necessary to climb the tree. There was not a moment to lose."

Ah, subterfuges of Fate! That he was caught
Stalking on a branch, exactly when extending his top hat.
That when hearing this news, the maiden swooned.

She was an unreasonable creature of the fairer sex.
She chose her Earth of tulle and gauze,
Of boudoir mirrors that were easily cracked,
Of faience chamberpots that leave only one ear
To the excavator's shovel. The Earth of midwives, mourners,
Of whispers *Between the Lips and the Cup,*
Or else between lips and a pastry
Devoured in wastelands by posthumous descendants.
An ordinary earth, after all. Priceless for many.
Oh may the earth lie lightly on her, though light it is never.

If not for that day, admit it, John Catchfly,
Your zeal would have grown tame among lampshades.
A passion, pure and manifest,
Would not have led you to your destiny,
Until at dawn on a meadow in the Tatra mountains,
In the Valley of White Water and Rówienka,
Looking at the red of the rising sun,
Obedient to the formula, you drank the elixir
And went down to where there is neither guilt nor complaint.

Tiny, I wandered with you in the unfathomed land
Beneath stalks of grass as thick as cedars,
In the din and blast of diaphanous, winged machines.
I would stand in the middle of a rugged leaf
And over the gloom of a swampy chasm
I pulled myself along a strand of gossamer.

You wrote down: "horrible conditions."
In sap, mush, glue, millions and millions
Of entangled legs, wings, and abdomens
Struggle to free themselves, weaken, stiffen forever.
The fat flesh of caterpillars being devoured alive
By the rapacious progeny of inquisitive flies,
Undulates its segments, and grazes unconcerned.
O humanitarian from the age of debates,
What sort of scientist are you, why do you feel
        compassion?
Is it proper to suddenly get incensed
When on a black, smoldering plain
You arrive at the gates of a burned-down city,
Witness and judge in a hall of dead ants?

You infected me with your pity for computers

Dressed in chitin cloaks, in transparent armor.
And in my child's imagination
I still bear your mark, O philosopher of pain.
But I don't hold a grudge, Dr. *honoris causa*
Of Heidelberg and Jena. I am glad
That the white of the ivory on your cane still shines
As if it has never been dimmed by fire
And someone still rode in carriages down the avenues.

I try to describe concisely what I experienced when instead of choosing the profession of a traveler–naturalist I turned toward other goals:

That's probably why I went on a pilgrimage.
The direction those will recognize who, for instance,
Having visited the caves near Les Eyzies,
Stopping perhaps at noon in Sarlat,
From there took the road that leads to Souillac
Where a bas-relief in a Romanesque portal
Tells the adventures of Monk Theophilus
From Adana in Cilicia, and where the prophet Isaiah
For eight centuries has persisted in a violent gesture
As if he were plucking the strings of an invisible harp.
And on and on, into winding dells, until suddenly
It appears high, so high, that jewel of wayfarers,
As desired as a nest in the top of a fir tree
Was in our boyhood: Roc Amadour.
But I'm not insistent. A road to Compostela
Or to Jasna Góra would instruct you as well.

Pursuing and passing by. Here a mossy rock
Runs, becomes more distinct at every curve,
Then fades in the distance. There, a river flashes
Beyond the trees and the arc of a bridge. But, remember,

Neither the view will stop us, nor the kingfisher
Stitching together the two banks with the bright thread of its
     flight,
Nor the maiden in the tower, though she lures us with a smile
And blindfolds us before she leads us to her chamber.
I was a patient pilgrim. And so I notched
Each month and year on my stick, since it neared me to my aim.

Yet when at last I arrived after many years
What happened there, many would know, I think,
Who in the parking lot at Roc Amadour
Found a space and then counted the steps
To the upper chapel, to make sure that this was it,
And saw a wooden Madonna with a child in a crown,
Surrounded by a throng of impassive art lovers.
As I did. Not a step further. Mountains and valleys
Crossed. Through flames. Wide waters. And unfaithful memory.
The same passion but I hear no call.
And the holy had its abode only in denial.

III. Lauda

A certain eminent alchemist wrote of that country that it is to be found wherever it has been placed by the first and most important need of the human mind, the same need that called into being geometry and science, philosophy and religion, morality and art. The above-mentioned alchemist—he was an ally of Descartes— also wrote that the name of the country could be Saana or Armageddon, Patmos or Lethe, Arcadia or Parnassus.

No, there should be no space here,
Though I talk to you and you stand before me
In a sun somewhat similar,
In a night almost the same,
And even a raindrop behaves here as it does there.

This space is different. Herald angels singing,
And in the street the three kings bowing,
And under an arcade lions kneeling
To announce a miracle.

And we, locked in amber, with trumpets, viols,
We run, we sing, we praise the days gone by
Because now we see them clearly, without pain.

And suddenly in my hand a scepter,
Or a child's rattle, so that I can accompany myself,
Since all shame has forsaken me,
And I can confess that I suffered after all.

Well, not exactly, not a scepter, a whipstock.
In fact a flyswatter, so that I sit at home
Listening by the window because a neighbor might drop in,
But it's quiet except for the creak of the well-beam.

I was born there and came from the noble class.
We were better than the yeomen of Lauda or Wędziagoła.
I was baptized, I renounced the Devil
In the parish of Opitołoki, district of Kiejdany.

My calling is to swat flies and meditate,
Or to order Jurkszys to prepare the phaeton
So I can go gadding through Girele Forest
To pay my respects to my kinsmen, the Silvestrowiczes.
Also the Dowgirds or the Dowgiełłos.

To be moderately happy. Our country is quiet,
Though not very rich. Few people use a coach.
It costs too much, it takes four horses,
So it always sits there in the carriage house.

To hunt after first snow. The first star will appear soon,
I stamped snow off my boots in the entrance hall,
The table is set for Christmas Eve and the cakes are soaked in
     honey,
My dear Jadwiga knows just how to please me.

If I hadn't been sent off to school in Wilno,
What would have been gained? Nothing.
I wouldn't anyway have been put to rest in Swiętobrość
In Šventybrastis, at the Holy Ford,
Where my ancestors are buried
And where the little boy was always startled by the horses' habit
Of stopping for a drink in midstream.

Now I feel as if I had flung a stone
From the Golden Gate Bridge, from which a suicide
Flies as in his dream, smaller than a gull.

As if I woke from an afternoon nap
And found myself in a smock of gold brocade.

It was written in the secret code of the genes.
Or I, a nobleman, played chess on the banks of the Niewiaża
With a devil insufficiently baptized, a plenipotentiary
Of telluric powers not well known.

I cannot swear that this happened to me precisely in either the nineteenth or the
twentieth century because it is not certain, and besides of no importance. In that
country things that happened yesterday or four hundred years ago don't differ
very much. The place is something else, requiring more not less concreteness,
and recalling it I try to eschew invention. Even if I were gathering images of the
earth from many countries on two continents, my imagination could cope with
them only by assigning them to positions to the south, north, east, or west of the
trees and hills of one district. In my district and the neighboring one of Kowno,
every little river, every town and settlement had its own dignity and was treated
with respect by historians. Thanks to them, I am able to record the following
notes.

Lauda: The word does not come from the medieval Italian song of praise, *lauda*,
to which my title perhaps alludes; nor does it have to do with the laws of the
Polish Diet, called in the plural *lauda*. This Lauda is the Lithuanian Liauda and is
not related to the Latin *laudare*. The small river Liaudé flows through it and feeds
the river Niewiaża on its way to receiving five tributaries: the Nekelpa, the
Garduva, the Kemsrotas, the Nykis, and the Viešnanta. As to the settlements of
Lauda, one might invoke *The Deluge* of the novelist Sienkiewicz, but a literary
fiction has dubious value as an historical source. The *Lietuvių Enciklopedija*, a
monumental work in thirty volumes (Boston, 1953–1963), says this: "Liauda. The
name of a group of villages on the right bank of the Niewiaża, mainly on the line
of the Počiuneliai-Dotnuva, district of Kedainiai. About the gentry of Liauda
much can be learned from the late sixteenth century court records of the
Rosienie region; these consist mostly of deeds of sale and other documents. At
that time a large belt on the right bank of the Niewiaża, inhabited by yeomen
farmers belonging to the broad estate of Veliuona, was called Liauda."
    This estimable work continues: "The name derived originally from the little
river Liaudė. The manor of Liauda and its fields are situated by A. Salys close to
the church in Počiuneliai (west of Krakenava). It is possible that there were other

manors of Liauda. The origin of these gentry villages has been explained in many ways. Closest to the historical truth seems to be H. Łowmiański, who advanced the thesis that the petty gentry of these communities had been settled there by the Grand Duke of Lithuania as early as the fourteenth century and were at constant war with the Teutonic Knights. They were responsible for the defense and supply of castles along the river Niemen. At a time when Teutonic Knights continually ravaged settlements on the right bank of the Niemen up to Veliuona, Liauda and the gentry from the region of Dotnuva provided the castles with fighting men. Until the eighteenth century these gentry villages were divided into separate areas, each with several farms, belonging to the estate of Veliuona."

"The nobles better than Lauda"—it was an actual title—refers to those nobility whose social position was higher than that of the yeomen farmers who composed the village gentry, but lower than that of the aristocracy and half-aristocracy. Perhaps that is not quite accurate, since gentry farms were of unequal size; besides, when the name was used in its older, larger meaning, all those who lived there could be ranked as Lauda. My mother was born where her mother was, and where I was also to be born, at the manor of Szetejnie, or Šeteiniai, on the left bank of the Niewiaża three kilometers from Świętobrość, or Šventybrastis, close to Lauda. My mother was the daughter of Zygmunt Kunat (whose name was also spelled with two *t*s, as was the name of a man who figured in the *Lietuvių Enciklopedija*, Stanislaw Kunatt, an émigré and economist, professor at the École des Batignolles in Paris) and of Józefa Syruć. Whether the document from 1595 quoted below, published in *Istorijos Archyvas*, volume 1, collected by K. Jablonskis (Kaunas, 1934) refers to my ancestors is impossible to ascertain for sure, but it is probable to the extent that the name Syrutis, though found among the peasants in modern times, did not exist among the nobility except in my family; in any case, the document would support placing the family in Lauda. It is written in the Cyrillic alphabet:

> I, Sebastyn Yurevich Volotkevich, countie bailiff of the Samogitian Lande, Veliuona countie, prove by this my receipt that I, in the present yere a thousand fyve hunderth ninetie five, thirtie day of January, was summoned in the cause of Lady Barbara Sirut, daughter of Wojciech Kovsha, widow of Jan Venclavovich Sirut, who is landed in the Samogitian Lande, to her demesne, her manour scituated in the Samogitian Lande, Veliuona Countie, called Lauda, which saied Lady before mee bailiff and two wytnessing knights gayve and graunted and bequethed that manour of Lauda with all meases, feldes, medowes, pastures, woodes, graungies, waters, tithes, profettes, domestics, labourers, and tenants, by her last will,

to her son Adam Janovich Sirut, landed squire in the Samogitian Lande, which saied Sir Adam Sirut, before mee bailiff and wytnesses took possession of the saied manour, demesne and its people and was intromitted by mee, and by the dissposition of Lady Sirut, having written down all dependants and domestics in this myne receipt, considering it as a valid register and inventorie, hereby I enumerate: [A register follows.]

Wędziagoła: Lithuanian *Vandžiogala.* A town south of Kiejdany in the district of Kowno, 25 kilometers from Kowno, 12 kilometers from Bobty, 11 kilometers from Labunava. The name also signified the second—after Lauda—cluster of gentry farms and manors. As to the history of the town of Wędziagoła, we read in the *Lietuvių Enciklopedija:* "Vandajagel, Wendjagel, Vendigalin. In the second half of the fourteenth century, a large line of defense ran west from V. through Bobtai, Ariogala, and Batakiai, which protected the more densely populated middle of the country from attacks by the Teutonic Knights. On a small section of the line, 8 km. in length, between V. and Labunava, there were barricades of fallen trees in twelve places. In the year 1382 or 1384, M. Schulzbach, a Teutonic Knight, second in command at Ragaina, entered Lithuania to help Vytautas against Skirgaila, and encountered there a crowd of people who had gathered to celebrate a feast. He was forced by them into armed encounter and a battle; 120 Lithuanians were killed in the fighting in that holy place, 300 were taken prisoner and forced to the other side of the Niemen.

"In the growing settlement in 1664, Jan and Mariona (née Łopaciński) Rostowski (or Rostworowski) erected a wooden church invoking the name of the Holy Trinity."

We read also that in 1863 the vicar of Wędziagoła, Father Antoni Kozłowski, was arrested and sent to Siberia. Also we find the following information: "The manor in V., which belonged once to Chłopicki, was purchased by Hartowski in 1890. In 1918 the Polonized inhabitants of V. and the region tried to proclaim an independent republic, the 'Republic of Wędziagoła.' "

My father was born in Serbiny near Wędziagoła, the son of Artur Miłosz and Stanisława née Lopaciński. My mother's sister married Zdzisław Jurewicz (or Juriewicz, creating many difficulties, considering that *ie* in Lithuanian reads "ia") from near Bobty. I mention this in view of the same names repeating themselves in records of the region.

Opitołoki: Usually thus in the old documents. Lithuanian *Apýtalaukis.* A church and a manor 5 kilometers north of Kiejdany on the left bank of the Niewiaża. In the *Lietuvių Enciklopedija* we find the following description: "On the slope of a hill a small church with one tower in the baroque style, erected by the bailiff of Ariogala and magistrate of Samogitia, Piotr Szukszta, in 1635, and a few buildings, and, half a mile from the river, a palace in the park. The palace was built in the middle of the nineteenth century in the classical style in the shape of a flattened letter H with Corinthian and Ionic columns and three reliefs. In the framing of the windows there are Renaissance and baroque elements. Inside attention should be paid to elegant stoves and gypsum rosettes. In the vestibule, as late as the time of the Second World War, there was furniture (a big table, chairs, a cupboard, coat racks, and so on) made from the horns of game animals. They were bought by the manor's owner in Paris during the World Exhibition for 5,000 rubles. Part of the furniture is in the museum in Kiejdany. After the Second World War the palace was converted into a home for veterans. In 1802 a school was established in the manor. A. is mentioned as early as 1371 in the chronicle of Livonia. Later, it was owned by Piotr Szukszta, who endowed the church built by him with ninety acres of land. Next Kazimierz Zawisza founded an altar and a crypt for his family. A. also belonged to the Karps, the Tyszkiewiczes, and from the last quarter of the nineteenth century to the Zabiełłos, who abandoned the center of the palace and allowed the park to grow wild, until 1940."

My certificate of baptism, written in Russian, came from Opitołoki. I've never been in the palace. Piotr Szukszta, probably the same magistrate of Samogitia, made an inventory of his movable possessions, which I give here, following the *Istorijos Archyvas* of 1934, so that this year and the year 1587 may be placed on an equal footing:

The inventorie of moveables and household stuffe being in the Opitołoki house and those wch are to be taken with mee to Warsaw, the yere thousande fyve hundert eightie seven, the seventh day of June:

Surcote of brown linen clothe lyned with marten; surcote of shymmeringe colour lyned with fox; surcote black with napp lyninge; surcote of grene clothe. Zhupan grey damskeene, zhupan of quilte; zhupan of browne linen clothe; zhupan of cherrie linen clothe. Doublet of red clothe; doublet of grene clothe.

Spones twelfe, in them fyve thalers less sixpence; spones six, in them two thalers; cuppes four, in them four thalers; baskot for aquavit sixteen pennies. Sabre of Lady Bieniasz, twentie pence.

Pewter: big bowles three, smaller bowles ten, platters eleven, disshes two, plates two dozen, ageyn plates nine, basone for washinge hands one, boxe for butter one, jugs big and smalle six, quart pots four, big bottel, medium bottel, halve bottels four, saltseller one, candell sticks two.

Brasse: bowles three, jugs two, bottel one, kettle to pour water, brasse candell sticks seven, latten candell sticks two; brewing kyfe, the second in Orwistów; medium kyfe, the second in Orwistów; smaller kyfe, the second in Orwistów; three legged cawdrons two; big panne one, smaller pannes two, skyllets two; gallon potts with bulges six.

Big iron chaynes two; chayne in kitchen.

Armours four, cuirasses four, couters four, helmets four, sabres newe two, broad swoords newe two, the third old, harquebuses newe two, the third old, bird musket of Sir Gineyt, simple muskets three, spear one, buckler one.

Hussard saddles two, Tartar saddle one, harnesses three, carte rope newe one, horse collars three. Coach newe hoopt, chariot hoopt, coach old hoopt, wagon bare unhoopt. Turkish head stalls two.

Horses: grey amblynge stallion; grey amblyng old; cart horses blacke two, other cart horses—horse from Luszczyk, Orwistów colt, mare, young fallow stallion, mare, baye little horse.

To Sir Stecki hundert fiftie threescores; to Sir Szembel twentie threescores for four cuppes; to Miss Regina twentie threescores; to Sir Tomas seven threescores for silver gilt belt; with Sir Bobrownicki fifteen threescores; with Sir Peliuc eightie threescores; with Sir Wojciech my brother four threescores. With Sir Borysowicz nine threescores; with Sir Mikolaj Koncza six threescores.

Chaste with letters, seeled, in which letters of Opitołoki and Orwistów of Sir my brother seeled, together the Medingiany priviledge on parchment and other small old letters with Sir my brother.

Rye on feldes of Opitołoki and Orwistów well sowne, likewise spring rye, out of which God willinge the next yere debts may be paied.

Chatteyl in Opitołoki: Yoke oxen, eight, to Paul for plowinge one, to Michael in Orwistów one. Cows twelfe, ageyn young. Ewes old twentie, lambs fourteen.

Chatteyl in Orwistów: Yoke oxen eight; with homager Tomas two: of which one ox must be geeven heem next yere for plowinge. Cows and hecfordes seventeen. Ewes and rams fortie and seven. Ageyn young, calves one yere old and of this yere.

Othere small thinges, togeather with not recorded additions to the recorded. This inventorie written with my hand writinge and sealed with my seal I leave.

[In Old Byelorussian] On that inventory one seal is affixed and a signature of hand in these words: Piotr Szukszta with his hand.

Świętobrość: The word *brasta* means "ford." Lithuanian *Šventybrastis.* A church and a few houses on the left bank of the Niewiaża, on the same road that leads through Opitołoki but farther north, 15 kilometers from Kiejdany, but within the Kiejdany district. From the *Lietuvių Enciklopedija:* "Though localities in the neighborhood of S., like Kalnaberże, Šlapaberże, and Dotnuva, were known to the Teutonic Knights and attacked on their raids into Lithuania, the chronicles do not mention S. According to legend, S. was once a pagan holy place. At the beginning of the Second World War, five fine oaks, up to 37 m. high, with a circumference of 3.5–5.8 m., were still standing. The name S. was likely derived from the Lithuanian *šventas,* Polish *święty,* which means 'holy,' and from the little river ford by which it is situated. The first wooden church of Our Lord's Transfiguration was built in 1774 by the owner of the manor Zawiszyn, Ignacy Zawisza. In 1880 Janowski enlarged it, adding a wing and a belfry. In 1915 two huge bells were taken from the belfry and carried to Russia. In 1863 in the neighborhood of S., near the village of Daniliškiai, the Russians fought a battle with detachments of insurrectionaries. In the battle, twenty-five insurgents were killed, eleven wounded, and eight taken prisoner. On the twentieth of October 1863, Father A. Mackiewicz, commanding a detachment of the insurrectionaries, attacked the Russians in this place, and seized twenty poods of gunpowder and other weaponry. Near the church of S., by the river Niewiaża and the little river Brasta, there are graves of fallen insurgents. To commemorate them, a wooden cross was raised, and replaced by a concrete monument in 1938. In 1928 the church was renovated. S. is a branch of the Apýtalaukis parish."

Passing it every day on a street from which you can glimpse the Pacific through San Francisco Bay, I dropped into the Museum of Modern Art to have a look at an exhibition of the projected cities of the future. These were models of buildings, every one of which would hold a million inhabitants. So I cannot expect a Temple of Sybil to survive in which my right shoe will be preserved and the loss of my left shoe a reason for lament. But we should not discount the curiosity of computers, a company of which will reflect on everything—among other obscurities, my origin and descent, and they will have to tackle the knotty problem of what country I should be assigned to. Considering certain features of their analytic program, their difficulties are easy to foresee—because the historical Samogitia stretched from the Baltic Sea to the river Niewiaża. Across the river on the eastern, that is to say, the left bank, another region called Aukštota began, and I was born on the left bank. Consider, however, my ties with Lauda, which was dependent on the castle at Veliuona; consider the undoubted fact that Wędziagoła is the historical Samogitia, and also the fact that Piotr Szukszta from Opitołoki (the wrong side of the river) was a Samogitian magistrate; above all, though, a sensible computer would not neglect climate and landscape (indications of how these data are to be assimilated will not be given here), which alone allow us to decide whether one comes from Samogitia or Aukštota.

In Wilno, the state high school for boys, called King Sigismund August's, on Bouffałowa Street (on the corner of Mała Pohulanka Street), had as chairman of its matriculation committee in 1929 a Professor Marian Massonius from Stefan Batory University, an old man, bald, with a long beard, about whom *The Philosophy of Poland: A Dictionary of Writers* (Warsaw, 1971) records the following: "In reference to Polish philosophy, Massonius maintained that the Polish mind has a basically empirical tendency and is inclined to inductive thinking and 'quite unfriendly to a speculative or fantastic style of thought.' He considered the positivist tendency as typical of Polish philosophy; Polish metaphysics, according to him, was shaped by the more romantic Lithuanian influences."

And now we are joined in a ritual.
In amber? In crystal? We make music.
Neither what once was nor what ever will be.
Only what persists when the world is over.

LENTEN SONG
Now my hands are gone to sleep.
A drowsy tingling takes my feet.
Sight and hearing lie no more.
Smell and taste lose their allure.
There is neither near nor far.
Everything is great and small.

I ran a long time on the earth
And shouldered through a fiery gulf.

I judged others, judged their worth,
Knowing nothing of myself.
That a meaning would not flare
In the long and wakeful night
Gave me grief, and then despair,
But the words would yield no light.

Mirrors, shadows on a screen,
All I'd thought and all I'd seen.
My face perhaps was honest clay.
Even now it fades away.
The light shuddered and went out,
Leaving self-love in the dark.

OVERSEAS SONG
In one of the more obscure African tongues
I fashioned my verses.
Even the *Commedia* is merely comic
Once its tribe disperses.

Whisked to the shores of motley continents
Among dragon scales of the sea
I saw myself from far away and above
As an island or a tree.

What had to be has been, although not quite.
The Wilno student hoped for grander deeds.
From him who earned little, it will be taken.
Minor triumphs, forgettable defeats.

My betters also tried to tune their voices.
Their names are entangled in grass.

I alone remain, filtering order from chaos,
For my mind was clear and perverse.

Above me every day the late Empire's eagles,
The planet perishing, provinces on fire.
Let the poor devils in that molten glare
Make sense of the elemental riot.

Who can blame me for seeking a native land
Here or perhaps nowhere,
Mixing dialects and provincial idioms
With an oceanic choir?

This transparent amber in my palm—
We are in it, with a fiddle's quaver,
And a song and guests stately in their dance
Will gladden us forever.

It's time, since we have meditated long enough, to give our assessment of a character who appears here, an assessment made without particular sympathy but without prejudice. We do not intend to make a clinical report; that is not, of course, possible. It is possible, nevertheless, to hope that impartiality will guide us.

He was a young man, quite able to learn, but without talent.
Others were talented, his friend the poet Theodore, for example,
Who much later moved to the same apartment house at 5 Podgórna
    Street,
Where our subject had been growing crookedly in an ugly apartment,
    with rubber plants.
There Theodore took three bullets in the stomach
At close range, because of which he was spared the need
To cross so many borders. He didn't grasp at a slim tree

In the street of a great city when the houses revolved and tumbled
On an escapee who shouts, "Where am I? Where am I?"
He didn't acquire a number of skills, not only superfluous
But harmful since they use up our time and our will.
Also he was spared the buffoonery of endless compromise
And of punishing himself with drunken babble.

The young man was cleverly constructed.
He was inhabited by a vulgar and lunatic ego.
He demanded love, admiration, the murmurs of praise,
Though power would have satisfied him only
If he had been invited by the tyrant of Syracuse
To use his resources to create a perfect state.
(He read *The Magic Mountain* then:
And he always took the side of Naphta, who glorified terror.)

Nevertheless, despite everything or because of it,
Inside he had nothing but fear.
Fear of others' eyes, fear of touch, fear of human morals,
Fear of life greater than fear of death,
And scornfulness and high fastidiousness.

So the young man meditated on the degeneration of families,
How the blood of obscure boyars of Samogitia was being spoiled
Until it produced a mutation of monsters and cripples,
A schizophrenic soul in a stupid and gluttonous body.
He nursed a grudge against his father because of his defeat,
For one should not travel on the Arctic Ocean and in the Sayan
    Mountains and in Brazil
Just to become a District Engineer
And to comfort oneself with vodka after a tour of muddy roads.
It was thus that the young man received inspiration,
Which is usually understood wrongly.

Neither rhythm nor incantation can supply the words.
He searched and he searched, and the years passed.

Talent is something else. Talent is exactly what Theodore had.
But talent seduces us with temporal rewards,
And now when the grave of Theodore is eroded,
When Draugas has died by his own hand in Canada,
And Nika is an old woman and will die in Australia,
Theodore will be remembered because of one poem.
Dictated—because it is not the skill of the hand
That writes poetry, but water, trees,
And the sky which is dear to us even though it's dark,
And to parents and parents of those parents since time immemorial.
And here we set down this poem, as though it bore an inscription:
"The last poor bard of the Grand Duchee."

÷

LITHUANIA, my native land. Simply and fervently
I repeat the words of our prayer.
Land of unfertile earth, of cornflowers and thistles,
Of white churches on flattened shores,
Of large mists and a sad sky,
Of lakes rustling with reeds.

LITHUANIA. With bitter lips,
Lacking in hope or faith,
I murmur and invoke your name,
And deep wind rocks the poplars
And rattles the leaves of leaning trees.

Through hungry roads leading out to the fallows,
By houses thrown into a coffin of rotting walls,
The cattle return home in the evening

And a huge sun like a red jar pours
Live blood on the thick clouds.

LITHUANIA. Land of persistent bad weather,
Torn by winds as the shore cliffs are,
Damaged by centuries and gods,
Draw swords from the sky's white sheaths,
Pour down hail, let it strike in abundance,
Give us pathos and put fire in our mouths!

Silence!

—TEODOR BUJNICKI

Bibliography of Polish Literature, The New Korbut, in its eighth volume gives the following biographical note under the heading "Jucewicz Ludwik Adam": "Pseud. and crypt.: L.A.J.; L. from Pok . . . ; Ludwik from Pokiewie. Poet, ethnographer. Born 1810 in Pokiewie in Samogitia. Theological studies in seminary at Wilno. Became a priest in 1837 and obtained a vicarage at Świadość. Around 1839 broke with Catholicism, switched to Orthodoxy, and married. In 1841 edited an annual called *Linksminė* (which means 'rainbow'). In 1844 became a teacher at the district school of Lepel. Died there in 1846."

Father Jucewicz is considered one of the first Lithuanian ethnographers. He collected songs, proverbs, and folk legends. He wrote in Polish, but also translated Mickiewicz and other poets into Lithuanian. The manor of Pokiewie where he was born was situated in the district of Szawle. The note does not permit us to guess the reason for his switching to Orthodoxy, nor the responsibility of music in it. The vicar of Świadość was perhaps unaware that the shared reading of poetry by people of different sexes or moments spent together at the clavichord have detrimental consequences, as is demonstrated by Paolo and Francesca in Dante's Hell and also by Gustav in *Forefather's Eve*. Thus he would often go to the house of his nearby neighbors, the landowners Żurawskis, and fell fatally in love with their daughter Malwina.

I was already familiar with some of the writings of Father Jucewicz in childhood. His *Lithuania Described as to Its Old Monuments, Mores, and Customs,* published by Ludwik of Pokiewie (Wilno, 1846), contains in its introduction an encomium to the Lithuanian language, expresses regret that foreign (i.e., Polish) customs and a foreign tongue have been adopted, and enumerates briefly "the more important works which have appeared in public in the Lithuanian language," beginning with Protestant tracts and Jakób Wujek's *Postylla* (Sermons), the translation of which by Father Nicholas Dauksza, dedicated to the bishop of Samogitia, Prince Melchior Giedroyc, was printed at the press of the Jesuit Academy in 1599. The author also says: "The second person to provide so great a service to native literature is Father Konstanty Szyrwid, Jesuit, eminent Lithuanian philologist and preacher. The style of his sermons is correct, his language is always pure and free from foreign borrowings." For "not only among Protestants were there zealous proponents of the Christian faith and friends of village folk. Not long ago, in our Roman Church, there was a great man of noble lineage, a descendant of Lithuanian monarchs, a man who, serving the altar, reached a venerable age in his vocation, in his saintliness, in (if I am permitted to use an expression of one of the great Polish writers) his very eyes, and in the silver-white hair that adorned his patriarchal brow and descended to his shoulders, priest most deserving of respect, shepherd to the Samogitian flock, Józef Arnólf Prince Giedroyc! To him we owe a translation of the New Testament into our native tongue."

The author also pays homage to Donelajtis, the author of a poem called *Four Seasons*, and praises the Lithuanian poetry of his own era: Szymon Staniewicz, Dyonizy Paszkiewicz, and the clergyman Antoni Drozdowski, and he proclaims the following: "There have not been until now any historical works in Lithuanian. I have only heard that Count Jerzy Plater wrote a history of Lithuania in the national language, but because of the premature death of that young lover of things of the fatherland, it hasn't yet appeared in print. We nourish the hope (be it not deceived!) that the honorable spouse of the dead man won't hide the manuscript and will publish it as soon as possible. It will be one of the most beautiful flowers of our literature, a wreath which will hang in the temple of memory and fame!"

The spouse didn't hang the wreath, because, we may suppose, she was numbered among the indifferent to whom Father Jucewicz addressed the following appeal:

"But for the misfortune that few people understand our language and even fewer can speak it, we could yet rid ourselves of that prejudice which we have against our national speech. Even Lithuanian poets of today, alas, write not in Lithuanian! It is time to rid ourselves of these inveterate habits! It is time to return to our senses and to blend knowledge of foreign language with knowledge of the one spoken by our great-grandfathers—*because language is the property of a nation, and no one should forget the speech of his ancestors!*"

I arrive, Father Ludwik, a woodpecker knocking in the pines.
After years of sound and fury, a colt stirred in the stable.
You see, I have lost the habit of candlesticks with sconces.
No one among the bards returned to the speech of his ancestors.
Whoever forgot its sound forgot it forever.
And there were many others later, various names you don't know.
Mr. Norwid, for instance, and Mr. Gombrowicz, both from
    Samogitia.
We are not Lithuanian poets, neither myself nor the Lithuanian
    Theodore.
Only in far-off cities, over a Greek or a Sanskrit dictionary,
Did I rub my brow, as if I were sure I had heard that word
By the river at harvest time, in a graveyard on All Souls' Day.
I lived a long life there, several times a hundred years.
On my conscience the fate of serfs and servants.
Who except me has pondered the life of Jasiulis
And his wife, and their son Gregory, and their four daughters,
And Matulis, Pranialis, Ambrożej, and their sisters Polonija,
Rajna, Dosjuda, and Bujkis? And Mik Żemojtiewicz
And his wife Kasiula, and Ławryn and Miłoszajtis?
Who sifts in his hand their ashes, changed now into words?
And this is not, Father Ludwik, some false humility.
It was, let me make a comparison, like tearing apart a cloud.
For human ways deceive us with their warmth and bubbling noises.
The truth of the earth is not that. We know it in flesh and blood.
Having the memory of many lives, I was not as defenseless as others.
I was able to choose what was small because the great passes in just the
    same way.
Let me put my books there where your proverbs are,
On shelves smelling of ginger, by the Lithuanian statutes.

Ludwik Adam Jucewicz calls Dyonizy Paszkiewicz, who signed his poems Dyonizas Poszka, "the most zealous worker for national glory." He was a Samogitian nobleman and he founded a museum of native artifacts in the interior of an immense oak called Baublis which grew on his estate at Bordzie.

> Is great Baublis still alive, whose heart,
> Dug out by centuries, could hold a cart
> Or twelve good people for a wedding feast?

The bard Mickiewicz asked, though he must have known that Baublis had withered from old age and was cut down in 1811.

Father Ludwik had a good opinion of Poszka's epigrams, and quotes one of them, "heard myself from the mouth of the poet."

"The subject was provided by the following event: neighbors were driving to Paszkiewicz at carnival time; a carriage that had been driven ahead had had an accident, rolling over, and a lady sitting in it lost a bag containing a beloved golden snuffbox. An officer named Linde who was following on horseback had failed to notice it and smashed it to bits. Upon arrival, the lady recounted to the Lithuanian bard with great pathos the whole tragic story of her snuffbox. Paszkiewicz responded: If you so much regret your snuffbox, put in the place where it ended its existence a monument, and on it this little poem which I will provide to you:

> Cze buwa tabakiera,
> O dabarczios niera.
> Nes tas Linde passiutis,
> Praważiavo nepajutis."

The Lithuanian orthography is not perfect and the contents not very sophisticated. It means more or less this: Here there was a snuffbox, and now it is not, because that crazy Linde smashed it without noticing.

By the Great Kowno Highway. Where seals bark in the clouds
And sailboats glide through the gate of sheer rock, coming from the
    sea.
In this temporal place of our pilgrimage,
By neither human persuasion nor enforcement nor instigation,

Knowinge that nothinge is more certyn in the world than death,
I bequethe for future times and graunte for human needs
Myne demesne with all wilderness belonging to the estate,
With forests, woodes, lakes, with buried ribbons of pretty ladies,
And a snuffbox of pure gold, with myself as I was,
A wanderer from town to town, with everything
I signed by my propre hand,
And be it so that we or our descendents leave for foreign landes,
Let these verses be preserved, even on cheap paper,
As testimony that it's no use to kick against the pricks,
For we wanted to have this for ourselves and it turned out otherwise,
What was accepted in bitterness and misery turned into praise,
From a complaint hardly spoken there grew up thanksgiving,
So that by our owne free choice and will we partake,
Hayving heard and adored the worde of God,
Following the example of our old and pious ancestors,
Both of Lithuania and Russ,
In our unremovable demesne, safe from terrestrial adventure.

IV. Over Cities

1

If I am responsible
It is not for everything.
I didn't support the theses of Copernicus.
I was neither for nor against in Galileo's case.
My ships have never left the pond to sail the seas.
When I was born, locomotives ran on rails
Moving in a jumble of wheels and pistons,
And the echo of an express train rang wide
Through forests no longer primeval.
The district was inhabited by folk, Jews, and gentry.
You went by horse cart to buy kerosene, herring, and salt,
But in the towns they were using electricity.
It was said that someone had invented the wireless telegraph.
Books were already written. Ideas thoroughly discussed.
The ax was put to the tree.

2

"He that leadeth into captivity, shall go into captivity": thus began my age on the planet Earth. Later on I became a teacher in a city by a great sea and I had just turned away from the blackboard on which they could read, scribbled in my crooked writing: "Maximus the Confessor" and the dates "580–662." A multitude of their faces before me, these boys and girls, born when I was composing the first stanza of a threnody to be read at a memorial service, grew up before I managed to finish the poem. Then, putting aside my chalk, I addressed them in the following words:

"Yes, it is undeniable that extraordinary fates befell our species, precisely those from which Maximus the Confessor wanted to protect us, suspecting as he did the devilish temptation in the truth of reason. Yet while we hear everyone advising us to understand clearly causes and effects, let us beware of those perfectly logical though somewhat too eager arguments. Certainly, it is distressing not to know where this force that carries us away comes from or where it leads. But let us observe restraint and limit ourselves to statements which in our intention will be statements and nothing else. Let us formulate it thus: yes, the Universal is devouring the Particular, our fingers are heavy with Chinese and Assyrian rings, civilizations are as short-lived as weeks of our lives, places which not long ago were celebrated as homelands under oak trees are now no more than States on a map, and each day we ourselves lose letter after letter from our names which still distinguish us from each other."

3

Once upon a time they inhabited the land. The high and low sun
    divided their year.
In fog and mist after St. Michael's, when the angel announces to the
    seed,
Through the four Sundays of Advent and Ember days
Until the blind, the lame, and the crippled rejoice, the power
    trembles,
The sages of the world trudge through the snow protecting myrrh,
    frankincense, and gold.
Frost makes the trees crack in the woods, candles are brought home
    on Candlemas,
He wanders by Genezaret, time for their bearish dances.
The double bass and the drum at Shrovetide until Ash Wednesday.
And lo our little sun / / warms the frozen earth again
Riding past green corn / / palm in hand / / the King enters Jerusalem.

4

It is a ship in the likeness of a trireme or an Egyptian sailboat.

In any case the same as in the days when gods used to call from island to island, their hands cupped to their mouths.

Driven by a small motor, it comes near on a Pacific swell.

And in the rustle of the surf, runs aground high on the beach.

They are running, a crowd of them. On the deck, on the mast, their motley nakedness.

Until the whole ship is covered with a swarm opening and closing its wings,

With men and women from the end of the twentieth century.

Waking up I understood the meaning or, rather, I almost did.

5
A life unendurable but it was endured.
Cattle being driven to pasture in early spring. Speech betrays me here:
I don't know what to call a strip of land fenced with poles
That leads from the last huts of the village up to the forest.
(I have always lacked words and have not been a poet
If a poet is supposed to take pleasure in words.)
So, here is the eldest shepherd and his bags,
And his cross-gartered legs and the longest whipstock.
Two striplings with him. One is carrying a birch-bark trumpet,
The other an old-fashioned pistol, its barrel fixed with a string.
Really seen. Near Širvintai or Grinkiškai.
Long before I entered the monastery,
The light over an always radiant sandstone column,
The same today as in the time of Franconian kings,
Because I wanted to earn a day of comprehension,
Or even a single second, when those three
Would also reveal themselves, each in his unique essence.

6
I was long in learning to speak, now I let days pass without a word.

Incessantly astonished by the day of my birth, once only from the beginning to the end of time.

Born of a foolhardy woman with whom I am united, and whom I, an old man, pity in my dreams.

Her funny dresses, her dances, so utterly lost yet so close again.

And to call her a different name than I called her once, childishly unique.

Means to gauge, forget, number myself as well.

O what happened and when to *principium individuationis*?

Where is the calamus by the river with its scent, mine alone, and for no one else?

Through what meadows burned brown does she run with me in her arms

Carrying me to safety, away from the teeth of a beast?

My memory is shut, I don't know who I really was.

Have I fulfilled anything, have I been of use to anyone?

And she, who offered me to Our Lady of Ostrabrama,

How and why was she granted what she asked for in her prayer?

A handless performer with his collection of butterflies,

A fisherman by a lake, proud of his nets, the best in the county,

A gardener growing plants from beyond the seas.

Everything taken away. Crossed out. All our treasures.

So that we are alone at the trial in the dark

And hear her steps nearby, and think she has forgiven.

7

Sir Hieronymus took me by the arm and led me to the park
Where, at the turn of the lane, before a moss-covered Ceres,
A view opened upon meadows, the river, and the whole valley
Up to the towers of a church in the town beyond the forest.
And he was snapping his snuffbox and unhurriedly telling
Of his adventures in St. Petersburg or Naples,
Wittily describing the various countries.
He dealt at length with the swamps of Polesine
Which he once crossed on his way to Ravenna
From Venice, and argued that Jesuits from that province
Named similar Lithuanian swamps: Polesia.
Then he reminisced about Count de Saint-Germain
Or about the lost Book of Hieroglyphic Figures.
Just then the sun was setting over our land.
And he had hardly put his handkerchief into his pocket
When the birds began to sing as in early morning
And the full light of daybreak burst into noon.
Quicker and quicker. A century in half an hour.
And where is Sir Hieronymus? Where did I go? Here there is no one.

V. A Short Recess

1

Life was impossible, but it was endured.
Whose life? Mine, but what does that mean?

During recess, biting into a sandwich wrapped in paper
I stand under the wall in chubby meditation.

And I would have been someone I have never been.
And I would have obtained what I have never obtained.
Jackdaws beyond the window would have been remembered
By another I, not the one in whose words I am thinking now.

And if they say that all I heard was the rushing of a Heraclitean river
That will be enough, for the mere listening to it wore me down.
Scribes in dim rooms calculated on their abacuses.
Or perhaps men drove herds amid the smoke of distant fires.
Abandoned clothes kept for a moment the shape of arms and
    shoulders.
Pine needles fell onto a plush teddy bear.
And already new peoples with their numerous carts and a cannon.
What else could I be concerned with in Ostrogothic camps?

If only my early love had come true.
If only I had been happy walking down Harbor Street
(Which, anyway, did not lead to a harbor
But only to wet logs beyond the sawmills).
Had I been counted among the elders of our city,
And traveled abroad on an assignment.
Had we concluded an alliance with Ferrara.

Whoever is born just once on earth
Could have been that man whom Isis visited in a dream
And have gone through an initiation
To say afterward: I saw.
I saw the radiant sun at midnight.
I trod Proserpina's threshold.
I passed through all the elements and returned.
I came into the presence of the gods below and the gods above
And adored them face to face.

Or a gladiator, a slave
Under an inscription on a level stone:
"i was not, i was, i am not, i do not desire."

2
—Most distinguished voyager, from where do you hail?

—My city, in a valley among wooded hills
Under a fortified castle at the meeting of two rivers,
Was famous for its ornate temples:
Churches, Catholic and Orthodox, synagogues and mosques.
Our country cultivated rye and flax, it rafted timber as well.
Our army was composed of a lancer regiment,
Dragoons and a regiment of Tartar horsemen.
The postal stamps of our State
Represented phantasms
Sculpted long ago by two artists,
Friends or enemies, Pietro and Giovanni.
Our schools taught dogmatics,
Apologetics, sentences from the Talmud and Titus Livius.
Aristotle was highly regarded,

Though not as highly as sack races and jumping over fires
On Saint John's Eve.

—Most distinguished voyager, what was your eon like?

—Comic. Terror is forgotten.
Only the ridiculous is remembered by posterity.
Death from a wound, from a noose, from starvation
Is one death, but folly is uncounted and new every year.
I took part, I tied neckties
For no purpose and danced dances for no purpose.
A customer, a buyer of sweaters and pomade,
A mimicker, a shy guest,
A fop impressed by his reflection in shop windows.
I was overgrown by the bark of unconsciousness.
I tried hard to imagine another earth and could not.
I tried hard to imagine another heaven and could not.

3
There is an understanding and a covenant
Between all those whom time has defeated and released.
They tap their hammers, put curl paper in their hair,
Walk crooked sidewalks on urgent errands.
Cripples, harlots, swindlers, potentates.
And the duration of their city has no end,
Though they will no longer buy or sell
Nor take for themselves a husband or wife,
In mirrors they are not visible to themselves, or to anyone.
Their linen, wool, calico, and sateen
Sent back to them, as it should be, a little later,
Roll up and shimmer and gently rustle
Under the immovable light of street lamps or sun.
Forgiving each other and forgiven,

My fellow messengers, a taciturn retinue,
Though they never stop busying themselves in their streets and
    marketplaces,
Simultaneously (as we are wont to say) here and there.

4
I wanted glory, fame, and power.
But not just in one city of modest renown.
So I fled to countries whose capitals
Had boulevards lustrous beneath incandescent lamps
And, here and there, the outlines of Ionic columns.
I did not learn to value the honors one received there.
A sandy plain showed through every form.
So I ran farther, to the center of Megalopolis
In the belief that there was a center, though there was none.
I would have wept over my exposed delusion
Had the custom of regretting our offenses been preserved.
At best I would prostrate myself
And turn to my silent retinue:
Tell me, why should it be me, why exactly me?
Where are the others whose love was real and strong?
Should he remain faithful who didn't want to be faithful?

5
I made a pledge, what kind, I don't remember.
I wore a silver scout badge, then a gold one.
I took an oath, in mystical lodges, in underground assemblies
Swearing by the freedom of the people, or perhaps by brotherhood.
I wasn't to be obedient to my slogans or my chiefs.
Some lazy earthly spirits from under the roots of trees
Had obviously made other arrangements
Having a little laugh at the expense of my morals.
Engaged in weighty discussion on killing for the common good

My clear-eyed companions glanced distractedly
As I passed their table, a naive lute player.
And while they sat at their chess games (the winner was to execute the
    verdict)
I believed they were taking part in the tournaments for fun.
How I envied them: so magnificent,
So free from what I guarded as my shameful secret:
That, like the mermaid from Andersen's tale
I tried to walk correctly but a thin pain
Reminded me that I was foolish to try to imitate people.

6
And there was a holiday in Megalopolis.
Streets were closed to traffic, people walked in a procession.
The statue of a god slowly moved along:
A phallus four stories high
Surrounded by a crowd of priests and priestesses
Who tossed about in a whirling dance.
A service was also being celebrated in Christian churches
Where the liturgy consisted of discussion
Under the guidance of a priest in Easter vestment
On whether we should believe in life after death,
Which the president then put to the vote.
So I betook myself to an evening party
In a glass house at the edge of a mountain,
Where, silent, they stood observing a landscape of the planet:
A sparkling plain of metal or salt,
Absinthe lands furrowed by erosions,
White observatories far away on the summit.
The sun was setting in cardinal crimson.

After shootings and bitterness and songs and lamentations
It is not I who is going to tear at bandages and break seals.

What if I was merely an ignorant child
And served the voices that spoke through me?

Who can tell what purpose is served by destinies
And whether to have lived on earth means little
Or much.

VI. The Accuser

You say a name, but it's not known to anyone.

Either because that man died or because
He was a celebrity on the banks of another river.

> Chiaromonte
> Miomandre
> Petöfi
> Mickiewicz

Young generations are not interested in what happened
Somewhere else, long ago.

And what about your teachers who repeated:
Ars longa, vita brevis?

Their laurel-crowned deceptions will soon be over.

Do you still say to yourself: *non omnis moriar?*

Oh yes, not all of me shall die, there will remain
An item in the fourteenth volume of an encyclopedia
Next to a hundred Millers and Mickey Mouse.

A traveler. Far away. And a low sun.
You sit in a ditch and to your bearded mouth
You raise a slice of bread cut off with a penknife.
And there, splendor. Parades. Carriages. Youth all in flowers.
A short while ago you were one of them. Now you are watching.
Your sons ride there and do not know you.

You don't like this subject. Fine. Let's change it then.
What about those medieval dialogues before daybreak.
My most gracious and honorable body,
I, your soul, you declaim, I command you:
It's time to get up, check the date.
There are many tasks to be done today.
Serve me a little longer, just a bit.
I don't know what is going on in your dark tunnels,
At what moment you'll deny and overthrow me,
On what day your cosmos will congeal and collapse.

And you hear in reply: a bone cracks,
Murky blood grumbles, accelerates its rhythm,
Pain answers close in sign language,
A megalithic gurgle, whisper, indictments.

Confess, you have hated your body,
Loving it with unrequited love. It has not fulfilled
Your high expectations. As if you were chained to
Some little animal in perpetual unrest,
Or worse, to a madman, and a Slavic one at that.

What beauty. What light. An echo.
You lean from the window of a train, behind the house of the
    signalman
Children wave their kerchiefs. Woods flow by. An echo.
Or she, in a long dress embroidered in gold,
Steps down and down the stairs, your beloved.

The so-called sights of the earth. But not many.
You started on a journey and are not sated.
Spring dances go on but there is no dancer.

In truth, perhaps you never took part in all that.
A spirit pure and scornfully indifferent,
You wanted to see, to taste, to feel, and nothing more.
For no human purpose. You were a passerby
Who makes use of hands and legs and eyes
As an astrophysicist uses shiny screens,
Aware that what he perceives has long since perished.
"Tender and faithful animals." How is one to live with them
If they run and strive, while those things are no more?

Do you remember your textbook of Church History?
Even the color of the page, the scent of the corridors.
Indeed, quite early you were a gnostic, a Marcionite,
A secret taster of Manichean poisons.
From our bright homeland cast down to the earth,
Prisoners delivered to the ruin of our flesh,
Unto the Archon of Darkness. His is the house and law.
And this dove, here, over Bouffalowa Street
Is his as you yourself are. Descend, fire.
A flash—and the fabric of the world is undone.

This sin and guilt. And to whom should you complain?
I know your microscopes, your many labors,
And your secrets and your life spent
In the service of self-will, not out of self-will.

One summer day, one summer day.
A little armchair adorned with a garland of peonies and jasmine.
Your short legs dangle. All applaud.
A choir of peasants sings a song.

Until you reach the crossroads. There will be two paths.
One difficult and down, another easy and up.

Take the difficult one, simple Johnny. Again two paths.
One difficult and up, another easy and down.
Go up and it will lead you to the castle.

The road weaves upward accompanied by a drum and a flute,
Round and round the bends, where the scent is more and more
　　honeyed.
Plaited beehives, their straw shines like brass,
Sunflowers in rows, thyme.
And there, four turrets: facing east, west, north, and south.
When you enter the gate it's as if they were waiting for you.
Complete silence in a rose garden,
Around it, an expanse of green hills,
Of blue-green, up to the very clouds.

A pebble grates on the path. And presto! you fly as in dreams.
Black and white griffins on marble floors,
Parquetry of dim rooms. Yes, you were expected.
You don't have to say who you are. Everyone here knows and loves
　　you.
Eyes meeting eyes, hands touching hands. What communion.
What timeless music of saved generations.

And whoever that man is, from Provence, judging by his dress,
His words, when he addresses beautiful ladies, old men, and youths,
Are yours as well, as if he and you had long been one:
"Behold the sword that separates Tristan and Iseult.
Revealed to us was the contradiction between life and truth.
In the forgetting of earthly years is our movement and peace.
In our prayer for the last day is our consolation."

There was no castle. You were simply listening to a record.
A needle, swaying lightly on a black frozen pond,

Led the voices of dead poets out into the sun.
Then you thought in disgust:

Bestiality
Bestialité
Bestialità

Who will free me
From everything that my age will bequeath?
From infinity plus. From infinity minus.
From a void lifting itself up to the stars?

Throats.
Choking.
Fingers sinking.
Into flesh.
Which in an instant will cease to live.
A naked heap.
Quivering.
Without sound.
Behind thick glass.

And what if that was you, that observer behind thick glass?

Well, it happened long ago, in Ecbatana.
In Edessa, if you prefer. Be it as it may, a chronicle
In which nothing is certain and no evidence
Against any of you. Or against you alone.

You all rushed to arrange your households.
To smash tablets. Cart them away. Blood
Was washed from the walls with soap, sand, and chlorine.

In a barber's chair somewhere in a southern city.
Summer heat, jingling, a tambourine.
And a pythoness on the sidewalk
Rocks her swarthy belly in a ring of onlookers.
While here they trim your gray hair and sideburns
O Emperor.
Franz Josef.
Nicholas.
Ego.

—Yet I have learned how to live with my grief.

—As if putting words together has been of help.

—Not true, there were others, grace and beauty,
I bowed to them, revered them,
I brought them my gifts.

—And all you do is repeat:
If only there were enough time.
If only there were enough time.

You would like to lead a gathering of people
To a ritual of purification through the columns of a temple.

A ritual of purification? Where? When? For whom?

VII. Bells in Winter

Once, when returning from far Transylvania
Through mountain forests, rocks, and Carpathian ridges,
Halting by a ford at the close of day
(My companions had sent me ahead to look
For passage), I let my horse graze
And out of the saddlebag took the Holy Scripture;
The light was so gracious, murmur of streams so sweet,
That reading Paul's epistles, and seeing the first star,
I was soon lulled into a profound sleep.

A young man in ornate Greek raiment
Touched my arm and I heard his voice:
"Your time, O mortals, hastens by like water,
I have descended and known its abyss.
It was I, whom cruel Paul chastised in Corinth
For having stolen my father's wife,
And by his order I was to be excluded
From the table at which we shared our meals.
Since then I have not been in gatherings of the saints,
And for many years I was led by the sinful love
Of a poor plaything given to temptation,
And so we doomed ourselves to eternal ruin.
But my Lord and my God, whom I knew not,
Tore me from the ashes with his lightning,
In his eyes your truths count for nothing,
His mercy saves all living flesh."

Awake under a huge starry sky,
Having received help unhoped for,

Absolved of care about our paltry life,
I wiped my eyes wet with tears.

No, I have never been to Transylvania.
I have never brought messages from there to my church.
But I could have.
This is an exercise in style.
The pluperfect tense
Of countries imperfective.

But what I am going to tell you now is not invented.
The narrow street, just opposite the university
Was called, in fact, Literary Lane.
On the corner, a bookstore; but not books, just sheaves of paper
Up to the very ceiling. Unbound, tied with string,
Print and handwriting, in Latin, Cyrillic script,
In Hebrew letters. From a hundred, three hundred years ago.
Now it seems to me like quite a fortune.
From this bookstore you could see a similar one
Facing it. And their owners
Were similar, too: faded beards
Long black caftans, red eyelids.
They hadn't changed since the day Napoleon passed through the town.
Nothing has changed here. The privilege of stones?
They always are, for that is the way they like it. Beyond the second store
You turn along a wall and pass a house
Where a poet, famous in our city,
Wrote a tale about a princess named Grażyna.
Next, a wooden gate studded with nails
As huge as fists. Under the vault, to the right,
Stairs smelling of oil paint, where I live.

Not that I myself chose Literary Lane.
It just happened, there was a room for rent,
Low-ceilinged, with a bay window, an oak bed,
Heated well that severe winter by a stove
That used to devour logs brought from the hallway
By the old servant woman, Lisabeth.

There is, it would seem, no reason
(For I have departed to a land more distant
Than one that can be reached by roads leading through woods and
    mountains)
To bring that room back here.

Yet I belong to those who believe in *apokatastasis*.
That word promises reverse movement,
Not the one that was set in *katastasis*,
And appears in the Acts 3, 21.

It means: restoration. So believed: St. Gregory of Nyssa,
Johannes Scotus Erigena, Ruysbroeck, and William Blake.

For me, therefore, everything has a double existence.
Both in time and when time shall be no more.

And so, one morning. In biting frost,
All is cold and gray. And in that sleepy haze
A span of air suffused with carmine light.
Banks of snow, roadways made slippery by sleighs
Grow rosy. As do wisps of smoke, puffs of vapor.
Bells jingle nearby, then farther away, shaggy horses
Covered with hoarfrost, every hair distinct.
And then the pealing of bells. At Saint John's

And the Bernardines', at Saint Casimir's
And the Cathedral, at the Missionaries'
And Saint George's, at the Dominicans'
And Saint Nicholas's, at Saint Jacob's.
Many many bells. As if the hands pulling the ropes
Were building a huge edifice over the city.

So that Lisabeth wrapped up in her cape could go to
    morning Mass.

I have thought for a long time about Lisabeth's life.
I could count the years. But I prefer not to.
What are years, if I see the snow and her shoes,
Funny, pointed, buttoned on the side,
And I am the same, though the pride of the flesh
Has its beginning and its end.

Pudgy angels are blowing their trumpets again.
And him, the stooped priest in his chasuble
I would compare today to a scarab
From the Egyptian division of the Louvre.
Our sister Lisabeth in the communion of saints—
Of witches ducked and broken on the wheel
Under the image of the cloud-enfolded Trinity
Until they confess that they turn into magpies at night;
Of wenches used for their masters' pleasure;
Of wives who received a letter of divorce;
Of mothers with a package under a prison wall—
Follows the letters with her black fingernail,
When the choirmaster, a sacrificer, a Levite
Ascending the stairs, sings: *Introibo ad altare Dei.*
Ad Deum qui laetificat juventutem meam.

Prie Dievo kurs linksmina mano jaunystė.

Mano jaunystė.
My youth.
As long as I perform the rite
And sway the censer and the smoke of my words
Rises here.

As long as I intone:
Memento etiam, Domine, famulorum famularumque tuarum
Qui nos praecesserunt.

Kurie pirma musu nuėjo.

What year is this? It's easy to remember.
This is the year when eucalyptus forests froze in our hills
And everyone could provide himself with free wood for his
    fireplace
In preparation for the rains and storms from the sea.

In the morning we were cutting logs with a chain saw.
And it is a strong, fierce dwarf, crackling and rushing in the smell of
    combustion.
Below, the bay, the playful sun,
And the towers of San Francisco seen through rusty fog.

And always the same consciousness unwilling to forgive.

Perhaps only my reverence will save me.

If not for it, I wouldn't dare pronounce the words of prophets:

"Whatever can be Created can be Annihilated; Forms cannot;
The Oak is cut down by the Ax, the Lamb falls by the Knife,
But their Forms Eternal Exist forever. Amen. Hallelujah!

"For God himself enters Death's Door always with those that enter
And lies down in the Grave with them, in Visions of Eternity
Till they awake and see Jesus and the Linen Clothes lying
That the Females had woven for them and the Gates of their Father's
       House."

And if the city, there below, was consumed by fire
Together with the cities of all the continents,
I would not say with my mouth of ashes that it was unjust.
For we lived under the Judgment, unaware.

Which Judgment began in the year one thousand seven hundred
       fifty-seven.

Though not for certain, perhaps in some other year.
It shall come to completion in the sixth millennium, or next Tuesday.
The demiurge's workshop will suddenly be stilled. Unimaginable
       silence.
And the form of every single grain will be restored in glory.
I was judged for my despair because I was unable to understand this.

Berkeley, 1973–1974

HYMN

OF THE

PEARL

(Hymn o perle)

1981

A MAGIC MOUNTAIN

I don't remember exactly when Budberg died, it was either two years
    ago or three.
The same with Chen. Whether last year or the one before.
Soon after our arrival, Budberg, gently pensive,
Said that in the beginning it is hard to get accustomed,
For here there is no spring or summer, no winter or fall.

"I kept dreaming of snow and birch forests.
Where so little changes you hardly notice how time goes by.
This is, you will see, a magic mountain."

Budberg: a familiar name in my childhood.
They were prominent in our region,
This Russian family, descendants of German Balts.
I read none of his works, too specialized.
And Chen, I have heard, was an exquisite poet,
Which I must take on faith, for he wrote in Chinese.

Sultry Octobers, cool Julys, trees blossom in February.
Here the nuptial flight of hummingbirds does not forecast spring.
Only the faithful maple sheds its leaves every year.
For no reason, its ancestors simply learned it that way.

I sensed Budberg was right and I rebelled.
So I won't have power, won't save the world?
Fame will pass me by, no tiara, no crown?
Did I then train myself, myself the Unique,
To compose stanzas for gulls and sea haze,
To listen to the foghorns blaring down below?
Until it passed. What passed? Life.
Now I am not ashamed of my defeat.
One murky island with its barking seals
Or a parched desert is enough

To make us say: yes, *oui, si.*
"Even asleep we partake in the becoming of the world."
Endurance comes only from enduring.
With a flick of the wrist I fashioned an invisible rope,
And climbed it and it held me.

What a procession! *Quelles délices!*
What caps and hooded gowns!
Most respected Professor Budberg,
Most distinguished Professor Chen,
Wrong Honorable Professor Milosz
Who wrote poems in some unheard-of tongue.
Who will count them anyway. And here sunlight.
So that the flames of their tall candles fade.
And how many generations of hummingbirds keep them company
As they walk on. Across the magic mountain.
And the fog from the ocean is cool, for once again it is July.

Berkeley, 1975

THE VIEW

The landscape lacked nothing except glorification.
Except royal messengers who would bring their gifts:
A noun with an attribute and an inflected verb.
If only precious oaks would richly shine
When our brave students, on a path over the valley,
Walk and sing the "Ode to Joy."
If at least a solitary shepherd would carve letters in bark.

The landscape lacked nothing except glorification.
But there were no messengers. Thickets, dark ravines,
Forest overhanging forest, a kite wailed.
And who here could manage to institute a phrase?
The view was, who knows, probably pretty.

Far below, all was crumbling: castle halls,
Alleys behind the cathedral, bordellos, shops.
And not a soul. So where could the messengers come from?
After forgotten disasters I was inheriting the earth
Down to the shore of the sea, and above the earth, the sun.

Berkeley, 1975

CAESAREA

When we entered the waters of Caesarea
Or were sailing toward it, still straying through atlases,
Gulls were asleep on the smooth sounds between promontories,
A string of ducks flew along the delta in the morning mist.
Phantoms, towers beyond the smoke. A flickering and a sound like
    metal.
And galleons, of those who had made it to port long before,
Lay rotting at the gates of the city.

How many years were we to learn without understanding.
We roamed about the markets of Caesarea,
We crossed mountain chains and inland seas,
Getting acquainted with a multitude of its peoples and creeds and
    tongues.
Now, when Caesarea is bitterness for us
We are still not sure: were we led astray by the greed of our eyes,
Or did we so firmly believe that it had come true:
Our vocation, our very first calling.

Berkeley, 1975

STUDY OF LONELINESS

A guardian of long-distance conduits in the desert?
The one-man crew of a fortress in the sand?
Whoever he was. At dawn he saw furrowed mountains
The color of ashes, above the melting darkness,
Saturated with violet, breaking into fluid rouge,
Till they stood, immense, in the orange light.
Day after day. And, before he noticed, year after year.
For whom, he thought, that splendor? For me alone?
Yet it will be here long after I perish.
What is it in the eye of a lizard? Or when seen by a migrant bird?
If I am all mankind, are they themselves without me?
And he knew there was no use crying out, for none of them would
    save him.

Berkeley, 1975

A FELICITOUS LIFE

His old age fell on years of abundant harvest.
There were no earthquakes, droughts or floods.
It seemed as if the turning of the seasons gained in constancy,
Stars waxed strong and the sun increased its might.
Even in remote provinces no war was waged.
Generations grew up friendly to fellow men.
The rational nature of man was not a subject of derision.

It was bitter to say farewell to the earth so renewed.
He was envious and ashamed of his doubt,
Content that his lacerated memory would vanish with him.

Two days after his death a hurricane razed the coasts.
Smoke came from volcanoes inactive for a hundred years.
Lava sprawled over forests, vineyards, and towns.
And war began with a battle on the islands.

Berkeley, 1975

THE FALL

The death of a man is like the fall of a mighty nation
That had valiant armies, captains, and prophets,
And wealthy ports and ships over all the seas,
But now it will not relieve any besieged city,
It will not enter into any alliance,
Because its cities are empty, its population dispersed,
Its land once bringing harvest is overgrown with thistles,
Its mission forgotten, its language lost,
The dialect of a village high upon inaccessible mountains.

Berkeley, 1975

TEMPTATION

Under a starry sky I was taking a walk,
On a ridge overlooking neon cities,
With my companion, the spirit of desolation,
Who was running around and sermonizing,
Saying that I was not necessary, for if not I, then someone else
Would be walking here, trying to understand his age.
Had I died long ago nothing would have changed.
The same stars, cities, and countries
Would have been seen with other eyes.
The world and its labors would go on as they do.

For Christ's sake, get away from me.
You've tormented me enough, I said.
It's not up to me to judge the calling of men.
And my merits, if any, I won't know anyway.

Berkeley, 1975

SECRETARIES

I am no more than a secretary of the invisible thing
That is dictated to me and a few others.
Secretaries, mutually unknown, we walk the earth
Without much comprehension. Beginning a phrase in the middle
Or ending it with a comma. And how it all looks when completed
Is not up to us to inquire, we won't read it anyway.

Berkeley, 1975

PROOF

And yet you experienced the flames of Hell.
You can even say what they are like: real,
Ending in sharp hooks so that they tear up flesh
Piece by piece, to the bone. You walked in the street
And it was going on: the lashing and bleeding.
You remember, therefore you have no doubt: there is a Hell for
    certain.

Berkeley, 1975

AMAZEMENT

O what daybreak in the windows! Cannons salute.
The basket boat of Moses floats down the green Nile.
Standing immobile in the air, we fly over flowers:
Lovely carnations and tulips placed on long low tables.
Heard too are hunting horns exclaiming *hallali.*
Innumerable and boundless substances of the Earth:
Scent of thyme, hue of fir, white frost, dances of cranes.
And everything simultaneous. And probably eternal.
Unseen, unheard, yet it was.
Unexpressed by strings or tongues, yet it will be.
Raspberry ice cream, we melt in the sky.

Berkeley, 1975

IDEA

Afoot, on horseback, with bugles and baying hounds,
We looked down at last on the wilderness of the Idea,
Sulphur yellow like an aspen forest in late fall
(If the memory of a previous life does not deceive me),
Though it was not a wood, but a tangle of inorganic forms,
Chlorine vapor and mercury and iridescence of crystals.
I glanced at our company: bows, muskets,
A five-shot rifle, here and there a sling.
And the outfits! The latest fashions from the year one thousand
Or, for variety, top hats such as Kierkegaard,
The preacher, used to wear on his walks.
Not an imposing crew. Though, in fact, the Idea
Was dangerous to our kind no more, even in its lair.
To assault poor shepherds, farmhands, lumberjacks
Was its specialty, since it had changed its habits.
And the youngsters above all. Tormenting them with dreams
Of justice on earth and the Island of the Sun.

Berkeley, 1976

FILINA

A phantom laboratory smoked in the hills.
The fog ascended the terraces of light.
Driving on a long street I thought of you, Filina,
Who appear with the bounty of your froufrou skirts,
With your funny song:

> *My shoes are made of a mouse's cunt*
> *And so are the gloves I got from my aunt.*

And walk before a mirror tum-ta-tum
Then hurry down
To our carriage.

Fast horses take us down a poplar-lined road.
Anglers on holiday sit by the river.
We spread our tablecloth under an apple tree
And pour dark red wine into our silver goblet.

—And just where is this charming countryside?
—In ancient dukedoms far away, Filina.

And even if your ribbons were rather cheap
And your undergarments not very clean
That day and its white clouds remain forever
So that help comes to us from the earth, the real.

You are entrusted to the eternal keeping
That preserves a butterfly's trace in the air
And creates the earth anew to its liking
In which there is no irony or pain.

Filina, skirts rustling.
Mirrors disappearing.
Tum-ta-tum.

Berkeley, 1976

READING THE JAPANESE POET ISSA
(1762–1826)

A good world—
dew drops fall
by ones, by twos

A few strokes of ink and there it is.
Great stillness of white fog,
waking up in the mountains,
geese calling,
a well hoist creaking,
and the droplets forming on the eaves.

Or perhaps that other house.
The invisible ocean,
fog until noon
dripping in a heavy rain from the boughs of the redwoods,
sirens droning below on the bay.

Poetry can do that much and no more.
For we cannot really know the man who speaks,
what his bones and sinews are like,
the porosity of his skin,
how he feels inside.
And whether this is the village of Szlembark
above which we used to find salamanders,
garishly colored like the dresses of Teresa Roszkowska,
or another continent and different names.
Kotarbiński, Zawada, Erin, Melanie.
No people in this poem. As if it subsisted
by the very disappearance of places and people.

A cuckoo calls
for me, for the mountain,
for me, for the mountain

Sitting under his lean-to on a rocky ledge
listening to a waterfall hum in the gorge,
he had before him the folds of a wooded mountain
and the setting sun which touched it
and he thought: how is it that the voice of the cuckoo
always turns either here or there?
This could as well not be in the order of things.

In this world
we walk on the roof of Hell
gazing at flowers

To know and not to speak.
In that way one forgets.
What is pronounced strengthens itself.
What is not pronounced tends to nonexistence.
The tongue is sold out to the sense of touch.
Our human kind persists by warmth and softness:
my little rabbit, my little bear, my kitten.

Anything but a shiver in the freezing dawn
and fear of oncoming day
and the overseer's whip.
Anything but winter streets
and nobody on the whole earth
and the penalty of consciousness.
Anything but.

Berkeley, 1978

NOTES

ON THE NEED TO DRAW BOUNDARIES
Wretched and dishonest was the sea.

REASON TO WONDER
The ruler of what elements gave us song to praise birth?

ACCORDING TO HERACLITUS
The eternally living flame, the measure of all things, just as the measure
of wealth is money.

LANDSCAPE
Unbounded forests flowing with the honey of wild bees.

LANGUAGE
Cosmos, i.e., pain raved in me with a diabolic tongue.

SUPPLICATION
From galactic silence protect us.

JUST IN CASE
When I curse Fate, it's not me, but the earth in me.

FROM THE STORE OF PYTHAGOREAN PRINCIPLES
Having left your native land, don't look back, the Erinyes are behind you.

HYPOTHESIS
If, she said, you wrote in Polish to punish yourself for your sins, you will
be saved.

PORTRAIT
He locked himself in a tower, read ancient authors, fed birds on the terrace.

For only in this way could he forget about having to know himself.

CONSOLATION
Calm down. Both your sins and your good deeds will be lost in oblivion.

DO UT DES
He felt thankful, so he couldn't not believe in God.

THE PERFECT REPUBLIC
Right from early morning—the sun has barely made it through the dense maples—they walk contemplating the holy word: Is.

THE TEMPTER IN THE GARDEN
A still-looking branch, both cold and living.

HARMONY
Deprived. And why shouldn't you be deprived?
Those better than you were deprived.

STRONG OR WEAK POINT
You were always ready to fall to your knees!
Yes, I was always ready to fall to my knees.

WHAT ACCOMPANIES US
Mountain stream, footbridge with a rail
remembered down to the smallest burr on its bark.

THE WEST
On straw-yellow hills, over a cold blue sea,
black bushes of thorny oak.

INSCRIPTION TO BE PLACED OVER THE UNKNOWN GRAVE OF L.F.
What was doubt in you, lost, what was faith in you, triumphed.

EPITAPH
You who think of us: they lived only in delusion,
Know that we, the People of the Book, will never die.

MEMORY AND MEMORY
Not to know. Not to remember. With this one hope:
That beyond the River Lethe, there is memory, healed.

A GOD-FEARING MAN
So God heard my request after all, and allowed me to sin in his praise.

AIM IN LIFE
Oh to cover my shame with regal attire!

MEDICINE
If not for the revulsion at the smell of his skin,
I could think I was a good man.

LONGING
Not that I want to be a god or a hero.
Just to change into a tree, grow for ages, not hurt anyone.

MOUNTAINS
Wet grass to the knees, in the clearing, raspberry bushes taller than a
man, a cloud on the slope, in the cloud a black forest. And shepherds in
medieval buskins were coming down as we walked up.

IN REVERSE

On the ruins of their homes grows a young forest. Wolves are returning
and a bear sleeps secure in a raspberry thicket.

MORNING

We awoke from a sleep of I don't know how many thousand years.
An eagle flew in the sun again but it didn't mean the same.

ABUNDANT CATCH (LUKE 5.4–10)

On the shore fish toss in the stretched nets of Simon, James, and John.
High above, swallows. Wings of butterflies. Cathedrals.

HISTORY OF THE CHURCH

For two thousand years I have been trying to understand what It was.

Berkeley, 1978

BEFORE MAJESTY

It is bitter to praise God in misfortune,
thinking that He did not act, though He could have.

The angel of Jehovah did not touch the eyelids
of a man whose hand I hold,
I, a passive witness of this suffering for no cause.

Unanswered is our prayer, both his and mine.
Unanswered is my request: strike me
and in exchange give him an ordinary life.

A weak human mercy walks in the corridors of hospitals
and is like a half-thawed winter.

While I, who am I, a believer, dancing before the All-Holy?

Berkeley, 1978

A POETIC STATE

As if I were given a reversed telescope instead of eyes, the world moves away and everything grows smaller, people, streets, trees, but they do not lose their distinctness, are condensed.

In the past I had such moments writing poems, so I know distance, disinterested contemplation, putting on an "I" which is not "I," but now it is like that constantly and I ask myself what it means, whether I have entered a permanent poetic state.

Things once difficult are easy, but I feel no strong need to communicate them in writing.

Now I am in good health, where before I was sick because time galloped and I was tortured by fear of what would happen next.

Every minute the spectacle of the world astonishes me; it is so comic that I cannot understand how literature could expect to cope with it.

Sensing every minute, in my flesh, by my touch, I tame misfortune and do not ask God to avert it, for why should He avert it from me if He does not avert it from others?

I dreamt that I found myself on a narrow ledge over the water where large sea fish were moving. I was afraid I would fall if I looked down, so I turned, gripped with my fingers at the roughness of the stone wall, and moving slowly, with my back to the sea, I reached a safe place.

I was impatient and easily irritated by time lost on trifles among which I ranked cleaning and cooking. Now, attentively, I cut onions, squeeze lemons, and prepare various kinds of sauces.

Berkeley, 1977

DISTANCE

At a certain distance I follow behind you, ashamed to come closer.

Though you have chosen me as a worker in your vineyard and I
　　pressed the grapes of your wrath.

To every one according to his nature: what is crippled should not
　　always be healed.

I do not even know whether one can be free, for I have toiled against
　　my will.

Taken by the neck like a boy who kicks and bites

Till they sit him at the desk and order him to make letters,

I wanted to be like others but was given the bitterness of separation,

Believed I would be an equal among equals but woke up a stranger.

Looking at manners as if I arrived from a different time.

Guilty of apostasy from the communal rite.

There are so many who are good and just, those were rightly chosen

And wherever you walk the earth, they accompany you.

Perhaps it is true that I loved you secretly

But without strong hope to be close to you as they are.

Berkeley, 1980

WHEN AFTER A LONG LIFE

When, after a long life, it falls out
That he takes on a form he had sought
And every word carved in stone
Grows its hoarfrost, what then? Torches
Of Dionysian choruses in the dark mountains
From whence he comes. And half of the sky
With its snaky clouds. A mirror before him.
In the mirror the already severed, perishing
Thing.

Oregon, 1976

ON PILGRIMAGE

May the smell of thyme and lavender accompany us on our journey
To a province that does not know how lucky it is
For it was, among all the hidden corners of the earth,
The only one chosen and visited.

We tended toward the Place but no signs led there.
Till it revealed itself in a pastoral valley
Between mountains that look older than memory,
By a narrow river humming at the grotto.

May the taste of wine and roast meat stay with us
As it did when we used to feast in the clearings,
Searching, not finding, gathering rumors,
Always comforted by the brightness of the day.

May the gentle mountains and the bells of the flocks
Remind us of everything we have lost,
For we have seen on our way and fallen in love
With the world that will pass in a twinkling.

Lourdes, 1976

EARLY MORNING

Galloping horses
Of the departed century.

Day breaking,
Huge, over the world.
My torch fades and the sky glows.
I am standing by a rocky grotto above the hum of the river.
In the dawn radiance on the mountain a sliver of the moon.

Lourdes, 1976

A PORTAL

Before a sculpted stone portal,
In the sun, at the border of light and shade,
Almost serene. Thinking with relief: this will remain
When the frail body fades and presto, nobody.
Touching a grainy wall. Surprised
That I accept so easily my waning away,
Though I should not. Earth, what have I to do with thee?
With your meadows where dumb beasts
Grazed before the deluge without lifting their heads?
What have I to do with your implacable births?
So why this gracious melancholia?
Is it because anger is no use?

Berkeley, 1976

A Mirrored Gallery

(Page 1)
An old man, contemptuous, black-hearted,
Amazed that he was twenty such a short time ago,
Speaks.
     Though he would rather understand than speak.

He loved and desired, but it turned out badly.
He pursued and almost captured, but the world was faster than he was.
And now he sees the illusion.

In his dreams he is running through a dark garden.
His grandfather is there but the pear tree is not where it should be,
And the little gate opens to a breaking wave.

Inexorable earth.
Irrevocable law.
The light unyielding.

Now he climbs marble stairs
And the blossoming orange trees are fragrant
And he hears, for a while, the *tiuu* of birds,
But the heavy doors are already closing
Behind which he will stay for a very long time
In air that does not know winter or spring,
In a fluorescence without mornings and without sunsets.

The coffers of the ceiling imitate a forest vault.
He passes through halls full of mirrors
And the faces loom up and dissolve,
Just as Barbara, the princess, appeared to the king once
When a black mage had conjured her.

And all around him the voices are intoning,
So many that he could listen for centuries,
Because he wanted, once, to understand his poor life.

(Page 10)
Sacramento River, among barren hills, tawny,
And spurts of shallow wind from the bay
And on the bridges my tires drum out a meter.

Ships, black animals among the islands,
Gray winter on the waters and the sky.
If they could be called in from their far-off Aprils and countries,
Would I know how to tell them what is worst yet true—
The wisdom, not for them, that has come to me?

(Page 12)
He found on dusty shelves the pages of a family chronicle covered with barely legible writing, and again he visits the murky house on the Dvina where he had been once in his childhood, called The Castle because it had been built where, at the time of Napoleon, a castle of the Knights of the Sword had burned down, exposing dungeons in the foundations and a skeleton chained to the wall. It was also called The Palace, to distinguish it from the cottage in the park where Eugene used to move, together with his piano, for the winter. That relative of his had gone to Jesuit schools in Metz and made a career as a lawyer in the military courts of St. Petersburg, but left the service when he was asked to convert to Orthodoxy; after which he returned to The Castle and lived alone, maintaining relations with none of the neighbors nor with his family, except his sister Mrs. Jadwiga Iżycka, whom he loved. *"They conversed with the servants only in Polish or Byelorussian, holding the Russian language in abomination."* With rare guests, former colleagues from St. Petersburg, Eugene spoke French. *"He remained in The Castle, practically without leaving it, from 1893 to 1908. He used to read a great deal, also to*

write, but mostly, night and day, he played the piano. It was a cabinet model, a Korngoff of Warsaw make, for which he paid 1500 rubles in gold, in those times an enormous sum." If he went anywhere, it was on horseback to visit his sister at the neighboring Idolta, and they were often seen riding together through the forests, for she was fond of riding on an "amazon" saddle. But after her death, only a passerby, stopping at the park's gate and hearing his exquisite music, could have testified that the house was inhabited. Later on, no music was heard, *"though it was already autumn, and so people assumed that he still played, but in the far interior of The Palace where, because of the double windows, he could not be heard."* Then, suddenly, he convoked the family and even admitted priests. He was buried beside his sister in the family vault at Idolta. He left behind packages of manuscripts, of unknown contents, bound with string.

(Page 13)

I did not choose California. It was given to me.
What can the wet north say to this scorched emptiness?
Grayish clay, dried-up creek beds,
Hills the color of straw, and the rocks assembled
Like Jurassic reptiles: for me this is
The spirit of the place.
And the fog from the ocean creeping over it all,
Incubating the green in the arroyos
And the prickly oak and the thistles.

Where is it written that we deserve the earth for a bride,
That we plunge in her deep, clear waters
And swim, carried by generous currents?

(Page 14)

He reads in the chronicle: *"Soon after his death, he began to frighten people. From that time there was no peace in The Castle, for everybody would say that Pan Eugene was walking. Furniture moved, the desk in his room changed place, the piano played at night in his study, and there were weird goings-on in the library upstairs."* This unpleasant discovery was made by an agent of the Bank of Wilno, Mr. Mieczysław Jałowiecki, who was assessing the estate in connection with the heirs' endeavors to get a loan. They made a bed for him in Eugene's study, a large room with an oak parquet floor and windows facing the Dvina, where beside a piano and a desk there were bookcases for those books which Eugene wanted to have at hand without having to walk upstairs to the library; and one's attention was drawn by paintings and a valuable clock from the time of the Directorate, adorned with Napoleonic eagles. In the middle of the night the guest, ringing— in horror—the bell for the servants, tore off the thick woolen bell pull and, without waiting for rescue, jumped out of the window in his underwear, for which rashness he paid with pneumonia, since it was cold outside. Eventually everyone became accustomed to troubles in The Castle, but what happened to the new parish priest in Druja, Canon Father Weber, was unusual. He came to The Castle to pay a visit, and looking casually through albums of photographs suddenly stopped at one of them and asked whom it represented. When he heard from his hostess that the figure was her brother-in-law Eugene who had died two years before, he said, *"Strange, I don't know if I should mention it, Madam—perhaps it would be better not, for you may think I have lost my mind, saying such things—yet, whether you believe me or not, I must tell you that he was in my room at the monastery yesterday night."* And he told how, after having returned from an inspection of his parish, he went to bed early, and began to read to induce sleep, when he heard the door creaking, steps in the dining room and then in the living room which adjoined his chamber. The door opened and an unknown man entered, elegantly dressed, *"with the energetic bearing of a man of wealth, full of self-assurance,"* bareheaded and without an overcoat. Father Weber took him for one of the neighboring landlords whom he had not as yet met, arriving on some urgent business, and he began to excuse himself for being found so early in bed. The unknown man approached him silently, rested his hand on the marble top of the night table, and said, *"As proof that I was here, I leave my fingerprints."*

And then he turned and left. Without hurry, he crossed the unlit living room, then the dining room, opened the door to the corridor of the former monastery, and gradually his steps fell silent. Yet, as the priest was later able to assure himself, the door leading to the yard was locked, as was the gate to the street and the wicket in the gate. Eugene continued to remind people of himself until precisely that day in February 1914 when his brother Józef passed away. I wonder, thinks the reader, whether philosophy is really of any help against the passion of life? Perhaps all of wisdom is good for nothing if petty angers and ill feelings and family quarrels are so durable that they force us to walk after our death?

(Page 15)

> *Le Monde—c'est terrible*
> —CÉZANNE

Cézanne, I bring these three for an impossible meeting
to your workshop in Aix, into the fire of ocher and cinnabar.

This woman's name is Gabriela. I could show her
in a white dress with a sailor's collar
or as an old hag with protruding, gumless teeth.
Here she stands olive-gold, black-haired.

This is Eddy, an athlete from half a century ago.
He rests his hand on his hip as in the portrait
reproduced sometimes in art books.

And here is Mieczysław who painted him. Fingers yellow from
    tobacco,

he licks a cigarette paper, thinking about the next move of his brush.

They will be witnesses to my grief,
and to whom should I reveal it, if not to you?

Strength, skill, beauty, above all strength,
swinging one's shoulders, an easy gait
are what people value most highly, and justly so.
A movement in harmony with the universal movement, deftness,
whatever the world is, makes one happy.
To be like him when he bends into the crouch of a discus thrower,
when he urges his horse into a gallop, slips at dawn from the window
of the redhaired wife of Mr. Z!

I envied him as only a sixteen-year-old can do.
Until, not soon, after the big war,
news of him reached me. He had not perished in battle.
In a new State, under the rule of a debased language,
he poisoned himself with gas out of loathing for the everyday lie.

If glory of flesh falls into the earth,
into the general oblivion. If I, the mind,
have such power over him that at my order
he appears, though he is no one until the end of the world,
have I triumphed? Is not that a miserable revenge?

Whatever was desired, Cézanne,
was changing like the trunk of a Provençal pine when you tilted your
    head.
The color of her dress and skin: the yellow, the rouge,
the sienna raw and burnt, the green Veronese,

words like tubes of color ready-made and alien.
And Gabriela remains only that.

I want to know where it goes, that moment of
    enchantment,
to what heaven above, to the bottom of what abyss,
to what gardens growing beyond space and time.
I want to know where the house of an instant of seeing is,
when it's liberated from the eye, in itself forever,
the one you pursued day after day
circling a tree with your easels.

Mieczysław had his workshop in the city of Warsaw.
Your tardy disciple, he nearly achieved,
as he used to tell me, blowing on his cold fingers
that war winter, a clay jar and an apple.
He looked at them constantly and constantly they filled his
    canvases.

And I believe he would have snatched from things a moment of
    seeing,
had he observed the rules of the artist
who must be indifferent to good and evil,
to joy and pain and the laments of mortals,
a haughty servant, as he is, of only one aim.

But he used his workshop to help people
and hid Jews there, for which the penalty was death.
He was executed in May 1943,
thus giving his soul for his friends.

And it is bitter to sing in praise of the mind, Cézanne.

The three names are real and because of that they exert control. Had they been changed, the road to fictionalizing would, immediately, have been opened. Yet the more he tries to be precise, the more entangled he gets in devices of human speech. And it is enough to put those three, quite arbitrarily, together, and suddenly what is untellable in them is strengthened, composing itself into an autonomous tale. But yes, also in reality they stood together once, in a photo, not alone, with others, before the house in Krasnogruda, and each one of them lived in the thoughts of his neighbor. He tries now to guess how he thinks of them. Eddy is a panic of remembered shames: not saving a goal, kicking down the jumping bar, falling from a horse, things which should not be known by anybody. When he learned that Eddy married shortly before the war, that he and his wife were inseparable, that they survived those years together and, by mutual consent, committed suicide in 1951 or 1952, he felt, yes, relief, as if the disappearance of a man compared to whom he felt himself inferior elevated him. As for Gabriela, her presence is nearly as intense as that of the river on whose banks he was born and where he, three years old, saw her, a teenager, for the first time. A golden net on ultramarine, or green, green Veronese, an acrid sweetness of honeycombs brought in in a clay bowl, a neck like the necks of musical instruments—she was never expected to be all this for him, constantly rescued, taken out of time. And about Mieczysław he thinks that even if a life was refused to him in which he could win as an artist and all his paintings were burned except for the portrait of Eddy which he painted in his youth, at least he was happy once, arranging an apartment with Julia in the quarter of modern buildings or wandering with her in the Gorce mountains at the end of the nineteen twenties, when Warsaw artists and literati loved mountaineering lore, naive paintings on glass, and folk songs. He does not know why, but there is some consolation in that, just as there is in the little song Mieczysław hummed, sometimes, with a kind of embarrassed emotion:

"Round and round
The little sun is going
The little sun is going
And our Catherine
Is riding to her wedding
Is riding to her wedding
Is riding, is riding
And lifting her hands
And lifting her hands
Asking Jesus
Asking Jesus
To make her happy."

He thinks that the word *past* does not mean anything, for if he can keep those three so strongly before his eyes, how much stronger than his is an unearthly gaze.

(Page 17)
A portrait of Schopenhauer consorts, who knows why, with a portrait of Ela who, adorned by the painter with a Renaissance hat similar, probably, to those worn by ladies on the deck of the *Titanic*, smiles enigmatically. "Ah, philosopher," the wanderer addresses him, "I have found out why they dislike you. Who, after all, wants to be told that truth is a rebellion of the mind against its utilitarian vocation? That fate is aristocratic in allocating the gifts of intellect, and that they, completely average, chasing illusion, are supposed to bow to the fewest of the few and admit their own inferiority? *'He is rather like a theatergoer, for separated from everything he watches the drama.'* One in how many millions, the artist and philosopher? And myself too, had I known in advance what was in store for me, wouldn't I have chosen life and happiness? Even now, when I know that what remains of the life and happiness of my contemporaries is nothing? It is easy to guess why you were not liked and never will be. No one had ever so forcefully opposed the child and the genius to the rest of them, always under the power of blind will, of which the essence is sexual desire; no one has ever so forcefully explained the genius of children: they are

onlookers, avid, gluttonous, minds not yet caught by the will of the species, though I would add, led too by Eros, but an Eros who is still free and dances, knowing nothing of goals and service. And the gift of the artist or philosopher likewise has its secret in a hidden hostility toward the earth of the adults. Your language—O philosopher—so logical and precise in its appearance, disguised more than it revealed, so they really had no access to you. Admit it, your only theme was time: a masque on midsummer night, young girls in bloom, ephemerid generations born and dying in a single hour. You asked only one question—is it worthy of man to be seduced and caught?"

(Page 18)
Lovers walk in the morning on a path above the village, they look down into the valley, dazzled by themselves and by their part in the earth of the living.

Brookwater below, green meadows, and on the opposite slope the forest tiers up steeply.

They go where a black woodpecker flickers among the firs and the scent of new clover rises from the edge of the gorge.

And now they have found a footbridge among the trees, a true bridge with a handrail, that leads somewhere, on the other side.

And when they walk down, they see in a frame of pines the roofs of two towers, green copper glistening, and they hear the thin voice of a little bell.

That cloister, small cars high above it on the road, and, in the sun, the echo and then silence.

As the beginning of a revelation—what kind they don't know—because it will never advance beyond its beginning.

"Philosopher, you were too severe for their short-lived élans of the ego, though even then they looked at things as if the vainglory of existence were in the past. And I concede, your words confirmed what I had experienced myself: '. . . *the quiet contemplation of the natural object actually present, whether a landscape, a tree, a mountain, a building or whatever it may be; in as much as he loses himself in this object, i.e., forgets even his individuality, his will, and only continues to exist as the pure subject, the clear mirror of the object, so that it is as if the object alone were there, without anyone to perceive it, and he can no longer separate the perceiver from the perception but both have become one, because the whole consciousness is filled and occupied with one single sensuous picture; if thus the object has to such an extend passed out of all relation to the will, then that which is so known is no longer the particular thing as such; but it is the Idea, the eternal form, the immediate objectivity of the will at this grade; and, therefore, he who is sunk in this perception is no longer individual, for in such perception the individual has lost himself; but he is* pure, *will-less, powerless, timeless subject of knowledge.'* "

(Page 20)
The earth in its nakedness of hard lava carved by river beds, the vast earth, void, from before the vegetation.

And the river they came to, called by adventurers Columbia, rolls down her waters, a cold and liquid lava as gray as if there were neither sky nor white clouds above.

Nothing here, except the winds of the planet raising dust from the eroded rock.

And, after a hundred miles, they reach the building on the plateau, and when they enter it, an old dream of a volcanic desert comes true;

For this is a museum, preserving the embroideries of princesses, the cradle of a crown prince, photographs of the cousins and nieces of a forgotten dynasty.

The wind beats loudly against the brass door, while the parquets squeak under the portraits of Czar Nicholas and of the Romanian queen, Maria.

What madman chose this place to dispose the souvenirs of his adoration, lilac-colored scarves and dresses in crêpe de chine?

For the eternal bitterness of the lost fleshliness of lovely girls traveling with their families to Biarritz.

For the degradation of touches and whispers by the mutterings of strewn pumice and basalt gravel.

Until even regret wears thin, and a deaf-dumb abstract ache remains?

His name was Sam Hill and he was a millionaire. On the windy heights where the Columbia River, flowing down out of the Rocky Mountains, had carved canyons for itself in volcanic layers from the time of the Pliocene, and where, a little later, men traced a border between central Washington and central Oregon, he started to build an edifice in 1914 which was to serve as a museum honoring his friend Maria of Romania. A beauty on the throne, eldest daughter of the Duke of Edinburgh and Saxe-Coburg-Gotha and of the Great Princess of Russia, Mary, thus cousin to both King George and Czar Nicholas II, she was eighteen when, in 1893, she married Prince Ferdinand Hohenzollern-Sigmaringen, the Romanian Crown Prince. It was rumored that she had *une cuisse légère*, i.e., a light thigh. Whatever the truth was, Sam Hill named his building Maryhill, uniting her name to his, and the inauguration of the museum in 1926 took place with the active participation of the royal guest. The few tourists who wander that way are able to take a look at her in Romanian folk dress; also to marvel at her sculptured throne, her spinning wheel, and her loom. Her toilets are preserved in the showcases, the walls adorned with portraits of her relatives, predominantly the Czar's family.

(Page 24)
If not now, when?
Here is the Phoenix airfield,
I see the cones of volcanic mountains
And I think of all I have not said,
About the words *to suffer* and *sufferance* and how one can bear a lot
By training anger until it gets tired and gives up.
Here is the island Kauai, an emerald set among white clouds,
Warm wind in the palm leaves, and I think of snow
In my distant province where things happened
That belong to another, inconceivable life.
The bright side of the planet moves toward darkness
And the cities are falling asleep, each in its hour,
And for me, now as then, it is too much.
There is too much world.

Waiting indefinitely. Every day and in every hour, hungry. A spasm in the throat, staring at the face of every woman passing in the street. Wanting not her but all the earth. Inhaling, with dilated nostrils, the smells of the bakery, of roasting coffee, wet vegetables. In thought devouring every dish and drinking every drink. Preparing myself for absolute possession.

(Page 25)
You talked, but after your talking all the rest remains.
After your talking—poets, philosophers, contrivers of romances—
Everything else, all the rest deduced inside the flesh
Which lives and knows, not just what is permitted.

I am a woman held fast now in a great silence.
Not all creatures have your need for words.
Birds you killed, fish you tossed into your boat,
In what words will they find rest and in what Heaven?

You received gifts from me; they were accepted.
But you don't understand how to think about the dead.
The scent of winter apples, of hoarfrost, and of linen:
There are nothing but gifts on this poor, poor earth.

A dark Academy. Assembled are instructresses in corsets, grammarians of petticoats, poets of unmentionables with lace. The curriculum includes feeling the touch of silk against the skin, listening to the rustle of a dress, raising the chin when the aigrette on the hat sways. They teach the use of what is customary: long gloves up to the elbows, a fan, lowered eyelashes, bows, as well as human speech, so that a faience chamberpot, even if a painted eye looks up roguishly from the bottom, is called a *vessel*, a brassiere lifting the breasts bears the name *soutiengorge*, and, in the spirit of French great-grandmothers who remembered the red coats of English soldiers, a menstruation is announced as *"the English have arrived."* The superior method and goal lies in a hardly noticeable smile, for everything is only make-believe: sounds of orchestras and promenades, paintings in gilded frames, hymns, chorals, marble sculptures, speeches of statesmen, and the words of chronicles. In reality there is only a sensation of warmth and gluiness inside, also a sober watchfulness when one advances to meet that delicious and dangerous thing that has no name, though people call it *life*.

(Page 27)
How many before me crossed over the frontier of words
Knowing the futility of speech after a century of phantoms
Which were terrifying but meant nothing?

What am I to do with the conductor of the Trans-Siberian Railway,
With the lady to whom a traveler offered a ring from Mongolia,
With singing expanses of telephone wires
And lush coupés and a station after the third bell?

They are all standing in front of the porch, dressed in white,
And through sooty pieces of glass they look at the eclipse
In the summer of 1914 in the Kowno gubernia.
And I am there, not knowing how or what will happen.
But they do not know either how or what will happen,
Or that this boy, now one of them,
Will wander as far as a precipice across the frontier of words,
Once, at the end of his life, when they will be no more.

(Page 29)
In the shadow of the Empire, in Old Slavonic long-johns,
You better learn to like your shame because it will stay with you.
It won't go away even if you change your country and your name.
The dolorous shame of failure. Shame of the muttony heart.
Of fawning eagerness. Of clever pretending.
Of dusty roads on the plain and trees lopped off for fuel.
You sit in a shabby house, putting things off until spring.
No flowers in the garden—they would be trampled anyway.
You eat lazy pancakes, the soupy dessert called "Nothing-served-cold."
And, always humiliated, you hate foreigners.

(Page 31)
Pure beauty, benediction: you are all I gathered
From a life that was bitter and confused,
In which I learned about evil, my own and not my own.
Wonder kept seizing me, and I recall only wonder,
Risings of the sun over endless green, a universe
Of grasses, and flowers opening to the first light,

Blue outline of the mountain and a hosanna shout.
I asked, how many times, is this the truth of the earth?
How can laments and curses be turned into hymns?
What makes you need to pretend, when you know better?
But the lips praised on their own, on their own the feet ran;
The heart beat strongly; and the tongue proclaimed its adoration.

(Page 34)
And why all this ardor if death is so close?
Do you expect to hear and see and feel there?
But you know the earth is like no other place:
What continents, what oceans, what a show it is!
In the hall of pain, what abundance on the table.
The music endures, but not the music-maker:
No velvet of his survives, not even a garter.
And space-age men, in thickets, lift bows to fiddles,
Drink in their villages, squabble, let dice rattle
With the dead perched on a giddy carousel.

And I have lived a life that makes me feel unable
To bring myself to write an accusation.
Joy would spurt in amid the lamentation.
So what, if, in a minute I must close the book:
Life's sweet, but it might be pleasant not to have to look.

Pages Concerning the Years of Independence

(Page 35)
It is much easier to reach the Columbia River which empties into the Pacific, or to pitch a tent at the Athabaska River flowing to polar lakes, than to penetrate that zone marked by the zigzag silver lines on the collar of his father's uniform. It is the spring of the year nineteen hundred twenty, they live on Embankment Street, just by the Church of Saint Jacob, and who would have supposed that one man could preserve inside himself, so vividly, that aroma of flowers, benches, vespers? In a britzka with a soldier on the driver's seat they ride along the Wilia to Antokol and beyond, out of town, where sappers have been stationed on the banks of the river. And everything is green, batteries painted that special olive-green seen now for the first time, and an armored car, and the green outside the window when his father sings:

> *"On the banks of the river Loire,*
> *There was my birth and my cradle.*
> *Two kinds of goods flow from that land:*
> *Beautiful ribbons and rifles."*

What is that song about? About weapons sent from France? About an armored car? And they sing this, also:

> *"At a faraway river, where he fell in battle,*
> *A white rose blossoms on his grave."*

And also on Embankment Street, only at its other end, close to the harbor, Mrs. Burchardt, standing on the left side—he remembers—of the piano, draws from her long neck the melody of another soldier's song, difficult to understand:

> *"The echoes of cafés came back to him."*

On the walls of houses by the Wilia he reads: "Piłsudski" and thinks, "Why did they write *ds* instead of *dz* as it should be in Polish?" And Mrs. Strawinski and Mrs. Niezabitowski; and Mary Pawlikowski's brother Dan who became an aviator; Witold is far away with his regiment of cavalry; Nina, that crazy girl, joined, they say, a unit of dragoons. When Dr. Swieżynski cut out his tonsils, it was painful, but for an instant only and then one was allowed to eat a lot of ice cream, something he remembers much later, sitting in the dentist's chair when Dr. Hallat laughs: "You certainly are no complainer!" Ice cream, cherries; summer is already here, larger and larger headlines in the newspapers, more and more whispered conversations. Ever since, the breaking of the front has meant for him what his memory absorbed then: dusty roads under the glow of artillery fire, military trains, wandering, panics. The very idea of defeat will always be for him a scorched highway leading to Niemenczyn, packed with carts, wagons, britzkas. He will also be able to say, without distortion: I know how the streets of a city grow empty, while eyes peep from behind half-closed shutters. At dusk their wagon, loaded with belongings and fodder for the horses, climbs the serpentine curves of the road leading through Ponary toward Landwarów; when he looks back, the city is dark. What those serpentine curves in the road became for him later when he was a student, he cannot recall precisely now, nor can he verify the circumstances, for there is nobody to ask. It was long ago and all of them are dead. It should not be that way, but it is: even the silvery zigzag lines on the collar of his father's uniform appear only when the melody of a little song returns:

> *"On the banks of the river Loire,*
> *There was my birth and my cradle."*

(Page 36)
The war was over and the stars, serene.

The impoverished country of fields and poplars had managed to protect the wings of the storks nesting on its huts and the bread marked with a sign of the cross.

No one would be cutting down alleys of linden or surrounding villages at dawn to deport people in long trains to the East.

Artisans thatching roofs with straw, village blacksmiths, coopers preparing tubs for the cabbage-pickling season were constantly busy, as were musicians at weddings.

Everyday poverty was preserved, barefooted little shepherds were making fires on the stubble, geese gaggled on the meadows, and wooden hoists at the wells creaked.

Black towns, that on fair-days wore multicolored blankets and nibbled oats from a bag, were lighting candles at sundown on Friday.

Wooden spokes clattered at night through the fields, and a glow came from the sunsets, not from awakening cities.

A student from a Galician high school, a farmhand, a landowner's son, and a young peasant lay under the sod, leaving their homeland to the doings of the King-Spirit.

The victor, a nobleman with a *ds* in his non-Polish name, was biting his moustache and saying nothing.

> *"He went out into the fields, black earth and rye*
> *Spread wide before his freedom-loving eye."*

If only, as his father had done, he could busy himself with the rotation of crops, with planning the next day's work for servants and field hands!

"High-roofed front porches, floors of slick wet clay"

If only he had the power of the peasant-king, judge under the apple trees!

"In the silence before the dawn of life,
O golden rose, you lift me to yourself."

No State was truly his; no tribe desired his union of nations.

"And he, pursued by a great Genesic cry"

No country was his; there was only this other country, the one he got too late.

"I am like a beggar stopped on a road"

The stars over his head were not serene, but what he read in them would be of no avail to anybody.

A coffin under a white eagle deposited in the royal tombs, but the heart elsewhere, in his city, his own capital.

Such then was the inheritor of the Boleslavian crown—after whom again the homelessness of vanquished generations?

"As though a smile were the only thing we owed
These holy songs—and to their gift of blood."
                              —"THE KING SPIRIT"

(Page 37)

TO JÓZEF CZECHOWICZ

It is possible that the dead do not need reports from the Earth, and see in one symbol all that occurred later.

Yet I presume you have some trace of interest, at least as to your own continued stay among the living.

Therefore I try to describe how you appear now, on this other continent, in the sudden lightning of your afterlife.

A dark-haired young boy in a blue infantry uniform, a cap with a little white eagle, and puttees.

Because you were a soldier for two weeks in the Nineteen Twenty, and wrote about it, and the actors in your play were dressed in that same uniform.

That play which Horzyca succeeded in putting on stage, before our desks in that creaky office on Dąbrowski Square disintegrated.

Before you perished from a bomb, Szulc in Auschwitz, Szpak from a bullet because he refused to be closed in the ghetto, Janina Włodarkiewicz from a heart attack in New York.

So I am not surprised at your being dressed that way as you circle around me, when I record your poems in the Language Lab or play them back from a tape.

Lives taken away, lands defiled, sins: and your note, pure above the abyss.

From iron beds, rheumatic basements, disheveled laments and wailings, a calico misery,

From shit-houses in the yard, tomatoes on the windowsill, vapor over washtubs, greasy checkered notebooks—

How could that modest music for young voices soar, transforming the dark fields below?

Sleepy fields, some marigolds and mallows, in the garden of my *Matusia*, my dear Mama.

You were set apart by a flaw in your blood, you knew about Fate; but only the chant endures, nobody knows about your sorrow.

And this is what tormented me in those years I lived after you; a question: Where is the truth of unremembered things?

Where are you behind your words, and all who are silent, and a State now silent though it once existed?

The Wormwood Star

(Page 38)
Now there is nothing to lose, my cautious, my cunning, my hyperselfish cat.

Now we can make confession, without fear that it will be used by mighty enemies.

We are an echo that runs, skittering, through a train of rooms.

Seasons flare and fade, but as in a garden we do not enter anymore.

And that's a relief, for we do not need to catch up with the others, in the sprints and the high jump.

The Earth has not been to Your Majesty's liking.

The night a child is conceived, an obscure pact is concluded.

And the innocent receives a sentence, but he won't be able to unravel its meaning.

Even if he consults ashes, stars, and flights of birds.

A hideous pact, an entanglement in blood, an anabasis of vengeful genes arriving from swampy millennia,

From the half-witted and the crippled, from crazed wenches and syphilitic kings

At mutton's leg and barley and the slurping of soup.

Baptized with oil and water when the Wormwood Star was rising,

I played in a meadow by the tents of the Red Cross.

That was the time assigned to me, as if a personal fate were not enough.

In a small archaic town ("The bell on the City Hall clock chimed midnight, as a student N . . ." and so on).

How to speak? How to tear apart the skin of words?
What I have written seems to me now not that.
And what I have lived seems to me now not that.

When Thomas brought the news that the house I was born in no longer exists,

Neither the lane nor the park sloping to the river, nothing,

I had a dream of return. Multicolored. Joyous. I was able to fly.

And the trees were even higher than in childhood, because they had been growing during all the years since they had been cut down.

The loss of a native province, of a homeland,

Wandering one's whole life among foreign tribes—

Even this

Is only romantic, i.e., bearable.

Besides, that's how my prayer of a high school student was answered, of a boy who read the bards and asked for greatness which means exile.

The Earth has not been to Your Majesty's liking,

For a reason having nothing to do with the Planetary State.

Nonetheless I am amazed to have reached a venerable age.

And certainly I have experienced miraculous narrow escapes for which I vowed to God my gratitude,

So the horror of those days visited me as well.

(Page 39)

He hears voices but he does not understand the screams, prayers, blasphemies, hymns which chose him for their medium. He would like to know who he was, but he does not know. He would like to be one, but he is a self-contradictory multitude which gives him some joy, but more shame. He remembers tents of the Red Cross on the shore of a lake at a place called Wyshki. He remembers water scooped out of the boat, big gray waves and a bulb-like Orthodox church which seems to emerge from them. He thinks of that year, 1916, and of his beautiful cousin Ela in the uniform of an army nurse, of her riding through hundreds of versts along the front with a handsome officer, whom she has just married. Mama, covered with a shawl, is sitting by the fireplace at dusk with Mr. Niekrasz whom she knows from her student days at Riga, and his epaulets glitter. He had disturbed their conversation, but now he sits quietly and looks intently at the bluish flames, for she has told him that if he looks long enough he will see a funny little man with a pipe in there, riding around.

(Page 40)

What should we do with the child of a woman? ask the Powers
Above the Earth. The barrel of a cannon
Leaps, recoiling. Again. And a plain flares up
As far as the horizon. Thousands of them, running.
In the park on the lake shore tents of the Red Cross

Among hedges, flower beds, vegetable gardens.
Now, into a gallop: the nurse's veil, streaming.
A pitch-black stallion rearing; stubble, ravines.
At the river bank, red-bearded soldiers rowing.
Opens, through the smoke, a forest of broken firs.

(Page 41)
Our knowledge is not profound, say the Powers.
We come to know their pain but without compassion.
We wonder at the radiance under the clouds,
At the humility of the Mother, Substance, the Earth, a virgin.
Why should we care about living and dying?

(Page 42)
On all fours they crawled out of the dugout. Dawn.
Far away, under a cold aurora, an armored train.

(Page 43)
He walks, not like the soldier in the song, worn and weary, through the fields and forest dreary, but through many rooms in which the sounds and colors of forms that have come into being crackle, glitter, and boil up. Here a band of bagpipers sequestered in a medieval village climbs a grassy slope toward a plateau where they are going to play to the battle; there the flood waters of the river Wilia have risen so high that they reach the steps of the cathedral, and, under the sharp light of April, rowboats painted with blue, white, and green stripes cruise around under the cathedral tower; over there, little boys gathering raspberries have stumbled on a cemetery overgrown with hopbines and bend down to decipher names: Faust, Hildebrand. Indeed, why should we care about living and dying?

(Page 44)
Ladies of 1920 who served us cocoa.
Grow strong for the glory of Poland, our little knights, our eagles!

"Jackets carmine, buttons bright." And the lancers enter the city gate.
Ladies from the Polish Circle, ladies from the Auxiliary Corps.

(Page 45)
To the museum I carted frock-coats laced with silver,
Snuffboxes of speakers from chambers of deputies.
The hooves of draft horses clattered on the asphalt,
In the empty streets the smell of putrefaction.
We kept guzzling vodka, we drivers.

(Page 46)
"Mère des souvenirs, maîtresse des maîtresses." Vlad drove him from the bus
station in a carriage called a *dokart*, and nobody there knew or cared that
the name meant "dogcart." A road through a windy, treeless upland, full
of potholes and not much traveled. Below to the right, a middle-sized
lake, farther on, an isthmus: on one side, an eye of water among green
fields; on the other, a large shimmering expanse set among hills of
juniper and postdiluvian rock. The white spot of a grebe in the middle
of that scaling brightness. They turned left onto a dirt road from which
one more lake was visible, passed through a village in a dell at its end,
and turned up through a forest of pine, fir, and hazel scrub, which meant
they were practically home.

"—Who is going to reproach me for lack of precision, who would
recognize the places or the people? My power is absolute, everything
there belongs to one man now, who once, a student from Wilno, arrived
there in a dogcart. I decide whether or not I want to tell, for instance,
who Vlad was, that before World War I he studied engineering in
Karlsruhe; or who Aunt Florentyna was, that in the time of her youth an
old forest still formed a huge natural wall on the three kilometers of
holms and slopes between this and the other, immense lake, and that it
was she who used to buy those French novels in yellow covers: Bourget,
Gyp, Daudet. What to select, what to leave out depends on my will, and
I wonder at my reluctance to indulge in fiction, as if I believed that one

could faithfully reconstruct what once was. And why Florentyna? It is hard to take in: that I am allowed now to address her informally, though then I would not have dared, and that she is not an old lady but simultaneously a young girl and a child and all of them. What do I have to do with her, in her corsets and bustle skirts, unimaginable in her physical needs, taking her daughters to Warsaw, Paris, Venice, and Biarritz? And yet it was precisely my reflecting on her that introduced me to the kingdom of the purely empirical. How she had to make do: instead of having a manager and servants, her daughters get up at dawn— kneeboots, sheepskin coats—go to the stable, to the pigsty, assign work to farmhands, in winter supervise the threshing until evening. And for three months every year, there is no manor, just a boardinghouse for paying guests; in Kathleen's kitchen a fire burns from four in the morning until late at night, Vlad pounds on the piano for hours, and they, those guests, dance. She had also to accept a tacit change in customs; she had to decide not to notice whether her daughters had men with the blessing of marriage or without, so that, besides Vlad, someone else would live on the premises, George or some other boy. Everything was as it was, unspoken, so that an inevitable dailiness turned the strictest principles into those human inventions which evaporate without any- one bothering to say yes or no. There were no trips to church, except sometimes for Florentyna's sake. And she, with her two not-too-Catholic daughters, became my hidden thought about the sheer relativity of beliefs and convictions, which cannot resist the law of things."

And really, for him, spinning this monologue, why shouldn't what he learned there be enough? He had thought that he found himself there by chance and for the time being, that it was just a preface to something, but later on, too, there was nothing more than a preface and for the time being.

(Page 47)
For some hundred years that fabric, fleecy,
Thick as felt, was used to manufacture robes,

So you can't tell whether it is the end or the beginning of the
    twentieth century,
Now, when she, sitting before her mirror, opens the folds of her
    gown,
Bright yellow on the rose bronze of her breasts.
Nor has the brush in her hand changed its shape.
And the window frame belongs to any time,
And the view onto ash trees bent by the wind.
And who is she, in this one flesh only,
Inhabiting this one moment?
By whom is she to be seen
If she is deprived even of her name?
Her skin in the third person is for nobody,
Her most smooth skin in the third person does not exist.
And look—from behind the trees clouds rush in
Bordered with coppery lace, and all this
Stalls, hardens, and rises into light.

(Page 48)
Northern sunset, beyond the lake a song of harvesters.
They move about, tiny, binding the last sheaves.
Who has the right to imagine how they return to the village,
And sit down by the fire and cook and cut their bread?
Or how their fathers lived in huts without chimneys,
When every roof would smoke as if on fire?
Or how the land was once, before being given to the winds,
Quiet, the lakes like eyes in the untouched forest?
And who has the right to guess how the sun will set in the future
Over a prison train or the sleep of rigs on building sites,
To make himself a god who looks into their windows
And shakes his head and walks off full of pity because he knows so
    much?

You, my young hunter, had better just ease your canoe from the shore
And pick up the killed mallard before it gets dark.

(Page 49)
In a night train, completely empty, clattering through fields and woods,
a young man, my ancient self, incomprehensibly identical with me,
tucks up his legs on a hard bench—it is cold in the wagon—and in his
slumber hears the clap of level crossings, echo of bridges, thrum of
spans, the whistle of the locomotive. He wakes up, rubs his eyes, and
above the tossed-back scarecrows of the pines he sees a dark-blue
expanse in which, low on the horizon, one blood-red star is glowing.

(Page 50)

THE WORMWOOD STAR

Under the Wormwood Star bitter rivers flowed.
Man in the fields gathered bitter bread.
No sign of divine care shone in the heavens.
The century wanted homage from the dead.

They traced their origin to the dinosaur
And took their deftness from the lemur's paw.
Above the cities of the thinking lichen,
Flights of pterodactyls proclaimed the law.

They tied the hands of man with barbed wire.
And dug shallow graves at the edge of the wood.
There would be no truth in his last testament.
They wanted him anonymous for good.

The planetary empire was at hand.
They said what was speech and what was listening.
The ash had hardly cooled after the great fire
When Diocletian's Rome again stood glistening.

Berkeley, 1977–1978

BYPASSING RUE DESCARTES

Bypassing rue Descartes
I descended toward the Seine, shy, a traveler,
A young barbarian just come to the capital of the world.

We were many, from Jassy and Koloshvar, Wilno and Bucharest,
    Saigon and Marrakesh,
Ashamed to remember the customs of our homes,
About which nobody here should ever be told:
The clapping for servants, barefooted girls hurry in,
Dividing food with incantations,
Choral prayers recited by master and household together.

I had left the cloudy provinces behind,
I entered the universal, dazzled and desiring.

Soon enough, many from Jassy and Koloshvar, or Saigon or Marrakesh
Would be killed because they wanted to abolish the customs of their
    homes.

Soon enough, their peers were seizing power
In order to kill in the name of the universal, beautiful ideas.

Meanwhile the city behaved in accordance with its nature,
Rustling with throaty laughter in the dark,
Baking long breads and pouring wine into clay pitchers,
Buying fish, lemons, and garlic at street markets,
Indifferent as it was to honor and shame and greatness and glory,
Because that had been done already and had transformed itself
Into monuments representing nobody knows whom,
Into arias hardly audible and into turns of speech.

Again I lean on the rough granite of the embankment,
As if I had returned from travels through the underworlds
And suddenly saw in the light the reeling wheel of the seasons
Where empires have fallen and those once living are now dead.

There is no capital of the world, neither here nor anywhere else,
And the abolished customs are restored to their small fame
And now I know that the time of human generations is not like the
    time of the earth.

As to my heavy sins, I remember one most vividly:
How, one day, walking on a forest path along a stream,
I pushed a rock down onto a water snake coiled in the grass.

And what I have met with in life was the just punishment
Which reaches, sooner or later, the breaker of a taboo.

Berkeley, 1980

ACCOUNT

The history of my stupidity would fill many volumes.

Some would be devoted to acting against consciousness,
Like the flight of a moth which, had it known,
Would have tended nevertheless toward the candle's flame.

Others would deal with ways to silence anxiety,
The little whisper which, though it is a warning, is ignored.

I would deal separately with satisfaction and pride,
The time when I was among their adherents
Who strut victoriously, unsuspecting.

But all of them would have one subject, desire,
If only my own—but no, not at all; alas,
I was driven because I wanted to be like others.
I was afraid of what was wild and indecent in me.

The history of my stupidity will not be written.
For one thing, it's late. And the truth is laborious.

Berkeley, 1980

RIVERS

Under various names, I have praised only you, rivers!

You are milk and honey and love and death and dance.

From a spring in hidden grottoes, seeping from mossy rocks

Where a goddess pours live water from a pitcher,

At clear streams in the meadow, where rills murmur underground,

Your race and my race begin, and amazement, and quick passage.

Naked, I exposed my face to the sun, steering with hardly a dip of the
     paddle—

Oak woods, fields, a pine forest skimming by,

Around every bend the promise of the earth,

Village smoke, sleepy herds, flights of martins over sandy bluffs.

I entered your waters slowly, step by step,

And the current in that silence took me by the knees

Until I surrendered and it carried me and I swam

Through the huge reflected sky of a triumphant noon.

I was on your banks at the onset of midsummer night

When the full moon rolls out and lips touch in the rituals of kissing—

I hear in myself, now as then, the lapping of water by the boathouse

And the whisper that calls me in for an embrace and for consolation.

We go down with the bells ringing in all the sunken cities.

Forgotten, we are greeted by the embassies of the dead,

While your endless flowing carries us on and on;

And neither is nor was. The moment only, eternal.

Berkeley, 1980

UNATTAINABLE

EARTH

(Nieobjęta ziemia)

✠

1986

THE GARDEN
OF EARTHLY DELIGHTS

1. Summer

In the July sun they were leading me to the Prado,
Straight to the room where *The Garden of Earthly Delights*
Had been prepared for me. So that I run to its waters
And immerse myself in them and recognize myself.

The twentieth century is drawing to its close.
I will be immured in it like a fly in amber.
I was old but my nostrils craved new scents
And through my five senses I received a share in the earth
Of those who led me, our sisters and lovers.

How lightly they walk! Their hips in trousers, not in trailing dresses,
Their feet in sandals, not on cothurni,
Their hair not clasped by a tortoiseshell buckle.
Yet constantly the same, renewed by the moon, Luna,
In a chorus that keeps praising Lady Venus.

Their hands touched my hands and they marched, gracious,
As if in the early morning at the outset of the world.

2. A Ball

It is going on inside a transparent ball
Above which God the Father, short, with a trimmed beard,
Sits with a book, enveloped in dark clouds.
He reads an incantation and things are called to being.
As soon as the earth emerges, it bears grasses and trees.
We are those to whom green hills have been offered
And for us this ray descends from opened mists.
Whose hand carries the ball? Probably the Son's.
And the whole Earth is in it, Paradise and Hell.

3. Paradise

Under my sign, Cancer, a pink fountain
Pours out four streams, the sources of four rivers.
But I don't trust it. As I verified myself,
That sign is not lucky. Besides, we abhor
The moving jaws of crabs and the calcareous
Cemeteries of the ocean. This, then, is the Fountain
Of Life? Toothed, sharp-edged,
With its innocent, delusive color. And beneath,
Just where the birds alight, glass traps set with glue.
A white elephant, a white giraffe, white unicorns,
Black creatures of the ponds. A lion mauls a deer.
A cat has a mouse. A three-headed lizard,
A three-headed ibis, their meaning unknown.
Or a two-legged dog, no doubt a bad omen.
Adam sits astonished. His feet
Touch the foot of Christ who has brought Eve
And keeps her right hand in his left while lifting
Two fingers of his right like the one who teaches.
Who is she, and who will she be, the beloved
From the Song of Songs? This Wisdom-Sophia,
Seducer, the Mother and Ecclesia?
Thus he created her who will conceive him?
Where then did he get his human form
Before the years and centuries began?
Human, did he exist before the beginning?
And establish a Paradise, though incomplete,
So that she might pluck the fruit, she, the mysterious one,
Whom Adam contemplates, not comprehending?
I am these two, twofold. I ate from the Tree

Of Knowledge. I was expelled by the archangel's sword.
At night I sensed her pulse. Her mortality.
And we have searched for the real place ever since.

4. Earth

Riding birds, feeling under our thighs the soft feathers
Of goldfinches, orioles, kingfishers,
Or spurring lions into a run, unicorns, leopards,
Whose coats brush against our nakedness,
We circle the vivid and abundant waters,
Mirrors from which emerge a man's and a woman's head,
Or an arm, or the round breasts of the sirens.
Every day is the day of berry harvest here.
The two of us bite into wild strawberries
Bigger than a man, we plunge into cherries,
We are drenched with the juices of their wine,
We celebrate the colors of carmine
And vermilion, as in toys on a Christmas tree.
We are many, a whole tribe swarming,
And so like each other that our lovemaking
Is as sweet and immodest as a game of hide-and-seek.
And we lock ourselves inside the crowns of flowers
Or in transparent, iridescent bubbles.
Meanwhile a flock of lunar signs fills the sky
To prepare the alchemical nuptials of the planets.

5. Earth Again

They are incomprehensible, the things of this earth.
The lure of waters. The lure of fruits.
Lure of the two breasts and long hair of a maiden.
In rouge, in vermilion, in that color of ponds
Found only in the Green Lakes near Wilno.
And ungraspable multitudes swarm, come together
In the crinkles of tree bark, in the telescope's eye,
For an endless wedding,
For the kindling of the eyes, for a sweet dance
In the elements of the air, sea, earth, and subterranean caves,
So that for a short moment there is no death
And time does not unreel like a skein of yarn
Thrown into an abyss.

AFTER PARADISE

Don't run anymore. Quiet. How softly it rains
On the roofs of the city. How perfect
All things are. Now, for the two of you
Waking up in a royal bed by a garret window.
For a man and a woman. For one plant divided
Into masculine and feminine which longed for each other.
Yes, this is my gift to you. Above ashes
On a bitter, bitter earth. Above the subterranean
Echo of clamorings and vows. So that now at dawn
You must be attentive: the tilt of a head,
A hand with a comb, two faces in a mirror
Are only forever once, even if unremembered,
So that you watch what is, though it fades away,
And are grateful every moment for your being.
Let that little park with greenish marble busts
In the pearl-gray light, under a summer drizzle,
Remain as it was when you opened the gate.
And the street of tall peeling porticoes
Which this love of yours suddenly transformed.

THE HOOKS OF A CORSET

In a big city, on the boulevards, early. The raising of jalousies and marquees, sprinkled slabs of sidewalk, echo of steps, the spotted bark of trees. My twentieth century was beginning and they walked, men and women; it is now close to its end and they walk, not exactly the same but pattering the same way with shoes and high-heeled slippers. The impenetrable order of a division into the male and female sex, into old and young, without decrease, always here, instead of those who once lived. And I, breathing the air, enchanted because I am one of them, identifying my flesh with their flesh, but at the same time aware of beings who might not have perished. I, replacing them, bearing a different name yet their own because the five senses are ours in common, I am walking here, now, before I am replaced in my turn. We are untouched by death and time, children, myself with Eve, in a kindergarten, in a sandbox, in a bed, embracing each other, making love, saying the words of eternal avowals and eternal delights. The space wide open, glittering machines up above, the rumble of the *métro* below. And our dresses under heaven, tinfoil crowns, tights, imitation animal hair, the scales of lizard-birds. To absorb with your eyes the inside of a flower shop, to hear the voices of people, to feel on your tongue the taste of just-drunk coffee. Passing by the windows of apartments, I invent stories, similar to my own, a lifted elbow, the combing of hair before a mirror. I multiplied myself and came to inhabit every one of them separately, thus my impermanence has no power over me.

÷

INSCRIPT

"And he sets off! and he watches the river of vitality flowing, so majestic and so brilliant. He admires the eternal beauty and astonishing harmony of life in the capitals, harmony so providentially maintained in the turmoil of human freedom. He contemplates the landscapes of big cities, landscapes caressed by mists or struck by the sun. He delights in beautiful carriages, proud horses, the spic-and-span cleanliness of grooms, the dexterity of footmen, the beauty of undulating women, in pretty children happy to be alive and well dressed; to put it briefly, in universal life. If a fashion, the cut of dresses changes slightly, if knotted ribbons or buckles are dethroned by a cockade, if the bonnet grows larger and the chignon descends to the nape of the neck, if the waistline goes up and the skirt is simplified, do not doubt that *his eagle's eye* even at a great distance will take notice. A regiment is passing, perhaps on its way to the end of the world, throwing into the air its enticing flourish, light as hope: and already Mr. G. saw, examined, analyzed the arms, the gait, and the physiognomy of that unit. Shoulder-belts, sparklings, music, resolute looks, heavy and ponderous moustaches, all that penetrates him pell-mell; and in a few minutes a poem which results from it will be composed. And already his soul lives with the life of that regiment which is marching as one animal, a proud image of joy in obedience!

"But evening comes. It is the bizarre and ambiguous hour when the curtains of the sky are drawn, when the cities light up. The gas makes a spot on the crimson of the sunset. Honest or dishonest, reasonable or crazy, people say to themselves: 'At last the day is over!' Wise men and rascals think of pleasure and everybody runs to a chosen place to drink the cup of oblivion. Mr. G. will remain to the last wherever the light still glows, poetry resounds, life teems, music vibrates; wherever a passion can pose for his eye, wherever the natural man and the man of convention show themselves in a strange beauty, wherever the sun witnesses the hurried pleasures of a *depraved animal.*"

—*CHARLES BAUDELAIRE,*
"*Constantin Guys, Painter of Modern Life*"

✝

I am engaged in a serious operation, devoted to it exclusively, and for that reason I am released from the reproach of shirking my social duties. In the Quartier Latin, when bells ring for the New Year 1900, I am the one who walks uphill on rue Cujas. A gloved hand is linked to my arm and the gas hisses in the streetlamps. Her flesh which has turned to dust is as desirable to me as it was to that other man and if I touch her in my dream she does not even mention that she has died long ago. On the verge of a great discovery I almost penetrate the secret of the Particular transforming itself into the General and of the General transforming itself into the Particular. I endow with a philosophical meaning the moment when I helped her to undo the hooks of her corset.

÷

INSCRIPT

"She was fond of tailored dresses from Vienna, very modest but rustling with linings made of iridescent taffeta; she would carry a rarely used lorgnon on a long chain interspersed with tiny pearls, and a bracelet with pendants. Her movements were slow and somewhat affected, she offered her hand to be kissed with a studied gesture, probably under her calm she was concealing the timidity characteristic of her whole family. Her jewelry, cigarette case, and perfume bore the stamp of an individual and fastidious taste. Her literary preferences were rather revolutionary and progressive. Much more vividly and sincerely than did Lela, she took an interest in her reading but in fact books were for her accessories to her dress, like a hat or an umbrella. Aunt Isia was the first to introduce Doroszewicze to the fashionable Tetmajer, then she brought the photographs of Ghirlandaio's and Botticelli's paintings from Italy and talked about the school of the early Renaissance, finally she took a liking to Przybyszewski and his style, and would often say: 'Do you want white peacocks?—I will give you white peacocks. Do you want crimson amethysts?—I will give you crimson amethysts.' "

—*JANINA ŻÓŁTOWSKA,*
Other Times, Other People (Inne czasy, inni ludzie)

÷

Rustling taffetas. At sunset in a park by the Prypet River.
The party sets out for a walk on a path lined with flowers.
The fragrance of nicotianas, phlox, and resedas.
Great silence, the empty expanse of rising waters.
Meanwhile the servants bring in lamps, set the table for supper.
And the dining room windows lit the agaves on the lawn.

Lela, Marishka, Sophineta! Lenia, Stenia, Isia, Lilka!
Is it fair that I will never talk with you
In a language not disguised by etiquette
As less than language and not reduced to table chatter
But austere and precise like a thought
That attempts to embrace the poor lives of beings?

I walk about. No longer human. In a hunting outfit.
Visiting our thick forests and the houses and manors.
Cold borscht is served and I am abstracted
With disturbing questions from the end of my century,
Mainly regarding the truth, where does it come from, where is it?
Mum, I was eating chicken with cucumber salad.

My pretty ones, abducted, beyond will and guilt.
My awareness harrows me as well as my silence.
All my life I gathered up images and ideas,
I learned how to travel through lost territories,
But the moment between birth and disappearance
Is too much, I know, for the meager word.

Strings of wild ducks fly over the Respublica's waters.
Dew falls on Polish manners imported from Warsaw and Vienna.
I cross the river in a dugout to the village side.

Barking dogs greet me there and the bell of an Orthodox
    church.

What would I like to tell you? That I didn't get what I looked for:
To gather all of us naked on the earthly pastures
Under the endless light of suspended time
Without that form which confines me as it once confined you.

Seeing the future. A diviner. In a soft merciful night.
When pigweed grows on the paths of a cut-down garden
And a narrow gold chain on a white neck,
Together with the memory of all of you, perishes.

÷

INSCRIPT

"In the Ukraine several hundred gardens of various sizes survived the fall
of the Respublica and of the gentry whose presence was marked
everywhere by old trees, lawns and decorative shrubbery. Once, in the
eastern Carpathians, in a remote valley distant by a whole day's walk
from the nearest settlement, I noticed, lost among hazels, one of those
decorative shrubs characteristic of gardens from the beginning of the last
century. Parting raspberries and vines I found a few old stones and
bricks. Even in that wilderness the settlers had remained faithful to the
horticultural passion of the old Respublica."

—*PAWEŁ HOSTOWIEC,*
    In the Valley of the Dniester (W dolinie Dniestru)

What did I really want to tell them? That I labored to transcend my
place and time, searching for the Real. And here is my work done
(commendably?), my life fulfilled, as it was destined to be, in grief. Now
I appear to myself as one who was under the delusion of being his own

while he was the subject of a style. Just as they were, so what if it was a different subjection. "Do you want white peacocks?—I will give you white peacocks." And we could have been united only by what we have in common: the same nakedness in a garden beyond time, but the moments are short when it seems to me that, at odds with time, we hold each other's hands. And I drink wine and I shake my head and say: "What man feels and thinks will never be expressed."

ANNALENA

It happened that sometimes I kissed in mirrors the reflection of my face; since the hands, face and tears of Annalena had caressed it, my face seemed to me divinely beautiful and as if suffused with heavenly sweetness.

—O. MILOSZ, *L'AMOUREUSE INITIATION*

I liked your velvet yoni, Annalena, long voyages in the delta of your legs.

A striving upstream toward your beating heart through more and more savage currents saturated with the light of hops and bindweed.

And our vehemence and triumphant laughter and our hasty dressing in the middle of the night to walk on the stone stairs of the upper city.

Our breath held by amazement and silence, porosity of worn-out stones and the great door of the cathedral.

Over the gate of the rectory fragments of brick among weeds, in darkness the touch of a rough buttressed wall.

And later our looking from the bridge down to the orchard, when under the moon every tree is separate on its kneeler, and from the secret interior of dimmed poplars the echo carries the sound of a water turbine.

To whom do we tell what happened on the earth, for whom do we place everywhere huge mirrors in the hope that they will be filled up and will stay so?

Always in doubt whether it was we who were there, you and I, Annalena, or just anonymous lovers on the enameled tablets of a fairyland.

YELLOW BICYCLE

When I ask her what she wants,
She says, "A yellow bicycle."
                    —ROBERT HASS

As long as we move at a dancing gait, my love,
Leaving the car by the place where a yellow bicycle stands, leaning
    against a tree,
As long as we enter the gardens at a dancing gait,
Northern gardens, full of dew and the voices of birds,
Our memory is childish and it saves only what we need:
Yesterday morning and evening, no further.
But then we recalled a girl who had a yellow bicycle like that
And used to talk to it in caressing words.
Later on, among flower beds between box hedges,
We saw a little statue and a plate with the sculptor's name.
We were descending by terraces toward a lake
Which is like a lake from an old ballad,
Smooth, between the peninsulas of spruce forests.
Thus common human memory visited us again.

INTO THE TREE

*And he placed at the east of the garden of Eden Cherubim, and a flaming
sword which turned every way, to keep the way to the tree of life.*
—GENESIS 3, 24

And he looked up and said, "I see men as trees, walking."
—MARK 8, 24

The tree, says good Swedenborg, is a close relative of man.
Its boughs like arms join in an embrace.
The trees in truth are our parents,
We sprang from the oak, or perhaps, as the Greeks maintain, from the ash.

Our lips and tongue savor the fruit of the tree.
A woman's breast is called apple or pomegranate.
We love the womb as the tree loves the dark womb of the earth.
Thus, what is most desirable resides in a single tree,
And wisdom tries to touch its coarse-grained bark.

I learned, says the servant of the New Jerusalem,
That Adam in the garden, i.e., mankind's Golden Age,
Signifies the generations after the pre-adamites
Who are unjustly scorned though they were gentle,
Kind to each other, savage yet not bestial,
Happy in a land of fruits and springwaters.

Adam created in the image and in the likeness
Represents the parting of clouds covering the mind.
And Eve, why is she taken from Adam's rib?
—Because the rib is close to the heart, that's the name of self-love,
And Adam comes to know Eve, loving himself in her.

Above those two, the tree. A huge shade tree.

Of which the counselor of the Royal Mining Commission says the following in his book *De amore conjugiali:*

"The Tree of Life signifies a man who lives from God, or God living in man; and as love and wisdom, or charity and faith, or good and truth, make the life of God in man, these are signified by the Tree of Life, and hence the eternal life of the man. . . . But the tree of science signifies the man who believes that he lives from himself and not from God; thus that love and wisdom, or charity and faith, or good and truth, are in man from himself and not from God; and he believes this because he thinks and wills, and speaks and acts, in all likeness and appearance as from himself."

Self-love offered the apple and the Golden Age was over.
After it, the Silver Age, the Bronze Age. And the Iron.

Then a child opens its eyes and sees a tree for the first time.
And people seem to us like walking trees.

ONE MORE DAY

Comprehension of good and evil is given in the running of the blood.
In a child's nestling close to its mother, she is security and warmth,
In night fears when we are small, in dread of the beast's fangs and in
    the terror of dark rooms,
In youthful infatuations where childhood delight finds completion.

And should we discredit the idea for its modest origins?
Or should we say plainly that good is on the side of the living
And evil on the side of a doom that lurks to devour us?
Yes, good is an ally of being and the mirror of evil is nothing,
Good is brightness, evil darkness, good high, evil low,
According to the nature of our bodies, of our language.

The same can be said of beauty. It should not exist.
There is not only no reason for it, but an argument against.
Yet undoubtedly it is, and is different from ugliness.

The voices of birds outside the window when they greet the morning
And iridescent stripes of light blazing on the floor,
Or the horizon with a wavy line where the peach-colored sky and the
    dark-blue mountains meet.
Or the architecture of a tree, the slimness of a column crowned with
    green.

All that, hasn't it been invoked for centuries
As a mystery which, in one instant, will be suddenly revealed?
And the old artist thinks that all his life he has only trained his hand.
One more day and he will enter the core as one enters a flower.

And though the good is weak, beauty is very strong.
Nonbeing sprawls, everywhere it turns into ash whole expanses of
    being,

It masquerades in shapes and colors that imitate existence
And no one would know it, if they did not know that it was ugly.

And when people cease to believe that there is good and evil
Only beauty will call to them and save them
So that they still know how to say: this is true and that is false.

WINTER

The pungent smells of a California winter,
Grayness and rosiness, an almost transparent full moon.
I add logs to the fire, I drink and I ponder.

"In Ilawa," the news item said, "at age 70
Died Aleksander Rymkiewicz, poet."

He was the youngest in our group. I patronized him slightly,
Just as I patronized others for their inferior minds
Though they had many virtues I couldn't touch.

And so I am here, approaching the end
Of the century and of my life. Proud of my strength
Yet embarrassed by the clearness of the view.

Avant-gardes mixed with blood.
The ashes of inconceivable arts.
An omnium-gatherum of chaos.

I passed judgment on that. Though marked myself.
This hasn't been the age for the righteous and the decent.
I know what it means to beget monsters
And to recognize in them myself.

You, moon, You, Aleksander, fire of cedar logs.
Waters close over us, a name lasts but an instant.
Not important whether the generations hold us in memory.
Great was that chase with the hounds for the unattainable meaning of
    the world.

And now I am ready to keep running
When the sun rises beyond the borderlands of death.

I already see mountain ridges in the heavenly forest
Where, beyond every essence, a new essence waits.

You, music of my late years, I am called
By a sound and a color which are more and more perfect.

Do not die out, fire. Enter my dreams, love.
Be young forever, seasons of the earth.

A BOY

Standing on a boulder you cast a line,
Your bare feet rounded by the flickering water
Of your native river thick with water lilies.
And who are you, staring at the float
While you listen to echoes, the clatter of paddles?
What is the stigma you received, young master,
You who are ill with your apartness
And have one longing: to be just like the others?
I know your story and I learned your future.
Dressed as a Gypsy girl I could stop by the river
And tell your fortune: fame and a lot of money,
Without knowledge, though, of the price to be paid
Which one does not admit to the envious.
One thing is certain: in you, there are two natures.
The miserly, the prudent one against the generous.
For many years you will attempt to reconcile them
Till all your works have grown small
And you will prize only uncalculated gifts,
Greatheartedness, self-forgetful giving,
Without monuments, books, and human memory.

IN SALEM

Now you must bear with your poor soul.
Guilt only, where you proudly stood.
Diplomas, honors, parchment scrolls,
Lectures at Harvard, doctor's hood:
Tongues in which nothing loudly calls.

I walk somewhere at the world's end,
In Wilno, by a bridge called Green.
An old woman reads postcards I send
From Baton Rouge or Oberlin.
We both have reasons to lament.

Dreams visit me year after year,
They are expendable, J.W.
What might have been is just thin air,
A loss we long ago outgrew.
So why do we talk and why do we care?

You know that tangible things escape
The art of words and tricks of mind.
Early I guessed what was my fate,
The sentence was already signed
At Haven Street and the Outgate.

In Salem, by a spinning wheel
I felt I, too, lived yesterday,
My river Lethe is the Wilia,
Forest bonfires like censers sway,
So many names and all unreal.

1913

I betook myself to Italy right after the harvest.
That year 1913 the McCormick harvester
For the first time moved across our fields
Leaving behind stubble altogether unlike that
Left by the sickle or the scythe of the reapers.
On the same train, but in third class,
My factotum Yosel rode to his kin in Grodno.
I had my supper there, in the refreshment room,
At a long table under rubber plants.
I recollected the high bridge over the Niemen
As the train wound out of an Alpine pass.
And I woke up by the waters, grayish blue
In the radiance of the pearly lagoon,
In the city where a traveler forgets who he is.
By the waters of Lethe I saw the future.
Is this my century? Another continent,
With Yosel's grandson we sit together
Talking of our poet friends. Incarnated,
Young again, yet identical with my older self.
What strange costumes, how strange the street is,
And I myself unable to speak of what I know.
No lesson for the living can be drawn from it.
I closed my eyes and my face felt the sun,
Here, now, drinking coffee in Piazza San Marco.

AT DAWN

How enduring, how we need durability.
The sky before sunrise is soaked with light.
Rosy color tints buildings, bridges, and the Seine.
I was here when she, with whom I walk, wasn't born yet
And the cities on a distant plain stood intact
Before they rose in the air with the dust of sepulchral brick
And the people who lived there didn't know.
Only this moment at dawn is real to me.
The bygone lives are like my own past life, uncertain.
I cast a spell on the city asking it to last.

AT NOON

At a mountain inn, high above the bulky green of chestnuts,
The three of us were sitting next to an Italian family
Under the tiered levels of pine forests.
Nearby a little girl pumped water from a well.
The air was huge with the voice of swallows.
Ooo, I heard a singing in me, ooo.
What a noon, no other like it will recur,
Now when I am sitting next to her and her
While the stages of past life come together
And a jug of wine stands on a checkered tablecloth.
The granite rocks of that island were washed by the sea.
The three of us were one self-delighting thought
And the resinous scent of Corsican summer was with us.

RETURN TO KRAKÓW IN 1880

So I returned here from the big capitals,
To a town in a narrow valley under the cathedral hill
With royal tombs. To a square under the tower
And the shrill trumpet sounding noon, breaking
Its note in half because the Tartar arrow
Has once again struck the trumpeter.
And pigeons. And the garish kerchiefs of women selling flowers.
And groups chattering under the Gothic portico of the church.
My trunk of books arrived, this time for good.
What I know of my laborious life: it was lived.
Faces are paler in memory than on daguerreotypes.
I don't need to write memos and letters every morning.
Others will take over, always with the same hope,
The one we know is senseless and devote our lives to.
My country will remain what it is, the backyard of empires,
Nursing its humiliation with provincial daydreams.
I leave for a morning walk tapping with my cane:
The places of old people are taken by new old people
And where the girls once strolled in their rustling skirts,
New ones are strolling, proud of their beauty.
And children trundle hoops for more than half a century.
In a basement a cobbler looks up from his bench,
A hunchback passes by with his inner lament,
Then a fashionable lady, a fat image of the deadly sins.
So the Earth endures, in every petty matter
And in the lives of men, irreversible.
And it seems a relief. To win? To lose?
What for, if the world will forget us anyway.

THE CITY

The city exulted, all in flowers.
Soon it will end: a fashion, a phase, the epoch, life.
The terror and sweetness of a final dissolution.
Let the first bombs fall without delay.

PREPARATION

Still one more year of preparation.
Tomorrow at the latest I'll start working on a great book
In which my century will appear as it really was.
The sun will rise over the righteous and the wicked.
Springs and autumns will unerringly return,
In a wet thicket a thrush will build his nest lined with clay
And foxes will learn their foxy natures.

And that will be the subject, with addenda. Thus: armies
Running across frozen plains, shouting a curse
In a many-voiced chorus; the cannon of a tank
Growing immense at the corner of a street; the ride at dusk
Into a camp with watchtowers and barbed wire.

No, it won't happen tomorrow. In five or ten years.
I still think too much about the mothers
And ask what is man born of woman.
He curls himself up and protects his head
While he is kicked by heavy boots; on fire and running,
He burns with bright flame; a bulldozer sweeps him into a clay pit.
Her child. Embracing a teddy bear. Conceived in ecstasy.

I haven't learned yet to speak as I should, calmly.

With not-quite truth
and not-quite art
and not-quite law
and not-quite science

Under not-quite heaven
on the not-quite earth
the not-quite guiltless
and the not-quite degraded

CONSCIOUSNESS

1. Consciousness enclosed in itself every separate birch
And the woods of New Hampshire, covered in May with green haze.
The faces of people are in it without number, the courses
Of planets, and things past and a portent of the future.
Then one should extract from it what one can, slowly,
Not trusting anybody. And it won't be much, for language
   is weak.

2. It is alien and useless to the hot lands of the living.
Leaves renew themselves, birds celebrate their nuptials
Without its help. And a couple on the bank of a river
Feel their bodies draw close right now, possessed by a nameless power.

3. I think that I am here, on this earth,
To present a report on it, but to whom I don't know.
As if I were sent so that whatever takes place
Has meaning because it changes into memory.

4. Fat and lean, old and young, male and female,
Carrying bags and valises, they defile in the corridors of an airport.
And suddenly I feel it is impossible.
It is the reverse side of a Gobelin
And behind there is the other which explains everything.

5. Now, not anytime, here, in America
I try to isolate what matters to me most.
I neither absolve nor condemn myself.

The torments of a boy who wanted to be nice
And spent a number of years at the project.

The shame of whispering to the confessional grille
Behind which heavy breath and a hot ear.

The monstrance undressed from its patterned robe,
A little sun rimmed with sculptured rays.

Evening devotions of the household in May,
Litanies to the Maiden,
Mother of the Creator.

And I, conscience, contain the orchestra of regimental brasses
On which the moustachioed ones blew for the Elevation.

And musket volleys on Easter Saturday night
When the cold dawn had hardly reddened.

I am fond of sumptuous garments and disguises
Even if there is no truth in the painted Jesus.

Sometimes believing, sometimes not believing,
With others like myself I unite in worship.

Into the labyrinth of gilded baroque cornices
I penetrate, called by the saints of the Lord.

I make my pilgrimage to the miraculous places
Where a spring spurted suddenly from rock.

I enter the common childishness and brittleness
Of the sons and daughters of the human tribe.

And I preserve faithfully the prayer in the cathedral:
Jesus Christ, son of God, enlighten me, a sinner.

6. I—consciousness—originate in skin,
Smooth or covered with thickets of hair.

The stubby cheek, the pubes, and the groin
Are mine exclusively, though not only mine.
And at the same instant, he or she—consciousness—
Examines its body in a mirror,
Recognizing a familiar which is not quite its own.

Do I, when I touch one flesh in the mirror,
Touch every flesh, learn consciousness of the other?

Or perhaps not at all, and it, unattainable,
Perceives in its own, strictly its own, manner?

7. You will never know what I feel, she said,
Because you are filling me and are not filled.

8. The warmth of dogs and the essence, inscrutable, of doggishness.
Yet I feel it. In the lolling of the humid tongue,
In the melancholy velvet of the eyes,
In the scent of fur, different from our own, yet related.
Our humanness becomes more marked then,
The common one, pulsating, slavering, hairy,
Though for the dogs it is we who are like gods
Disappearing in crystal palaces of reason,
Busy with activities beyond comprehension.

I want to believe that the forces above us,
Engaged in doings we cannot imitate,
Touch our cheeks and our hair sometimes
And feel in themselves this poor flesh and blood.

9. Every ritual, astonishing human arrangements.
The dresses in which they move, more durable than they are,
The gestures that freeze in air, to be filled by those born later,

Words that were pronounced by the dead, here and still in use.
And erotic: they guess under the fabric
Dark triangles of hair, are attentive to convexities in silk.
Faithful to the ritual because it differs so much from their natures,
And soars above them, above the warmth of mucous membrane,
On the incomprehensible borderline between mind and flesh.

10. Certainly, I did not reveal what I really thought.
Why should I reveal it? To multiply misunderstandings?
And reveal to whom? They are born, they mature
In a long pause and refuse to know what comes later.
Anyway I won't avert anything. All my life it was like that:
To know and not be able to avert. I must give them reason.
They have no use for lives lived sometime in the future
And the torments of their descendants are not their concern.

ON PRAYER

You ask me how to pray to someone who is not.
All I know is that prayer constructs a velvet bridge
And walking it we are aloft, as on a springboard,
Above landscapes the color of ripe gold
Transformed by a magic stopping of the sun.
That bridge leads to the shore of Reversal
Where everything is just the opposite and the word *is*
Unveils a meaning we hardly envisioned.
Notice: I say *we;* there, every one, separately,
Feels compassion for others entangled in the flesh
And knows that if there is no other shore
We will walk that aerial bridge all the same.

FATHER CH.,
MANY YEARS LATER

Father Chomski, the vicar of Vaidotai parish,
Died at the age of ninety-seven, worrying till the end
About his parishioners, for no one would succeed him.

On the shore of the Pacific, I, his former pupil,
Was translating the Apocalypse from Greek into Polish,
Finding it the proper season for that labor.

They had to hold up his hands on both sides
When he raised the host and the wine above the altar.

He had been beaten by thugs of the Empire
Because he refused to bow before the world.

And I? Didn't I bow? The Great Spirit of Nonbeing,
The Prince of this World, has his own devices.

I did not want to serve him. I always labored
In order to at least delay his victory.

So that God might be resplendent with his angelic crowd,
He who is all-powerful but whose mill grinds slow.

He who in the huge war is defeated every day
And does not give signs through his churches.

To whom in our school chapel I vowed faithfulness
While Father Chomski approached on tiptoe and put out candles.

And yet I could not distinguish Him from the rhythm of my blood
And felt false reaching beyond it in my prayer.

I was not a spiritual man but flesh-enraptured,
Called to celebrate Dionysian dances.

And disobedient, curious, on the first step to Hell,
Easily enticed by the newest idea.

Hearing all around me: it is good to experience,
It is good to feel, be bold, free yourself from guilt.

Wanting to absorb everything, comprehend everything,
And darkness proved to be forebearing toward me.

Did I toil then against the world
Or, without knowing, was I with it and its own?

Helping the Ruler to tread with his iron boot
An earth that did not merit any better?

÷

And yet it wasn't so, o my accomplice in sin,
Eve under the apple tree, in the delightful garden.

I loved your breasts and your belly and your lips.
How to comprehend your otherness and sameness?

Convex and concave, how do they complement
     each other?
How is it that we feel and think alike?

Our eyes seeing the same, our ears hearing the same,
Our touch making and unmaking the same world.

Not one, divided in two, not two, united in one:
The second I, so that I may be conscious of myself.

And together with you eat fruits from the Tree of Knowledge
And by twisting roads make our way through deserts.

÷

By twisting roads from which one sees, below, the golden domes of rising
and sinking cities, mirages of undulating streets, hunters pursuing gazelles, a
pastoral scene by a stream, ploughs at noon resting in the fertile fields, so
much and in such variousness, with a music in the air of pipes and flutes,
with voices calling, voices that once were. Twisting roads, uncounted
centuries, but could I renounce what I received, consciousness, knowledge,
a never-fulfilled striving toward the aim? Even if it was fated that the aim,
of which for a long time nothing was known, would hold our expectations
up to ridicule. To renounce, to close, and to mortify sight, hearing, and
touch, to break free that way and not have to fear anymore that something
will be taken away from us—no, I did not know how to do that.

÷

I sit down now and write in my defense.
The witnesses are old things, undimmed, dense

With the life of human hands: the intense reds
In stained glass, stone lacework, marble heads,

The dark gold calligraphies of magic, traces
Of red in alchemical script, marmoreal laces,

Maps on which the lands of faery glimmer,
Globes wrapped in black velvet and a shimmer

Of stars, the slow spokes of a millwheel
By a waterfall, lute songs, a bell's peal.

There I had my home, my refuge, my Exodus
From the Egypt of cosmic unreachableness.

÷

All I have is the dexterity of my hands. I was *homo faber*, originator, maker,
fabricator, builder. The sky above me was too big, its numberless stars
deprived me of my singularity. And the line of time infinitely retreating and
infinitely extending annihilated each moment of my life. But when I hit a
log in its very center with an ax and saw suddenly the white of the split
wood, when I carved close-grained pear wood with a chisel, or painted
Ledum palustre or *Graphalium uliginosum* on soft thick paper that held the
color, or boiled elixirs according to an old recipe, then the Dragon of the
Universe, the great Egypt of inexorable galactic rotations, had no power
over me, because I was guided and protected by Eros, and whatever I was
doing grew immense and stood in front of me, here, right now.

÷

And thus, willy-nilly, you sang my song?
And gave me everything beautiful and strong?

What comes from nothing and returns to it? This:
Strength, exultation, abundance, and bliss.

You danced a blind dance on the edge of a pit.
Blood gave you the rhythm. You chose to submit,

No truth in all that. It's nothing but fever.
The earth is mine forever and ever.

÷

That voice, persecuting me, to be honest, every day.

I am unable to imagine myself among the disciples of Jesus
When they wandered through Asia Minor from city to city
And their words were preparing the Empire's collapse.

I was in the marketplace between amphoras of wine,
Under the arcade where tasty flitches of meat sizzled on a spit.
The dancers danced, the wrestlers gleamed with oil.
I was choosing among bright fabrics sold by merchants from overseas.

Who will refuse to pay homage to the statutes of Caesar
If by his grace we are granted a reprieve?

I could not understand from whence came my stubbornness

And my belief that the pulse of impatient blood
Fulfills the designs of a silent God.

INITIATION

Vanity and gluttony were always her sins
And I fell in love with her in the phase of life
When our scornful reason is the judge of others.

Then I went through a sudden initiation.
Not only did our skins like each other, tenderly,
And our genitals fit once and for all,
But her sleep at arm's length exerted its power
And her childhood in a city she visited dreaming.

Whatever was naive and shy in her
Or fearful in the disguise of self-assurance
Moved me, so that—we were so alike—
In an instant, not judging anymore,
I saw two sins of mine: vanity, gluttony.

ELEGY FOR Y. Z.

Never forget that you are a son of the King.
                    —MARTIN BUBER

A year after your death, dear Y. Z.,
I flew from Houston to San Francisco
And remembered our meeting on Third Avenue
When we took such a liking to each other.
You told me then that as a child you had never seen a forest,
Only a brick wall outside a window,
And I felt sorry for you because
So much disinheritance is our portion.
If you were the king's daughter, you didn't know it.
No fatherland with a castle at the meeting of two rivers,
No procession in June in the blue smoke of incense.
You were humble and did not ask questions.
You shrugged: who after all am I
To walk in splendor wearing a myrtle wreath?
Fleshly, woundable, pitiable, ironic,
You went with men casually, out of unconcern,
And smoked as if you were courting cancer.
I knew your dream: to have a home
With curtains and a flower to be watered in the morning.
That dream was to come true, to no avail.
And our past moment: the mating of birds
Without intent, reflection, nearly airborne
Over the splendor of autumn dogwoods and maples;
Even in our memory it left hardly a trace.
I am grateful, for I learned something from you,
Though I haven't been able to capture it in words:
On this earth, where there is no palm and no scepter,
Under a sky that rolls up like a tent,
Some compassion for us people, some goodness
And, simply, tenderness, dear Y. Z.

P.S. Really I am more concerned than words would indicate.
I perform a pitiful rite for all of us.
I would like everyone to know they are the king's children
And to be sure of their immortal souls,
I.e., to believe that what is most their own is imperishable
And persists like the things they touch,
Now seen by me beyond time's border:
Her comb, her tube of cream, and her lipstick
On an extramundane table.

ANKA

In what hat, from what epoch,
Is Anka posing in the photograph,
Above her brow the wing of a killed bird?
Now she is one of them, beyond the threshold
Where there are no men, no women,
And the prophet does not give separate sermons
To the ones covered with shawls
So that their long hair does not provoke lust,
And to the tanned, bearded men in draped burnouses.
Saved from the furnaces of World War II,
Trying on dresses in reflected mirrors
And blouses and necklaces and rings,
With a hairstyle and makeup for the wars of her career,
Happy to go to bed or just talk over wine,
The owner of a beautiful apartment, full of sculpture.
Left to herself till the end of the world,
How does she manage now, fleshless?
And what could the prophet find to say, when he has no thought
Of the hair under a shawl and the secret
Fragrance of skin and of ointments?

THEODICY

No, it won't do, my sweet theologians.
Desire will not save the morality of God.
If he created beings able to choose between good and evil,
And they chose, and the world lies in iniquity,
Nevertheless, there is pain, and the undeserved torture of creatures,
Which would find its explanation only by assuming
The existence of an archetypal Paradise
And a pre-human downfall so grave
That the world of matter received its shape from diabolic power.

TABLE I

Only this table is certain. Heavy. Of massive wood.
At which we are feasting as others have before us,
Sensing under the varnish the touch of other fingers.
Everything else is doubtful. We too, appearing
For a moment in the guise of men or women
(Why either-or?), in preordained dress.
I stare at her, as if for the first time.
And at him. And at her. So that I can recall them
In what unearthly latitude or kingdom?
Preparing myself for what moment?
For what departure from among the ashes?
If I am here, entire, if I am cutting meat
In this tavern by the wobbly splendor of the sea.

TABLE II

In a tavern by the wobbly splendor of the sea,
I move as in an aquarium, aware of disappearing,
For we are all so mortal that we hardly live.
I am pleased by this union, even if funereal,
Of sights, gestures, touches, now and in ages past.
I believed my entreaties would bring time to a standstill.
I learned compliance, as others did before me.
And I only examine what endures here:
The knives with horn handles, the tin basins,
Blue porcelain, strong though brittle,
And, like a rock embattled in the flow
And polished to a gloss, this table of heavy wood.

MY-NESS

"My parents, my husband, my brother, my sister."
I am listening in a cafeteria at breakfast.
The women's voices rustle, fulfill themselves
In a ritual no doubt necessary.
I glance sidelong at their moving lips
And I delight in being here on earth
For one more moment, with them, here on earth,
To celebrate our tiny, tiny my-ness.

THANKFULNESS

You gave me gifts, God-Enchanter.
I give you thanks for good and ill.
Eternal light in everything on earth.
As now, so on the day after my death.

POET AT SEVENTY

Thus, brother theologian, here you are,
Connoisseur of heavens and abysses,
Year after year perfecting your art,
Choosing bookish wisdom for your mistress,
Only to discover you wander in the dark.

Ai, humiliated to the bone
By tricks that crafty reason plays,
You searched for peace in human homes
But they, like sailboats, glide away,
Their goal and port, alas, unknown.

You sit in taverns drinking wine,
Pleased by the hubbub and the din,
Voices grow loud and then decline
As if played out by a machine
And you accept your quarantine.

On this sad earth no time to grieve,
Love potions every spring are brewing,
Your heart, in magic, finds relief,
Though Lenten dirges cut your cooing.
And thus you learn how to forgive.

Voracious, frivolous, and dazed
As if your time were without end
You run around and loudly praise
Theatrum where the flesh pretends
To win the game of nights and days.

In plumes and scales to fly and crawl,
Put on mascara, fluffy dresses,
Attempt to play like beast and fowl,

Forgetting interstellar spaces:
Try, my philosopher, this world.

And all your wisdom came to nothing
Though many years you worked and strived
With only one reward and trophy:
Your happiness to be alive
And sorrow that your life is closing.

To find my home in one sentence, concise, as if hammered in metal. Not to enchant anybody. Not to earn a lasting name in posterity. An unnamed need for order, for rhythm, for form, which three words are opposed to chaos and nothingness.

Berkeley—Paris—Cambridge, Massachusetts, 1981—1983

NEW POEMS

1985–1987

A PORTRAIT WITH A CAT

A little girl looks at a book with a picture of a cat
Who wears a fluffy collar and has a green velvet frock.
Her lips, very red, are half opened in a sweet reverie.
This takes place in 1910 or 1912, the painting bears no date.
It was painted by Marjorie C. Murphy, an American
Born in 1888, like my mother, more or less.
I contemplate the painting in Grinnell, Iowa,
At the end of the century. That cat with his collar
Where is he? And the girl? Am I going to meet her,
One of those mummies with rouge, tapping with their canes?
But this face: a tiny pug nose, round cheeks,
Moves me so, quite like a face that I, suddenly awake
In the middle of the night, saw by my side on a pillow.
The cat is not here, he is in the book, the book in the painting.
No girl, and yet she is here, before me
And has never been lost. Our true encounter
Is in the zones of childhood. Amazement called love,
A thought of touching, a cat in velvet.

Berkeley, 1985

MARY MAGDALEN AND I

The seven unclean spirits of Mary Magdalen
Chased from her by the Teacher with his prayer
Hover in the air in a bat-like flight,
While she, with one leg folded in,
Another bent at the knee, sits staring hard
At her toe and the thong of her sandal
As if she had just noticed such an odd thing.
Her chestnut-brown hair curls in rings
And covers her back, strong, almost virile,
Resting on her shoulder, on a dark-blue dress
Under which her nakedness phosphoresces.
The face is heavyish, the neck harboring
A voice that is low, husky, as if hoarse.
But she will say nothing. Forever between
The element of flesh and the element
Of hope, she stays still. At the canvas's corner
The name of a painter who desired her.

Berkeley, 1985

A SKULL

Before Mary Magdalen, albescent in the dusk,
A skull. The candle flickers. Which of her lovers
Is this dried-up bone, she does not try to guess.
She remains like that, for an age or two
In meditation, while sand in the hourglass
Has fallen asleep—because once she saw,
And felt on her shoulder the touch of His hand,
Then, at daybreak, when she exclaimed: "Rabboni!"
I gather dreams of the skull for I am it,
Impetuous, enamored, suffering in the gardens
Under a dark window, uncertain whether it's mine
And for no one else, the secret of her pleasure.
Raptures, solemn oaths. She does not quite remember.
And only that moment persists, unrevoked,
When she was almost on the other side.

Berkeley, 1985

IN A JAR

Now, with all my knowledge, honorable newts,
I approach the jar in which you live
And see how you float up vertically to the surface
Showing your bellies of vermilion color,
Color of flame, that makes you akin
To the alchemists' salamander living in fire.
Perhaps that's the reason why I caught you
In a pond between pines when white April clouds race,
And carried you to town, proud of my trophy.
You vanished so long ago, I ponder the moment
When you lived unaware of hours and years.
I address you, I give you existence—
Even a name and a title in the princedom of grammar—
To protect you by inflection from nothingness.
Myself no doubt held by powers who observe me
And transfer me to some grammatical hyper-form,
While I wait with the hope that they seize me and carry me up
So that I last like an alchemists' salamander in fire.

South Hadley, 1985

ALL HALLOWS' EVE

In the great silence of my favorite month,
October (the red of maples, the bronze of oaks,
A clear-yellow leaf here and there on birches),
I celebrated the standstill of time.

The vast country of the dead had its beginning everywhere:
At the turn of a tree-lined alley, across park lawns.
But I did not have to enter, I was not called yet.

Motorboats pulled up on the river bank, paths in pine needles.
It was getting dark early, no lights on the other side.

I was going to attend the ball of ghosts and witches.
A delegation would appear there in masks and wigs,
And dance, unrecognized, in the chorus of the living.

South Hadley, 1985

THIS ONLY

A valley and above it forests in autumn colors.
A voyager arrives, a map led him here.
Or perhaps memory. Once, long ago, in the sun,
When the first snow fell, riding this way
He felt joy, strong, without reason,
Joy of the eyes. Everything was the rhythm
Of shifting trees, of a bird in flight,
Of a train on the viaduct, a feast of motion.
He returns years later, has no demands.
He wants only one, most precious thing:
To see, purely and simply, without name,
Without expectations, fears, or hopes,
At the edge where there is no I or not-I.

South Hadley, 1985

A CONFESSION

My Lord, I loved strawberry jam
And the dark sweetness of a woman's body.
Also well-chilled vodka, herring in olive oil,
Scents, of cinnamon, of cloves.
So what kind of prophet am I? Why should the spirit
Have visited such a man? Many others
Were justly called, and trustworthy.
Who would have trusted me? For they saw
How I empty glasses, throw myself on food,
And glance greedily at the waitress's neck.
Flawed and aware of it. Desiring greatness,
Able to recognize greatness wherever it is,
And yet not quite, only in part, clairvoyant,
I knew what was left for smaller men like me:
A feast of brief hopes, a rally of the proud,
A tournament of hunchbacks, literature.

Berkeley, 1985

FOR JAN LEBENSTEIN

Certainly we have much in common,
We who grew up in baroque cities
Without asking what king has founded a church
We passed every day, what princesses lived
In the palace, what were the names of architects, sculptors,
Where they came from and when, what made them famous.
We preferred to play ball in front of ornate porticoes,
To run past bay windows and marble stairs,
Later on, benches in shadowy parks were dearer to us
Than a throng of gypsum angels overhead.
And yet something remained: our liking for tortuous line,
Our high spirals of contraries, flame-like,
And dressing our women in abundantly draped silks
To brighten the dance of skeletons.

Berkeley, 1985

WITH HER

Those poor, arthritically swollen knees
Of my mother in an absent country.
I think of them on my seventy-fourth birthday
As I attend early Mass at St. Mary Magdalen in Berkeley.
A reading this Sunday from the Book of Wisdom
About how God has not made death
And does not rejoice in the annihilation of the living.
A reading from the Gospel according to Mark
About a little girl to whom He said: "Talitha, cumi!"
This is for me. To make me rise from the dead
And repeat the hope of those who lived before me,
In a fearful unity with her, with her pain of dying,
In a village near Danzig, in a dark November,
When both the mournful Germans, old men and women,
And the evacuees from Lithuania would fall ill with typhus.
Be with me, I say to her, my time has been short.
Your words are now mine, deep inside me:
"It all seems now to have been a dream."

Berkeley, 1985

OLD WOMEN

Arthritically bent, in black, spindle-legged,
They move, leaning on canes, to the altar where the Pantocrator
In a dawn of gilded rays lifts his two fingers.
The mighty, radiant face of the All-Potent
In whom everything was created, whatever is on the earth and in
 Heaven,
To whom are submitted the atom and the scale of galaxies,
Rises over the heads of His servants, covered with their shawls
While into their shriveled mouths they receive His flesh.

A mirror, mascara, powder, and cones of carmine
Lured every one of them and they used to dress up
As themselves, adding a brighter glow to their eyes,
A rounder arch to their brows, a denser red to their lips.
They opened themselves, amorous, in the riverside woods,
Carried inside the magnificence of the beloved,
Our mothers whom we have never repaid,
Busy, as we were, with sailing, crossing continents.
And guilty, seeking their forgiveness.

He who has been suffering for ages rescues
Ephemeral moths, tired-winged butterflies in the cold,
Genetrixes with the closed scars of their wombs,
And carries them up to His human Theotokos,
So that the ridicule and pain change into majesty
And thus it is fulfilled, late, without charms and colors,
Our imperfect, earthly love.

Rome, 1986

HOW IT SHOULD BE IN HEAVEN

How it should be in Heaven I know, for I was there.
By its river. Listening to its birds.
In its season: in summer, shortly after sunrise.
I would get up and run to my thousand works
And the garden was superterrestrial, owned by imagination.
I spent my life composing rhythmical spells
Not quite aware of what was happening to me.
But striving, chasing without cease
A name and a form. I think the movement of blood
Should continue there to be a triumphant one,
Of a higher, I would say, degree. That the smell of gillyflower,
That a nasturtium and a bee and a ladybug
Or their very essence, stronger than here,
Must summon us just the same to a core, to a center
Beyond the labyrinth of things. For how could the mind
Stop its hunt, if from the Infinite
It takes enchantment, avidity, promise?
But where is our, dear to us, mortality?
Where is time that both destroys and saves us?
This is too difficult for me. Peace eternal
Could have no mornings and no evenings,
Such a deficiency speaks against it.
And that's too hard a nut for a theologian to crack.

Rome, 1986

CAFFÉ GRECO

In the eighties of the twentieth century, in Rome, via Condotti
We were sitting with Turowicz in the Caffé Greco
And I spoke in, more or less, these words:

—We have seen much, comprehended much.
States were falling, countries passed away.
Chimeras of the human mind besieged us
And made people perish or sink into slavery.
The swallows of Rome wake me up at dawn
And I feel then transitoriness, the lightness
Of detaching myself. Who I am, who I was
Is not so important. Because others,
Noble-minded, great, sustain me
Anytime I think of them. Of the hierarchy of beings.
Those who gave testimony to their faith,
Whose names are erased or trampled to the ground
Continue to visit us. From them we take the measure,
Aesthetic, I should say, of works, expectations, designs.
By what can literature redeem itself
If not by a melopoeia of praise, a hymn
Even unintended? And you have my admiration,
For you accomplished more than did my companions
Who once sat here, the proud geniuses.
Why they grieved over their lack of virtue,
Why they felt such pangs of conscience, I now understand.
With age and with the waning of this age
One learns to value wisdom, and simple goodness.
Maritain whom we used to read long ago

Would have reason to be glad. And for me: amazement
That the city of Rome stands, that we meet again,
That I still exist for a moment, myself and the swallows.

Rome, 1986

AND YET THE BOOKS

And yet the books will be there on the shelves, separate beings,
That appeared once, still wet
As shining chestnuts under a tree in autumn,
And, touched, coddled, began to live
In spite of fires on the horizon, castles blown up,
Tribes on the march, planets in motion.
"We are," they said, even as their pages
Were being torn out, or a buzzing flame
Licked away their letters. So much more durable
Than we are, whose frail warmth
Cools down with memory, disperses, perishes.
I imagine the earth when I am no more:
Nothing happens, no loss, it's still a strange pageant,
Women's dresses, dewy lilacs, a song in the valley.
Yet the books will be there on the shelves, well born,
Derived from people, but also from radiance, heights.

Berkeley, 1986

ON PARTING WITH MY WIFE, JANINA

Women mourners were giving their sister to fire.
And fire, the same as we looked at together,
She and I, in marriage through long years,
Bound by an oath for good or ill, fire
In fireplaces in winter, campfires, fires of burning cities,
Elemental, pure, from the beginnings of the Earth,
Was taking away her streaming hair, gray,
Seized her lips and her neck, engulfed her, fire
That in human languages designates love.
I thought nothing of languages. Or of words of prayer.

I loved her, without knowing who she really was.
I inflicted pain on her, chasing my illusion.
I betrayed her with women, though faithful to her only.
We lived through much happiness and unhappiness,
Separations, miraculous rescues. And now, this ash.
And the sea battering the shore when I walk the empty boulevard.
And the sea battering the shore. And ordinary sorrow.

How to resist nothingness? What power
Preserves what once was, if memory does not last?
For I remember little. I remember so very little.
Indeed, moments restored would mean the Last Judgment
That is adjourned from day to day, by Mercy perhaps.

Fire, liberation from gravity. An apple does not fall,
A mountain moves from its place. Beyond the fire-curtain,
A lamb stands in the meadow of indestructible forms.
The souls in Purgatory burn. Heraclitus, crazy,
Sees the flame consuming the foundations of the world.
Do I believe in the Resurrection of the Flesh? Not of this ash.

I call, I beseech: elements, dissolve yourselves!
Rise into the other, let it come, kingdom!
Beyond the earthly fire compose yourselves anew!

Berkeley, 1986

POWERS

Though of weak faith, I believe in forces and powers
Who crowd every inch of the air.
They observe us—is it possible that no one sees us?
Just think: a cosmic spectacle and absolutely no one?
There is proof, my consciousness. It separates itself,
Soars above me, above other people, above earth,
Obviously kindred to those powers,
Able, as they are, to see with detachment.
Whether they help us, harm us, under what conditions,
Or whether they are allowed only to see, who knows.
They laugh and feel pity. In that they are quite human
But also superhuman, for neither a day nor a year
Nor a century will encompass them. Kindergartens, playgrounds
Are their beloved domain. Boys, girls, on the run,
Or throwing a ball, an outline of what they will be
In their faces, gestures. Later, decked with jewels,
Garishly painted, sleepy, with a loop of smoke at their lips,
Or those in white aprons, in gauze masks,
Or the white-breasted, feeding. And they, with their glory of roosters,
At meetings, pot-bellied players for power, at drinking
Contests, dull-eyed. Beds, blankets, his and her
Incomprehensible, to tell the truth, hastes.
My pussy cat. My puppy dog. Froggies.
Most green little frogs. Winnie the Poohs. Rabbits.
Their language is always the same, nourished by fairy tale.
And what's that to powers? How can pure spirits
Comprehend from the inside pungency, scent, touching
Rough hair, of, for instance, a Titianesque color?
Let's assume, though, they can. Still, really obscure
For them are cemeteries. Slanting toward the sea
Which shows blue behind the trees, or toward the sunrise,
Or flat, beyond a gray river. What a perfection
Of the Irrevocable! What a total otherness

Offensive to beings from the circuit of consciousness
And for that reason enticing, so elementary
That what remains is to ask repeatedly: "Why?"
And the powers flow, whir among the tombstones,
"Who ordered them to die, who needs it?"
They exclaim, pondering, in constant amazement.
Because their thought, clear, tends to harmony,
Knows the ideal shapes, respects order
In which whatever exists must exist forever.

Berkeley, 1987

The Trans-Siberian Railway

On the Trans-Siberian Railway I traveled to Krasnoyarsk,
With my Lithuanian nurse, with my mama; a two-year-old
    cosmopolitan,
A participant in the promised European era.
My dad hunted marals in the Sayan Mountains,
Ela and Nina were running on the beach in Biarritz.

Yes, this happened in 1913. The past hundred years were then considered as merely a preface to a truly European and even cosmopolitan epoch. French novels in yellow covers were read on the Danube and the Vistula, on the Dnieper and the Volga. McCormick harvesters were working in the fields of the Ukraine. Oscar Wilde had hardly become a magnet for budding aesthetes before young rebels found the herald of the liberated masses in Walt Whitman, while the Parisian boheme learned about the enigmatic Slavic soul from *ballets russes* and Dostoevsky's novels. Again and again some refined poet would go on a pilgrimage to Moscow, the holy city, to listen there to the sound of bells. A society of many countries would meet in summer at the waters in Marienbad or on the Côte d'Azur, families would send their consumptive sons and daughters to the sanatoriums in Davos. Poets began to praise international express trains and one of them wrote a poem entitled "La Prose du Trans-Siberien." Thus, in St. Petersburg, putting my foot on the running board of an automobile glimmering with black enamel, and then crossing the Urals, I was in harmony with the spirit of the age. It was at that time that a young civil engineer, Aleksander Milosz, alumnus of Riga Polytechnic, hunted in the taiga of the Sayan Mountains, where the river Yenissei, in its upper run, flowing to the north, toward the plains and the glacial ocean, carved a gorge. It was mating season of Siberian deer called marals, their bellowings resounded and echoed among forest slopes where lemon-yellow birches contrasted with the dark green of cedars. The young man was light-footed, he leaped effortlessly across moss-covered rocks and breathed in the cold autumn air with delight. Nearly identical with him now, I feel the ease of his stalking, the thrust of his hand, and a certainty, at the moment of shooting, that he did not miss. And perhaps the community of our experiences, considerable, as we are parts of the same species, is enough to make me for a short while a fifteen-year-old Ela when she runs to meet a swelling, rustling wave of the Atlantic? Or when she stands naked before a mirror, unplaits her black tress, pretty, and aware she is pretty, touches the brown disks on her breasts and in a flash experiences a revelation which excludes her from everything she had been taught: curtseying, bows, sailor's collars, petticoats, behavior at the table, governesses, sleeping cars, gentlemen with their moustaches combed into spikes, women in corsets and tournures, of whom one says either "ladies" or "cocottes," the catechism, the list of sins before confession, music lessons, French verbs, pretended naiveté, politeness toward servants, knowledge of the amount of your dowry. Revelation: it is not like that at all, in reality it is completely different. One should not tell this to anybody, only to oneself. How good it is to touch oneself and not to believe them even a bit, and everywhere, in the sun, in the white clouds above the sea, in the rustling of the waves, in one's own body to feel this: completely different.

Beyond the Urals

Day after day the plain. Mountains, again the plain.
The samovar purrs incessantly. The merchants in their coupé
Drink their *tchay* from painted wooden cups.
The archaeologist Valuev tells my mother of excavations
    in Mongolia,
Then engages in an endless quarrel with Peterson,
Too difficult for her to follow, though she went to school
And attended Zdziechowski's lectures in Kraków.

The Arkonia and Veletia fraternities
Parading at midnight in the city of Riga,
With them my pretty mommy, for she liked to drink
Though she was pregnant with me—perhaps I was affected?
Now she passes through the Urals (Like statues of the Apostles!
—Exclaims my nurse from the Kiejdany district)
And travels to join her husband (strange expression: to join a husband).

Valuev:
Nobody wants the truth. Man cannot bear the truth.
It's not in his measure. Flee, take refuge
In the incense smoke, in icons, in priests' chantings,
In your goodness, false, in relics, legends,
As long as you are with others who pretend as you do.
But it's ended. And what lasted for centuries is perishing.
Shamans of islands and continents shake their rattles
But won't wake, won't wake the Killed One.
I see moldy altars, temples changed into museums,
I hear a triumphant song, they don't know it's a song of mourning.
They will rub their eyes in the blinding light of "it's over,"

Search for the smashed tablets with the letters of good and evil.
While the lofty thought says: "Let what's destined to fall, fall.
Let the new race receive the gift, its mortality.
Let it rule the earth, dance upon ruins."

Peterson:
That's teenage melodrama. The old draws to its close
So the new is not here. Yet surely it will come.
We will put an end to religion. But also to philosophy and art.
For philosophy and art are born of our fear of death.
They are not needed by gods who live forever.
The human spirit will soon create itself anew.
Just as it began by stealing fire.
And will clearly perceive its goal, proportional to man's greatness:
To win victory over death and to become gods.
The promise will be fulfilled, the dead will rise.
We will bring back to life our fathers, thousands of generations.
We will populate Mars, Venus, and other planets.
No songs of mourning for man, happy and good.

Valuev:
—Why good?

Peterson:
—Because evil, in other words egoism, is due to the shortness of life.
Whoever has limitless time, ceases to be predatory.

Valuev:
Ha!

Peterson was obviously familiar with the writings of Nicolas Fedorovich
Fedorov (1828–1903), who announced that through the progress of

science man would cease to be a mortal being. Then his main moral duty would be to use science to revive his forefathers, i.e., all people who have ever lived on the earth.

Both Valuev and Peterson were executed in 1918.

First Performance

The orchestra tuned its instruments to perform *The Rite of Spring.*
You hear those marches of woodwinds, the rumble of cymbals and
    drums?
Dionysus arrives, the long-exiled Dionysus returns.
The rule of the Galilean is ended.
More and more pale, fleshless, moon-like,
He fades away, leaving to us dark cathedrals
With the colored water of stained glass and hand bells for Elevation.
The noble-minded rabbi who announced that he would live forever
And would save his friends, raising them from ashes.
Dionysus arrives, he glimmers, olive-gold, among the ruins of
    Heaven.
His cry, of earthly ecstasy, is carried by the echo in the praise of death.

The Northern Route

The fame of Fridtjof Nansen, explorer, was so great that his very presence on the steamer *Correct*, which in the summer of 1913 navigated the northern route from Norway to Siberia, was sufficient to assure publicity to the voyage. This was not the first expedition along the northern shores of the Euro-Asiatic continent, yet the Siberian Company of Norway financed it in the hope that it would become the first of the annual sailings. Johan Samuelsen was the ship's captain, Hans Johansen its ice pilot, the passengers were Jonas Lied, director of the Siberian Company, Joseph Gregorievitch Loris-Melikov, secretary of the Russian legation in Christiania, an industralist by the name of Stepan Vasilievitch Vostrotin, and Fridtjof Nansen. A book by the latter about his Siberian journey appeared in English translation in 1914. He says there:

"The future possibilities of Siberia may almost be called unlimited; but their development is attended with difficulties, which are mainly due to the great distances. In Central Siberia the railway route—whether westward to the Baltic or eastward to the Pacific—is so long as to render the freight on the chief products of the country, such as grain, timber, etc., prohibitive, since the cost of carriage to the markets may easily equal the value of the goods.

"If regular annual sailings could be established, in spite of the ice, between the Yenissei estuary and Europe, so that in the future the immense quantities of produce could be sent by this cheaper route, it would naturally be of the greatest importance to the future development of the whole Central Siberia. Therefore the people of that country are keenly interested in everything that may promote this affair. And without being aware of it—speaking of myself, in any case—many eyes were doubtless fixed upon our voyage and what it might lead to." (Fridtjof Nansen, *Through Siberia, The Land of the Future,* New York, London, 1914)

I recognize them. They stand on the deck
Of the steamer *Correct* when it entered the Yenissei estuary.
The swarthy one, in the leather jacket of an automobilist,
Is Loris-Melikov, diplomat. The fat one, Vostrotin,
Owner of a gold mine and a deputy to the Duma.
Beside them a lean blond man, my father. And the bony Nansen.
The photograph hangs in our apartment in Wilno,
Five Podgórna Street. By the jars
In which I rear newts. What can happen
In ten years? The end? The beginning? of the world.
My father, then. I don't know why he traveled
In the summer of 1913 to the gloomy wastes
Of the northern lights. What a confusion
Of times. And places. Here I am, uneasy,
In the midst of the California spring, for things do not fit together.
What do you want? I want it to exist. But what? That which is no
    more.
Even your newts? Yes, even my newts.

Revolutionaries

"But they complained of the entirely unoccupied, inactive life they had to lead. There was nothing for them to do, except to read. No work for them was to be had there. They might have found some amusement at least in hunting, but that was out of the question, as the exiles are not allowed to have arms. The only other thing was a little fishing when they had the chance, and, otherwise, they had to let the summers and winters slip by as best they could, till their time was up and they were free again to return to life and the world." (Fridtjof Nansen, *Through Siberia, The Land of the Future*)

Leaders of mankind, noble revolutionaries,
Throw pebbles into the water, look at the Yenissei current,
Play the guitar, teach themselves languages,
Read *Das Kapital*, yawn, wait.
Certain of victory. For the man-god will arrive.
His mind as clear as two and two make four.
It leaves aside the irrelevant and aims at the goal
Which is power. Not of kings and caesars.
All the continents and seas. His dominion
Over mortal beings on the earth and in Heaven.
The avenger and educator. There, in their capitals,
Let the torpid animals sleep, unaware
Of what is prepared already. Compassion is not his hobby.
They, dull and languid, will be exercised
Till, in dread, obedience and fearful hope,
They will lose the human nature in which they take refuge,
Though it does not exist. Till their mask falls off
And they enter the heights, transformed by agony.

A Parisian Scene

"Then he tells me their names, as they enter, one after another, those who are habitual guests here: Lucienne, sweet and elegant, moving like a shadow, without a word; charming Alice, with an ever-present smile on her lips; big Yolande in a hat rakishly cocked, one of those who belong to our Inter-Slipper Club; Andrée, dignified, squeezes your hand, without insisting; frouu . . . a tempest of rustling skirts, little cries of a startled bird . . . it is Jeanne who appears, in a hat adorned with one red plume. Everything turns upside down when she passes through the café hall and disappears at the staircase leading to the first floor." (A clipping from a Parisian newspaper, in *Inédits secrets* of Blaise Cendrars)

The Titanic

"There was peace, and the world had an even tenor to its ways. True enough from time to time there were events—catastrophes—like the Johnstown Flood, the San Francisco Earthquake, or floods in China—which stirred the sleeping world, but not enough to keep it from resuming its slumber. It seems to me that the disaster about to occur was the event, which not only made the world rub its eyes and awaken, but woke it with a start, keeping it moving at a rapidly accelerating pace ever since, with less and less peace, satisfaction and happiness. To my mind the world of today awoke April 5, 1912." (John B. Thayer, one of the surviving passengers of the *Titanic*, in Wyn Craig Wade, *The Titanic: End of a Dream*, 1979)

Events—catastrophes of which they learned and those others of which they did not want to know. In Johnstown, Pennsylvania, a flood in 1889 took 2,300 lives; 700 persons perished in the San Francisco earthquake of 1906. Yet they did not notice the earthquake at Messina in Sicily (1908), around 84,000 victims, or the Russian-Japanese War. There is no reason to wonder, as even passengers on the Trans-Siberian Railway a few years after 1905 did not think of thousands and thousands of the killed rolling in the muddy currents of the river Amur, or of the ships that were sinking at Tsushima amid the loud cries of sailors swarming in the backwash of a wave. What remained was only the waltz "On the Hills of Manchuria" played by throaty gramophones with a big horn.

Bigger and bigger, more and more rapid, more and more perfect.
Till they built the biggest ship since the beginning of the world.
Her power, 50,000 horse
(Imagination suggests a gigantic team:
50,000 horses pull a chariot-pyramid).
And she went on her first voyage,
Announced with fat print on the front pages of newspapers,
Unsinkable, a floating palace.

Hundreds of servants ready at your beck and call,
Kitchens, elevators, barbershops,
Halls lit by electricity of daylight brightness,
For gentlemen and ladies in evening dresses
A band playing ragtime.

The ship carries 1,320 passengers, together with servants and the crew,
    2,235 people.

Around one o'clock after midnight a feeble rasp, like grazing against
    glass,
But no shock. The machines were stopped. Silence.
The night freezing cold and clear, the stars ablaze.
The surface of the sea smooth, like a lake of oil.
After this meeting with a medium-sized iceberg
The deck begins to lean forward.
Many of those who were already asleep had no time to dress.
And those who set out in the lifeboats
See a long shape with rows of brightly lit cabins
Going down gradually, a swarming of tiny figures,
Hear music—that is the band, in tuxedos,
Standing by the rail and playing a hymn
To the God of mercy, peace, and everlasting love.
Then, acceleration. The first of the four funnels
Disappears underwater, the stern heaves up
Covered with people, the rudder, like a cathedral
Emerging from the depths of the sea, hangs in the air,
A column of black smoke bursts from inside the ship
And everything sinks, softly swallowed
With an underwater groan or thunder.

Then the echo of a scream above water,
A thousand-voiced call for help. It sounded from far off,

Says a witness, like an orchestra of crickets in summer,
Loud at first, then more and more hushed.
Till, after an hour, it subsided. They did not drown, they froze to
    death
Swimming in their lifebelts. The number of victims
Was 1,522. Some would be found later
In the ship lanes. For instance a corpse of a woman, moving quickly
Under its sail—a nightgown blown by the wind.

Here are the words of the hymn played by the *Titanic* band:

> *God of mercy and compassion,*
> *Look with pity on my pain;*
> *Hear a mournful broken spirit*
> *Prostrate at Thy feet complain . . .*
> *Hold me up in mighty waters,*
> *Keep my eyes on things above—*
> *Righteousness, divine atonement,*
> *Peace, and everlasting love.*

Sarcastic Joseph Conrad was not for "a music to get drowned by." He
wrote: "It would be finer if the band of the *Titanic* had been quietly
saved, instead of being drowned while playing—whatever tune they
were playing, the poor devils . . . There is nothing more heroic in being
drowned very much against your will, off a holed, helpless, big tank in
which you bought your passage, than in quietly dying of colic caused by
the imperfect salmon in the tin you bought from your grocer."

Of what were they afraid? Why that ah ah ah in newspapers,
commissions, inquiries, street ballads, pamphlets, and an ominous-
sentimental legend? The *Titanic*, the end of an era? Is it because there is
no more feeling of security? That nothing protects them, neither money
nor changing for dinner every evening, nor the aroma of cigars, nor
Progress? Neither mores, nor polite and faithful servants, nor Greek and

Latin in school, nor law, nor churches, nor science, nothing. And has there ever been anything that offered protection? Fatality, nameless and pitiless, could it be averted? O civilized humanity! O spells, O amulets!

Berkeley, 1985

FEAR-DREAM
(1918)

Orsha is a bad station. In Orsha a train risks stopping for days.
Thus perhaps in Orsha I, six years old, got lost
And the repatriation train was starting, about to leave me behind,
Forever. As if I grasped that I would have been somebody else,
A poet of another language, of a different fate.
As if I guessed my end at the shores of Kolyma
Where the bottom of the sea is white with human skulls.
And a great dread visited me then,
The one destined to be the mother of all my fears.

A trembling of the small before the great. Before the Empire.
Which constantly marches westward, armed with bows, lariats, rifles,
Riding in a troika, pummeling the driver's back,
Or in a jeep, wearing fur hats, with a file full of conquered countries.
And I just flee, for a hundred, three hundred years,
On the ice, swimming across, by day, by night, on and on.
Abandoning by my river a punctured cuirass and a coffer with king's grants.
Beyond the Dnieper, then the Niemen, then the Bug and the Vistula.

Finally I arrive in a city of high houses and long streets
And am oppressed by fear, for I am just a villager
Who only pretends to follow what they discuss so shrewdly
And tries to hide from them his shame, his defeat.

Who will feed me here, as I walk in the cloudy dawn
With small change in my pocket, for one coffee, no more?
A refugee from fictitious States, who will want me here?

Stony walls, indifferent walls, bitter walls.
By order of their reason, not my reason.
Now accept it. Don't kick. You are not going to flee any further.

Berkeley, 1985

IN A BUGGY AT DUSK

To ride in a buggy at dusk. Well-worn ruts.
The road goes past a farm in a dell by a lake.
The roofs nestling together, raw linen spread on the meadow.
Nets drying, smoke rising from the chimney.

What silence. Who are they? Are they among the saved or damned,
Sitting down to supper under pictures of the saints?
And Thomas Aquinas writes about them in his cell,
Nonstop, as punishment no doubt, he was too angelic.
Perhaps I write as punishment, too? I wanted to bow
To the Light, to Majesty, only that, no more.
And here are mere people, their customs, their houses,
A defenseless family, a year on the calendar.

The goal of an artist: to be free from violent joys and sorrows for which
he had time enough during his past life. At breakfast not to think
anything except that he will go to his workshop, where stretched
canvases are ready. He works on a few of them simultaneously, intrigued
by a surprise emerging out of the movements of the brush. He knows
what he looks for, what he strives for. And that is the whole reality, a
detail seen once but constantly escaping, its nameless essence not
touched by anybody. Practically this means to re-create trees, landscapes,
people, animals, but always with the hope that the brush will find a
proper trail.

The brush but also the pen. Perhaps some attempts succeed better,
others less well. Why a hut by the lake and with it Thomas Aquinas? He
presumably said before his death: "Everything I wrote seems to me
straw." Which should be understood as renouncing a gigantic edifice
laboriously erected with syllogisms because it was too human and thus
is no more than mist, nothing when we look at it backward, facing the
last thing, almost before the highest throne. Yet who knows whether we
are allowed to renounce transient, fleeting forms in the name of an

absolute desire. In my youth I did not expect that I would be one day so fascinated by people, by their everyday existence in time, by that day, by that year—which do not augur anything good for the hut by the lake. No, we cannot look straight at the sun. On the other hand we should not imitate the guests in the royal palace from Baal Shem-Tov's tale, who forgot why they arrived there.

A HASSIDIC TALE
From various countries, districts, villages, cities
We were invited to the palace of the king.
His ponds and his gardens astonished us
As well as the choruses of birds and trees of every species.
Wandering through the rooms we saw marvels,
Gold, and silver, and pearls and precious stones.
Days and weeks were too short for looking.

While the guests scattered through the maze of rooms
I insisted on searching for the king's chamber
And was led in. Suddenly all those things
Vanished. They had been conjured up
By Him, the All-Radiant, master of Illusion.

Berkeley, 1985

1945

—You! the last Polish poet!—drunk, he embraced me,
My friend from the Avant-Garde, in a long military coat,
Who had lived through the war in Russia and, there, understood.

He could not have learned those things from Apollinaire,
Or Cubist manifestos, or the festivals of Paris streets.
The best cure for illusions is hunger, patience, and obedience.

In their fine capitals they still liked to talk.
Yet the twentieth century went on. It was not they
Who would decide what words were going to mean.

On the steppe, as he was binding his bleeding feet with a rag
He grasped the futile pride of those lofty generations.
As far as he could see, a flat, unredeemed earth.

Gray silence settled over every tribe and people.
After the bells of baroque churches, after a hand on a saber,
After disputes over free will, and arguments of diets.

I blinked, ridiculous and rebellious,
Alone with my Jesus Mary against irrefutable power,
A descendant of ardent prayers, of gilded sculptures and miracles.

And I knew I would speak in the language of the vanquished
No more durable than old customs, family rituals,
Christmas tinsel, and once a year the hilarity of carols.

Berkeley, 1985

SIX LECTURES IN VERSE

Lecture I

How to tell it all? Referring to what chronicles?
Imagine a young man walking by a lake shore
On a hot afternoon. Dragonflies, diaphanous,
Over the rushes as always. But nothing of what's to come
Has yet arrived. Understand: nothing.
Or perhaps it has, but is unfulfilled.
Bodies assigned for wounds, cities for destruction,
Pain of uncounted numbers, each pain one's own.
Concrete for crematoria, States for partitioning,
Assassins drawn by lot: you, and you, and you.
Yes. And the jet. The transistor. The video.
Men on the moon. He walks and doesn't know.

He comes to a little bay, a kind of beach.
People on vacation are there sunbathing.
Gentlemen and ladies, bored, talk about
Who is sleeping with whom, bridge, and a new tango.
That young man is me. I was him, perhaps still am
Though half a century has passed. I remember and don't remember
How they and he were at odds. He is different, alien.
Prisoners of his mind, they flash by and vanish.
He scorns then, a judge, observer.
Thus the sickliness of adolescence
Divines the sickness of an era
That will not end well. Those who are unaware
Deserve to be punished: they wanted only to live.

A wave, bits of reed on gravel, white clouds.
Beyond the water, village roofs, a wood. And imagination.
In it, Jewish towns, a train crossing the flatlands.
Abyss. The earth is swaying. Does it sway only now

When I throw open the labyrinths of time,
As if to know meant to comprehend,
And beyond the window hummingbirds perform their dance?

I should have . . . I should have what fifty-five years ago?
I should have lived in joy. In harmony. In faith. In peace.
As if that had been possible. And later, stupefaction:
Why hadn't they been wiser? It all appears now as a sequence
Of cause and effect. No, that too is doubtful.
Everyone's responsible who ever breathed—
Air? Unreason? Illusion? Idea?
Like everyone who lived there and then, I didn't see clearly.
This I confess to you, my young students.

Lecture II

Mothers and sisters, tender wives and lovers.
Think of them. They lived and had names.
I saw on a radiant Adriatic beach
Between the Wars, a girl so beautiful
I wanted to stop her in the irrevocable moment.
Her slenderness clasped by a silk bathing suit
(Before the era of plastic), color of indigo
Or ultramarine. Her eyes, violet,
Hair, blond touched with russet. Daughter of patricians,
Of a lordly clan perhaps, striding confidently.
Fair-haired young men, as handsome as she,
Served as her retinue. Sigrid or Inge
From a house scented with cigars, well-being, order.

"Don't go off, fool. Better to take refuge
In hieratic sculptures, church mosaics, rosy gold auroras.
Stay as an echo on waters at sunset.
Don't destroy yourself, don't trust. Not splendor and glory,
But an apish circus calls you, your tribal rite."

So I could have told her. An essence, a person?
A soul, unique? While day of birth
And place of birth, like a planetary house,
Control what she'll be: seduced by her love
Of native customs, by her obedient virtue.

Dante was wrong, alas. It doesn't happen that way.
The verdict is collective. Eternal damnation
Should have afflicted all of them, yes, all.
Which is no doubt impossible. Jesus has to face
Flowery teapots, coffee, philosophizing,

Landscapes with deer, the sound of the clock on the town hall.
Nobody will be convinced by him, black-eyed,
A hooked nose, the dirty clothes
Of a convict or slave, one of those drifters
The State justly catches and disposes of.
Now, when I know so much, I have to forgive
My own transgressions, not unlike theirs:
I wanted to equal others, behave just like them.
To shut my ears, not to hear the call of prophets.
That's why I understand her. A snug home, a garden,
And from the depths of Hell, a fugue of Bach.

Lecture III

Poor humanity is camping on train station floors.
Caps with earflaps, babushkas, quilted jackets, sheepskins.
They sleep side by side, waiting for a train. Cold blows in through the
    doorway.
New arrivals shake off snow, adding to the mud.

I know it's not for you, that knowledge of Smolensk, Saratov.
And better it is not. If one can, let him avoid
Compassion, that ache of imagination.
So I won't labor this. Just fragments, an outline.
They appear. The guards. Three men and one woman.
The leather of their long boots is soft, first-class,
Coats of expensive fur. Movements arrogant, confident.
Leading on leash their German shepherds. Look at her,
Large, still sleepy, well fucked in bed,
Glancing scornfully from under a beaver cap.
Doesn't she clearly show who holds the power here,
Who takes the prize? Ideological,
If you prefer. For nothing here is professed,
All is disguised in a ritual phrase,
Though the fear is real, people obedient,
And where are these four coming from, in a snowstorm,
Real barbed wire, watchtowers of a camp.

At the Congress for the Defense of Culture in Paris
In spring 1935, my fellow student,
Wandering across Europe, Günther from Marburg,
Chuckled. An admirer of Stefan George,
He would write poems on knightly valor
And carried a pocket edition of Nietzsche.
He was to die, perhaps near Smolensk.

From whose bullet? One of those here asleep.
Of the guard with the dogs? Of a camp inmate?
Of this Nadia or Irina? About them, he knew nothing.

Lecture IV

Reality, what can we do with it? Where is it in words?
Just as it flickers, it vanishes. Innumerable lives
Unremembered. Cities on maps only,
Without that face in the window, on the first floor, by the market,
Without those two in the bushes near the gas plant.
Returning seasons, mountain snows, oceans,
And the blue ball of the Earth rotates,
But silent are they who ran through artillery fire,
Who clung to a lump of clay for protection,
And those deported from their homes at dawn
And those who have crawled out from under a pile of bodies,
While here, I, an instructor in forgetting,
Teach that pain passes (for it's the pain of others),
Still in my mind trying to save Miss Jadwiga,
A little hunchback, librarian by profession,
Who perished in the shelter of an apartment house
That was considered safe but toppled down
And no one was able to dig through the slabs of wall,
Though knocking and voices were heard for many days.
So a name is lost for ages, forever,
No one will ever know about her last hours,
Time carries her in layers of the Pliocene.
The true enemy of man is generalization.
The true enemy of man, so-called History,
Attracts and terrifies with its plural number.
Don't believe it. Cunning and treacherous,
History is not, as Marx told us, anti-nature,
And if a goddess, a goddess of blind fate.
The little skeleton of Miss Jadwiga, the spot
Where her heart was pulsating. This only
I set against necessity, law, theory.

Lecture V

"Christ has risen." Whoever believes that
Should not behave as we do,
Who have lost the up, the down, the right, the left, heavens, abysses,
And try somehow to muddle on, in cars, in beds,
Men clutching at women, women clutching at men,
Falling, rising, putting coffee on the table,
Buttering bread, for here's another day.

And another year. Time to exchange presents.
Christmas trees aglow, music,
All of us, Presbyterians, Lutherans, Catholics,
Like to sit in the pew, sing with others,
Give thanks for being here together still,
For the gift of echoing the Word, now and in all ages.

We rejoice at having been spared the misfortune
Of countries where, as we read, the enslaved
Kneel before the idol of the State, live and die with its name
On their lips, not knowing they're enslaved.
However that may be, The Book is always with us,
And in it, miraculous signs, counsels, orders.
Unhygienic, it's true, and contrary to common sense,
But they exist and that's enough on the mute earth.
It's as if a fire warmed us in a cave
While outside the golden rain of stars is motionless.
Theologians are silent. And philosophers
Don't even dare ask: "What is truth?"
And so, after the great wars, undecided,
With almost good will but not quite,
We plod on with hope. And now let everyone
Confess to himself. "Has he risen?" "I don't know."

Lecture VI

Boundless history lasted in that moment
When he was breaking bread and drinking wine.
They were being born, they desired, they died.
My God, what crowds! How is it possible
That all of them wanted to live and are no more?

A teacher leads a flock of five-year-olds
Through the marble halls of a museum.
She seats them on the floor, polite boys
And girls, facing a huge painting,
And explains: "A helmet, a sword, the gods,
A mountain, white clouds, an eagle, lightning."
She is knowing, they see for the first time.
Her fragile throat, her female organs,
Her multicolored dress, creams, and trinkets
Are embraced by forgiveness. What is not embraced
By forgiveness? Lack of knowledge, innocent unconcern
Would cry for vengeance, demand a verdict
Had I been a judge. I won't be, I'm not.
In splendor the earth's poor moment renews itself.
Simultaneously, now, here, every day
Bread is changed into flesh, wine into blood,
And the impossible, what no one can bear,
Is again accepted and acknowledged.

I'm consoling you, of course. Consoling myself also.
Not very much consoled. Trees-candelabra
Carry their green candles. And magnolias bloom.

This too is real. The din ceases.
Memory closes down its dark waters.
And those, as if behind a glass, stare out, silent.

Berkeley, 1985

PROVINCES

(Dalsze okolice)

✣

1991

BLACKSMITH SHOP

I liked the bellows operated by rope.
A hand or foot pedal—I don't remember which.
But that blowing, and the blazing of the fire!
And a piece of iron in the fire, held there by tongs,
Red, softened for the anvil,
Beaten with a hammer, bent into a horseshoe,
Thrown in a bucket of water, sizzle, steam.

And horses hitched to be shod,
Tossing their manes; and in the grass by the river
Plowshares, sledge runners, harrows waiting for repair

At the entrance, my bare feet on the dirt floor,
Here, gusts of heat; at my back, white clouds.
I stare and stare. It seems I was called for this:
To glorify things just because they are.

ADAM AND EVE

Adam and Eve were reading about a monkey in a bath,
Who jumped into the tub, imitating her mistress
And started to turn faucets: Aï, boiling hot!
The lady arrives running, in a robe, her white breasts
Huge, with a blue vein, dangle.
She rescues the monkey, sits at her dressing table,
Calls for her maid, it's time to go to church.

And not only about that were Adam and Eve reading,
Resting a book on their naked knees.
Those castles! Those palaces! Those towering cities!
Planetary airfields between pagodas!
They looked at each other, smiled,
Though uncertainly (you will be, you will know)
And the hand of Eve reached for the apple.

EVENING

An instant of low white clouds before the rising of the moon,
Perfectly immobile on the line of the sea.
The apricot translucence with edges of ash
Darkens, wanes, sets into gray vermillion.

Who is seeing this? The one who doubts his existence.
He strides along the beach, wants to dwell in memory
And to no avail. He is irretrievable, like clouds.
Lungs, liver, sex, not me, not mine.

Masks, wigs, buskins, be with me!
Transform me, take me to a gaudy stage
So that for a moment I can believe I am!

O hymn, O palinode, melopoea,
Sing with my lips, you stop and I perish!

And thus he slowly sinks into the night
Okeanic. No longer held here
By sunrises or the rising of the moon.

CREATING THE WORLD

Celestials at the Board of Projects burst into laughter
For one of them has designed a hedgehog,
Another, not to be left behind, a soprano:
Eyelashes, a bust, and ringlets, plenty of ringlets.

It is superb fun in the ocean of seething energy,
Among bursts and clacks announcing electric currents.
Buckets of proto-colors gurgle, proto-brushes labor,
A mighty whirl of almost galaxies beyond nearly windows
And pure radiance that has never experienced clouds.

They blow conches, somersault in proto-space,
In their realm of archetypes, the seventh heaven.
The earth is practically ready, its rivers sparkle,
Forests cover it, and every single creature
Waits for its name. Thunder strolls the horizon
But the herds in the grass do not lift their heads.

Towns come to be, narrow streets,
A chamberpot poured out a window, laundry.
And immediately freeways to the airport,
A monument at crossroads, a park, a stadium
For thousands when they get up and roar: Goal!

To invent length, width, height,
Two times two and the force of gravity
Would be quite enough, but on top of it, panties
With lace, a hippopotamus, the beak of a toucan,
A chastity belt with its terrible teeth,
A hammerhead shark, a visored helmet,
Plus time, that is, a division into was and will be.

Gloria, gloria, sing objects called to being.
Hearing them, Mozart sits down at the pianoforte
And composes music which had been ready
Before he himself was born in Salzburg.

If only it all could last, but no way.
It iridesces, passes, turns inside a soap-bubble
Together with an invocation Celestials address to the mortals:

"Oh, dizzy tribe, how not to look at you with pity!
Your bright rags, your dances
Seemingly profligate but in truth pathetic,
Mirrors in which you leave a face with earrings,
Painted eyelids, eyelashes with mascara.
Oh, to have so little, nothing except feasts of love!
How feeble your defense against the abyss!"

And the sun rises and the sun sets,
And the sun rises and the sun sets
While they go on running, running.

LINNAEUS

He was born in 1707 at 1:00 a.m. on May 23rd,
when spring was in beautiful bloom, and cuckoo
had just announced the coming of summer.
                —FROM LINNAEUS'S BIOGRAPHY

Green young leaves. A cuckoo. Echo.
To get up at four in the morning, to run to the river
Which steams, smooth under the rising sun.
A gate is open, horses are running,
Swallows dart, fish splash. And did we not begin with an
    overabundance
Of glitterings and calls, pursuits and trills?
We lived every day in hymn, in rapture,
Not finding words, just feeling it is too much.

He was one of us, happy in our childhood.
He would set out with his botanic box
To gather and to name, like Adam in the garden
Who did not finish his task, expelled too early.
Nature has been waiting for names ever since:
On the meadows near Uppsala, white, at dusk
Platanthera is fragrant, he called it *bifolia*.
Turdus sings in a spruce thicket, but is it *musicus*?
That must remain the subject of dispute.
And the botanist laughed at a little perky bird
For ever *Troglodytes troglodytes L.*

He arranged three kingdoms into a system.
Animale. Vegetale. Minerale.
He divided: classes, orders, genuses, species.
"How manifold are Thy works, O Jehovah!"
He would sing with the psalmist. Rank, number, symmetry
Are everywhere, praised with a clavecin
And violin, scanned in Latin hexameter.

We have since had the language of marvel: atlases.
A tulip with its dark, mysterious inside,
Anemones of Lapland, a water lily, an iris
Faithfully portrayed by a scrupulous brush.
And a bird in foliage, russet and dark blue,
Never flies off, retained
On the page with an ornate double inscription.

We were grateful to him. In the evenings at home
We contemplated colors under a kerosene lamp
With a green shade. And what there, on earth,
Was unattainable, over much, passing away, perishing,
Here we could love, safe from loss.

May his household, orangery, the garden
In which he grew plants from overseas
Be blessed with peace and well-being.
To China and Japan, America, Australia,
Sailing-ships carried his disciples;
They would bring back gifts: seeds and drawings.
And I, who in this bitter age deprived of harmony
Am a wanderer and a gatherer of visible forms,
Envying them, bring to him my tribute—
A verse imitating the classical ode.

IN MUSIC

Wailing of a flute, a little drum.
A small wedding cortege accompanies a couple
Going past clay houses on the street of a village.
In the dress of the bride much white satin.
How many pennies put away to sew it, once in a lifetime.
The dress of the groom black, festively stiff.
The flute tells something to the hills, parched, the color of deer.
Hens scratch in dry mounds of manure.

I have not seen it, I summoned it listening to music.
The instruments play for themselves, in their own eternity.
Lips glow, agile fingers work, so short a time.
Soon afterwards the pageant sinks into the earth.
But the sound endures, autonomous, triumphant,
For ever visited by, each time returning,
The warm touch of cheeks, interiors of houses,
And particular human lives
Of which the chronicles make no mention.

INCARNATED

In that country he was an officer of cavalry.
He used to frequent good families, even the countess P.
He had boots well polished, a breakfast served
By his orderly, a smart boy from a village.
Girls. More of them than anywhere, the garrison was huge.
Some of them on their own, in rented rooms,
Others in the care of a polite madame
Who greets you under a pink lamp shade
And recommends the hot Irma, the milkwhite Katherine.
A horse dances under him at a review, bells ring,
The clergy strolls in a procession, children pour a powder of flowers.
Life there was as it should be. The seasons
Decked the streets with brightness, with the copper of leaves, with
     white.
Peasants from the neighborhood, in sheepskin overcoats
Belted with colorful wool, in bast shoes,
Thongs on the leggings, displayed their products.
Nothing beyond that can be said. He lived, once,
On the pages of chronicles, under a different wind,
Under a different conjunction of stars, though on the same
Earth which, as they say, is a goddess.

MISTER HANUSEVICH

Hanusevich wants Nina. But why? Why?
He has tantrums, blubbers when drunk.
Nina laughs. Is he not funny?
Fat and all nerves, he has big ears
And flaps them, a real elephant.

A dark-blue cloud stands over San Francisco
When I drive along Grizzly Peak,
And far out, beyond the Golden Gate, the ocean gleamed.

Aï, my dead of long ago! Aï, Hanusevich, aï, Nina!
Nobody remembers you, nobody knows about you.

Hanusevich had his estate somewhere near Minsk.
The region was taken by the Bolsheviks, so he lives in Wilno.
When he was young, his mommy let him have flings.
He caroused with chanteuses, pretended to be a big shot,
Would send telegrams in Russian: "*Arriving with ladies*
Meet with music troikas champagne"
And a signature: *Count Bobrinskii.*

Chanteuses. I see now their satin underskirts
And black panties with lace. Breasts, too big, too small,
Worries, touching themselves in mirrors, tardy menses.
Later on they changed into *sestritsas* in the windows of hospital trains
(On their brows, bound with a veil, the sign of the red cross).

Nina is not for Hanusevich. Look how she walks.
She rolls from side to side, like a sailor.
A whole year in the saddle, in a cavalry regiment.
What sort of marriageable young lady is she?

What did you find in her, Mister Hanusevich
That you got so romantic? Always pretending,
Perhaps you adorned her with your fantasies.
And, it is true, your funny ears
Nearly transparent, with red veins,
Move, and in your eyes, nearly always, fright.

Once upon a time there was Hanusevich. And there was Nina.
Once only, from the beginning till the end of the world.
It is I who perform, late, this ceremonial wedding.
And around me striped, emerald-eyed beasts,
Ladies from journals of fashion, shamans of lost tribes,
Or, with a secret smile, a grave *sestritsa*,
Appear among white clouds, assist.

PHILOLOGY

To the memory of Kostanty Szyrwid, S.J.,
professor of the Jesuit academy in Wilno and a
Lithuanian preacher who published in 1612 the first
Lithuanian-Latin-Polish dictionary.

He is running, lifting a little the skirt of his winter cloak.
His stockinged ankles, snow and crows.
He caught it and has it, keeps it in his mouth: a word
He has heard as a child by his native river
Near dug-outs in rushes, foot bridges, hazel bushes,
And the pointed roofs of wooden huts.
Along the arcades of the seminary to his cell,
He is running to write it down with a goose pen
Next to the register of Latin words. He coughs; logs in the fireplace,
Smoke. And the Academy Societatis Jesu
Soars above the streets and the angels
Take flesh in stone and gypsum in the mode Barocco.
With stains of sweat under armpits, how many shirts,
How many skirts covering swarthy, shadowy bellies—
And pants, generations of pants, of jerkins,
Of breeches, of cloaks and burlaps on naked skin!
Bagpipes and violins, they danced on the green,
Love meetings, touchings, teasing games.
And all of them knew the same words
Which exist, endure, though they died long ago;
As if not from the earth, from the night, from the flesh
Words arrive, but from lofty ethereal domains,
Visiting him, her, an old man, a child,
Submitted to their own law, of genitive, dative,
Obedient for centuries to a preposition.
I open a dictionary as if I summoned the souls
He enchanted into mute signs on a page,
And I try to visualize him, a lover,
To have some comfort in my mortality.

AND YET

And yet we were so like one another
With all our misery of penises and vaginas,
With the heart beating quickly in fear and ecstasy,
And a hope, a hope, a hope.

And yet we were so like one another
That lazy dragons stretching themselves in the air
Must have considered us brothers and sisters
Playing together in a sunny garden,
Only we did not know that,
Enclosed in our skins, each separately,
Not in a garden, on the bitter earth.

And yet we were so like one another
Even though every leaf of grass had its fate
Just as a sparrow on the roof, a field mouse,
And an infant that would be named John or Teresa
Was born for long happiness or shame and suffering
Once only, till the end of the world.

AT YALE

I

We were drinking vodka together, Brodsky, Venclova
With his beautiful Swedish girl, myself, Richard,
Near the Art Gallery, at the end of the century
Which woke up as if from a heavy slumber
And asked, in stupefaction: "What was that?
How could we? A conjunction of planets?
Or spots on the sun?"
       —For history
Is no more comprehensible. Our species
Is not ruled by any reasonable law.
The boundaries of its nature are unknown.
It is not the same as I, you, a single human.

—Thus mankind returns to its beloved pastimes
During the break. Taste and touch
Are dear to it. Cookbooks,
Recipes for perfect sex, rules
Lowering cholesterol, methods
Of quickly losing weight—that's what it needs.
It is one (from colorful magazines) body
That every morning runs along park lanes,
Touches itself in a mirror, checks its weight.
Et ça bande et ça mouille—to put it briefly.
Are we that? Does it apply to us? Yes and no.

—For, visited by dictators' dreams,
Don't we soar above them who are light-headed
And unwilling to think of the punishment that
  awaits
All those who are too much in love with life?

—Not so light-headed after all, they worship
In their new temples, and mortality,
Having been overcome by the craft of artists,
Comforts them in the halls of museums.

—So the time came again for adoring art.
The names of gods are forgotten, instead, the masters
Soar in the clouds, Saint Van Gogh, Matisse,
Goya, Cézanne, Hieronymus Bosch,
Together with a cluster of the smaller ones, the acolytes.
And what would they say had they stepped down on earth,
Invoked in photographs, newspapers, TV?
Where are those nights growing dense in the loneliness of a workshop,
Which protected, transformed the refugees from the world?

—All form—says Baudelaire—
Even the one created by man,
Is immortal. There was once an artist
Faithful and hard working. His workshop
Together with all he had painted, burned down,
He himself was executed. Nobody has heard of him.
Yet his paintings remain. On the other side of fire.

—Whenever we think of what fulfills itself
By making use of us, we are somewhat uneasy.
A form is accomplished, exists, though before it was not,
And we have nothing more to do with it. Others, generations,
Will chose what they want, accepting or destroying it.
And instead of us, real, they will need just names.

—But suppose all our internal dirt
And nuttiness and shame, a lot of shame,

Were not forgotten—would we prefer that?
They want to find in us their improved selves:
Instead of comic flaws, flaws monumentalized,
And secrets revealed, provided they are not too depressing.

II

"I have heard that Balzac (and who would not listen with respect to every anecdote, even the most insignificant, having to do with that genius?) one day found himself before a fine painting representing winter, a quite melancholy landscape, heavy with hoarfrost, with huts here and there, and sickly peasants. After having contemplated a small house out of which meager smoke ascended, he exclaimed: 'How beautiful it is! But what do they do in that hut? What do they think about, what are their worries? Did they have a good harvest? Certainly they have payments coming due?'

"Let people laugh at M. de Balzac. I do not know who the painter was who had the honor of making vibrate, speculate, and worry the soul of the great novelist, but it seems to me that he gave us, with his adorable naïvete, an excellent lesson in criticism. I often will appraise a painting uniquely by the sum of ideas or reveries which it brings to my mind."

—BAUDELAIRE

III

Yale Center for British Art—J.M.W. Turner (1775–1851):
"Chateaux de St. Michel, Bonneville, Savoy, 1803."

White clouds pass each other above the mountains.
And here a road in the sun, long shadows,
Low embankments, sort of a little bridge,
In a warm-brown color, the same as the tower
Of a *chateau*, which shoots up
On the dark right side, from behind the trees.
A second *chateau* far away, on the upland,
In a white blur, over a wooded slope
That descends towards the road and the hamlet in the valley
With its flock of sheep, poplars, the third
Chateau, or perhaps a romanesque church tower.
And most important: a peasant woman in a red
Skirt, a black bodice, a white
Blouse, carrying something (laundry to the stream?),
Hard to see her face—it is no more than a dot.
Yet she walked there, seen by the painter
And remained forever, only to make possible
The fulfillment of his own, revealed just to him,
Harmony in yellow, blue, and russet.

IV

To tell the truth, a rather miserable stream,
A little more abundant at the dam by the mill,
Enough to lure boys. Their angling tackle
Is quite sloppy. A branch, not a fishing rod
In the hand of the one who stands. Others slouch
Staring at their floats. Over there, in a boat
The younger ones are playing. If only blue
Were that water, but the clouds of England,
As always ragged, announce rain
And this brief clearing is the color of lead.
This is supposed to be romantic, i.e., picturesque.
Yet not for them. We are free to guess
Their patched trousers, patched shirts
As well as their dream of escaping from the village.
But let it be, after all. We recognize the right
To change everything that is sadly real
Into a composition on canvas, which has for its subject
Air. Its changeability, sudden leaps,
Cloudy turmoils, a wandering ray.
No slightest promise of Eden. Who would like to live here?
Let us pay tribute to the painter, so faithful
To bad weather, who chose it, and remains with it.

V

Yale University Art Gallery—Jean Baptiste Corot (1796–1875):
"Port in La Rochelle," ca. 1851.

His name is luminosity. Whatever he saw
Would bring to him, would humbly offer
Its interior without waves, its silence, its calm,
Like a river in the haze of an early morning,
Like a mother of pearl in a black shell.
So, too, this port, in an afternoon hour
With its slumbering sails, its heat,
Where we wandered perhaps, heavy with wine,
Unbuttoning our waistcoats, for him was airy.
It revealed radiance in the disguise of a moment.
These small figures are real till today:
Here are three women, another is riding
A donkey, a man is rolling a barrel,
Horses in their collars, patient. He, holding his palette,
Called out to them, summoned them, led them away
From the poor earth of toil and bitterness
Into this velvety province of goodness.

BEINECKE LIBRARY

He had his home, posthumous, in the town of New Haven,
In a white building, behind walls
Of translucent marble like turtle shell,
Which seep yellowish light on ranges of books,
Portraits and busts in bronze. There precisely
He decided to dwell when nothing any more
Would be revealed by his ashes. Though there, too,
Had he been able to touch his manuscripts
He would have been surprised by the destiny
Of such a complete change into letters, that no one
Could guess who he really was. He rebelled, screamed
And faithfully fulfilled what had been preordained,
Discovering empirically that his biography
Had been carefully arranged against his will
By powers with whom it's hard to conclude an alliance.
Has he done more evil or more good? This only
Must be important. The rest, artistry,
Does not count anyway, as they, our posterity, know
Any time the pulse is normal, breathing easy,
The day sunny, and a rosy tongue
Checks in a little mirror the dense carmine of the lip.

THE THISTLE, THE NETTLE

Let the sad terrestrials remember me,
recognize me and salute: the thistle and the tall nettle,
and the childhood enemy, belladonna.
    —O. V. DE L. MILOSZ, *"Les Terrains Vagues"*

The thistle, the nettle, the burdock, and belladonna
Have a future. Theirs are wastelands
And rusty railroad tracks, the sky, silence.

Who shall I be for men many generations later?
When, after the clamor of tongues, the award goes to silence?

I was to be redeemed by the gift of arranging words
But must be prepared for an earth without grammar,

For the thistle, the nettle, the burdock, the belladonna,
And a small wind above them, a sleepy cloud, silence.

RECONCILIATION

Late, the time of humbling reconciliation
With himself, arrived for him.
"Yes"—he said—"I was created
To be a poet and nothing more.
I did not know anything else to do,
Greatly ashamed but unable to change my fate."

The poet: one who constantly thinks of something else.
His absentmindedness drives his people to despair.
Maybe he does not even have any human feelings.

But, after all, why should it not be so?
In human diversity a mutation, variation
Is also needed. Let us visit the poet
In his little house in a somewhat faded suburb
Where he raises rabbits, prepares vodka with herbs,
And records on tape his hermetic verses.

ABODE

The grass between the tombs is intensely green.
From steep slopes a view onto the bay,
Onto islands and cities below. The sunset
Grows garish, slowly fades. At dusk
Light prancing creatures. A doe and a fawn
Are here, as every evening, to eat flowers
Which people brought for their beloved dead.

A NEW PROVINCE

You would like to hear how it is in old age?
Certainly, not much is known about that country
Till we land there ourselves, with no right to return.

1. I looked around. That it befell others,
This I can understand, but why me?
What do we have in common? Wrinkled, grayhaired,
With their canes they shuffle along, no one is expecting them.
Perhaps a young girl sees me the same way,
Though I see myself differently in the mirror.

2. Don't talk of peace. Dragged against my will,
Afraid of being abandoned any moment
By him who every day adorned the world with colors,
Put oil on my muscles, and dictated words:
Eros has never before seemed to me so mighty
And the earth of new generations so eternal.

3. How to have peace? So many faces,
They lived and vanished. "Where are you?"
I ask and try to remember
The shape of lips, of eyelids, a warm touch.
But with every new day memory is less and less eager.
So, man, I say to myself, you want to be free of dreams?

4. The course of my dying seems to me amusing.
Weakness of legs, the heart pounding, hard to go uphill.
Myself beside my refractory body.
In the clarity of my mind, as in a mountain nest.
And yet humiliated by difficulty in breathing,
Vanquished by the loss of my hair and teeth.

5. I acquired wisdom, I drink a late wine,
Truth about others and truth about myself.
Often in despair, and I ask now why.
So what if I was lame and uncertain?
Life got fulfilled, in a better or worse manner,
And a garden of forgiveness gathered all of us.

6. I would not like to be young, though I'm envious.
They do not ever know how happy they are.
They should greet a sunrise with hymns,
Compose every day a song of songs.
Yet I could not be free from myself,
Again I would get entangled in my fate and genes.
It's better that such misery is given only once.

7. I visit regions unknown until now,
Of which there is no word in learned books.
A thousand-year-old tree lasts only one day,
A butterfly is stopped in the air for ever,
A little Roman girl in an atrium flashes and disappears
At a dark turn of time without dates.
How oddly they are divided, those two tribes:
Women learning about the comic shames of men,
Men learning about the comic shames of women.
Under the feet of passersby, kings: dried-up insects,
Rue de la Vrillère, real, as long as Kot Jelenski was alive.
Once he said: "I will take you to the tomb of Cleopatra,"
And pointed it out, "Here you are," as we stood in the Passage
    Vivienne.

(According to a persistent Parisian legend, Napoleon brought from Egypt the mummy of Cleopatra and, not knowing what to do with it, officials buried it in the present Passage Vivienne.)

8. *Mavet, mors, mirtis, thanatos, smrt.*
And thus it ends, the state of affairs,
All I used to list as my own.
And thus it ends, the state of mind.
Absolute cold. How will I pass through that door?
I search for what is most strongly opposed to *smrt.*
I think it is music. Of the Baroque.

9.—Oh, if only what I beg for would come true!
I would give for it half of my life!
And later it comes true. Followed by bitterness and pity.
So don't beg, mortals! You will be heard.

10. Poetry will remain after you. You were a great poet.
—But in fact, I have known only a chase.
As then, when I was awakened by quacking, gaggling in a
    farm yard
And the garish sun called me to run
Barefoot, on a still wet blackness of paths.
Was it not like that many years later, when I would start up
Every morning, knowing that so much was to be discovered
In a wilderness engraved by my pen?
I had to find a core that makes all things real,
Always hoping to reach it the next day.

11. Poetry will remain after you. A few verses, durable.
—Possibly, but that's not a strong consolation.
Who would ever have believed that the only remedy for sorrow
Would prove to be both acrid and not too effective.

12. "I walk in the disguise of an old, fat woman,"
Wrote Anna Kamienska shortly before her death.
Yes, I know. We are a lofty flame

Not identical with a clay jar. So let us write with her hand:
"Slowly I am withdrawing from my body."

(Two poets appear, girls seventeen years old.
One of them is she. They are still in high school.
They came from Lublin to a master. That is, me.

We sit in a Warsaw apartment with a view onto fields.
Janka serves tea. Politely, we crunch cookies.
I don't talk about the graves in an empty lot close by.)

13. I would prefer to be able to say: "I am satiated,
What is given to taste in this life, I have tasted."
But I am like someone in a window who draws aside a curtain
To look at a feast he does not comprehend.

READING THE NOTEBOOK OF
ANNA KAMIENSKA

Reading her, I realized how rich she was and myself, how poor
Rich in love and suffering, in crying and dreams and prayer.
She lived among her own people who were not very happy but
    supported each other,
And were bound by a pact between the dead and the living renewed
    at the graves.
She was gladdened by herbs, wild roses, pines, potato fields
And the scents of the soil, familiar since childhood.
She was not an eminent poet. But that was just:
A good person will not learn the wiles of art.

YOUTH

Your unhappy and silly youth.
Your arrival from the provinces to the city.
Misted-over windowpanes of streetcars,
Restless misery of the crowd.
Your dread when you entered a place too expensive.
But everything was too expensive. Too high.
Those people must have noticed your crude manners,
Your outmoded clothes, and your awkwardness.

There were none who would stand by you and say,

You are a handsome boy,
You are strong and healthy,
Your misfortunes are imaginary.

You would not have envied a tenor in an overcoat of camel hair
Had you guessed his fear and known how he would die.

She, the red-haired, because of whom you suffered tortures,
So beautiful she seemed to you, is a doll in fire,
You don't understand what she screams with her lips of a clown.

The shapes of hats, the cut of robes, faces in the mirrors,
You will remember unclearly like something from long ago
Or like what remains from a dream.

The house you approached trembling,
The apartment that dazzled you—
Look, on this spot the cranes clear the rubble.

In your turn you will have, possess, secure,
Able to be proud at last, when there is no reason.

Your wishes will be fulfilled, you will gape then
At the essence of time, woven of smoke and mist,

An iridescent fabric of lives that last one day,
Which rises and falls like an unchanging sea.

Books you have read will be of use no more.
You searched for an answer but lived without answer.

You will walk in the streets of southern cities,
Restored to your beginnings, seeing again in rapture
The whiteness of a garden after the first night of snow.

IN COMMON

What is good? Garlic. A leg of lamb on a spit.
Wine with a view of boats rocking in a cove.
A starry sky in August. A rest on a mountain peak.

What is good? After a long drive water in a pool and a sauna.
Lovemaking and falling asleep, embraced, your legs touching hers.
Mist in the morning, translucent, announcing a sunny day.

I am submerged in everything that is common to us, the living.
Experiencing this earth for them, in my flesh.
Walking past the vague outline of skyscrapers? anti-temples?
In valleys of beautiful, though poisoned, rivers.

A PHOTOGRAPH

Few tasks more difficult
Than to write a treatise
On a man who looks
At an old photograph.

Why he does it
Is incomprehensible
And his feelings
Cannot be explained.

Seemingly it's simple:
She was his love.
But here precisely
Questions begin.

If she is tangible
So strongly present
In her skin and her dress,
Her nails and hair,

Was she then a cloud
Or a river wave,
And did she return
to nonexistence?

Or, on the contrary
Is she still a substance,
A thing with duration
Separate and eternal?

We are taught in schools
About the unity of life—

Of plants and protozoa,
Of insects and humans—

Which incessantly
Renews itself and falls
Into our common
Fatherland—abyss.

Thence comes compassion
For every living thing—
Without distinction
Between human and nonhuman.

But how, then, to preserve
That golden privilege
Of an immortality
Given to us only?

Already we hear
Theologians say:
"Being disintegrates,
Substance escapes us."

Meditating over
Her photograph
He repeats to himself
Words of a Zen poet:

"What is our I?
A short-lived ball

Of earth and water,
Of fire and wind."

And, inconceivable,
He addresses her,
Perfectly certain
That she hears him:

"O maiden of the Lord,
Promised to me,
With whom I was to have
At least twelve children,

"Obtain for me the grace
Of your strong faith.
We living are too weak
Without your assistance.

You are for me now
The mystery of time
i.e., of a person
Changing and the same,

Who runs in the garden
Fragrant after the rain
With a ribbon in your hair
And lives in the beyond.

You see how I try
To reach with words
What matters most
And how I fail.

Though perhaps this moment
When you are so close
Is precisely your help
And an act of forgiveness."

LASTINGNESS

That was in a big city, no matter what country, what language,
A long time ago (blessed be the gift
Of spinning a tale out of a trifle,
In the street, in a car—I write it down not to lose it).
Perhaps not a trifle, a crowded night café
Where every evening a famous chanteuse used to sing.
I was sitting with others in smoke, a clatter of beer glasses.
Ties, officers' uniforms, deep décolletés of women,
Wild music of their folklore, probably from the mountains.
And that singer, her throat, a pulsating stem,
Her dancing movement, the black of her hair, white of her skin,
The imagined scent of her perfumes.
What have I learned since, what have I discovered?
States, customs, lives, gone.
No trace of her or of that café.
And only her shade with me, her frailty, beauty, always.

EITHER-OR

If God incarnated himself in man, died and rose from the dead,
All human endeavors deserve attention
Only to the degree that they depend on this,
I.e., acquire meaning thanks to this event.
We should think of this by day and by night.
Every day, for years, ever stronger and deeper.
And most of all about how human history is holy
And how every deed of ours becomes a part of it,
Is written down for ever, and nothing is ever lost.
Because our kind was so much elevated
Priesthood should be our calling
Even if we do not wear liturgical garments.
We should publicly testify to the divine glory
With words, music, dance, and every sign.

If what is proclaimed by Christianity is a fiction
And what we are taught in schools,
In newspapers and TV is true:
That the evolution of life is an accident,
As is an accident the existence of man,
And that his history goes from nowhere to nowhere,
Our duty is to draw conclusions
From our thinking about the innumerable generations
Who lived and died deluding themselves,
Ready to renounce their natural needs for no reason,
To wait for a posthumous verdict, every day afraid
That for licking clean a pot of jam they go to eternal torment.

If a poor degenerate animal
Could have reached so far in his fantasies
And peopled the air with radiant beings,
Rocky chasms with crowds of devils,
The consequences of it must be, indeed, serious.

We should go and proclaim without cease
And remind people at every step of what we are:
That our capacity for self-delusion has no limits
And that anybody who believes anything is mistaken.
The only gesture worthy of respect is to complain of our transience,
Of the one end for all our attachments and hopes,
As if by threatening indifferent Heaven,
We fulfilled that which distinguishes our species.

Not at all! Why either-or?
For centuries men and gods have lived together,
Supplications have been made for health or a successful journey.
Not that one should constantly meditate on who Jesus was.
What can we, ordinary people, know of the Mystery?
Not worse than our neighbors and kin,
We pay homage to it every Sunday.
It is better that not everyone is called to priesthood.
Some are for prayers, others for their sins.
It's a pity that their sermons are always so boring
As if they themselves no more understood.
Let scientists describe the origin of life.
Perhaps it's true, but is all that for human beings?

Day follows night, trees bloom in the spring—
Such discoveries are certainly less harmful.
May we not care about what awaits us after death
But here on earth look for salvation,
Trying to do good within our limits,
Forgiving the mortals their imperfection. Amen.

TWO POEMS

The two poems placed here together contradict each other. The first renounces any dealing with problems which for centuries have been tormenting the minds of theologians and philosophers; it chooses a moment and the beauty of the earth as observed on one of the Caribbean islands. The second, just the opposite, voices anger because people do not want to remember, and live as if nothing happened, as if horror were not biding just beneath the surface of their social arrangements.

I alone know that the assent to the world in the first poem masks much bitterness and that its serenity is perhaps more ironic than it seems. And the disagreement with the world in the second results from anger which is a stronger stimulus than an invitation to a philosophical dispute. But let it be, the two poems taken together testify to my contradictions, since the opinions voiced in one and the other are equally mine.

Conversation with Jeanne

Let us not talk philosophy, drop it, Jeanne.
So many words, so much paper, who can stand it.
I told you the truth about my distancing myself.
I've stopped worrying about my misshapen life.
It was no better and no worse than the usual human tragedies.

For over thirty years we have been waging our dispute
As we do now, on the island under the skies of the tropics.
We flee a downpour, in an instant the bright sun again,
And I grow dumb, dazzled by the emerald essence of the leaves.

We submerge in foam at the line of the surf,
We swim far, to where the horizon is a tangle of banana bush,
With little windmills of palms.
And I am under accusation: That I am not up to my oeuvre,
That I do not demand enough from myself,
As I could have learned from Karl Jaspers,
That my scorn for the opinions of this age grows slack.

I roll on a wave and look at white clouds.

You are right, Jeanne, I don't know how to care about the salvation of
    my soul.
Some are called, others manage as well as they can.
I accept it, what has befallen me is just.
I don't pretend to the dignity of a wise old age.
Untranslatable into words, I chose my home in what is now,
In things of this world, which exist and, for that reason, delight us:
Nakedness of women on the beach, coppery cones of their breasts,

Hibiscus, alamanda, a red lily, devouring
With my eyes, lips, tongue, the guava juice, the juice of *la prune de
    Cythère,*
Rum with ice and syrup, lianas-orchids
In a rain forest, where trees stand on the stilts of their roots.

Death you say, mine and yours, closer and closer,
We suffered and this poor earth was not enough.
The purple-black earth of vegetable gardens
Will be here, either looked at or not.
The sea, as today, will breathe from its depths.
Growing small, I disappear in the immense, more and more free.

Guadeloupe

A Poem for the End of the Century

When everything was fine
And the notion of sin had vanished
And the earth was ready
In universal peace
To consume and rejoice
Without creeds and utopias,

I, for unknown reasons,
Surrounded by the books
Of prophets and theologians,
Of philosophers, poets,
Searched for an answer,
Scowling, grimacing,
Waking up at night, muttering at dawn.

What oppressed me so much
Was a bit shameful.
Talking of it aloud
Would show neither tact nor prudence.
It might even seem an outrage
Against the health of mankind.

Alas, my memory
Does not want to leave me
And in it, live beings
Each with its own pain,
Each with its own dying,
Its own trepidation.

Why then innocence
On paradisal beaches,

An impeccable sky
Over the church of hygiene?
Is it because *that*
Was long ago?

To a saintly man
—So goes an Arab tale—
God said somewhat maliciously:
"Had I revealed to people
How great a sinner you are,
They could not praise you."

"And I," answered the pious one,
"Had I unveiled to them
How merciful you are,
They would not care for you."

To whom should I turn
With that affair so dark
Of pain and also guilt
In the structure of the world,
If either here below
Or over there on high
No power can abolish
The cause and the effect?

Don't think, don't remember
The death on the cross,
Though every day He dies,
The only one, all-loving,
Who without any need
Consented and allowed

To exist all that is,
Including nails of torture.

Totally enigmatic.
Impossibly intricate.
Better to stop speech here.
This language is not for people.
Blessed be jubilation.
Vintages and harvests.
Even if not everyone
Is granted serenity.

Berkeley

SPIDER

The thread with which he landed stuck to the bottom of the bathtub
And he desperately tries to walk on the glossy white
But not one of his thrashing legs gets a hold
On that surface so unlike anything in Nature.
I do not like spiders. Between me and them there is enmity.
I have read a lot about their habits
Which are loathsome to me. In a web
I have seen the quick run, a lethal stabbing
With poison that, in some species,
Is dangerous also for us. Now I take a look
And leave him there. Instead of running water
To end this unpleasantness. For, after all, what can we,
People, do except not to harm?
Not to pour toxic powder on the road of marching ants,
Save stupid moths rushing to the light
By putting a windowpane between them and the kerosene lamp
By which I used to write. Name this at last,
I tell myself: Reluctance to think to the end
Is lifesaving for the living. Could lucid consciousness
Bear everything that in every minute,
Simultaneously, occurs on the earth?
Not to harm. Stop eating fish and meat.
Let oneself be castrated, like Tiny, a cat innocent
Of the drownings of kittens every day in our city.

The Cathari were right: Avoid the sin of conception
(For either you kill your seed and will be tormented by conscience
Or you will be responsible for a life of pain).
My house has two bathrooms. I leave the spider
In an unused tub and go back to my work
Which consists in building diminutive boats
More wieldy and speedy than those in our childhood,
Good for sailing beyond the borderline of time.

Next day I see my spider:
Dead, rolled into a black dot on the glittering white.

I think with envy of the dignity that befell Adam
Before whom creatures of field and forest paraded
To receive names from him. How much he was elevated
Above everything that runs and flies and crawls.

FAR AWAY

Great love makes a great grief.
                    SKARGA

1

The chronicler is breathing, his heart is beating.
This is rare among chroniclers, for they are usually dead.
He tries to describe the earth as he remembers it
I.e., to describe on that earth his first love,
A girl bearing some ordinary name
From whom he will never again receive a letter
And who astonishes him by her strong existence
So that she seems to dictate what he writes.

It happened a long, long time ago.
In a city which was like an oratorio
Shooting with its ornate towers up to the sky
Into the white clouds, from among green hills.
We were growing there next to each other, unaware of it,
In the same legend: about a subterranean river
Nobody has ever seen, about a basilisk
Under a medieval tower, about a secret passage
Which led from the city to a remote island
With the ruins of a castle in the middle of the lake.
Every spring we took the same delight in the river:
Ice is breaking, it flows, and look, ferry boats
Painted in blue and green stripes,
And majestic raft trains drift to the sawmills.

In the sun of April we were walking in the crowd.
Expectation was timid, nameless.
And only now, when every "he loves me, loves me not"
Is fulfilled, when ridicule and grief
Are alike and I am at one
With those girls and boys, saying farewell,

I realize how strong their love was for their city.
Though they were unaware, it was to last them a lifetime.
They were destined to live through the loss of their country,
To search for a souvenir, a sign, something that does not perish.
And had I to offer a gift to her, I would choose this:
I would place her among the dreams of architecture,
There, where St. Ann and the Bernardins,
St. John and the Missionaries meet the sky.

2

In the scent of savory, there where the path
Winds down towards the alders and the rushes
Of a small lake, in the sun, beehives.
The unchanging bees of our forest country
Work, as always, on the day we perish.

She was quick. She shouted: "Now!
No time to lose!"—and they grabbed the children,
They ran that path, from the house, by the alders, into the swamp.
The soldiers came out of the birch grove, were surrounding the
     house,
They had left their truck in the woods, so as not to scare people away.
"They did not think to let the dog loose,
It would have certainly led them to us."
Thus our country was ending, still generously
Protective with its osiers, mosses, wild rosemaries.
Long trains were moving eastward, towards Asia,
With the laments of those who knew they would not return.

Bees fly, heavy, to their mead breweries,
White clouds drift slowly, reflected in the lake.
Our heritage will be handed to unknown people.
Will they respect the hives, nasturtiums by the porch,
Carefully weeded patches, the slanting apple trees?

3

But yes, the restaurant's name was "A Cozy Nook."
How could I have forgotten! Does it mean
I did not want to remember? And the city was falling
Into its sleepy moulting, into a long season
Of people I could not imagine. It hardly, hardly
Returns. Why in my poems is there so little
Autobiography? Where did it come from, the idea
To hide what is my own as if it were sick?
Then, in the "Cozy Nook" I was still one
Of the gentlemen, students, and officers, before whom
Little Matthew's waiters would put a carafe
Of vodka straight from the ice, misty with dew,
And to be adult made you proud,
Just as you felt proud coming of good stock.
This took place in a Europe of swamps and pine forests,
Of horse carts creaking on sandy highways.
Little Matthew, obliging, circulated among the tables.
Was he to become an informer? Or has he gone
To a gulag on one of the Siberian rivers?

4

How stupid is the business of the State.
I should not write about it and yet I do.
For, after all, one pities people.

Here where I live they buy and sell
Every hour of the day and night.
In halls sprinkled with bluish light they heap
Fruits brought from five continents,
Fish and meats from the East and West,
Snails and oysters summoned against the clock,
Liquors fermented in sultry valleys.
I have nothing against the Polynesias in shop windows,
Against a virgin nature at a modest price.
And if I object, I keep it to myself, it's simpler.

I am not from here. From a remote province,
From a remote continent
Where I had learned the nature of the State.

By a river in the evening, our choral singing.
We were living beyond marshes, beyond woods,
Thirty kilometers from the nearest railway station,
In manors, yeomen's lodges, farmhouses, hamlets.
Our singing was about division: this here
Is ours, that over there is alien, here poverty, there wealth,
Here ploughing, there trading, here virtue, there sin,
Here faithfulness to the ancestors, there treason,
And the worst of all, if one should sell his forest.
The oaks stood there for ages, now they were falling

With thunderous echoes, so that the earth trembled.
And then the road to our parish church
Led no more through shade with songs of birds
But through empty and silent clearings,
And that was like a presage of every kind of loss.
We implored the protection of the Miraculous Virgin,
We accompanied organ music with Latin chants.
Generation after generation we lived against the State
Which would not overcome us either with threat or punishment.
Till a perfect State appeared on the earth.

The state is perfect if it takes away
From every man his name, sex, dress, and manner,
And carries them at dawn, insane with fear,
Where, no one knows, to steppes, deserts,
So that its power is revealed
And, wallowing in their filth,
Hungry, humiliated, men renounce their right.
What did we know of this? Nothing at all.
And later on there were none among us
Who would be able to tell the world about this new knowledge.
The age passes, memory passes. Nobody will find
Letters begging for help, graves without crosses.

INHERITOR

Listen, perhaps you will hear me, young man.
Noon. Crickets sing as they did for us
A hundred years ago. A white cloud passes,
Its shadow runs beneath it, the river glitters.
Your nakedness. The echo
Of a tongue unknown to you, here, in the air,
Our words addressed to you, gentle and guiltless
Son of invaders. You do not know
What happened here. You do not seek
Faith and hope as they were practiced here,
You walk by smashed stones with the fragments of a name.
Yet this water in the sun, the scent of calamus,
The same ecstasy of discovering things
Unite us. You will find again
The sacredness they tried to expel forever.
Something returns, invisible, frail and shy,
Adoring, without name, and yet fearless.
After our despair, your hottest blood,
Your young and avid eyes succeed us.
Our heir. Now we are allowed to go.
Again, listen. Echo. Faint. Fainter.

GATHERING APRICOTS

In the sun, while there, below, over the bay
Only clouds of white mist wander, fleeting,
And the range of hills is grayish on the blue,
Apricots, the whole tree full of them, in the dark leaves,
Glimmer, yellow and red, bringing to mind
The garden of Hesperides and apples of Paradise.
I reach for a fruit and suddenly feel the presence
And put aside the basket and say: "It's a pity
That you died and cannot see these apricots,
While I celebrate this undeserved life."

COMMENTARY
Alas, I did not say what I should have.
I submitted fog and chaos to a distillation.
That other kingdom of being or non-being
Is always with me and makes itself heard
With thousands of calls, screams, complaints,
And she, the one to whom I turned,
Is perhaps but a leader of a chorus.
What happened only once does not stay in words.
Countries disappeared and towns and circumstances.
Nobody will be able to see her face.
And form itself as always is a betrayal.

MEDITATION

With an ancient love worn down by pity, anger, and solitude.
—O. V. DE L. MILOSZ

Lord, it is quite possible that people, while praising you, were
    mistaken.
You were not a ruler on a throne to whom from here below prayers
    and the smoke of incense ascend.
The throne they imagined was empty and you smiled bitterly
Seeing that they turn to you with the hope
That you will protect their crops from hail and their bodies from
    illness,
That you save them from pestilence, hunger, fire and war.
A wanderer, camping by invisible waters, you would keep a little flame
    hardly visible in darkness.
And sitting by it, pensive, you would shake your head.
So much you wanted to help them, glad any time you succeeded,
You felt compassion for them, forgiving them their mistake,
Their falsity, of which they were aware, pretending they did not
    know it,
And even their ugliness, as they gathered in their churches.
Lord, my heart is full of admiration and I want to talk with you,
For I am sure you understand me, in spite of my contradictions.
It seems to me that now I learned at last what it means to love people
And why love is worn down by loneliness, pity, and anger.
It is enough to reflect strongly and persistently on one life,
On a certain woman, for instance, as I am doing now
To perceive the greatness of those—weak—creatures
Who are able to be honest, brave in misfortune, and patient till the
    end.
What can I do more, Lord, than to meditate on all that
And stand before you in the attitude of an implorer
For the sake of their heroism asking: Admit us to your glory.

ON A BEACH

The sea breaks on the sands, I listen to its surge and close my eyes,

Here on this European shore, in the fullness of summer, after the big wars of the century.

The brows of new generations are innocent, yet marked.

Often in a crowd a face resembling—he could be one of the destroyers

If he were born a little earlier but he doesn't know it.

Chosen, as his father was, though not called.

Under my eyelids I keep their eternally young cities.

The shouts of their music, the rock pulsating, I am searching for the core of my thought.

Is it only what can't be expressed, the "ah" mumbled every day—:

The irretrievable, indifferent, eternal vanishing?

Is it pity and anger because after the ecstasy and despair and hope beings similar to gods are swallowed by oblivion?

Because in the sea's surging and silences one hears nothing about a division into the just and the wicked?

Or was I pursued by images of those who were alive for a day, an hour, a moment, under the skies?

So much, and now the peace of defeat, for my verse has preserved so little?

Or perhaps I have only heard myself whispering: "Epilogue, epilogue"?

Prophecies of my youth fulfilled but not in the way one expected.

The morning is back, and flowers are gathered in the cool of the garden by a loving hand.

A flock of pigeons soars above the valley. They turn and change color flying along the mountains.

Same glory of ordinary days and milk in a jug and crisp cherries.

And yet down below, in the very brushwood of existence, it lurks and crawls,

Recognizable by the fluttering dread of small creatures, it, implacable, steel-gray nothingness.

÷

I open my eyes, a ball flies past, a red sail leans on a wave which is blue in the gaudy sun.

Just before me a boy tests the water with his foot, and suddenly I notice he is not like others.

Not crippled, yet he has the movements of a cripple and the head of a retarded child.

His father looks after him, that handsome man sitting there on a boulder.

A sensation of my neighbor's misfortune pierces me and I begin to comprehend

In this dark age the bond of our common fate and a compassion more real than I was inclined to confess.

RETURN

In my old age I decided to visit places where I wandered long ago in my early youth.

I recognized smells, the outline of postglacial hills and oval-shaped lakes.

I forced my way through a thicket where a park was once, but I did not find the traces of the lanes.

Standing on the shore while the wave shimmered lightly as it did then, I was incomprehensibly the same, incomprehensibly different.

And yet I will not repudiate you, unlucky youngster, nor dismiss the reasons for your sufferings as foolish.

He to whom the pitiless truth of existence is suddenly unveiled, cannot but ask: How can it be?

How can it be, such an order of the world—unless it was created by a cruel demiurge?

There is nothing to esteem in the fattened wisdom of adults, and acquiescence trained in slyness is disgraceful.

Let us honor a protest against the immutable law and honor revolvers in the hands of adolescents when they refuse to participate for ever.

And then—was it not like this?—a woman's hand covers our eyes and a gift is offered: brown shields of her breasts, the ebony tuft of her belly.

How the heart beats! Only for me such happiness? Nobody knows, nobody guesses the golden marvel of her body.

Only for you? I nod and look at the lake—only for you, and thus since the millennia, so that the beauty of the earth be exalted.

And now, after a long life, grown slyly just and made wise by mere searching, I ask whether all that was worthwhile.

When doing good we also do evil, the balances evening out, that's all, and a blindly accomplished destiny.

Nobody here, I did not feel troubled spirits flying by, only the wind was bending the bullrushes, so I could not say to her: You see.

Somehow I waded through; I am grateful that I was not submitted to tests beyond my strength, and yet I still think that the human soul belongs to the anti-world.

Which is real as this one is real and horrible and comic and senseless.

I toiled and kept choosing the opposite: a perfect Nature lifted above chaos and transience, a changeless garden on the other side of time.

* * *

Large finger-like leaves of an Hawaiian fern
Seen against the sun and my joy
At the thought that they will be when I am no more.
I try to grasp what that joy signifies.

GOOD NIGHT

No duties. I don't have to be profound.
I don't have to be artistically perfect.
Or sublime. Or edifying.
I just wander. I say: "You were running,
That's fine. It was the thing to do."
And now the music of the worlds transforms me.
My planet enters a different house.
Trees and lawns become more distinct.
Philosophies one after another go out.
Everything is lighter yet not less odd.
Sauces, wine vintages, dishes of meat.
We talk a little of district fairs,
Of travels in a covered wagon with a cloud of dust behind,
Of how rivers once were, what the scent of calamus is.
That's better than examining one's private dreams.
And meanwhile it has arrived. It's here, invisible.
Who can guess how it got here, everywhere.
Let others take care of it. Time for me to play hooky.
Buena notte. Ciao. Farewell.

DECEMBER 1

The vineyard country, russet, reddish, carmine-brown in this season.
A blue outline of hills above a fertile valley.
It's warm as long as the sun does not set, in the shade cold returns.
A strong sauna and then swimming in a pool surrounded by trees.
Dark redwoods, transparent pale-leaved birches.
In their delicate network, a sliver of the moon.
I describe this for I have learned to doubt philosophy
And the visible world is all that remains.

DANTE

To be so poor. No earth, no abyss,
A revolving wheel of seasons.
People walk under the stars
And disintegrate
Into ash or a stellar dust.
Molecular machines work faultlessly, self-propelled.
Lilium columbianum opens its tiger-striped flowers
And in an instant they shrink into a sticky pulp.
Trees grow up, straight up in the air.

O alchemist Alighieri, how distant
From your harmony is that crazy sequence,
That cosmos at which I wonder and in which I vanish,
Not knowing anything about the immortal soul,
My eyes riveted to unpopulated screens.

Colorful slippers, ribbons, rings
Are sold as always on the bridge over the Arno.
I choose a gift for Theodora,
Elvira or Julia, whatever the name
Of her with whom I sleep and play chess.
In a bathroom, sitting at the edge of a tub
I look at her, flesh-colored in greenish water.
Not at her, at nakedness, which taken from us,
Abstracted, makes our bodies not our own.

Ideas, words, emotions abandon us
As if our ancestors were a different species.
It's more and more difficult to compose love songs,
Wedding canzoni, a solemn music.

And only, as once for you, this remains real:
La concreata e perpetua sete,

The inborn and the perpetual desire
Del deiformo regno—for a God-like domain,
A realm or a kingdom. There is my home.
I cannot help it. I pray for light,
For the inside of the eternal pearl, *L'etterna margarita.*

MEANING

—When I die, I will see the lining of the world.
The other side, beyond bird, mountain, sunset.
The true meaning, ready to be decoded.
What never added up will add up,
What was incomprehensible will be comprehended.

—And if there is no lining to the world?
If a thrush on a branch is not a sign,
But just a thrush on the branch? If night and day
Make no sense following each other?
And on this earth there is nothing except this earth?

—Even if that is so, there will remain
A word wakened by lips that perish,
A tireless messenger who runs and runs
Through interstellar fields, through the revolving galaxies,
And calls out, protests, screams.

KAZIA

A two-horse wagon was covered with tarpaulin stretched on boughs of hazel and in that manner we had been voyaging a couple of days, while my eyes kept starting out of my head from curiosity. Especially when we left the flat region of fields and woods for a country of hills and many lakes, of which I was to learn later that it was shaped thus by a glacier. That country revealed to me something not named, what might be called today a peaceful husbandry of man on the earth: the smoke of villages, cattle coming back from pasture, mowers with their scythes cutting oats and after-grasses, here and there a rowboat near the shore, rocked gently by a wave. Undoubtedly these things existed also elsewhere, but here they were somehow condensed into one modest space of everyday rituals and labors.

We were hospitably received for the night in a manor by a lake. My memory stops at the very border of returning there but cannot cross it and the name of the place does not appear, nor the name of our hosts, nothing except the name, Kazia, of that little girl at whom I looked, about whom I thought something, though how she looked I do not know anymore, all I know is that she was wearing a sailor's collar.

And so it is, against expectation, that Kazia or another girl, a complete stranger, accompanies us for years and we constantly ask ourselves what happened to her. For, after all, we are able, by concentrating our attention, to raise her, so to say, to the square and to make her important to us disinterestedly, since nothing sentimental colors our imaginings. This is a meditation on one of our contemporaries, how she did not choose a place or time to be born into such and such family. There is no help, I entangle her in everything that has happened since that moment, thus, the history of the century, of the country, of that region. Let us assume that she married, had a child, then was deported to Asia, starving, infected with lice, tried to save herself and her child, worked hard, discovering a dimension of existence which is better left in silence, for our notions of decency and morality have nothing to do with it. Let us assume she learned about the death of her husband in a gulag, found herself in Iran, had two husbands more, lived successively in Africa, in England, in America. And the house by the lake followed her in her dreams. Of course in my fantasies I imagine a day and a place of our meeting as two adults, which has never occurred, perhaps our affair, her nakedness, her hair, dark I am pretty certain, our basic resemblance, of a couple having the same tribe, language, manners. We have been paying too much attention to what separates people; in truth we could have been, we, the two of us, married, and it would have been fine, and our biographies would have faded in human memory as they fade now, when I have no idea what she really felt and thought, and am unable to describe it.

A PHILOSOPHER'S HOME

Pondering over the testimony of his predecessors he knew that he was entering the age of the mind. When, as they say, blood circulates more slowly, when outbursts of anger and desire are rarer and rarer, while our own existence is accepted without vain regrets, the time has arrived for liberating ourselves from the rituals of our contemporaries. Their judgements amused him. They were not founded on anything, heard once and repeated because of fashion, i.e., animal warmth. The names of their great were losing their appeal. Highly regarded works could not, at a new reading, conceal their blemishes and seemed mediocre.

Deprived of many illusions, the mind abandoned itself the more eagerly to voyaging amidst the phenomena, i.e., all things that appear to us by the intermediary of the senses. The door of a car slams and a woman in a green overcoat quickly runs up a few steps; votive candles are lit on the terrace of a Shintoist temple; a barman serves a drink to a man in a crumpled hat; a scream "ouch!" at hurting herself with a needle; at a florist, the cut ends of stems while the hand of the seller composes a bouquet; lean dogs in refuse-heaped outskirts under the smoke of mills; glittering multi-colored lines of freeways in a metropolis; the feet of a homeless man sticking out in a corridor of a metro. Circumstances and coincidences, such as are or might have been, all those "because ofs," "if nots," and "if onlys." Also, an infinite number of theories, theses, beliefs, hypotheses, appeals, avowals in the sounds of speech, in the letters of a written language. The mind marvelled at that overflowing multiplicity: it sneaked into a secret session of the Venetian Council of Ten, participated in the invention of cuneiform writing, was entering a crusader's tent and looking at the head of a sleeping woman, was flying over a clearing on the plateau of an island where our brethren the cannibals performed their dances.

Simultaneous multiplicity, in every minute and second of the existence of the world, but also another kind, extending across years, centuries, a thousand and a million years, and millions of years. And everywhere the mind was allowed to travel; light and fleshless, it was soaring over the earth before man, watching eruptions of volcanoes and the pastures of dinosaurs.

Meditating on that privilege of the mind, he was astonished by the lack of its resemblance to the body which soon would die, but also by its, the mind's, greed which can never be satisfied. For the more it wanted to embrace, the more those things which escaped it grew in size. And that disparity between striving and achieving was the source of the pious awe of philosophers, at least of the school to which he himself wished to belong.

Is it possible, he asked himself, that this spectacle of the incredible multitude of forms, each of them appearing in a definite point of time, proper to it only, is it possible that this breath-taking spectacle is played for nobody? Does not the mind, as it possesses a never assuaged desire for detail, show by its very nature its affinity to an absolute mind, a witness present in every moment of space-time? Indeed, this theatre must have a spectator, even if the actors are not aware of him, just as a blade of grass is not aware of human eyes which look at it. Let us repeat then a maxim more important now than at any other time: *esse* is *percipi*, to be is to be perceived.

COMMENTARY

Philosophers have a measure of time that is different from that of ordinary mortals. They converse with Plato, listen to the arguments of Thomas Aquinas, visit Spinoza's study. The philosopher who speaks in *A Philosopher's Home* has been, however, shaped in the first place by what surrounded him in the twentieth century. It is not difficult to notice that his gluttony for images has much in common with the eye of a movie camera, and he probably quite often travelled merely by sitting before a screen. The camera did not only provide him with pictures taken in various countries of the earth, for it plunged into the depths of the sea, into the interstellar spaces, and even reached other planets. Wherever he turned, he saw photographs of people upon the background of rural and urban landscapes, he caught and retained moments of their labors and leisure, of their loves and wars. Espying their denuded bodies, in health and beauty, in withering and illness, in starvation and in agony from wounds, in the triumphs of victory in sports. He must have also liked pornographic photographs and films which dissolve our individual features in a universally practiced activity of incomparable ludicrousness.

And books—for he undoubtedly glimpsed into the kind of books not accessible to any of his distinguished predecessors. They described and illustrated life in ancient China and ancient Egypt, Greece, the islands of Polynesia. He was becoming acquainted with the shapes of clay vats for wine, with various types of sails, with colors of wedding dresses, with the art of constructing siege-trains and making a silver handle for brushes to paint the eyelids. The history of our species opened to him as read anew from remnants of mosaics, from the contents of a tomb where the dead had reposed in silence and peace for three thousand years, from newly found poems whose authors will forever remain nameless. Or he wondered at the incessant changeability of the so-called live nature whose scenes from millennia before were described by zealous partisans of the theory of evolution.

From what he says we can also deduce that he had visited museums and galleries of art where the hand of an artist stops a year, a day, an instant and all he touched persists though it happened long ago. We may suspect him of having the habits of a stroller through galleries and guess in his reasoning the hidden passion of a collector, or the curator of an immense museum of things once seen.

Thus, paradoxically, the twentieth century directed the philosopher towards the idea of an Eye (we remember the eye in a triangle) which is the eye of a universal witness, even, who knows, of a super-curator of the universe or the owner of a movie camera absolutely perfect, for it is pointed towards everything. Even if philosophers of old meditated upon the omniscience of God, besides trying in vain to solve the riddle of Providence, no one of them chose for a point of departure certain traits of our mind intensified by technology. They would humanize the Highest, ascribing to Him human feelings and human will, but they never tried to endow Him with the passionate zeal of a photo-reporter.

FACING

THE RIVER

(Na brzegu rzeki)

1995

AT A CERTAIN AGE

We wanted to confess our sins but there were no takers.
White clouds refused to accept them, and the wind
Was too busy visiting sea after sea.
We did not succeed in interesting the animals.
Dogs, disappointed, expected an order,
A cat, as always immoral, was falling asleep.
A person seemingly very close
Did not care to hear of things long past.
Conversations with friends over vodka or coffee
Ought not be prolonged beyond the first sign of boredom.
It would be humiliating to pay by the hour
A man with a diploma, just for listening.
Churches. Perhaps churches. But to confess there what?
That we used to see ourselves as handsome and noble
Yet later in our place an ugly toad
Half-opens its thick eyelid
And one sees clearly: "That's me."

A LECTURE

A certain student in the city of Paris
Coming from countries called Nowhere
Once got a ticket to a lecture
By a famous poet, of the Académie
    Française.

Duchesses and countesses
In gowns of high fashion
In exquisite coiffures
Were honoring the poet.
They, as everyone knew,
Organized for him those evenings
Attended by every person of
    distinction.

Paul Valéry looked exactly
Like his photographs:
A close-trimmed mustache,
A clear-eyed, attentive
Boy who had gone gray
And was, as always, quick.

He arranged pages on the table.
His hands were precise.
He read logical sequences
Of main and subordinate clauses,
Discussing permanent features
Of aesthetic experience
That confirm the eternal
Attraction of art.

His listener, that student,
Was busy elsewhere:

His hair stood on end,
His ear caught the screams of a hunt,
He was fleeing across frozen fields
Where behind rimed barbed wire
The miserable souls of his friends
And enemies would remain.

Yet he was clever enough
To admire the poet
For his polite acceptance
Of unpleasant circumstances:
These ladies of good will,
The snobs and their approbation,
The cannibalism and wars
Of his century.

For the speaker only pretended
To be among them, with them.
In truth, sitting in his workshop
He was counting verse syllables.
A servant of architecture,
A grower of crystals,
He shunned the unreasonable
Affairs of mortals.

And alas, alas, it passed—
The rejoicing and weeping,
Believing and despairing,
Debasement and terror.
Wind covered the signs with snow,
The earth took in the screams,
No one anymore remembers
How and when it occurred.

And only the sumptuous, golden
Decasyllabic verse
Lasts and will last for its own
Harmonious reason.
And I, late, am returning
With a shred of bitterness
To his cemetery by the sea,
In the always commencing noon.

WHY

Why hasn't it risen, the powerful hymn?
Of thanksgiving, of eternal glory?

Have not the prayers of the humiliated been heard?
The bereft of their possessions, the slandered, the murdered, the
    tortured behind barbed wire?

He broke the teeth from the jaw that devoured the humble.
He overthrew the strong one who was to rule for centuries.

Monuments of boastful theory lie between nettles.
Darkness descended on the infallible empire.

Is it because generations waited for justice in vain
That faith in superterrestrial verdicts has been abandoned?

And the unending valley of faces deprived of hope
Forbids rejoicing to those who are alive.

No *Te Deum* has been sung to praise the Lord of Hosts.
The name of the Hidden God is being pronounced in
    silence.

No painting represents the Warrior in shining armor,
The one who strolls in white clouds over a battlefield.

Who says: "Mine is the punishing arm,
I choose the one day and the one hour in a thousand years."

We were safe behind the shield of his protection.
Misfortunes besieged us but did not prevail.

Where are the solemn assemblies of peoples under a sky pierced by the
    lightning of the One and Holy?
Where is contrite meditation on His deed?

Fearful, they rub their eyes, knowing only that there is no limit to
    evil.
Enough to shout joyfully, and evil will return with force.

They still look for signs in the sky, for fiery circles, rods and crosses.
Remembering the word History, the second name of which is
    Annihilation.

CAPRI

I am a child who receives First Communion in Wilno and afterwards drinks cocoa served by zealous Catholic ladies.

I am an old man who remembers that day in June: the ecstasy of the sinless, white tablecloth and the sun on vases filled with peonies.

Qu'as tu fait, qu'as tu fait de ta vie?—voices call, in various languages gathered in your wanderings through two continents. What did you do with your life, what did you do?

Slowly, cautiously, now when destiny is fulfilled I enter the scenes of the bygone time,

Of my century, in which, and not in any other, I was ordered to be born, to work, and to leave a trace.

Those Catholic ladies existed, after all, and if I returned there now, identical but with another consciousness, I would look intensely at their faces, trying to prevent their fading away.

Also, carriages and rumps of horses illuminated by lightning or by the pulsating flow of distant artillery.

Chimneyless huts, smoke billowing on their roofs, and wide sandy roads in pine forests.

Countries and cities that must remain without name, for how can I explain why and how many times they changed their banners and emblems?

Early we receive a call, yet it remains incomprehensible, and only late do we discover how obedient we were.

The river rolls its waters past, as it did long ago, the church of St. Jacob, I am there together with my foolishness, which is shameful, but had I been wiser it would not have helped.

Now I know foolishness is necessary in all our designs, so that they are realized, awkwardly and incompletely.

And this river, together with heaps of garbage on its banks, with the beginning of pollution, flows through my youth, a warning against the longing for ideal places on the earth.

Yet, there, on that river, I experienced full happiness, a ravishment beyond any thought or concern, still lasting in my body.

Just like the happiness by the small river of my childhood, in a park whose oaks and lindens were to be cut down by the will of barbarous conquerors.

I bless you, rivers, I pronounce your names in the way my mother pronounced them, with respect yet tenderly.

Who will dare to say: I was called and that's the reason Might protected me from bullets ripping up the sand close by me, or drawing patterns on the wall above my head.

From a casual arrest just for elucidating the case, which would end with a journey in a freight car to a place from which the living do not return?

From obeying the order to register, when only the disobedient would survive?

Yes, but what about them, has not every one of them prayed to his God, begging: Save me!

And the sun was rising over camps of torture and even now with their eyes I see it rising.

I reach eighty, I fly from San Francisco to Frankfurt and Rome, a passenger who once traveled three days by horse carriage from Szetejnie to Wilno.

I fly Lufthansa, how nice that stewardess is, all of them are so civilized that it would be tactless to remember who they were.

On Capri a rejoicing and banqueting humanity invites me to take part in the festivity of incessant renewal.

Naked arms of women, a hand driving a bow across the strings, among evening gowns, glares and flashes open for me a moment of assent to the frivolity of our species.

They do not need a belief in Heaven and Hell, labyrinths of philosophy, mortification of the flesh by fasting.

And yet they are afraid of a sign that the unavoidable is close: a tumor in the breast, blood in the urine, high blood pressure.

Then they know for certain that all of us are called, and each of us meditates on the extravagance of having a separate fate.

Together with my epoch I go away, prepared for a verdict, that will count me among its phantoms.

If I accomplished anything, it was only when I, a pious boy, chased after the disguises of the lost Reality.

After the real presence of divinity in our flesh and blood which are at the same time bread and wine,

Hearing the immense call of the Particular, despite the earthly law that sentences memory to extinction.

REPORT

O Most High, you willed to create me a poet and now it is time for me to present a report.

My heart is full of gratitude though I got acquainted with the miseries of that profession.

By practicing it, we learn too much about the bizarre nature of man.

Who, every hour, every day and every year is possessed by self-delusion.

A self-delusion when building sandcastles, collecting postage stamps, admiring oneself in a mirror.

Assigning oneself first place in sport, power, love, and the getting of money.

All the while on the very border, on the fragile border beyond which there is a province of mumblings and wails.

For in every one of us a mad rabbit thrashes and a wolf pack howls, so that we are afraid it will be heard by others.

Out of self-delusion comes poetry and poetry confesses to its flaw.

Though only by remembering poems once written is their author able to see the whole shame of it.

And yet he cannot bear another poet nearby, if he suspects him of being better than himself and envies him every scrap of praise.

Ready not only to kill him but smash him and obliterate him from the surface of the earth.

So that he remains alone, magnanimous and kind toward his subjects, who chase after their small self-delusions.

How does it happen then that such low beginnings lead to the splendor of the word?

I gathered books of poets from various countries, now I sit reading them and am astonished.

It is sweet to think that I was a companion in an expedition that never ceases, though centuries pass away.

An expedition not in search of the golden fleece of a perfect form but as necessary as love.

Under the compulsion of the desire for the essence of the oak, of the mountain peak, of the wasp and of the flower of nasturtium.

So that they last, and confirm our hymnic song against death.

And our tender thought about all who lived, strived, and never succeeded in naming.

For to exist on the earth is beyond any power to name.

Fraternally, we help each other, forgetting our grievances, translating each other into other tongues, members, indeed, of a wandering crew.

How then could I not be grateful, if early I was called and the incomprehensible contradiction has not diminished my wonder?

At every sunrise I renounce the doubts of night and greet the new day of a most precious delusion.

LITHUANIA, AFTER FIFTY-TWO YEARS

A Goddess

Gaia, first-born daughter of Chaos,
Adorned with grasses and trees, gladdens our eyes
So that we can agree when naming what is beautiful
And share with all earthly wanderers our joy.

Let us give thanks in our own and our ancestors' name
For oaks and their rough-barked dignity,
For pines, their trunks flaming in the sun,
For clear green clouds of vernal birch groves
And for the candlesticks of the autumnal wilderness, aspens.

How many kinds of pear and apple trees in our gardens!
(Arranged as described in *The Northern Gardens* of Strumillo),
Currants, gooseberries, dogberries, barberries
For a great boiling of preserves
When the faces of our housewives are reddened by their long stay
 by the stove.

There was a separate corner for medicinal herbs,
Those which were grown at the advice of Gizycki's *Economical-
 Technological Herbarium.*
From them elixirs and ointments for the manor's pharmacy.

And mushroom gathering! Sturdy boletus in the oakwoods.
Strings of them, one by another, drying under the eaves.
A hunter's trumpet is heard when we search for milk cups
And our knives are stained yellow-red by their juices.

Gaia! Whatever happens, preserve at least your seasons.
Emerge from under the snows with the trickling of rivulets in springs,
Dress yourself for those who will live after us
If only in the green of mid-city parks
And the blossoming of dwarf apple trees in garden plots at the edge of cities.
I depose my petition, your lowly son.

The Manor

There is no house, only the park, though the oldest trees have been
    cut down.
And a thicket overgrows the traces of former alleys.
The granary has been dismantled, white, castlelike,
With cellars where the shelves harbored winter apples.
The same ruts as long ago on the sloping road,
I remembered where to turn but did not recognize the river.
Its color like that of reddish automobile oil,
No rushes and no lily pads.
The linden alley, dear to bees, is gone
And the orchards, a realm of wasps and hornets drunk with sweetness,
Disappeared, crumbled into thistles and nettles.
This place and I, though far away,
Simultaneously, year after year, were losing leaves.
Were covered with snow, were waning.
And again we are gathered in our common old age.

My interest turns to the smoke from a metal pipe instead of a chimney
Above a cabin haphazardly patched up with boards and bricks
In the green of weeds and bushes—I recognize *Sambucus nigra*.

Blessed be life, for lasting, poorly, anyhow.
They were eating their noodles and potatoes
And at least had the use of all the old gardens
To cut wood for burning in our long winters.

A Certain Neighborhood

I told nobody I was familiar with that neighborhood.
Why should I? As if a hunter with a spear
Materialized, looking for something he once knew.
After many incarnations we return to the earth,
Uncertain we would recognize its face.
Where there were villages and orchards, now nothing, fields.
Instead of old timber, young groves,
The level of the waters is lower, the swamp disappeared
Together with the scent of *ledum*, black grouse, and adders.
A little river should be here. Yes, but hidden in the brush,
Not, as before, amidst meadows. And the two ponds
Must have covered themselves with duckweed
Before they sank into black loam.
The glitter of a small lake, but its shores lack the rushes
Through which we struggled forward, swimming,
To dry ourselves afterwards, I and Miss X, and one towel, dancing.

A Naiad

The only proof of the existence of Miss X
Is my writing. As long as I am here
She lives not far from the places she loved.

Her hair was dark blond, nearly chestnut,
Of a tint common among the girls of our gentry.
Her eyes were gray, rarely blue,
More often greenish, the cut of her eyelids
Somewhat oriental. Her cheeks
Would have been protruding if not for her oblong face.
Yet in the arches of her eyebrows something Japanese.

If not for the secret of each singular *anima*
Scoffers would have been right, the trace of a human vanishes.

Yet she is here, in her country
Like an invisible naiad from Mickiewicz's ballad "I Love It."
She will be permitted to go away or rather to fly away
Simultaneously with my disappearance from this world.

Who?

Beyond the red traffic light, young chestnut leaves.
Who is the one who seeing it,
Where does he come from, where will he disappear to,
Who is the one, instead of him,
Who will be seeing the same but not the same thing,
Because of a different pulsation of the blood?

And limbs of huge trees over a steep road,
Leaning into each other, and in that lane,
Beyond the colonnade of trunks, an open brightness.
For whom is this? And how does it vary?
Is it present every time or just imaginary?

Be yourselves, things of this earth, be yourselves!
Don't rely on us, on our breath,
On the fancies of our treacherous and avid eye.
We long for you, for your essence,
For you to last as you are in yourselves:
Pure, not looked at by anybody.

CITY OF MY YOUTH

It would be more decorous not to live. To live is not decorous,
Says he who after many years
Returned to the city of his youth. There was no one left
Of those who once walked these streets.
And now they had nothing, except his eyes.
Stumbling, he walked and looked, instead of them,
On the light they had loved, on the lilacs again in bloom.
His legs were, after all, more perfect
Than nonexistent legs. His lungs breathed in air
As is usual with the living. His heart was beating,
Surprising him with its beating, in his body
Their blood flowed, his arteries fed them with oxygen.
He felt, inside, their livers, spleens, intestines.
Masculinity and femininity, elapsed, met in him
And every shame, every grief, every love.
If ever we accede to enlightenment,
He thought, it is in one compassionate moment
When what separated them from me vanishes
And a shower of drops from a bunch of lilacs
Pours on my face, and hers, and his, at the same time.

A MEADOW

It was a riverside meadow, lush, from before the hay harvest,
On an immaculate day in the sun of June.
I searched for it, found it, recognized it.
Grasses and flowers grew there familiar in my childhood.
With half-closed eyelids I absorbed luminescence.
And the scent garnered me, all knowing ceased.
Suddenly I felt I was disappearing and weeping with joy.

TRANSLATING ANNA SWIR ON AN ISLAND OF THE CARIBBEAN

By banana plants, on a deck chair, by the pool
Where Carol, naked, swims her laps
Of the crawl and the classical style, I interrupt her
Asking for a synonym. And again I am submerged
In the murmuring Polish, in meditation.

Because of the impermanence of the mind and the body,
Because of your tender embracing of our fate,
I call you in and you will be among people,
Though you have written in a poem: "There is no me."
"What a joy there is no me."
Which means neither: "I do not exist,"
Nor: "*Je n'existe pas*," and is pure Slavic:
"*Mene netu*," somewhat Oriental.

And, indeed, by praising being:
  The delight of touch in lovemaking, the delight of
   running on a beach,
  of wandering in the mountains, even of raking hay

You were disappearing, in order to be, unpersonally.

When I saw you for the last time
I understood why they liked neither you
Nor your poetry. With that white mane of yours
You could ride a broom, have a devil for a lover.
And you arrogantly proclaimed
Your philosophy of the big toe,
Of the female split, of the pulse, of the large intestine.

The definition of that poetry: Whatever we do,
Desiring, loving, possessing, suffering,
Is always only meanwhile.

For there must be something else, true and stable.
Though nobody knows what eternity is.

And the body is most mysterious,
For, so mortal, it wants to be pure,
Liberated from the soul which screams: "I!"

A metaphysical poet, Anna Swir
Felt best when she was standing on her head.

TO MY DAIMONION

I

Please, my daimonion, ease off just a bit,
I am still closing accounts and have much to tell.
Your rhythmical whispers intimidate me.
Today for instance, reading about a certain old woman
I saw again—let us call her Priscilla,
Though I am astonished that I can give her any name
And people will not care. So, that Priscilla,
Her gums in poor shape, an old hag,
Is the one to whom I return, in order to throw charms
And grant her eternal youth. I introduce a river,
Green hills, irises wet with rain
And, of course, a conversation. "You know," I say,
"I could never guess what was on your mind
And will never learn. I have a question
That won't be answered." And you, daimonion,
Just at this moment interfere, interrupt us, averse to
Surnames and family names' actualities,
Too prosaic and ridiculous, no doubt.

II

My daimonion, it is certain I could not have lived differently.
I would have perished if not for you. Your incantation
Would resound in my ear, fill me,
And I could only repeat it, instead of thinking
About my bad character, the decline of the world,
Or about a lost laundry ticket.
And it seems that while others loved,
Strove, hated, despaired,
I have only been busy with listening intently
To your unclear notes, to change them into words.
I had to accept my fate, called today karma,
For it was as it was, though I did not choose it—
And get up every day to honor the work,
Even if there is no guilt of mine in it and no merit.

III

Two five-year-old boys before the poster of a nightclub,
On which a buoyant girl adjusts her garter,
Say something to each other or just stare
At the saurian whiteness of the thigh.

Daimonion, remembering my childhood fears
On this earth of the adults, I grasped who you are.

In their night of distant shooting, fires on the horizon,
Coarse laughter, grapplings, harsh breathing,
The heart of a child is troubled. And you, a wanderer,
Your pity is so strong that you avert your face.

You are a friend of the innocent and the defenseless
Who long for the Kingdom, as was that young rich man
So pure that he blushed hearing a lewd word,
And really suffered from it, and probably for that reason
After his short life, they raised him on the altars.

THE WALL OF A MUSEUM

That was an imprinted effigy of a river:
The flow of a knotty main branch, twigs of confluence,
As if they wanted to merge,
Trees and swift water, the best things on earth.
The façade, inlaid with marble panels,
Towered over a plain of rotting streets,
Some of them, without end, stretched beyond the horizon,
Where, in the smoke of garbage cans, in leprous desolation,
The poor squat, intent on killing each other,
And, arms ready, police cars make rounds.
When the bus took us to a ritual at the museum,
We heard beyond the windows yells, jeering,
Then we were met by smiles and silence.

BIOGRAPHY OF AN ARTIST

So much guilt behind them and such beauty!
These landscapes, in the quiet splendor
Of early summer, toward evening, these coves
Of lakes amid lush green, when, for welcome,
Messengers come running, in saffron robes,
And bring gifts, huge balls made of light.
Or his portraits. Is not tenderness
Needed to drive a brush with such attention
Along the eyelids of a sorrowing eye
Through the furrow at lips closed by grief?
And how could he do it? Knowing what we know
About his life, every day aware
Of harm he did to others. I think he was aware.
Just not concerned, he promised his soul to Hell,
Provided that his work remained clear and pure.

THE GARDEN OF EARTHLY DELIGHTS: HELL

If not for the existence of Earth, would there be a Hell?
The instruments of torture are man-made:
Kitchen knives, choppers, drills, enemas.
And implements to create the hellish noise:
Trombones, drums, a mechanical flute, a harp
With a poor damned man entwined in its strings.
The waters in Hell are set by the cold of eternal winter.
Mass meetings, military parades on ice
Under the blood-red and smoke-dark glow of burning cities.
Fire blazing from windows—not sparks, human figures,
Small and black, fly out and then fall into a chasm.
Dirty taverns with wobbly tables. Women in kerchiefs
Cheap, you can have them for a pound of meat,
And a multitude of busy henchmen,
Deft, well trained in their trade.
Thus it's possible to conjecture that mankind exists
To provision and to populate Hell,
The name of which is duration. As to the rest,
Heavens, abysses, orbiting worlds, they just flicker a moment.
Time in Hell does not want to stop. It's fear and boredom together
(Which, after all, happens). And we, frivolous,
Always in pursuit and always with hope,
Fleeting, just like our dances and dresses,
Let us beg to be spared from entering
A permanent condition.

REALISM

We are not so badly off, if we can
Admire Dutch painting. For that means
We shrug off what we have been told
For a hundred, two hundred years. Though we lost
Much of our previous confidence. Now we agree
That those trees outside the window, which probably exist,
Only pretend to greenness and treeness
And that the language loses when it tries to cope
With clusters of molecules. And yet, this here:
A jar, a tin plate, a half-peeled lemon,
Walnuts, a loaf of bread, last—and so strongly
It is hard not to believe in their lastingness.
And thus abstract art is brought to shame,
Even if we do not deserve any other.
Therefore I enter those landscapes
Under a cloudy sky from which a ray
Shoots out, and in the middle of dark plains
A spot of brightness glows. Or the shore
With huts, boats, and on yellowish ice
Tiny figures skating. All this
Is here eternally, just because once it was.
Splendor (certainly incomprehensible)
Touches a cracked wall, a refuse heap,
The floor of an inn, jerkins of the rustics,
A broom, and two fish bleeding on a board.
Rejoice! Give thanks! I raised my voice
To join them in their choral singing,
Amid their ruffles, collets, and silk skirts,
One of them already, who vanished long ago.
And our song soared up like smoke from a censer.

ONE MORE CONTRADICTION

Did I fulfill what I had to, here, on earth?
I was a guest in a house under white clouds
Where rivers flow and grasses renew themselves.
So what if I were called, if I was hardly aware.
The next time early I would search for wisdom.
I would not pretend I could be just like others:
Only evil and suffering come from that.
Renouncing, I would choose the fate of obedience.
I would suppress my wolf's eye and greedy throat.
A resident of some cloister floating in the air
With a view on the cities glowing below,
Or onto a stream, a bridge and old cedars,
I would give myself to one task only
Which then, however, could not be accomplished.

WOE!

It is true, our tribe is similar to the bees.
It gathers honey of wisdom, carries it, stores it in honeycombs.
I am able to roam for hours
Through the labyrinth of the main library, floor to floor.
But yesterday, looking for the words of masters and prophets
I wandered into high regions
That are visited by practically no one.
I would open a book and could decipher nothing
For letters faded and disappeared from the pages.
Woe! I exclaimed—so it comes to this?
Where are you, venerable one, with your beards and wigs,
Your nights spent by a candle, griefs of your wives?
So a message saving the world is silenced forever?

At your home it was the day of making preserves.
And your dog, sleeping by the fire, would wake up,
Yawn and look at you—as if knowing.

PIERSON COLLEGE

The wrought iron of the gate at Pierson College
And my stint there, which resembles
Nothing in my past life. Forgetting
And remembering. Both, how strange.
That old professor with an accent,
Who gives a seminar on *The Possessed* and reads
In the Beinecke Library manuscripts:
Joseph Conrad's *Heart of Darkness*
Hurriedly written with a pencil, a neat
Script of the novel *Razumov*
Called later *Under Western Eyes.*
Is he identical with a boy
Who, starting from Bouffalowa Hill
Would walk Louis home along Mala Pohulanka
And then goes to Tomasz Zan Library
To get a book of sea adventures?
On the very edge. Just before falling:
Now, here. Before "I" changes into "he."

Quality passes into quantity at the century's end
For worse or better, who knows, just different.
Though for those students no Louis ever
Existed and the old professor's passionate tone
Is a bit ridiculous as if the fate of the world depended on truth.

SARAJEVO

—Perhaps this is not a poem but at least I say what I feel

Now that a revolution really is needed, those who once were fervent are quite cool.

While a country murdered and raped calls for help from the Europe which it had trusted, they yawn.

While statesmen choose villainy and no voice is raised to call it by name.

The rebellion of the young who called for a new earth was a sham, and that generation has written the verdict on itself,

Listening with indifference to the cries of those who perish because they are after all just barbarians killing each other

And the lives of the well-fed are worth more than the lives of the starving.

It is revealed now that their Europe since the beginning has been a deception, for its faith and its foundation is nothingness.

And nothingness, as the prophets keep saying, brings forth only nothingness, and they will be led once again like cattle to slaughter.

Let them tremble and at the last moment comprehend that the word Sarajevo will from now on mean the destruction of their sons and the debasement of their daughters.

They prepare it by repeating: "We at least are safe," unaware that what will strike them ripens in themselves.

TO ALLEN GINSBERG

Allen, you good man, great poet of the murderous century, who persisting in folly attained wisdom.

I confess to you, my life was not as I would have liked it to be.

And now, when it has passed, is lying like a discarded tire by the road.

It was no different from the life of millions against which you rebelled in the name of poetry and of an omnipresent God.

It was submitted to customs in full awareness that they are absurd, to the necessity of getting up in the morning and going to work.

With unfulfilled desires, even with the unfulfilled desire to scream and beat one's head against the wall, repeating to myself the command "It is forbidden."

It is forbidden to indulge yourself, to allow yourself idleness, it is forbidden to think of your past, to look for the help of a psychiatrist or a clinic.

Forbidden from a sense of duty but also because of the fear of unleashing forces that would reveal one to be a clown.

And I lived in the America of Moloch, short-haired, clean-shaven, tying neckties and drinking bourbon before the TV set every evening.

Diabolic dwarfs of temptations somersaulted in me, I was aware of their presence and I shrugged: It will pass together with life.

Dread was lurking close, I had to pretend it was never there and that I was united with others in a blessed normalcy.

Such schooling in vision is also, after all, possible, without drugs, without the cut-off ear of Van Gogh, without the brotherhood of the best minds behind the bars of psychiatric wards.

I was an instrument, I listened, snatching voices out of a babbling chorus, translating them into sentences with commas and periods.

As if the poverty of my fate were necessary so that the flora of my memory could luxuriate, a home for the breath and for the presence of bygone people.

I envy your courage of absolute defiance, words inflamed, the fierce maledictions of a prophet.

The demure smiles of ironists are preserved in the museums, not as everlasting art, just as a memento of unbelief.

While your blasphemous howl still resounds in a neon desert where the human tribe wanders, sentenced to unreality.

Walt Whitman listens and says, "Yes, that's the way to talk, in order to conduct men and women to where everything is fulfillment. Where they would live in a transubstantiated moment."

And your journalistic clichés, your beard and beads and your dress of a rebel of another epoch are forgiven.

As we do not look for what is perfect, we look for what remains of incessant striving.

Keeping in mind how much is owed to luck, to a coincidence of words and things, to a morning with white clouds, which later seems inevitable.

I do not ask from you a monumental *oeuvre* that would rise like a medieval cathedral over a French flatland.

I myself had such a hope, yet half-knowing already that the unusual changes into the common.

That in the planetary mixture of languages and religions we are no more remembered than the inventors of the spinning wheel or of the transistor.

Accept this tribute from me, who was so different, yet in the same unnamed service.

For lack of a better term letting it pass as the practice of composing verses.

A HUMAN FLY

Crowds, streetcars stopped—is it a demonstration?
In the city of Oakland, in the year 1919?
All of them, obviously, in hats, looking up.
No, not at a speaker. It is a human fly
Who climbs vertically the wall of a building.

O miserable human fly, arms spread aloft,
You move inch by inch, testing a handhold.
And below, those hats. Will he fall? Or make it?

They stand in the photograph, lovers of plebeian games,
Of matches in a ring, acrobatics under the tent of a wandering circus,
Of catch-as-catch-can, of blood in the arena.
I am not a lover of mankind, though I pretended,
As if my tender skin, my fastidiousness were not against.

—But these here, hot-blooded, how many eyes,
Muscles, varieties of chin, shapes of lips,
All must be dead.
They are shadows, no more.

—And it is just that such a short existence had been their store.

HOUSE IN KRASNOGRUDA

I

The woods reached water and there was immense silence.
A crested grebe popped up on the surface of the lake,
In deep water, very still, a flock of teals.
That's what was seen by a man on the shore
Who decided to build his house here
And to cut down the primeval oak forest.
He was thinking of timber he would float down the Niemen
And of thalers he would count by candlelight.

II

The ash trees in the park calmed down after the storm.
The young lady runs down a path to the lake
She pulls her dress over her head
(She does not wear panties though Mademoiselle gets angry),
And there is a delight in the water's soft touch
When she swims, dog-style, self-taught,
Toward brightness, beyond the shade of the trees.

III

The company settles into a boat, ladies and gentlemen
In swimming suits. Just as they will be remembered
By a frail boy whose lifeline is short.
In the evening he learns to dance the tango. Mrs. Irena
Leads him, with that smirk of a mature woman
Who initiates a young male.
Out the door to the veranda owls are hooting.

A POLKA-DOT DRESS

Her polka-dot dress—that's all I know of her.
Once, walking silently with my gun in a forest thicket
I stumbled upon her lying with Michael
On a blanket spread in the clearing.
A plump little thing,
They say she was an officer's wife.
Her name must have been Zosia.

To the black waters I arrived at dusk.
All of them are dead, it was long ago.

Peace to you, Zosia, and to your adventures.

Going on a vacation, is it not usual
To expect that something might happen:
A dark-haired man from the cards, or a blond one like Michael,
Just for some change in everyday yawning,
Calls to a girlfriend, cake in a tea shop.
We are induced to sin by boredom and curiosity,
But besides that we are innocent.

You should understand, Zosia, what trouble I have
When I want to think of your life attentively
And find here, where you are mine, what is unique
In you, though it's covered by common form.

Perhaps you helped build a barricade.
Perhaps you sacrificed yourself for a sick child.
Perhaps, suffering pain from a wound or illness,
You came to a high degree of resignation.
However it was, whether you perished with your burning city,

Or, old, wandered in it, not recognizing the streets,
I try to be everywhere with you, yet in vain.
And all I can do is touch your too-round breasts
Remembering your dress, red, with white polka-dots.

PLATO'S DIALOGUES

Always at the end of the week my father and I would go to the sauna on Tartar Street.

There was a solemnity in our being allotted narrow sofas in a common hall with compartments like those in a railway wagon.

And in our opening the door into everything different, dense steam darkening the light of the bulbs and making the naked figures hardly visible.

From a faucet one would fill a wooden bucket with cold water for dousing one's head, and carry it to the highest shelf, as high as one could bear, among the roars of naked males lashing themselves with birch rods.

Virile ambition required one to stay there till the skin, made oversensitive by heat, would feel every touch of the rod as a whiplash.

Emitting roars belonged to the rite and testified that one was reaching the limit of endurance.

Upon our return to the hall we would listen to conversations conducted by fat men, everyone on his sofa, wrapped in his sheet:

Permanent customers, well-to-do artisans, police officers, and Jewish merchants.

Their conversations would not deserve the name of Plato's dialogues, but almost.

UNDRESSING JUSTINE

On the Banks of the Niemen was published in 1888. This bucolic Polish novel is the work of Eliza Orzeszkowa, one of the "emancipated" women of that time. Although Orzeszkowa received only the superficial education proper to young ladies of the manor, political events catapulted her into an independent literary career. Because of a Polish uprising against Russia in 1863, her husband was deported to Siberia. The marriage—unsuccessful from the start—disintegrated, but divorce proceedings dragged on for years. Her farm was confiscated, and she herself, considered a dangerous democrat by the tzarist authorities, was placed under police surveillance; for most of her life she was forced to live in the provincial town of Grodno (in what is now Belarus). She turned to writing to sustain herself. A virtual prisoner, she acquired (through extensive reading in several languages) a wide education, and her stories and novels defended the cause of the underprivileged, that is, women and Jews. Her characters were drawn from the people she observed in her province—peasants, Jewish artisans, and the petty gentry.

On the Banks of the Niemen takes place in a village and its neighboring manor. In the manor lives a young woman named Justine, a poor cousin of the owner. Instead of looking to a marriage that would free her from her lowly position, she falls in love with Jan, a lad of the village, and marries him, thus affirming her readiness to labor with her hands and assume the status of a peasant. The novel is full of political allusions, somewhat toned down because of censorship. A few miles from the village, in the forest, is the mass grave of the insurrectionists of 1863, where many boys from the village are buried. Jan and Justine's visits to the grave strengthen the bond between them through the awareness of a common cause. They also pay visits to the preserved tomb of the founders of the village, Jan and Cecilia. According to legend, a girl of royal blood, a long, long time ago, eloped with a commoner, and the couple came to live in the primeval forest, gradually clearing it and settling with their progeny; all the inhabitants of the village bear the same name, Bohatyrowicz, and boast a coat of arms given to them by a king who, while hunting, stumbled by chance upon a flourishing settlement in the depths of the forest. These two graves carry the novel's message about the value of tradition, of an un-interrupted continuity, passed from generation to generation, of attachment to ancestral land.

÷

The candles burned out long ago, Justine.
Other people walk your paths by the Niemen.
While I enter into a union with you, quite amorous.
I touch the heavy black tresses
That you, just now, are loosening. I weigh in my palm
Your no doubt abundant breast. I look in the mirror
At your gray eyes and the deep red of your lips.
You are big, strong, broad-shouldered.
Twenty-four, you don't like to be called
Young lady. And your dreams are telling.
No reason to be ashamed in front of me, who comes from an
    epoch
That will be called shameless. Mrs. Orzeszkowa
Would stop her pen. Your romance with your cousin
Left to our guesses, the flow of blood,
Spots on the linen, passed over in silence.
Yet for me your fleshliness, Justine,
Is important, you have to appear entire
So that your pride and angry integrity
Shine, surprising. Where do they come from?
What dialogues go on between the body and soul?
In your land, good and evil were measured by the grave.
Who would remain faithful to it, who would not.
(In other words, a serious corrective
Was introduced into the tangle of motives and desires.)
That novel can't be summarized for foreign readers.

In you they would find only another woman
Proclaiming equality of classes, like George Sand.
And now, Justine, comes old age, a ready chapter.
But not to be written by Mrs. Eliza.
You gave birth to sons and daughters, grandchildren grew up.
You rest your hands on a gnarly cane, the mother of a tribe,
The last of your kin and your contemporaries.
In floury snow you see sledges, convoys of sledges.
You hear the shouts of soldiers, women's laments.
And you know, feel, that this is how it looks, the end
Of one earthly country. Never again an echo
Of a song sung on the Niemen, the flight of swallows.
Never again fruit harvests in the village orchards
The bars of cattle cars slam, one after another.
They carry you, by ancient trails, to a land of shadows and
    murders.
Though you never existed, let us light candles,
Here, in our study, or in our church.

And wax encrusts sconces and nations trade and whales dance near
Lahaina and the ungrateful generations raise their buildings and French
policemen get new capes and the sun rises once again and . . .

÷

I always think of Orzeszkowa with love and respect. She is for me an
example of a writer who served the good. She certainly knew much
about the dark side of human existence, but she preferred, for reasons
she considered superior, not to divulge that knowledge. Just as she rarely
let show her erudition. She described the small people of her province
with the sympathy of a person who appreciates simple, traditional
virtues.

A strange adventure befell me. I was reading—I don't know which
time—*On the Banks of the Niemen* and I found myself falling in love with

Justine. When she looked in the mirror, I was by her side, and it seemed to me that she could see my voyeur's eyes. I was thinking about her, and out of that thinking came a poem, "Undressing Justine." The novel, set in the nineteenth century, was not enough for me; my imagination suggested a later fate for the heroine. After all, the inhabitants of the village of Bohatyrowicze had before them World War I and the independent Poland of the interwar years, but also the abyss that opened in 1939 with the entrance of the Soviets. For me this was not history learned from textbooks; it's a thing torturing me still with tears of compassion. I counted years. In 1939, Justine would have been a very old woman, but her arrest and deportation to the East is by no means beyond the limits of probability, since some million and a half people were uprooted in that way.

I concede that I did not know that Orzeszkowa had not invented the village of Bohatyrowicze, or the legend of its founding, including the tomb of the first settlers Jan and Cecilia. Or that the tale of Justine, a girl from the manor, and Jan, a country lad, was based on a true story. All this I learned from an article that recounted a visit to present-day Bohatyrowicze. Moreover, I learned that my anxiety about Justine's fate was justified and my poem was just short of prophetic.

The reporter had heard the story from the mouth of an elder of the tribe, Stanislaw Bohatyrowicz, who lives in one of the few surviving houses in the village. Everything was as it was in Orzeszkowa, even the tomb of Jan and Cecilia, dated 1547, and the grave of the insurrectionists in the forest. "We used to go there often by the river. Now I am old and do not go there anymore, but I know from people that Father Lucian Radomski from Lunna (that is our parish) has cleaned up the grave with his parishioners, and that it's a nice place now. So there are traces of our remembering them, those who were buried there in 1863. They were many, and our boys from Bohatyrowicze also lie there. The manor in reality bore the name of Miniewicze. All that remains of it are ruins." Is that the same place that belongs to the

Korczynskis in the novel? "Yes, Mrs. Orzeszkowa only changed the names. All the rest is the same. That daughter of Kamienski in the novel, she was nearly a spinster. She fell in love with a boy from the village, and he with her. In the novel they are Jan and Justine. But, to be exact, he wasn't a Bohatyrowicz. He descended from us on his mother's side, and she married a certain Strzalkowski. So, you see, Mrs. Orzeszkowa changed the name. That 'Jan,' I remember, was a handsome boy, and he married the lady Kamienska from the manor. Later old Kamienski died, and 'Jan' became the owner of the estate. They had two children, a daughter and a son. Sophie entered a monastery. Perhaps she's still alive. She used to visit us, even after the war. And the son, Casimir, stayed here; he managed the estate, and before that he studied in Warsaw where he met his wife.

"Jan and Justine did not live in the manor, but very near. Jan built a house for them between the village and the manor. It's still standing, but it's quite dilapidated. And in 1939 when the Soviet troops came and our Poland was perishing, all the landowners in the neighborhood, including Casimir and his old father, were taken and executed, near here, in a village called Kwasowka. Then when the Germans invaded our region, Mrs. Justine exhumed their remains secretly and buried them in the cemetery at Lunna."

So, perhaps some peculiar currents circulate between a literary work, its readers, and the posthumous life of its characters. It was so long ago. The novel appeared in 1888. Such cataclysms rolled over the earth, and yet the reality of that time persists in gossip, in an orally transmitted tale, in correctives to the myth. Justine was not, in reality, a poor relation, but a daughter of the manor's owner, Kamienski, Korczynski in the novel, who had served many years in Siberia.

Mrs. Orzeszkowa is still spoken of in the village as an acquaintance. A woman of the younger Bohatyrowicz generation tells the reporter that the novelist found her grandfather a wife in a neighboring village. "So that beautiful Mary Obuchowicz in the novel, she's my grandmother.

She married Adam, my grandfather. When a son was born to them, Mrs. Orzeszkowa and her husband Nahorski were the godparents. They helped with his education. Later he perished in Katyn."

Probably a commentary is impossible, as, until now, no language has been invented comprehensible to both the living and the dead.

RETIRED

An old man, tapping with his cane, aware of his silence.

Which fills every corner of his body with a dense, burning lava.

And confirms the trustworthiness of the words of Jesus about a worm that does not die and fire that never goes out.

Surrounded by his children and grandchildren, he sits down in a wicker armchair on the porch of his house.

Voices of birds from the garden are for everyone, he muses, they do not care about me, neither do they know.

And I, instead of screaming and beating my head against the floor, admire the cloudless sky.

Soon that tale, never started, will pass away and I with it.

A cat sleeps in the sun, the world continues and does not need the signs of testimony.

For nothing would have resulted from them, except the realization that we are poor humans.

Guardians of prison trains, then prisoners ourselves, the torturers and the tortured.

Only I do not understand why I should constantly remember those things.

And accuse myself of events stronger than myself.

Longing for the thunderbolt of a stroke to liberate me from images of this earth.

An old man, serene, liked by his neighbors—he greets passersby, and envies them their innocence.

That is what they have, he muses, if they have not been submitted to a test.

WANDA

Wanda Telakowska (1905–1985), once a popular figure in artistic Warsaw, a painter specializing in color woodcuts, was renowned for her conspicuous stature, her organizing skills, and her sense of humor. In the interwar period she created pattern designs for the textile industry based on folk craft, in particular the handwoven fabrics of Eastern Poland. Her idea of beauty in things for everyday use stemmed in part from native sources (the theories of the poet Norwid), and in part from folk art. She received some backing for her project in government circles. Also a cooperative—called *Lad*, or *Harmony*—working along those lines, was founded in Warsaw.

The *oeuvre* of Telakowska, the colored woodcuts and the theoretical essays prepared by her for print, was consumed by fire during the Warsaw Uprising of 1944. After the war she saw the possibility of organizing state enterprises to produce, for internal use and for export, products of high artistic quality modeled on native handicraft. She met with resistance, and the transition from prototypes to mass production proved impossible. A collection of individual objects, sent to New York, was much admired by the big trading firms, which, however, wanted quantity. Telakowska traveled to America in 1948, hoping to secure markets for the export of textiles. She succeeded in interesting prospective buyers, but no supply from Poland was forthcoming. I tried to help her. Unfortunately, her case—of a socially minded person eager to serve her country—was typical of Poland at that time.

÷

And so, Wanda of a bygone Warsaw,
Let the living pretend they are not concerned
With death, which is too common, too ordinary.
But I don't understand how it is possible
To live and to know that the hour strikes,
And to wait quietly for one's turn.
Something needs to be done. Protest marches?
Wallowings, howlings, curses?

At least let there be a skeleton with a scythe,
Scissors of the Fates, or a star that plummets
When a soul departs. But there is nothing,
An obituary in two or three lines,
And then oblivion forever.

We did not become romantically involved.
Traveling, we would take two rooms.
Because sex is diabolic. I believed that then
And still maintain it. And whoever
Believes otherwise surrenders to the power
Of the Spirit of the Earth, who is not good.

We are allowed it, but only with our spouses.
And, besides, Wanda, you were not a temptation.
Huge, heavy, and not too pretty,
A good companion in coarse laughter at the table.
And beneath, another Wanda, timid and tenderhearted,
Mindful—though with shame—of her maidenhood.

In our sorrows we find solace in a project:
To make the State a helper of art.
Factories and mills were to create beauty
For everyday, as country looms once did.

The elegant wives of ministers listened.

(Oh, elegant wives of ministers!
Where are you? In what department of oblivion
Do you touch up your lips, snap your handbags?)

During the war I used to meet Wanda at the Iwaszkiewiczes in Stawisko.
From her accounts of wartime adventures I remember those testifying

to her presence of mind—for instance, when she found herself in the middle of a roundup at the edge of Mokotowski Field, by Polna Street. "They were taking everybody, they walked straight toward me. What could I do? At the last moment I squatted and lifted my skirt. The German gendarme felt, after all, awkward confronted with a woman pissing and passed by, pretending he did not see me." Or when she moved to the mountains after the Warsaw Uprising and lived in Zakopane with a peasant family. "They were banging on the door. I escaped to the yard. There was a shed with sheep. I had brought my fur-lined overcoat from Warsaw, so I turned it fur-side-up and got down on all fours among the sheep. The Germans took a look into the shed and went away."

To be a witness, try to remember.
That cannot be done. Nor am I doing it.
I only know it's gone, that city,
And on its ruins the illustrious Red Army.
Also Wanda, who tried to convince yokels
Who pick their noses behind their desks
That it's worthwhile, important, that the State should . . .

Dull and sluggish, without the gentry or the Jews,
They were doing something, not too much.
And all daring seemed to them lordly,
Too risky, fanciful.

While you, Wanda, were of those who were ready
To straighten the bent axis of the globe.
People, as usual, did not care.
And soon, old age. Perhaps, you kept in memory
That trip of ours to San Francisco,
Which we both had hope enough to undertake.

What use medals and crosses of merit?
You remained alone in your defeat,
Lonely, not needed, going blind.

To bear it. And human beings bear it.
And what can be said is always too late.

TO MRS. PROFESSOR IN DEFENSE OF
MY CAT'S HONOR AND NOT ONLY

My valiant helper, a small-sized tiger
Sleeps sweetly on my desk, by the computer,
Unaware that you insult his tribe.

Cats play with a mouse or with a half-dead mole.
You are wrong, though: it's not out of cruelty.
They simply like a thing that moves.

For, after all, we know that only consciousness
Can for a moment move into the Other,
Empathize with the pain and panic of a mouse.

And such as cats are, all of Nature is.
Indifferent, alas, to the good and the evil.
Quite a problem for us, I am afraid.

Natural history has its museums,
But why should our children learn about monsters,
An earth of snakes and reptiles for millions of years?

Nature devouring, nature devoured,
Butchery day and night smoking with blood.
And who created it? Was it the good Lord?

Yes, undoubtedly, they are innocent,
Spiders, mantises, sharks, pythons.
We are the only ones who say: cruelty.

Our consciousness and our conscience
Alone in the pale anthill of galaxies
Put their hope in a humane God.

Who cannot but feel and think,
Who is kindred to us by his warmth and movement,
For we are, as he told us, similar to Him.

Yet if it is so, then He takes pity
On every mauled mouse, every wounded bird.
Then the universe for him is like a Crucifixion.

Such is the outcome of your attack on the cat:
A theological, Augustinian grimace,
Which makes difficult our walking on this earth.

YOU WHOSE NAME

You whose name is aggressor and devourer.
Putrid and sultry, in fermentation.
You mash into pulp sages and prophets,
Criminals and heroes, indifferently.
My *vocativus* is useless.
You do not hear me, though I address you,
Yet I want to speak, for I am against you.
So what if you gulp me, I am not yours.
You overcome me with exhaustion and fever.
You blur my thought, which protests,
You roll over me, dull unconscious power.
The one who will overcome you is swift, armed:
Mind, spirit, maker, renewer.
He jousts with you in depths and on high,
Equestrian, winged, lofty, silver-scaled.
I have served him in the investiture of forms.
It's not my concern what he will do with me.

A retinue advances in the sunlight by the lakes.
From white villages Easter bells resound.

THIS WORLD

It appears that it was all a misunderstanding.
What was only a trial run was taken seriously.
The rivers will return to their beginnings.
The wind will cease in its turning about.
Trees instead of budding will tend to their roots.
Old men will chase a ball, a glance in the mirror—
They are children again.
The dead will wake up, not comprehending.
Till everything that happened has unhappened.
What a relief! Breathe freely, you who suffered much.

HAPPENINGS ELSEWHERE

"I can't possibly go to Hell, me, so nice and good,"
Exclaimed Adam, boy, when the devils clustered around him.
They were dressed in black and had red snouts.
They taunted him horribly, pricking his sides with pitchforks
(They used small ones for emergency purposes.)

"I did not believe devils exist,"
Moaned poor Adam, boy,
"I have met ones like you are but that was on the earth."

"He-he"—they answered—"nonexistence is our specialty.
And you, do you exist, you scrap? You existed an instant and basta.
Now you will take your seat with us in nothingness forever."

"What did I do"—lamented Adam, boy,
"What did I do, that you have me in your power?"

"You don't know? He-he, don't worry, you'll get the idea.
We have everything recorded, documented."

They were walking along a slope where they had caught him in his
    lonely march
By lying in ambush in an empty cabin, as frontier guards are wont to
    do,
In that no-man's-land, not far from the gates of Hell.

Mountains, bare, sulfur-colored, in the semidarkness
Descended toward a dim and uncertain plain.
They were leading him down, now he was silent.

Then a shot resounded, so loud it was probably earthly.
The echo rolled and hardly had it thundered away
When the devils began to shrink as if punctured and leaking air.

Then they disappeared completely and again he was alone.

Then one in a homespun jerkin, in long boots,
Swinging a shotgun from his shoulder, came close and stood above
    him.

—"You did a lot of mischief, Adam boy, you are always in trouble.
Where did you get the idea that you are innocent?
Did you really believe you could sin without guilt?
I am sent to announce the verdict.

"You'll be with the Hospitaliers. There, festering bedsores,
Vapors of decaying flesh, howlings,
And pain, crying for vengeance to Heaven,
Contradict continuously the goodness of God.
In other words, the cruel cosmic vaudeville goes on.
It's different from Hell, instead of nothingness
Uninterrupted duration and suffering.

"Once it was called Purgatory. And there you will serve,
Washing, lifting, cleaning up, listening.
And every day you will learn to know your guilt,
Until you concede that you deserve no better."

Then a messenger went ahead up the steepness,
Adam, boy, followed him, for, alone, he could not find the way.

A HALL

The road led straight to the temple.
Notre Dame, though not gothic at all.
The huge doors were closed. I chose one on the side,
Not to the main building—to its left wing,
The one in green copper, worn into gaps below.
I pushed. Then it was revealed:
An astonishingly large hall, in warm light.
Great statues of sitting women—goddesses,
In draped robes, marked it with a rhythm.
Color embraced me like the interior of a purple brown flower
Of unheard-of size. I walked, liberated
From worries, pangs of conscience and fears.
I knew I was there as one day I would be.
I woke up, serene, thinking that this dream
Answers my question, often asked:
How is it when one passes the last threshold.

AFTER ENDURING

The hypothesis of resurrection
Drawn by an eminent scientist from quantum mechanics,
Foresees our return to familiar places and people
After a billion or two billion earth years
(Which in the beyond-time equals one instant.)
I am glad I have lived long enough to witness the fulfillment of
    predictions
About a possible alliance of religion and science,
That was prepared by Einstein, Planck, and Bohr.
I do not take too seriously scientific phantasies,
Though I respect graphs and computations.
The same was expressed more concisely by Peter the Apostle,
When he said: *Apokatastasis panton,*
The renewal of all things.
Yet it is helpful: to be able to imagine
That every person has a code instead of life
In an eternal storage room, a supercomputer of the universe.
We disintegrate into rot, dust, microfertilizers,
But that code or essence remains
And waits, till at last it takes flesh.
And also, as the new corporeality
Should be cleansed of evil and afflictions,
The notion of Purgatory enters the equation.
Not different is what the faithful in a country church
Repeat in chorus asking for life eternal.
And I with them. Not comprehending
Who I will be when I wake after enduring.

BODY

The human condition is not pain only.
Yet pain rules us and has much power.
Wise thoughts fail in its presence.
Starry skies go out.

From the center of the anatomical atlas
Where liver-red and clear-red of lungs
Meet flesh-color of cloudlike intestines,
Heralds of pain proceed with their muted calls.
From defenseless guard posts at the frontier of the skin
Runs the alarm of being touched by steel or fire.

No chitinous or horn armor.
Nakedness under dresses and the masks of dancers.
And our obsession with undressing them on the stage
To know what they are when they pretend.

Scarlet liquor under the sun of the heart
Circulates, warms up, pulsates.
Visions, landscapes move to its rhythm
As does the brain, a gray moon, Luna.

On a gynecological chair open knees.
Defenseless viscera shattered by childbirth.
And the first scream, terror of exile into the world,
On a frozen river, in a stony city.

Julia, Isabel, Luke, Titus!
It's us, our kinship and mutual pity.
This body so fragile and woundable,
Which will remain when words abandon us.

IN SZETEJNIE

You were my beginning and again I am with you, here, where I learned the four quarters of the globe.

Below, behind the trees, the River's quarter; to the back, behind the buildings, the quarter of the Forest; to the right, the quarter of the Holy Ford; to the left, the quarter of the Smithy and the Ferry.

Wherever I wandered, through whatever continents, my face was always turned to the River.

Feeling in my mouth the taste and the scent of the rosewhite flesh of calamus.

Hearing old pagan songs of harvesters returning from the fields, while the sun on quiet evenings was dying out behind the hills.

In the greenery gone wild I could still locate the place of an arbor where you forced me to draw my first awkward letters.

And I would try to escape to my hideouts, for I was certain that I would never learn how to write.

I did not expect, either, to learn that though bones fall into dust, and dozens of years pass, there is still the same presence.

That we could, as we do, live in the realm of eternal mirrors, working our way at the same time through unmowed grasses.

II
You held the reins and we were riding, you and me, in a one-horse britzka, for a visit to the big village by the forest.

The branches of its apple trees and pear trees were bowed down under the weight of fruits, ornate carved porches stood out above little gardens of mallow and rue.

Your former pupils, now farmers, entertained us with talks of crops, women showed their looms and deliberated with you about the colors of the warp and the woof.

On the table slices of ham and sausage, a honeycomb in a clay bowl, and I was drinking *kvas* from a tin cup.

I asked the director of the collective farm to show me that village; he took me to fields empty up to the edge of the forest, stopping the car before a huge boulder.

"Here was the village Peiksva" he said, not without triumph in his voice, as is usual with those on the winning side.

I noticed that one part of the boulder was hacked away, somebody had tried to smash the stone with a hammer, so that not even that trace might remain.

III

I ran out in a summer dawn into the voices of the birds, and I returned, but between the two moments I created my work.

Even though it was so difficult to pull up the stick of *n*, so it joined the stick of *u* or to dare building a bridge between *r* and *z*.

I kept a reedlike penholder and dipped its nib in the ink, a wandering scribe, with an ink pot at his belt.

Now I think one's work stands in the stead of happiness and becomes twisted by horror and pity.

Yet the spirit of this place must be contained in my work, just as it is contained in you who were led by it since childhood.

Garlands of oak leaves, the ave-bell calling for the May service, I wanted to be good and not to walk among the sinners.

But now when I try to remember how it was, there is only a pit, and it's so dark, I cannot understand a thing.

All we know is that sin exists and punishment exists, whatever philosophers would like us to believe.

If only my work were of use to people and of more weight than is my evil.

You alone, wise and just, would know how to calm me, explaining that I did as much as I could.

That the gate of the Black Garden closes, peace, peace, what is finished is finished.

ROAD-SIDE
DOG

(Piesek przydrozny)

1 9 9 8

ROAD-SIDE DOG

I went on a journey in order to acquaint myself with my province, in a two-horse wagon with a lot of fodder and a tin bucket rattling in the back. The bucket was required for the horses to drink from. I traveled through a country of hills and pine groves that gave way to woodlands, where swirls of smoke hovered over the roofs of houses, as if they were on fire, for they were chimneyless cabins; I crossed districts of fields and lakes. It was so interesting to be moving, to give the horses their rein, and wait until, in the next valley, a village slowly appeared, or a park with the white spot of a manor in it. And always we were barked at by a dog, assiduous in its duty. That was the beginning of the century; this is its end. I have been thinking not only of the people who lived there once but also of the generations of dogs accompanying them in their everyday bustle, and one night—I don't know where it came from—in a pre-dawn sleep, that funny and tender phrase composed itself: a road-side dog.

PELICANS

I marvel at the incessant labor of pelicans.
Their low flights over the surface of the sea,
Poising in one place, suddenly diving
For a singled-out fish, the white splash—
All day, from six in the morning. What are views
For them, what is blue ocean, a palm tree, the horizon
(Where, at the ebb, like distant ships,
Rocks crop out and blaze,
Yellow, red, and purple)?
Don't come too close to the truth. Live with a representation
Of invisible beings who dwell above the sun,
Free, indifferent to necessity and hunger.

A BALL

He gives to the chief the head of an enemy
Whom he pounced on in the bushes by a stream
And hefted with his spear. —A scout
From the enemy village. It's a pity
It wasn't possible to capture him alive.
Then he would have been put on the sacrificial altar
And the whole village would have had a feast:
The spectacle of his being killed slowly.
They were rather tiny brown people
Presumably no more than a meter-fifty tall.
What remains of them are some ceramics,
Though they did not know the potter's wheel.
Something else, too: found in the tropical jungle
A granite ball, immense, incomprehensible.
How, without knowing iron, could they dress the granite,
Give it a perfectly spheric shape?
They worked it for how many generations?
What did it mean to them? The opposite
Of everything that passes and perishes? Of muscles, skin?
Of leaves crackling in a fire? A lofty abstraction
Stronger than anything because it is not alive?

WATERING CAN

Of a green color, standing in a shed alongside rakes and spades, it comes alive when it is filled with water from the pond, and an abundant shower pours from its nozzle, in an act, we feel it, of charity toward plants. It is not certain, however, that the watering can would have such a place in our memory, were it not for our training in noticing things. For, after all, we have been trained. Our painters do not often imitate the Dutch, who liked to paint still lifes, and yet photography contributes to our paying attention to detail and the cinema taught us that objects, once they appear on the screen, would participate in the actions of the characters and therefore should be noticed. There are also museums where canvases glorify not only human figures and landscapes but also a multitude of objects. The watering can has thus a good chance of occupying a sizable place in our imagination, and, who knows, perhaps precisely in this, in our clinging to distinctly delineated shapes, does our hope reside, of salvation from the turbulent waters of nothingness and chaos.

FROM MY DENTIST'S WINDOW

Extraordinary. A house. Tall. Surrounded by air. It stands. In the middle of a blue sky.

AUTUMN

Cathedral of my enchantments, autumn wind, I grew old giving
    thanks.

HELENE

Here we are on the other side.
Expeditions. Demesnes were leased out. Steam rose from the cinders.
It must be Helene over there, dancing between the flames.
Perhaps she knows now the secret of particular existence.
All my life I tried in vain to comprehend it.
You suffered much, Helene, and said nothing.
Hungry, you didn't even ask for help.
And hospitals, that bodily misery wanting to love itself;
Hating itself, it weeps in a dirty hallway.
Who would have thought, Helene, that our youth would turn out this
    way?
The garden glowed in the sun and summer lasted forever.
Later for a long time we learn how to bear what is borne by others.
And how to bless a moment if it is without pain.

HELENE'S RELIGION

On Sunday I go to church and pray with all the others.
Who am I to think I am different?
—Enough that I don't listen to what the priests blabber in their
    sermons.
Otherwise, I would have to concede that I reject common sense.
I have tried to be a faithful daughter of my Roman Catholic Church.
I recite the Our Father, the Credo and Hail Mary
Against my abominable unbelief.
It's not up to me to know anything about Heaven or Hell.
But in this world there is too much ugliness and horror.
So there must be, somewhere, goodness and truth.
And that means somewhere God must be.

YOKIMURA

Once I saw on TV a cemetery of unborn babies, with little graves on which Japanese women lit candles and laid flowers. I put myself for a moment in the place of one of them who was leaning over to put down a spray of chrysanthemums.

—My son, you were conceived in love, that's all I will ever know about you.

You might have heard from me about the terror of life on earth, but you were spared.

About how we are visited by misfortune and cannot understand why we, who are unique, must be struck like the others.

Perhaps you would have had a life like mine and, clenching your teeth, would have borne your fate for years, for one has to.

Suffering, I thought that perhaps you, my son, had inherited my accursed tenacity and capacity for self-delusion.

So then I felt relief, saying to myself that at least you were safe.

In nonbeing as in a cradle or a cocoon of silk down.

Who would you have been? Every day I would have trembled to know what was winning in you: a portent of greatness or of defeat—one tiny grain is enough to tip the balance.

Either people's gratitude and respect or an embittered man's four walls.

No, I am certain you would have been powerful and brave, as all those are who are begotten by love.

I made a decision, and I know that was how it had to be, and I did not blame anyone.

When I bite into a peach, when I look at the rising moon, when I rejoice at the sight of young cedar groves on the mountains, I taste everything in your stead, in your name.

AMERICA

A tawny and lead-gray current of swift river,
To which a man and a woman come, leading a yoke of oxen,
To found a city and to plant in the middle of it a tree.
Under this tree I used to sit at midday
And look at the low bank on the other side:
There, a marsh, rushes, a pond overgrown with duckweed
Shone as before, when those two, of unknown name, were alive.
I did not expect it would fall to me: the river, the city,
Here, nowhere else, the bench and the tree.

CHRISTOPHER ROBIN

In April of 1996 the international press carried the news of the death, at age seventy-five, of Christopher Robin Milne, immortalized in a book by his father, A. A. Milne, Winnie-the-Pooh, *as Christopher Robin.*

I must think suddenly of matters too difficult for a bear of little brain. I have never asked myself what lies beyond the place where we live, I and Rabbit, Piglet and Eeyore, with our friend Christopher Robin. That is, we continued to live here, and nothing changed, and I just ate my little something. Only Christopher Robin left for a moment.

Owl says that immediately beyond our garden Time begins, and that it is an awfully deep well. If you fall in it, you go down and down, very quickly, and no one knows what happens to you next. I was a bit worried about Christopher Robin falling in, but he came back and then I asked him about the well. "Old bear," he answered. "I was in it and I was falling and I was changing as I fell. My legs became long, I was a big person, I wore trousers down to the ground, I had a gray beard, then I grew old, hunched, and I walked with a cane, and then I died. It was probably just a dream, it was quite unreal. The only real thing was you, old bear, and our shared fun. Now I won't go anywhere, even if I'm called for an afternoon snack."

RIVERS

"So lasting they are, the rivers!" Only think. Sources somewhere in the mountains pulsate and springs seep from a rock, join in a stream, in the current of a river, and the river flows through centuries, millennia. Tribes, nations pass, and the river is still there, and yet it is not, for water does not stay the same, only the place and the name persist, as a metaphor for a permanent form and changing matter. The same rivers flowed in Europe when none of today's countries existed and no languages known to us were spoken. It is in the names of rivers that traces of lost tribes survive. They lived, though, so long ago that nothing is certain and scholars make guesses which to other scholars seem unfounded. It is not even known how many of these names come from before the Indo-European invasion, which is estimated to have taken place two thousand to three thousand years B.C. Our civilization poisoned river waters, and their contamination acquires a powerful emotional meaning. As the course of a river is a symbol of time, we are inclined to think of a poisoned time. And yet the sources continue to gush and we believe time will be purified one day. I am a worshipper of flowing and would like to entrust my sins to the waters, let them be carried to the sea.

THIS

(To)

✛

2000

I

THIS

If I could at last tell you what is in me,
if I could shout: people! I have lied by pretending it was not there,
It was there, day and night.

Only thus was I able to describe your inflammable cities,
Brief loves, games disintegrating into dust,
earrings, a strap falling lightly from a shoulder,
scenes in bedrooms and on battlefields.

Writing has been for me a protective strategy
Of erasing traces. No one likes
A man who reaches for the forbidden.

I asked help of rivers in which I used to swim, lakes
With a footbridge over the rushes, a valley
Where an echo of singing had twilight for its companion.
And I confess my ecstatic praise of being
Might just have been exercises in the high style.
Underneath was this, which I do not attempt to name.

This. Which is like the thoughts of a homeless man walking in an alien
city in freezing weather.

And like the moment when a tracked-down Jew glimpses the heavy
helmets of the German police approaching.

The moment when the crown prince goes for the first time down to the
city and sees the truth of the world: misery, sickness, age, and death.

Or the immobile face of someone who has just understood that he's
been abandoned forever.

Or the irrevocable verdict of the doctor.

This. Which signifies knocking against a stone wall and knowing that the wall will not yield to any imploration.

TO A HAZEL TREE

You do not recognize me, but it's me all the same,
The one who used to make my bows by cutting your brown
　　branches,
So straight and so swift in their reaching for the sun.
You grew large, your shade is huge, you send up new shoots.
It's a pity I'm not a boy anymore.
Now I could cut for myself only a stick, for, as you see, I walk with a
　　cane.

I loved your brown bark with its whitish tinge, its true hazel color.
I'm glad that some oaks and ashes have survived,
But I rejoice at seeing you, magical as always, with the pearls of your
　　nuts
With the generations of squirrels that have danced in you.

This is something of a Heraclitean meditation: I stand here
Remembering my bygone self and life as it was but also as it could
　　have been.
Nothing lasts, but everything lasts: a great stability,
And I try to locate my destiny in it.
Which, in truth, I did not want to accept.
I was happy with my bow, stalking at the edge of a fairy tale.
What happened to me later deserves no more than a shrug;
It is only biography, i.e., fiction.

POSTSCRIPTUM
Biography or fiction or a long dream.

Layers of white clouds on a fragment of sky between the brightness of
　　the birches.

A vineyard, yellow and rusty in the approaching dusk.
For a short time I was a servant and a wanderer.
Released, I come back by a never-taken road.

Szetejnie and Napa Valley, Autumn 1997

I DO NOT UNDERSTAND

Muchenhauz, Henryk, captain of Reiters of His Majesty, married in Kujany February 10, 1659, to Marguerite Horn and killed immediately after by his brother-in-law, also Horn.
—REGISTER OF THE REFORMED-EVANGELICAL PARISH IN KEYDANY

But Kujany is less than a mile from Szetejnie, and there, barefoot, I used to run along the river. So the minister must have had to come on a sledge (February!) from the town where the temple was located to perform the wedding. Could they not have gone to town themselves? And who owned the manor of Kujany? Muchenhauz? The Horns? And whence, in that crowd of motley nationalities around the Protestant Prince Radziwill, came those names? And why did Horn kill Captain Muchenhauz? Too much celebration and a drunken brawl? An incestuous love for Marguerite? And how? With the blow of a sabre? A thrust of sword? A pistol? And where was the Captain of Reiters of His Majesty buried? What happened to his widow, Marguerite? Whom did she marry? Every day I, myself a shadow, enter more deeply among shadows. Centuries pass, the names and spirits around me more and more numerous, unlike my youth when the rhythm of the blood barred access to bygone people. Now, close, I call them, imagine them, and my memory preserves the graininess of the dirt under my naked feet, the ruts of the roads with puddles after rain, and, above, the park and the manor of Kujany. How many there were, who lived in that neighborhood, in their flesh as I am in my flesh, and for that reason I cannot understand how life can change into death and lungs filled with the movements of breathing can be immobilized. I think often that it would be enough to take this teeny scrap of Earth and build on it an invisible tower of lives, up to the sky, now, when nobody can find their bones anymore. It's like the table at our student parties when I would suddenly stop being there and would see us all talking, laughing, as if we were changed already into those who had lived long ago.

MY GRANDFATHER SIGISMUND KUNAT

In the photograph of my grandfather Kunat when he was six is contained, in my opinion, the secret of his personality.

A happy little boy, youthfully sprightful, the bright and serene soul visible through his skin.

The photograph comes from the 1860s, and now I, in my old age, join that child at his play.

By a familiar lake into which he is now throwing pebbles, under ash trees that were to find their way into my poems.

The Kunats were ranked with the Calvinist gentry, which I snobbishly note down, since in our Lithuania Calvinists were counted among the most enlightened.

The family changed their denomination to Roman Catholic late, around 1800, yet I have not preserved any image of my grandfather in a pew at Swiętobrość.

He never spoke evil of priests, though, nor departed in anything from accepted norms of behavior.

A student at the Main School in Warsaw, he danced at balls and studied the books of the epoch of positivism.

He took seriously calls for "organic work" and for that reason established in Szetejnie a workshop for the manufacture of cloth, which is why I used to play in rooms crowded with presses for fulling.

He was exquisitely polite to everyone, great and small, rich and poor, and had the gift of listening with attention to everyone.

Oscar Milosz, who met him in Kaunas in 1922, called him "*un gentilhomme français du dixhuitième siècle*," a French gentleman of the eighteenth century.

This external polish did not tell the whole story; underneath he was hiding wisdom and genuine goodness.

Meditating on my hereditary flaws, I have moments of relief any time I think of my grandfather; I had to have taken something from him, so I cannot be completely worthless.

He was called a "Lithuanizer," and did he not build a school in Legmedis and pay for a Lithuanian teacher?

Everyone liked him, Poles, Lithuanians and Jews, he was held in esteem by neighboring villages—

Those villages which were, a few years after his death, deported to Siberia, so that now in their place there is only an empty plain.

Among all books he liked best the memoirs of Jalub Gieysztor, for they described in detail our valley of Niewiaza between Kiejdany and Krakinowo.

They did not interest me in my youth; all my attention was directed toward the future.

Now I read those memoirs avidly, for I have learned the value of the names of localities, turns in the road, hills, and ferries on the river.

How much one must appreciate the province, the home and dates and traces of bygone people.

A Californian wanderer, I have kept a talisman: a photograph of the hill in Świętobrość where, under the oaks, my grandfather Kunat is buried, and my great-grandfather Szymon Syruc, and his wife, Eufrozyna.

LAKE

Maidenly lake, fathomless lake,
Stay as you were once, overgrown with rushes,
Idling with a reflected cloud, for my sake
Whom your shore no longer touches.

Your girl was always real to me.
Her bones lie in a city by the sea.
Everything occurs too normally.
A unique love simply wears away.

Girl, hey, girl, we repose in an abyss.
The base of a skull, a rib, a pelvis,
Is it you? me? We are more than this.
No clock counts hours and years for us.

How could a creature, ephemeral, eternal,
Measure for me necessity and fate?
You are locked with me in a letter-crystal.
No matter that you're not a living maid.

AFTER TRAVELING

How strange life is! How incomprehensible! As if I returned from it as from a long journey and tried to remember where I had been and what I had done. I can't quite manage it, and the most difficult part is trying to see myself there. I had intentions, motivations. I made decisions, performed acts. Yet from here that man seems so irrational and absurd. As if he did not act, but was activated by forces that made use of him. For, after all, I wrote many books, here they are, and there he is; how to trace between him and them a line of continuity?

So, opaque to myself, I want to guess who I was for others, especially the women to whom I was bound by ties of love or friendship. Too late. We are like a marionette theater that's been put to sleep. The puppets lie in the tangle of their strings and convey no idea of what the spectacle was like.

THE HEAD

An immense head emerged slowly
from behind the hills across the river
and saw a boy with a fishing rod
who, his eyes fixed on the float,
had only one thought: will they bite?

What should we do with him? the head pondered,
giving instructions to the lofty spirits
who specialized in arranging a fate.

And so it is, the head says to itself
at the sight of an old man returned after many voyages
to that same place by the river.

Some of them believe that they themselves decide, accomplish.
This one at least knows he was a plaything of powers
diving and giggling in the air,
and only wonders now
how it all happened.

FORGET

Forget the suffering
You caused others.
Forget the suffering
Others caused you.
The waters run and run,
Springs sparkle and are done,
You walk the earth you are forgetting.

Sometimes you hear a distant refrain.
What does it mean, you ask, who is singing?
A childlike sun grows warm.
A grandson and a great-grandson are born.
You are led by the hand once again.

The names of the rivers remain with you.
How endless those rivers seem!
Your fields lie fallow,
The city towers are not as they were.
You stand at the threshold mute.

IN A CITY

That city was happy and much beloved.
Always in peonies and late lilacs.
Its baroque towers soaring toward the sky.
To return from an excursion and arrange bouquets in a vase.
To see from the window the street you once took going to school.
(On the wall sharply delineated zones of sun and shadow.)
Canoeing together on the lakes.
Romantic outings to islands overgrown with osiers.
Betrothal, and the wedding at St. George's.
Our fraternity of writers celebrating a baptism at my home.

Tournaments of musicians, orators, poets, suited my taste,
And the applause of the crowd when the Dragon's Parade passed on
  the street.

Every Sunday I sat in the patron's pew at church.
I wore a toga and a golden chain, the gifts of my fellow citizens.

I grew old, certain that my grandchildren would remain faithful to
  their city.

Would it were true. But I was blown away,
Beyond oceans and seas. Farewell, lost destiny.

Farewell, city of my sorrow, farewell, farewell.

II

AN HONEST DESCRIPTION OF MYSELF
WITH A GLASS OF WHISKEY AT AN AIRPORT,
LET US SAY, IN MINNEAPOLIS

My ears catch less and less of conversations, and my eyes have weakened, though they are still insatiable.

I see their legs in miniskirts, slacks, wavy fabrics.

Peep at each one separately, at their buttocks and thighs, lulled by the imaginings of porn.

Old lecher, it's time for you to the grave, not to the games and amusements of youth.

But I do what I have always done: compose scenes of this earth under orders from the erotic imagination.

It's not that I desire these creatures precisely; I desire everything, and they are like a sign of ecstatic union.

It's not my fault that we are made so, half from disinterested contemplation, half from appetite.

If I should accede one day to Heaven, it must be there as it is here, except that I will be rid of my dull senses and my heavy bones.

Changed into pure seeing, I will absorb, as before, the proportions of human bodies, the color of irises, a Paris street in June at dawn, all of it incomprehensible, incomprehensible the multitude of visible things.

FOR MY EIGHTY-EIGHTH BIRTHDAY

A city dense with covered passageways, narrow
little squares, arcades,
terraces descending to a bay.

And I, taken by youthful beauty,
bodily, not durable,
its dancing movement among ancient stones.

The colors of summer dresses,
the tap of a slipper's heel in centuries-old lanes
give the pleasure of a sense of eternal recurrence.

Long ago I left behind
the visiting of cathedrals and fortified towers.
I am like someone who just sees and doesn't pass away,
a lofty spirit despite his gray head and the afflictions of age.

Saved by his amazement, eternal and divine.

Genoa, 30 June 1999

A RUN

Joyful my run through dark parks in the fall,
When the paths are thick with pine needles and the rustle of leaves
And the meadows are emptying of picnickers,
And the livid eyes of the TV screens are darkening.

I've never felt such lightness of step.
Maybe long ago, in my mornings as a child.
Borne above ground, suffused by light,
I stride through the air and do not stop.

I'm unkindly greeted by this awakened state.
During the day, on my cane, asthmatic, I creep.
But the night sees me off at the travelers' gate,
And there, as at the outset, the world is new and sweet.

BY A STREAM

The murmur of clear water on stones
in a gully deep in a tall forest.
Ferns brighten in the sun on the banks,
the stacked, ungraspable shapes of leaves,
lancet-like, sword-like,
heart-like, shovel-like,
notched, serrated,
sawtoothed—who will express it?
And the flowers! Whitish umbels,
deep blue chalices, bright yellow stars,
roselets, clusters.
To sit and to watch
the bustle of bumblebees, the flight of dragonflies,
the takeoff of a flycatcher,
in the tangle of twigs the hurry of the black beetle.
It seems that I hear the voice of a demiurge:
"Either speechless rocks, as on the first day of creation,
or life, whose condition is death,
and this beauty which elates you."

O!

O happiness! To see an iris.

The color of indigo, as Ela's dress was once, and the delicate scent like that of her skin.

O what a mumbling to describe an iris that was blooming when Ela did not exist, nor our kingdoms or our countries!

O!

O lips half opened, eyes half closed, the rosy nipple of your unveiled nakedness, Judith!

And they, rushing forward in an attack with your image preserved in their memories, torn apart by bursts of artillery shells, falling down into pits, into putrefaction.

O massive gold of your brocade, of your necklace with its rows of precious stones, Judith, for such a farewell!

O!

Salvator Rosa (1615–1673)
A Landscape with Figures
YALE UNIVERSITY GALLERY

O the quiet of water under the rocks, and the yellow silence of the afternoon, and the flat white clouds reflected!

Figures in the foreground dressing themselves after bathing, figures on the other shore tiny and in their activities mysterious.

O most ordinary, taken from dailiness and elevated to a place like this earth and not like this earth!

O!

Edward Hopper (1882–1967)
A Hotel Room
THYSSEN COLLECTION, LUGANO

O what sadness unaware that it's sadness!
What despair that doesn't know it's despair!

A businesswoman, her unpacked suitcase on the floor, sits on a bed half
undressed, in red underwear, her hairdo irreproachable; she has a piece
of paper in her hand, probably with numbers.

Who are you? Nobody will ask. She doesn't know either.

WHEREVER

Wherever I am, at whatever place on earth, I hide from people the conviction that I'm not from here. It's as if I'd been sent, to extract as many colors, tastes, sounds, smells, to experience everything that is a man's share, to transpose what was felt into a magical register and carry it there, from whence I came.

VOYEUR

I was a peeping Tom wandering the earth.
The inside of the galactic bubble rustled and fermented.

There were lilac-colored flowers on her hat; she wore panties with
    lace.
We dined on a tablecloth marked with little sun dots.

Or her half-naked breasts in an Empire dress.
I'd change into a frock coat, wear the medal of some order
To be able to imagine their hardened tips.

I've always meditated on what women keep hidden:
In a foam of flounces, frills, and skirts,
The dark entrance to the garden of knowledge.

And then they died, and with them their silks and mirrors,
Dogesses, princesses, and serving maids.
I had a lump in my throat at the thought that they,
So beautiful, would turn to rot.

In truth, I didn't aspire to making love to them.
My eyes desired them and my eyes were hungry,
Invited to a comic spectacle
Where philosophy and grammar,
Poetics and mathematics,
Logic and rhetoric,
Theology and hermeneutics,
As well as all the teachings of wise men and prophets,
Gathered to compose a canticle of canticles
To a small, furry, untameable animal.

SO-CALLED LIFE

So-called life:
everything that provides material for a soap opera,
he didn't think was worth relating,
or maybe he wanted to tell it and couldn't.
He was surprised by the tangled tales of men and women,
stretching out to a flickering oblivion.
He himself only knew how to clench his teeth and bear it,
to wait, until old age took from the dramas their meaning,
and the soap opera of loves, hatreds, temptations
and betrayals, dropped off to sleep.

PRESCRIPTION

Everything but confessions. My own life
Annoys me so, I would find relief
In telling about it. And I would be understood
By those wretches—how many!—who wobble
In the streets of cities, drugged or drunk,
Sick with the leprosy of memory and the guilt of living.
So what restrains me? Shame
That my misfortunes are not picturesque enough?
Or contrariness. Wailing has become fashionable,
Unhappy childhoods, trauma, all the rest.
Even had I been ready for a Job's complaint,
It is better to keep silent, to praise the immutable
Order of things. No, something else
Forbids me to speak. Whoever suffers
Should be a teller of the truth. Should? How,
With all the disguises, comedy, self-pity?
Falseness of feeling results in a false phrase.
I value style too much to take the risk.

IN BLACK DESPAIR

In grayish doubt and black despair,
I drafted hymns to the earth and the air,
Pretending to joy, although I lacked it.
The age had made lament redundant.

So here's the question—who can answer it—
Was he a brave man or a hypocrite?

EXAMPLE

She is eighty and writes in her memoir:
"I had no time or energy for worries."
Her good example fortifies me.

The Wilia shines. Full moon. We make love
By the Students' Club landing.
That moment would console me more than once,
For there was in my life much bitterness.

To sing and to dance before the Lord!
Simply because complaint is good for nothing,
So she says, my brave, undaunted Irena.

AWAKENED

In advanced age, my health worsening, I woke up in the middle of the night, and experienced a feeling of happiness so intense and perfect that in all my life I had only felt its premonition. And there was no reason for it. It didn't obliterate consciousness; the past which I carried was there, together with my grief. And it was suddenly included, was a necessary part of the whole. As if a voice were repeating: "You can stop worrying now; everything happened just as it had to. You did what was assigned to you, and you are not required anymore to think of what happened long ago." The peace I felt was a closing of accounts and was connected with the thought of death. The happiness on this side was like an announcement of the other side. I realized that this was an undeserved gift and I could not grasp by what grace it was bestowed on me.

SUBMERGED

And yet not everyone is given a true old age.
Its property is meditation
On the pride of the flesh, that once
Burst in us, who were the same and yet so different.
It was all really comic:
Arranging one's hair before a mirror,
Worrying about whether your hat fit your face,
Wetting your lips with the end of your tongue
And passing a lipstick over them,
Knotting a tie with an air of the king of animals.

The Earth Spirit, how he played with us!
If the individual is form and the species matter,
As Duns Scotus seemed to believe,
We performed what was demanded and were submerged
In matter, as someone might say, up to our ears.

Later on, out of the mirage, a synthetic city rises.
Between its Gothic towers the flight of swallows.
An old man in the window
Who has seen many cities,
Nearly liberated, is laughing
And has no intention to go back anywhere.

VIPERA BERUS

I wanted to tell the truth
and did not succeed.
I tried confession
and I could not confess anything.
I did not believe in psychotherapy.
I knew I would lie too much.
So I carried in myself a coiled adder of guilt.
This is not for me an abstraction.
I stand in a marsh in Raudonka near Jaszuny
and the tail of an adder is just disappearing
in a clump of moss under a dwarf pine,
as I pull the trigger and spray lead from my shotgun.
Even today I do not know whether a single pellet
hit the hideous white belly
or the zigzag-striped back of *Vipera berus*.
In any case, it's easier to describe this
than the psyche's adventures.

TEXAS

I came back from Texas.
I had been reading my poems there.
Nowhere else than in America do they pay so well for reading poems.
Next to my signature I put the date 2000.

Old age clings to my feet like dense pitch.
The mind resists, but that signifies consciousness.
And what can I do with it, unveil it to whom?
The best strategy is to say nothing.

I have experienced the shame of the recollected illusion
of loving, hating, aspiring, striving.
And now I can hardly believe
that I managed to live through my life.

CRAFTSMAN

Craftsman, prepare your instruments.

A tall echo comes down the mountain; you hear the roaring of spring torrents.

The beauty of the earth reveals itself for the first time to children's eyes just as it did once to yours.

Craftsman, you are building a star that will journey in the sky of those now being born,

While you withdraw without regret, thinking how difficult it was to live a life.

And to learn that we do not get what we wanted, and that the two greatest virtues are resignation and persistence.

Also that consciousness brings no solace, since it is the consciousness of a clown turning somersaults on a stage, hungry for applause.

You acquired unwelcome knowledge, of yourself and others; you are filled to the brim with pity and with wonder.

May those who are destined to take up your labor start where you finished, master of vanquished despair.

Praising, renewing, healing. Grateful because the sun rose for you and will rise for others.

YOU, VANQUISHED

You, vanquished and expelled.
Year after year fixing your eyes on the photograph of a white manor
And a company in white summer dresses gathered before a porch.
Forgive me, young scion of a good family,
That I began to betray you as early as my years in school,
Setting out on a breakneck expedition into the realms of intellect
Where no canopy sheltering a holy monstrance
Sways above a crowd in procession on Corpus Christi Sunday.

Lunar wastelands, loneliness and anger,
Had, after all, their uses:
They allowed me to lift to the second degree
Both my province and you, dear shadows,
Who arrive at my summons,
Just because I was a man with a flaw,
Excluded from the habits of his forefathers,
And destined for a different kind of faithfulness.

SPECIMENS

Specimens do not know they are specimens.
They are flitting over a meadow
where a gentleman in a cork helmet
strides with a butterfly net.

How to convince a butterfly it is a specimen?
O master most fierce and rapacious! Maharaja!
O prophet Elijah! Habakkuk!
Depose your wings on the altar of science!

O Basilissa! Lady Macbeth! Titania! Lenore!
There is no need to be yourselves,
you could come to represent a species!

And last forever in a register
beside kings, monuments, and temples,

Together with a gentleman in a cork helmet, who walked
through a meadow in the year one thousand nine hundred of our era.

THE YEAR 1900

To get out of thoughts about one's own person:
the first advice in depression.
I move therefore to the year 1900.

Yet how to communicate with the city of the dead?
I watch mirrors, corridors of mirrors
reflected in mirrors.
There, a flicker of a hat with plumes,
or a white nakedness in the dark,
Mariona, Stefa, Lilka
combing their long hair.

If they had fallen out of time and space,
they would be where the emperor Tiberius is,
or bison hunters from twelve thousand years ago.
But they are still close; they move away
only gradually, year after year,
as if they were still participants in our indecent dance.

OBVIOUSLY

Of course I don't say what I really think.
Polite society deserves respect.
And one should not reveal in talk or print
The doleful secrets of our common flesh.
For we, the weak and helpless, have been dared
To lift ourselves an inch above our heads,
To be able to say to someone in despair,
"I've lived who also wished that I were dead."

MY SECRETS

All my miserable secrets
Will be, one by one, revealed.
What a meager life! they'll say,
And the path so steep!

IF

If I cannot ascend to Paradise—
clearly those circles are too high for me—
I would like to spend time in one of the regions of Purgatory
gaining liberation from the phantoms of my mind,
whose power, though I never trusted it completely,
I remember very well.
The agony before her window in an empty street,
Or the idealizing call for a perfect love,
Spiritual, nearly superterrestrial.
Should I laugh now or weep? Yet my body
carries these splinters of exaltation and unreason.
I would like even yet to see clearly,
To not lie to anybody, or to myself,
And to invoke, supposing they were there,
my good intentions.

III

ZONE OF SILENCE

Truth is a terrible thing. We should not share with anyone more than a given person is able to bear. Above all, we should not reveal our own truth, should not force anyone to accept it, to dispose anyone to know things that are beyond human strength.

—ZYGMUNT MYCIELSKI, *A QUASI-DIARY*

It didn't happen that way.
Yet no one dares to tell how it did happen.
I am old enough to remember,
and yet like others I repeat the socially acceptable words,
for I do not feel authorized
to reveal a truth too cruel for the human heart.

SELECTING IWASZKIEWICZ'S POEMS FOR AN EVENING OF HIS POETRY AT THE NATIONAL THEATER IN WARSAW

When a Polish romantic is sitting on the papal throne,
As if to prove that the powers governing poetry
Can be quite strange, simple tasks cease to be simple.
And I too feel the seriousness of my duty.
How do I present your verses, Jarosław,
To people who believe or want to believe
That history has a providential meaning?
Your poems, beautifully made, carry within them
Contents so funereal they can hardly be read
Without harming their admirers. Unfortunately it's so.
Isn't it the case that you succumbed to the temptation,
Deeply sweet, of relief through nonexistence,
Of escape into nothingness? Even if it's true
That after the dream of our species is done with,
Only the immense laughter of the void remains,
Even if we are nothing, lumps of mucus on a beach
Without limit, even then some glory is due
To the brave who raised a protest to the end
Against death, the destroyer of faith. So,
From among your poems I have chosen the ones
That add splendor to the speech of generations,
Which has been for us a home and fortress.
You brought out of your beloved Ukraine
The colors and scents of the steppe in bloom,
And gave us salt breezes from the Aegean Sea,
And the whites and golds of a Byzantine dusk.
Always hungry, astonished always by beauty,
You heard into the rhythms of day and nights
And made yourself an instrument of that music.
We still hear in your melodic phrasings,
Despite your doubt, that tone of depths.
And our lips repeat, not all that rarely,
The words and music of your Dionysian prayer.

ODE FOR THE EIGHTIETH BIRTHDAY OF POPE JOHN PAUL II

We come to you, men of weak faith,
So that you might fortify us with the example of your life
And liberate us from anxiety
About tomorrow and next year. Your twentieth century
Was made famous by the names of powerful tyrants
And by the annihilation of their rapacious states.
You knew it must happen. You taught hope:
For only Christ is the lord and master of history.

Foreigners could not guess from whence came the hidden strength
Of a novice from Wadowice. The prayers and prophecies
Of poets, whom money and progress scorned,
Even though they were the equals of kings, waited for you
So that you, not they, could announce, *urbi et orbi,*
That the centuries are not absurd but a vast order.

Shepherd given us when the gods depart!
In the fog above the cities the Golden Calf shines,
The defenseless crowds race to offer the sacrifice
Of their own children to the bloody screens of Moloch.
In the air, fear, a lament without words:
Since a desire for faith is not the same as faith.

Then, suddenly, like the clear sound of the bell for matins,
Your sign of dissent, which is like a miracle.
People ask, not comprehending, how it's possible
That the young of the unbelieving countries
Gather in public squares, shoulder to shoulder,
Waiting for news from two thousand years ago
And throw themselves at the feet of the Vicar
Who embraced with his love the whole human tribe.

You are with us and will be with us henceforth.
When the forces of chaos raise their voice
And the owners of truth lock themselves in churches
And only the doubters remain faithful,
Your portrait in our homes every day remind us
How much one man can accomplish and how sainthood works.

WHAT I LEARNED FROM JEANNE HERSCH

1. That reason is a gift of God and that we should believe in its ability to comprehend the world.

2. That they have been wrong who undermined our confidence in reason by enumerating the forces that want to usurp it: class struggle, libido, will to power.

3. That we should be aware that our being is enclosed within the circle of its perceptions, but not reduce reality to dreams and the phantoms of the mind.

4. That truth is a proof of freedom and that the sign of slavery is the lie.

5. That the proper attitude toward being is respect and that we must, therefore, avoid the company of people who debase being with their sarcasm, and praise nothingness.

6. That, even if we are accused of arrogance, it is the case that in the life of the mind a strict hierarchy is mandatory.

7. That intellectuals in the twentieth century were afflicted with the habit of *baratin*, i.e., irresponsible jabber.

8. That in the hierarchy of human activities the arts stand higher than philosophy, and yet bad philosophy can spoil art.

9. That objective truth exists; namely, out of two contrary assertions, one is true, one false, except in strictly defined cases when maintaining contradiction is legitimate.

10. That quite independently of the fate of religious denominations we should preserve a "philosophical faith," i.e., a belief in transcendence as a measure of humanity.

11. That time excludes and sentences to oblivion only those works of our hands and minds which prove worthless in raising up, century after century, the huge edifice of civilization.

12. That in our lives we should not succumb to despair because of our errors and our sins, for the past is never closed down and receives the meaning we give it by our subsequent acts.

OPPOSED TO EACH OTHER

On one side, the world; on the other, men and gods.

The world is immutable, inexorable, indifferent.

It is the stone that hurt your toe when you used to run barefoot.

Men and gods: an incessant motion of guilt and forgiveness.

Their warm throats pronounce the words of curse and blessing.

They are weak, changeable, they expect help from each other.

The loves of men and gods, sharpened by the danger of loss.

Their dresses, buskins, and masks prove that neither of them wants to stay in the order of Nature.

Both mortal and immortal, they live in their own realm high above the world.

Do not forget, you who are men or gods, what honors are due to you from the suns and galaxies of the world.

ZDZIECHOWSKI

Once more the irises are blooming.
When they bloom again, my age will be over.

The ocean in the morning is veiled in mist.

In the doorway open to the garden I am busy with not remembering.

Yet I cannot forget you, philosopher of despair

Who doubted the goodness of Creation.

I see a shady trail lined with birches between Wilno and Minsk, with a winding rut down the middle.

No automobiles then, or asphalt roads.

A horse carriage was sent to the railway station to pick up guests.

He might have hosted Vladimir Solviev at his manor and listened to what he would say about the reconciliation of Roman Catholicism and the Orthodox Church.

They might have discussed as well whether the ducks on the estate pond could attain salvation.

Whether an ant or a fly has been redeemed.

Who established on this earth the law of agony for living creatures?

Until today I have preserved his words:

"And with the years, as I moved further and further into life and the world, I realized more and more clearly and painfully that this world, considered as a whole, is disorder and unreason, not, as we have been taught, the work of reason: it did not come from the hand of God."

Here he walks to class on the streets of Kraków.
With him his contemporaries: tulle, velvet, satin
Touch the bodies of women that are like slender stalks
Of the perverse flora of Art Nouveau.
Glances and calls from inside the night.

In a cosmic battle the swords of the angels are flashing.
The Prince of Rebellion advances, the servants of light retreat.

Cruelty, stony,
How to explain it otherwise? Though he, a professor,
Could not say openly he believed in the devil's world.
Lonely at their feast of color and touch.

"There is no God—nature and history unanimously proclaim it. But that voice is submerged by the harmony of psalms and hymns, by an avowal coming from the depth of the human spirit, that the soul of man without God is like 'earth without water.' God is. Yet the fact of God's existence is beyond the grasp of thought preoccupied with the external world. *Le monde est irrationnel. Dieu est un miracle.*"

Only the sound of bells,
Only the glow of a monstrance,
Mortal voices pronouncing glory,
The floors at the Dominicans and Franciscans
Used by the feet of generations

Protect us. Even if illusion
Unites us in this belief in life eternal,
We, dust, give thanks for the miracle of faithful dust.

Your Magnificence, I approached you once, a boy, on the steps of the library under the Poczobutt Tower painted with signs of the zodiac.

In a city taken from the Bolsheviks by Polish cavalry, you waited, aware of "the approaching end."

You could be seen passing in a carriage, the hoofs of two horses clicked on the uneven pavement, you never accepted the automobile or the telephone.

With its dances, blooming lilacs and wild cherries, with floating wreaths on the river, the city was sinking.

You died just in time, your friends whispered, shaking their heads: "He was lucky."

The prophecy was fulfilled, whatever existed there sank, only church towers jutted up above the deep.

Perhaps I am like the one who, when there was no escape from deportation to a gulag, hid himself at the top of St. John's belfry and was saved.

A doe with two young, just born, has chosen to stay on the lawn outside my window.

Inexorable sequence of birth and death, Your Magnificence.

I trained myself a long time in the art of restraint.

More clever than you, I learned my century, pretending I knew a method for forgetting pain.

AGAINST THE POETRY OF PHILIP LARKIN

I learned to live with my despair,
And suddenly Philip Larkin's there,
Explaining why all life is hateful.
I don't see why I should be grateful.
It's hard enough to draw a breath
Without his hectoring about nothingness.

My dear Larkin, I understand
That death will not miss anyone.
But this is not a decent theme
For either an elegy or an ode.

ON THE DEATH OF A POET

The gates of grammar closed behind him.
Search for him now in the groves and wild forests of the dictionary.

ON THE INEQUALITY OF MEN

It is not true that we are just meat
that for a moment prattles, moves, desires.

The throngs of bare bodies on the beaches are wrong;
so are the crowds on the escalator in the metro.

We don't know who the person next to us is.
He may be a hero, a saint, a genius.

For the equality of men is an illusion
and the tables of statistics are a lie.

My own impulse to admire instructs me
in the existence of a hierarchy daily renewed.

I walk on an earth that harbors the ashes of an elect,
though they last no longer than the ashes of others.

I confess to my esteem and my gratitude,
as there is no reason to be ashamed of these noble feelings.

May I prove to be deserving of that high company,
And walk with them, holding the hem of the king's garment.

ALEKSANDER WAT'S TIE

That tie, knitted, with a thick knot
that matched perfectly a dark-colored shirt
and a tweed jacket, ravished me.

This was a really elegant fellow,
with his short-cropped black mustache.

We were introduced on Mazowiecka Street, a few steps
from Ziemianska restaurant and Mortkowicz's bookstore
(the only place in Warsaw that carried my *Three Winters*,
published in an edition of 300 copies).

Whoever believes in Providence must see an Eye:
A rider from the Pamir Mountains gallops, all in rose and purple.
Then Benvenue Street in Berkeley and Wat on the couch.
His astonishment as he tries to grasp his fate.
And I, a young provincial with a tape recorder
who, it seems, was destined to bear witness.

It's true we lived together
through that horrible New Year's Supper of 1950.

Poor Wat,
he suffered enough in Kazakhstan and Tajikistan.

A beautiful tie was of no avail,
nor the street of phantoms, Mazowiecka, in Warsaw.

TO ROBERT LOWELL

I had no right to talk of you that way,
Robert. An émigré's envy
Must have prompted me to mock
Your long depressions, weeks of terror,
Presumed vacations in the safety of the wards.
It was not from pride in my normalcy.
Insanity, I knew, was insinuating itself
In a thin thread into my very being
And only waited for my permission
To carry me into its murky regions.
And I was watchful. Like a lame man,
I used to walk upright to hide my affliction.
You didn't have to. For you it was permitted.
Not for me, a refugee on this continent
Where so many newcomers vanished without a trace.
Forgive me my mistake. Your will was of no use
Against an illness that held you like a stigma.
And beneath my anger was the vanity,
unjustifiable, of the humiliated. A bit belated,
I write to you across what separates us:
Gestures, conventions, idioms, mores.

PASTELS BY DEGAS

That shoulder. An erotic thing submerged in duration.
Her hands are entangled in undone plaits of red hair
So dense that, combed, it pulls, the head down,
A thigh, and under it the foot of another leg.
For she is sitting, her bent knees open,
And the movement of her arm reveals the shape of a breast.
Here undoubtedly. In a century, a year
That have vanished entirely. How to reach her?
And how to reach the other in her yellow robe?
She puts on mascara, humming a song.
The third lies on the bed, smokes a cigarette,
And looks through a fashion journal. Her muslin shirt
Shows a white roundness and pinkish nipples.
The painter's hat hangs on the entresol
With their dresses. He liked to stay here, chatting,
Sketching. Our human communion has a bitter taste
Because of the familiarity of touch, of avid lips,
The shape of loins, and talk of an immortal soul.
It flows and recedes. A wave, a sighing of surf.
And only a red mane flickered in the abyss.

ON POETRY, UPON THE OCCASION
OF MANY TELEPHONE CALLS AFTER
ZBIGNIEW HERBERT'S DEATH

It should not exist,
considering conception,
gestation and delivery,
quick growth,
decay and death.
What is all that to it?

It cannot inhabit
the chambers of the heart,
the meanness of the liver,
the sententiousness of the kidneys,
or the brain, with its dependence on the grace of oxygen.

It cannot exist, and yet it exists.

He, who served it,
is changed into a thing,
delivered to decomposition
into salts and phosphates,
sinks
into the home of chaos.

In the morning telephones ring.
Straw hats, sleek nylon, linens
tried in front of mirrors
before a day at the beach.
Vanity and lust
as always,
self-centered.

Liberated from the phantoms of psychosis,
from the screams of perishing tissue,

from the agony of the impaled one,

It wanders through the world,
Forever, clear.

UNDE MALUM

Where does evil come from?
It comes

from man
always from man
only from man
   —TADEUSZ ROZEWICZ

Alas, dear Tadeusz,
good nature and wicked man
are romantic inventions
you show us this way
the depth of your optimism

so let man exterminate
his own species
the innocent sunrise will illuminate
a liberated flora and fauna

where oak forests reclaim
the postindustrial wasteland
and the blood of a deer
torn asunder by a pack of wolves
is not seen by anyone
a hawk falls upon a hare
without witness
evil disappears from the world
and consciousness with it

Of course, dear Tadeusz,
evil (and good) comes from man.

ROZEWICZ

he took it seriously
a serious mortal
he does not dance

he lights two thick candles
sits before a mirror
amused by his face

he does not indulge
in the frivolity of form
in the comic abundance
of human beliefs

he wants to know for sure

he digs in black soil
is both the spade and the mole
cut in two by the spade

IV

GARDENER

Adam and Eve were created for another purpose
Than to bow to the prince and master of the world.

Beyond time there was another earth, sunlit,
Offered to both of them, for eternity and for bliss.

A gray-haired gardener tended the trees faithfully,
Though the world was less bright than he would have liked.

He looked at days and ages, as if through field glasses.
He looked at all his works, so well begun.

Which lust for knowledge was about to transform
Into the insatiable soul and the woundable flesh.

He warned, not thinking it would do much good.
For they were ready, and as if on their way.

Invisible among the leaves, he meditated sadly.
He saw bursts of fire. He saw bridges, ships, and houses.

An airplane in the night sky like a pulsating spark,
Beds with canopies, the blackened earth of a battlefield.

Oh my poor children. Were you in such a hurry to get there
Where a skull in the sand grins with its yellow teeth?

To enclose your loins in pants and crinolines,
To discover chains of cause and effect?

Here he comes, my adversary. He will tell you:
Try, just try, and you will be gods.

Lackeys of self-serving loves and crimes,
And gods indeed, though lame.

My miserable children, it's a very long road
Before a ruined garden begins to bloom again.

You will return down an alley of lindens to a porch,
And flower beds fragrant with salvia and thyme.

Did you really need to plunge into an abyss,
To compose systems rather than settling into the fairy tale

Over which I exert a permanent care?
For the Writ tells the truth: my face is a man's.

ONE AND MANY

The Prince of This World governs number.
The singular is the hidden God's dominion,
The Lord of rescues and exception's Father
Who from the start inhabited my errors.

One against the multiplication table.
Particular, free from the general.
Without hands or eyes yet real.
Who is, every day, though unrevealed.

Don't be afraid of the empty millennia,
Of the snake pits rank with death,
Flesh teeming in the thicknesses of decay,
Nor the mist of distant galaxies.

For the human voice will not cease to try
To forge a song for terror or glory.
Since all things for us are ultimate,
Alien, beautiful, though contradictory.

AN ALCOHOLIC ENTERS THE GATES OF HEAVEN

What kind of man I was to be you've known since the beginning,
since the beginning of every creature.

It must be horrible to be aware, simultaneously,
of what is, what was,
and what will be.

I began my life confident and happy,
certain that the Sun rose every day for me
and that flowers opened for me every morning.
I ran all day in an enchanted garden.

Not suspecting that you had picked me from the Book of Genes
for another experiment altogether.
As if there were not proof enough
that free will is useless against destiny.

Under your amused glance I suffered
like a caterpillar impaled on the spike of a blackthorn.
The terror of the world opened itself to me.

Could I have avoided escape into illusion?
Into a liquor which stopped the chattering of teeth
and melted the burning ball in my breast
and made me think I could live like others?

I realized I was wandering from hope to hope
and I asked you, All Knowing, why you torture me.
Is it a trial like Job's, so that I call faith a phantom
and say: You are not, nor do your verdicts exist,
and the earth is ruled by accident?

Who can contemplate
simultaneous, a-billion-times-multiplied pain?

It seems to me that people who cannot believe in you
deserve your praise.

But perhaps because you were overwhelmed by pity,
you descended to the earth
to experience the condition of mortal creatures.

Bore the pain of crucifixion for a sin, but committed by whom?

I pray to you, for I do not know how not to pray.

Because my heart desires you,
though I do not believe you would cure me.

And so it must be, that those who suffer will continue to suffer,
praising your name.

THE RITE

Yes, it's true, Berenike. Not more calm,
But more tolerant toward myself and others.

Not to expect from people
Qualities for which they were not created:
Harmonious reasoning, beliefs that don't contradict each other, actions
That confirm their faith, their firmness.

They seem so transparent, as if you saw right through them,
And yet dark forces whirl inside.
I think now of George, Arthur, Kitty,
Whose stories no one will ever tell.

What complications! The line of fate
Swerves, tumbles, leaps to the side,
Yet remains one thing in human memory.
Words they said casually, as jokes,
Are interpreted now as serious avowals,
And even if they wanted to testify,
Nothing would come of it:
the truth is beyond their grasp.

Such as we are, we kneel in our church.
Amid columns crowned with golden agapanthus
And gracefully dressed angels whose thin trumpets
Announce the news too big for us.

Our attention is short, says Berenike,
My thought returns, in spite of the liturgy,
To the mirror, the bed, the telephone, the kitchen.
It's unable to carry the city of Jerusalem
And the weight of two thousand years and the blood on the cross.

Yet we soar somehow, though burdened
With the smells of sauces, and the shouting in narrow streets,
And the look of red meat in butcher shops.
Above the altar, the church, the town, circling the turning earth.

And they, our neighbors, Berenike,
In the same pew, close, their consciousness,
My consciousness. The mystery
Of the transformation of my "I" into "we."

"You are the salt of the earth, you are the light of the earth,"
He said, and called us to his glory.
He, who won out over the immutable laws of the world.

I know he called, Berenike says,
But what about the doubters? Do they testify
By keeping silent out of love for his name?

Perhaps we should begin by worshipping a stone,
An ordinary fieldstone, its very being,
And pray without opening our lips.

PERSONS

He was the only poet of his small nation.
Before him no one knew how to put signs on paper.

He wrote down the spells of shamans and a tale of the beginning:
How the first people were born of flowers
And had wings that emanated light.
There were no lights at that time in the skies.

Then they ate a certain root and knew sin.
They lost their wings and everything grew dark.
Because they entreated, there came to be a sun and a moon.

The poet pondered what he should translate into his language:
Homer? the Bible? Rilke? the Marquis de Sade?

Or perhaps he should compose the national hymn
And devise a national banner with a picture of a bear?

÷

I meditate now on the insufficiency of language.
I am very old and, together with me, words, unpronounced, will
    disappear,
In which persons who died long ago might have had their home,
While I am unable to make them appear with the oval of that, their
    only, face,
with the shape of the eyebrows, the color of those eyes.
They wander somewhere in the valley of their passing,
Hardly distinguishable, in the uncounted multitude of centuries,
    tongues, generations.

And you with them, Claudine, who once wrote to me this:

"You are for me a man of a somewhat childish character (perhaps poets remain so all their lives), all of whose transgressions one forgives, whom one loves in spite of everything."

That man, who was myself, now sees suddenly a birch forest and both of us in the house of our neighbors, on a bench at a table, eating a supper

Not unlike a wedding feast, but it is too late to tell the story of our lives.

I call you, also, Roxana, though here again I would not like to provide my biographers a clue.

First, the heart beats quicker at the sound of a name, later only a tale about a man and a woman incarnated centuries ago.

Somewhere at a seaport we might have sat after many years, remembering our mutual fascination.

I would have told you what I had come to understand, though it did not amount to much,

About our unlimited ability to convince ourselves of our noble feelings.

About two self-loves wearing the twinned masks of lovers.

About how we abandon, against our will, a person we love and sentence a living being to death by cold.

And always you, Berenike, I tremble any time I pronounce your true name.

We were like a pair of ships calling each other in a fog; you did not see me nor did I see you.

The tragedy of recognizing an error, irremediable, and then even guilt falls away, finds its place among the bygone things.

Yes, when we were young, we couldn't conceive that such common misfortune could befall us, two superior minds.

I will be with you soon, on a plain of the subterranean kingdom, and you, silent, will come out to greet me.

Not much of a conversation for this transformed pair if I have nothing to say in my defense but to point to the written pages of my oeuvre.

But I hear a choir, it grows in strength and resonance, and I sing with the others.

The choir of men and women, turning the pages of the score in the Sun, just as they had done on Earth.

I feel relief thinking I was no better and no worse than many, and that together with them I wait for forgiveness.

From all sides voiceless tribes push on, innocent grass overwhelms the stones of graves.

IN A PARISH

Had I not been frail and half broken inside,
I wouldn't think of them, who are like myself half broken inside.
I would not climb the cemetery hill by the church
To get rid of my self-pity.
Crazy Sophies,
Michaels who lost every battle,
Self-destructive Agathas
Lie under crosses with their dates of birth and death. And who
Is going to express them? Their mumblings, weepings, hopes, tears of
    humiliation?
In hospital muck and the smell of urine,
With their weak and contorted limbs,
And eternity close by. Improper. Indecent.
Like a dollhouse crushed by wheels, like
An elephant trampling a beetle, an ocean drowning an island.
Our childishness and stupidity does nothing to fit us
For the sobriety of last things.
They had no time to grasp anything
Of their individual lives,
any *principium individuationis.*
Nor do I grasp it, yet what can I do?
Enclosed all my life in a nutshell,
Trying in vain to become something
Completely different from what I was.

Thus we go down into the earth, my fellow parishioners.
With the hope that the trumpet of judgment will call us by our
    names.
Instead of eternity, greenness and the movement of clouds.
They rise then, thousands of Sophias, Michaels, Matthews,
Marias, Agathas, Bartholomews.
So that at last they know why
And for what reason?

PRAYER

Approaching ninety, and still with a hope
That I could tell it, say it, blurt it out.

If not before people, at least before You,
Who nourished me with honey and wormwood.

I am ashamed, for I must believe you protected me,
As if I had for You some particular merit.

I was like those in the gulags who fashioned a cross from twigs
And prayed to it at night in the barracks.

I made a plea and You deigned to answer it,
So that I could see how unreasonable it was.

But when out of pity for others I begged a miracle,
The sky and the earth were silent, as always.

Morally suspect because of my belief in You,
I admired unbelievers for their simple persistence.

What sort of adorer of Majesty am I,
If I consider religion good only for the weak like myself?

The least-normal person in Father Chomski's class,
I had already fixed my sights on the swirling vortex of a destiny.

Now You are closing down my five senses, slowly,
And I am an old man lying in darkness.

Delivered to that thing which has oppressed me
So that I always ran forward, composing poems.

Liberate me from guilt, real and imagined.
Give me certainty that I toiled for Your glory.

In the hour of the agony of death, help me with Your suffering
Which cannot save the world from pain.

AFTER

Convictions, beliefs, opinions,
certainties, principles,
rules and habits have abandoned me.

I woke up naked at the edge of a civilization
which seemed to me comic and incomprehensible.

The vaulted halls of the post-Jesuit academy
where I had taken my classes
would not have been pleased with me.

Though I preserved a few sentences in Latin.

The river flows through a forest of oak and pine.

I stand in grass up to my waist,
Breathing in the wild scent of yellow flowers.

Above, white clouds. As is usual in my district,
an abundance of white clouds.

By the river Wilia, 1999

RAYS OF DAZZLING LIGHT

Light off metal shaken,
Lucid dew of heaven,
Bless each and every one
To whom the earth is given.

Its essence was always hidden
Behind a distant curtain.
We chased it all our lives
Bidden and unbidden.

Knowing the hunt would end,
That then what had been rent
Would be at last made whole:
Poor body and the soul.

LATE RIPENESS

Not soon, as late as the approach of my ninetieth year,
I felt a door opening in me and I entered
the clarity of early morning.

One after another my former lives were departing,
like ships, together with their sorrow.

And the countries, cities, gardens, the bays of seas
assigned to my brush came closer,
ready now to be described better than they were before.

I was not separated from people,
grief and pity joined us.
We forget—I kept saying—that we are all children of the King.

For where we come from there is no division
into Yes and No, into is, was, and will be.

We were miserable, we used no more than a hundredth part
of the gift we received for our long journey.

Moments from yesterday and from centuries ago—
a sword blow, the painting of eyelashes before a mirror
of polished metal, a lethal musket shot, a caravel
staving its hull against a reef—they dwell in us,
waiting for a fulfillment.

I knew, always, that I would be a worker in the vineyard,
as are all men and women living at the same time,
whether they are aware of it or not.

NOTES

This poem, written in Warsaw in April 1943, was first published in the underground anthology *Z Otchłani* (From the Abyss, 1944), dedicated to the Jewish tragedy by poets living "on the Aryan side." The anthology reached New York in spring 1945. Because there were several reprints and handwritten copies which changed the text slightly, there are various versions of the ending of the poem. These differing versions also appear in the translations into Hebrew. In this edition the probable first version is restored.

The adventures of this poem require special mention. "The World" is written in the style of school primers, in neatly rhymed stanzas. Its deliberately naive tone can hardly find an equivalent in English. Several translators have tried a hand at it. A fine version by Robert Hass and Robert Pinsky was published in my volume *The Separate Notebooks*. For this book, however, I opted for a version done by myself, less ambitious but literal.

Adrian Zieliński is a fictitious name, like J. Alfred Prufrock.

a boy "fascist": The Warsaw Uprising broke out on August 1, 1944, when the victorious Soviet army was approaching the city and the German army was retreating. The battles in the city—between the German army and Polish fighters—raged for over two months, and as a result Warsaw was totally destroyed. The insurgents, who were not pro-Soviet, were subsequently accused of being fascists.

The poem was written in 1950. One stanza was placed on the monument in Gdansk erected by Solidarity in 1980 to commemorate the workers killed by the police in 1970.

A TREATISE ON POETRY

Translator's Note

A Treatise on Poetry was begun in the winter of 1955 and finished in the spring of 1956. The first three parts were printed in the

June 1956 issue of the émigré journal *Kultura.* "Natura" appeared in December 1956.

A word on form: The poem is written in a rather strict meter. The English equivalent would probably be a plain, regular, and forceful blank verse. It also breaks from time to time into more lyric forms. In "Natura," for example, there are the small song "Inside the Rose"; "O City," a set of prophetic rhymed quatrains that carry echoes of the romantic and apocalyptic style of nineteenth-century Polish poetry; and an old-fashioned ode to the month of October which, in 1955–1956, glints with multiple ironies, since October was in People's Poland the occasion for public celebrations of the Russian Revolution. To give some sense of the surprise of these forms, it would have been desirable to find English equivalents. But because their tone is often complex and because they have philosophical bearing in the poem, it also seemed desirable to hew fairly closely to the literal meaning, at least in this first English translation. In general we have tried to suggest, without being bound to, an English pentameter. And in the lyrics, we have for the most part taken Vladimir Nabokov's advice: "Better a crude word-for-word translation than the prettiest paraphrase."

I. BEAUTIFUL TIMES

page III   "Beautiful Times"
The phrase translates *la belle epoque,* a term applied at the time to the beginning of the twentieth century, specifically the years preceding the outbreak of World War I in 1914.

page III   *Cabbies were dozing by St. Mary's tower*
St. Mary's Church dates from Kraków's most prosperous era: its construction, in the Gothic style, took some hundred years, from the middle of the fourteenth to the middle of the fifteenth centuries.

page III   *An* Ober *brings the paper on a stick*
Ober is short for *Ober kellner,* or headwaiter.

page III   *Muses, Rachels in trailing shawls*
Rachel is a character in a play in verse, *Wedding,* by Stanisław Wyspiański (1869–1907). The play was performed in 1901, became a sensation in the city and an event in the history of Polish theater. Rachel, the daughter of a Jewish innkeeper, is an intellectual, a bluestocking, and an admirer of poets.

page III   *(Dr. Freud, I hear, is also from Galicia)*
Sigmund Freud was born in Moravia, but his ancestors presumably lived in the neighboring province of Galicia, the northern district of the Hapsburg Empire which contained the cities of Kraków and Lvov.

was the author of *Seowka* (Little Words). His songs, irreverent, slightly obscene, spiced with vulgarisms from the street, were a turning point in the struggle against the aesthetic of Young Poland. Together with other Polish intellectuals, he was executed by the Nazis in 1941.

page 115   *On Oleandry field the locks of the carbines*
Some young men in Kraków were engaged in private military training on fields outside the city, in the period just before the outbreak of World War I.

II. THE CAPITAL

page 116   *You, alien city on a dusty plain, / Under the cupola of the Orthodox cathedral*
To leave a permanent monument to its dominance, Russia built in the central square of the city an enormous Orthodox cathedral, which served only its own troops: the population was predominantly Roman Catholic.

page 116   *The Cavalry Guard was your soldier of soldiers*
This passage of the poem uses Russian expressions difficult to translate. "Allaverdy" was a bawdy song that had originated in the Caucasus and was sung by drunken Russian officers. The Cavalry Guards were elite troops of the czar's empire.

page 116   *An ensign elopes with a railwayman's daughter*
The reference is to an actual event. A girl of rare beauty, the daughter of a Polish railwayman, eloped with a young Russian ensign, who took her to Russia. Subsequently, she married an American multimillionaire who bought her Le Théâtre des Champs-Elysées in Paris.

page 116   *At Czerniakowski Street, at Górna and Wola*
Fragments from two Warsaw street songs popular around the time of World War I are telescoped here into three lines of verse.

page 116   *And you are ruled, City, from a citadel*
The czarist authorities considered Warsaw a dangerous city, full of clandestine activities and uprisings. They built the Citadel to control it.

page 116   *Cossack horses prick their ears*
The Cossacks were used against political demonstrations. The lyric comes from a socialist song.

page 116   *A saber, rifles from French army surplus*
The war between Poland and the Soviet army was very unpopular in the capitals of Europe. As a result, the Polish army had difficulty acquiring arms and was poorly equipped.

<table>
<tr><td>page 117</td><td>They don't know that, one day, harsh brasses will play / The "Internationale" above their graves
Soviet troops entered Warsaw twenty-five years later, in January 1945, and established a Communist government. Many former anti-Soviet militants were destined to serve the new rulers.</td></tr>
</table>

<table>
<tr><td>page 117</td><td>He could never believe in permanence
The creator of independent Poland and chief of the newly restored state was Józef Piłsudski (1867–1935).</td></tr>
</table>

<table>
<tr><td>page 117</td><td>Till not one stone, O city, remains / Upon a stone
The total devastation of Warsaw was inflicted when Hitler, after the battles in the city had died out, ordered that city be "razed without a trace"—by dynamiting the houses street by street.</td></tr>
</table>

<table>
<tr><td>page 117</td><td>A poet needs, first, to issue from good stock
I speak here of a group of poets called Skamander, after a magazine they started after World War I. They came from the intelligentsia and were the first generation of poets of urban origin in a basically rural country. Their origins reflected the ethnic mix of Poland. Julian Tuwim (1894–1953) descended from progressive Jewish intellectuals of the city of Łoda; Jan Lechón (1899–1956), family name Leszek Serafinowicz, came from burghers of Armenian origin. Antoni Słonimski (1895–1976) counted among his ancestors a Jewish scientist and inventors, as well as medical doctors. Jarosław Iwaszkiewicz (1894–1980) came from the Polish intelligentsia in the Ukraine. Kazimierz Wierzyński (1894–1969) was of German ancestry. United by friendship and mutual appreciation, they conquered the public and became the most highly regarded poets of the years between the wars.</td></tr>
</table>

<table>
<tr><td>page 118</td><td>Noisy at the Picadore
World War II and the ensuing political events were to separate friends. Tuwim succeeded in leaving Poland at the beginning of the war and heard from New York the news of his mother's death at the hands of the Nazis and of the mass murders that amounted to the end of Polish Jewry. He had always been a romantic revolutionary, and before the war at his poetry readings in small, predominantly Jewish towns he used to recite poems of the French Revolution ("Ça ira!"). This is what is meant by "a sound belated by a hundred years." Most of his audiences perished in the Shoah. Those who survived left for Israel or western countries. Some of those who remained threw in their lot with the Communist state.</td></tr>
</table>

<table>
<tr><td>page 118</td><td>The ball at the Senator goes on and on
This is an allusion to a ball famous in Polish literature. In Forefather's Eve, by Adam Mickiewicz (1798–1855), Poland's</td></tr>
</table>

national poet, a high Russian official in an occupied Polish city gives a ball which the reluctant Polish elite is expected to attend.

page 118   *Lechón-Herostrates trampled on the past*
In his youth, in 1918, Lechón wrote a poem titled "Herostrates," in which he identified with a Greek from Ephesus who set fire to the temple of Diana there in 350 B.C. The poem was an outburst of joy at a new era. Lechón was in Paris at the outbreak of World War II, became a political emigre in New York, and committed suicide there in 1956 by jumping from a skyscraper.

page 118   *Or on religion, Polish, not Catholic*
Or-Ot was the pseudonym of Artur Oppman (1869–1931), a poet whose traditional rhymed syllabic verse was extolled by Lechón.

page 118   *What of Słonimski, sad and noble-minded?*
Antoni Słonimski was, basically, a rationalist and a partisan of the scientific world view. Słonimski spent the war in London, but returned to Warsaw in 1950, only to join within a few years the liberal opposition against censorship and the violation of human rights.

page 118   *Iwaszkiewicz built his house of brilliant stones*
In his youth, the least appreciated of the Skamander poets because of his aestheticism, he drew few admirers (I was one of them) for his musical verse, which was sensuous and rich in color. During the war Iwaszkiewicz stayed in Poland. His house near Warsaw was the center of underground cultural life and, occasionally, a refuge for people endangered by the Nazis, including many Jews. After Poland was "liberated" by the Soviet Army and a government of Polish Communists installed, Iwaszkiewicz, though he had no illusions as to the character of the new regime, consciously chose the role of collaborator and allowed himself to be used as a figurehead by the government's propaganda machine.

page 119   *Not morally superior, just more proud*
This passage refers to Kazimierz Wierzyński, who, during World War II and afterward, lived as a political émigré on the East Coast of America. Uncompromising, he never returned to Poland. His youthful poems are exuberant, in contrast to his later work.

page 119   *There had never been such a Pléiade!*
"La Pléiade" was the famous group of seven French writers of the sixteenth century.

page 120   *Nor did Broniewski win their admiration*
Władysław Broniewski (1897–1962) was a Communist poet

whose verse resembled, strangely enough, revolutionary songs of the nineteenth century.

page 121

In the swarm of the Kraków avant-garde
The Constructivist avant-garde had their home in Kraków, where they published the magazine *Zwrotnica* (The Switch) in the nineteen twenties. They regarded metaphor as the basic building material of the poem. At the same time, they moved away from the poetry of personal feeling and strove for a kind of objectivity, rejected the metrical poetry of Skamander and searched for new rhythms. The most important among them, Julian Pryzboś (1901–1970), was a rationalist, faithful to the world view of modern science.

page 122

One of those who understood pretended
Can a poet remain detached while all around him people are animated by the same powerful nationalistic passion? Konstanty Ildefons Gałczyński (1905–1953) answered that question in the negative. As the extreme right dominated public opinion, he offered to it his considerable literary gifts and became its bard. He threatened liberals and radicals with "a night of long knives." After the war, which he survived in a POW camp, he became, however, the bard of Communist Poland.

page 122

Let it be stated here clearly: the Party / Descends directly from the fascist Right
Oboz Narodowo-Radkalny (O.N.R.) was the extreme rightist party. The Communist Party became its successor when it made its appeal to Polish nationalism.

page 122

Gałczyński tied these elements together
As in neighboring Nazi Germany, the Polish rightists were anti-philistine, populist, and racist. Horst Wessel was the author of the Nazi hymn.

page 123

Czechowicz, the bucolic, was quite different
The leading poet of the new generation, Józef Czechowicz (1903–1939) rejected regular meter and punctuation and followed his ear, which was sensitive to folk songs and Christmas carols, as well as to Polish bourgeois lyrics and dances of the seventeenth century. His poetry is undulant, subdued, close to dream. He was killed by a German bomb in September 1939 in his native city of Lublin, where he is buried.

page 123

Not one nation but a hundred nations
Lucien Szenwald (1909–1944) became a Communist in his early youth. He was self-taught but erudite, and translated poetry from English and ancient Greek. After the partition of Poland, he

moved to the Soviet zone, underwent military training in Siberia and became a political officer in the Red Army. He is the author of an ode to Mother Siberia. In 1944, when his unit was fighting in Poland, he was killed in an automobile accident.

page 123   *The book has a title:* Afloat in the Forest
The full title of that book for young people is *Afloat in the Forest, or a Voyage among the Treetops by Captain Mayne-Reid.* The first edition was published in 1889. Thomas Mayne-Reid (b. 1818) is an author not known today to American readers, but his books for young readers about a romanticized America were once (together with those of the German writer Karl May) staple readings in many European countries, including Poland and Russia.

page 124   *And, if he survives destruction, it is he/Who will preserve with tenderness his guides*
The author expresses in these lines his gratitude to his predecessors, poets whom he read in his adolescence, including some less well-known names: Józef Wittlin (1896–1976), in his youth the author of expressionist verses on hunger; Stanisław Baliński (1898–1984), who published a slim volume of verse on Persia; Adam Ważyk (1905–1982), translator of Guillaume Apollinaire; as well as Maria Pawlikowska-Jasnorzewska (1894–1945), perhaps a Polish Sappho. "Ursula" was the daughter of a major Polish poet, Jan Kochanowski (1530–1584). Her untimely death is the subject of his best-known poem, "Laments." In one of Pawlikowska's poems, the recorded voice of Caruso complains, asking *"Perchè?"*

page 125   *The last poem of the epoch went to print*
Its author, Władysław Sebyła (1902–1940), belonged to a group around the magazine *Kwadryga.* He rejected the poetics of Skamander, searching instead for a technique capable of expressing philosophic meanings. He was influenced by the patron saint of modern intellectual poetry, Cyprian Kamil Norwid (1821–1883), who having been rejected by his contemporaries, was rediscovered nearly two decades after his death in Paris in a hospice for the destitute. Sebyła was drafted at the beginning of the war and served as a noncommissioned officer. Taken prisoner by the Soviet army and interned in a POW camp, he was executed in the famous massacre of Polish officers in Katyn Woods near Smolensk in April 1940. By the order signed by Stalin on March 5, 1940, 24,600 Polish prisoners were executed.

page 125   *Swiatowid*
A pagan Slavic deity with four faces whose statues survived until the twelfth century.

Barrage balloons hang like ripened fruit
This is a faithful description of the night preceding the outbreak
of war, which started on September 1, 1939, with Hitler's dawn
attack on Poland.

In the original text, the "watchman on duty" is anonymous,
but it is easy to guess that I speak of myself. In this translation, I
changed "he" to "I."

III. THE SPIRIT OF HISTORY

In Masovian forests, on needle-covered paths
The Nazi administration introduced food rationing in the cities,
but the rations allotted were not sufficient for survival. This led
to high prices and smuggling. Often peasant smugglers had to
cross borders illegally between the new administrative regions,
such as this border between territories incorporated into the
Reich and those incorporated in the General Government.

*In the town, a bullet is carving a dry trace / In the sidewalk near bags of
homegrown tobacco*
Black market goods, including tobacco, were usually displayed
on the sidewalks and suddenly disappeared at the approach of a
police patrol.

Stanisław, or Henryk, sounds the bottom with a pole
In summer the Vistula is shallow. Old-fashioned steamboats with
paddle wheels had to move slowly, probing the bottom. "One
meter" indicates the water level.

Do we know you as the Spirit of the Earth
In Goethe's *Faust* the Spirit of the Earth was Nature, which
governed with the law of universal necessity.

Clandestine bulletins in a green bag
The underground press in occupied Poland was a phenomenon
unique in Europe, both for its wide circulation and for the number
of its printing shops. It reflected a large spectrum of political
opinion, including those of the right and the extreme right.

The twenty-year-old poets of Warsaw
This was a generation of poets who were children when the war
broke out. They grew up in conditions of terror and indigence,
took courses at a clandestine university, started to write poems
and copied them with primitive techniques. Their story is
heroic, heartrending, and absurd. Their small review *Art and
Nation* voiced the ideology of Polish nationalism ("Imperial
Poland"). Its editors perished one by one, in Auschwitz, in street
executions, in combat.

page 131

Copernicus: the statue of a German or a Pole?
A statue of Nicolaas Copernicus, seated, a globe in his hand, stands in the center of Warsaw. It bears an inscription in Polish: "To Copernicus—Compatriot." The Germans erased the inscription and replaced it with one in German. In 1943 three poets, from the group in question, decided to lay flowers in the national colors at the foot of the monument. It was a students' prank. An exchange of shots with the German police ensued and one of them, Wacław Bojarski, was mortally wounded.

page 131

Trzebiński, the new Polish Nietzsche
Andrzej Trzebiński (1922–1943) was brilliant, especially as an essayist. He belonged to the extreme right. Arrested by the Gestapo, he died in one of the numerous street executions. The victims, before being shot, had their mouths plastered shut.

page 131

Baczyński's head fell against his rifle
Krzysztof Kamil Baczyński (1921–1944) was killed on a barricade during one of the first days of the Warsaw Uprising of 1944.

page 131

Gajcy, Stroiński were raised to the sky
Tadeusz Gajcy (1922–1944) is considered, together with Baczyński, the most gifted poet among his contemporaries. He died just as his talent came into its own. In the Warsaw Uprising, together with a friend, the poet Zdzisław Stroiński (1921–1944), he was in an action in a neighborhood which was the scene of particularly fierce battles. The street changed hands several times. The Germans dug a tunnel, mined the building the poet's unit was defending, and blew it up. "On the shield of an explosion": in ancient Greece the emblem of heroic death.

page 132

Under a linden tree, as before, daylight
The linden tree calls to mind a poem written by Jan Kochanowski (1530–1584), who used to write under its shade when, after his travels through Italy and France, he settled on his country estate.

page 132

Now He, expected, for a long time awaited, /Raised up the smoke of a thousand censers
The Warsaw Uprising began on August 1, 1944. No one, including its commanders, expected that the battles would last until October 2, 1944. The death toll reached 250,000.

page 133

When they put a rope around my neck
In speaking of the Shoah, stress is usually put on the destruction of, not the life of, the communities destroyed. Polish Jews had behind them a long and rich tradition of religious writing, art, architecture, and traditions of self-rule. In the interwar years their cultural life thrived. They created a network of schools that taught in Yiddish and Hebrew and Polish, published a multitude

of newspapers of various political orientations, created a Yiddish theater, formed sports clubs, built hospitals and orphanages. The majority spoke Yiddish, which contributed to a protracted debate about language in school. The Zionists pressed for Hebrew, assimilationists for Polish, socialists for preserving the Yiddish of the working classes. The Polish language was adopted by a considerable number and there were even Zionist Polish-language newspapers. It was also a time when the leading figures in Polish literature and theater and art were Jewish. Poland was, however, plagued by anti-Semitic movements of the extreme right. The first president of independent Poland, Gabriel Narutowicz, accused of having been elected by "the Jewish vote," was assassinated by a nationalist fanatic in 1922.

The Jewish community was strongly diversified. It had its wealthy at the very top and its masses living in dismal poverty. The Germans usually chose to locate the ghettos in the poorest Jewish neighborhoods. In Poland the Shoah amounted to the extermination of a whole nation of Polish Jews. It was not one event among others. The shock left durable psychological and moral traces. The passage of time seems to change nothing in this respect. On the contrary, the Polish Jews are still vividly present in their absence.

page 133	*When they give me an injection of phenol* Phenol is a chemical compound derived from benzene. It was used by the Nazis in the concentration camps to kill the weaker prisoners.
page 135	Winter will end This small lyric is Jewish in origin; its author is anonymous. The author of this poem came across it in a short story by the Polish Jewish writer Artur Sandauer.
page 136	Light Nanking silk our shoulders adorn This quatrain comes from a poem by Adam Mickiewicz written in 1818, "Winter in the City."
page 136	Say what you desire / *Tell us your hungers and your thirsts* These lines are taken from Mickiewicz's verse drama *Forefather's Eve*. They are pronounced by a shaman summoning the souls of the dead on All Souls' Day, a rite mixing Christian and pagan elements.
page 136	*Poetry is well served by warm porcelains* This line and the following six slightly rewrite lines taken from Mickiewicz's poetry.
page 137	*Mickiewicz is too difficult for us* Here the peasants speak. The heritage of the gentry and the Jews is alien to them.

These lines refer to Christmas carols arranged by the avant-garde poet Tytus Czycewski (1883–1945), who drew from folk music in his poetry as composers like Béla Bartók and Karol Szymanowski did in their music. These fragments are taken from Czycewski's "Pastoreki" ("Pastorals"), published in 1925. Christmas carols in Poland date mostly from the seventeenth century.

IV. NATURA

page 140   Sunt mihi Dei Acherontis propitii!

May the gods of Acheron favor me! The triple name of Jehovah be praised! Spirits of fire, of water, of earth, protect me! This magical incantation is taken from *Doctor Faustus* by Christopher Marlowe (1564–1593).

page 140   *The* Socrates of snails . . . / Musician of pears

These epithets are borrowed from Wallace Stevens's "The Comedian as the Letter C." Stevens stressed the ability of man to inhabit "supreme fictions" created by his mind.

page 141   *To keep the oars from squeaking in their locks*

The author describes here a real event: how one evening on a lake in northern Pennsylvania he waited to see a beaver.

page 143   *Belinda of the big foot, Julia, Thaïs*

This enumeration of women's names imitates François Villon's: "But where are the snows of yesteryear?"

page 143   *Peace to the princesses under the tamarisks*

An allusion to a French poem by Oscar Milosz, "Karmomama." It was inspired by a statuette of an Egyptian princess of that name in the Louvre.

page 143   *Time lifted above time by time*

This line refers to T. S. Eliot's "Burnt Norton" in the *Four Quartets*.

page 144   O City, O Society

The city invoked is Paris. The author had lived there and would often take the suburban train from the station St.-Lazare.

page 147   *You will hear not one word spoken of the court / of Sigismund Augustus*

The reign of this king (1550–1572) was the golden age of Polish poetry. It was the time of Jan Kochanowski, whose play on a subject taken from Homer, *The Dismissal of the Greek Envoys,* was performed at court.

page 147   *Herodotus will repose on his shelf, uncut*

Herodotus (b. 484 B.C.) was, of course, the first European historian.

| page 147 | *Let names of months mean only what they mean* |
| | In some European countries the names of the months are associated with political events. October is the month of the Bolshevik Revolution in Russia, which was helped by the cannons of the ironclad ship *Aurora*. November for the Poles always suggests the 1830 uprising against czarist Russia. It was begun by young rebels, officers stationed in Warsaw. |

ODE

| page 148 | O October |
| | There is a sort of perversity in writing an ode to October simply as an autumn month, when historically it denotes the Russian Revolution, an event which had grave consequences for the whole twentieth century. |

| page 148 | When a Polish engineer glimpses near West Point |
| | The forests of New York recall a Polish participant in the American revolution, Tadeusz Kościusko (1746–1817), who built the fort's defenses. |

| page 148 | Blowing a buffalo horn above the rebel camp |
| | Poles who fought the Russians in 1863. |

| page 149 | *Neither the eternal moment / Attracted us* |
| | T. S. Eliot in *Four Quartets* speaks of "the still point of the turning world." |

| page 150 | *Spirits of the air, of fire, of water* |
| | The last passage of the poem describes travel by ship to Europe in 1950. |

| page 151 | Iam Cytherea choros ducit |
| | Already Cytherean Venus leads choruses, dancing under the rising moon. |

KING POPIEL AND OTHER POEMS

| page 170 | *"In Milan"* |
| | In this translation the last line of the Polish original has been omitted. In English it reads: |

> "Whoever has not touched the earth . . ." Few have understood this.

The quotation refers to a passage in *Forefather's Eve* by Adam Mickiewicz: "Whoever has not touched the earth will never be in Heaven." It is spoken by the phantom of a girl who died a virgin. Perhaps this poem alters Mickiewicz's meaning.

page 181   *"Far West"*
                "Gently, my lambs, move gently": a line, slightly changed, from
                the Polish baroque poet Jan Gawiński (1622–1684).

page 182   *"Throughout Our Lands"*
                Cabeza: Spanish explorer Alvar Núñez Cabeza de Vaca (ca. 1490–ca.
                1560). A member of a disastrous expedition to Florida in 1527–1528,
                he returned to civilization after long wanderings among Indian tribes.

BOBO'S METAMORPHOSIS

page 203   *"Three Talks on Civilization"*
                The persona is somehow identical with an archreactionary and
                cynical master of diplomatic games in the nineteenth century,
                Metternich. In 1820 he wrote a letter to Czar Alexander I,
                warning him against the romantic youth influenced by the ideas
                of Jean-Jacques Rousseau.

CITY WITHOUT A NAME

page 214   *"City Without a Name"*
                The title refers to the capital of Lithuania, Wilno in Polish,
                Vilnius in Lithuanian.

page 214   *Ponary Hills*
                Hills near Wilno covered with lush oak forests, the place for holiday
                excursions by students. During World War II the Nazis chose a
                large clearing in these hills for their mass executions and killed
                around 120,000 people, eighty percent of whom were Jewish.

page 214   *Vagabonds, Pathfinders*
                The Club of Vagabonds was a colorful student organization in
                the 1930s. *Pathfinder* was the title of a volume of poems by a local
                avant-garde poet, Aleksander Rymkiewicz.

page 214   *Kontrym*
                Kazimierz Kontrym (1792–1836), a librarian at the university library
                in Wilno. As a Freemason he acted as an intermediary between the
                city's Freemasonic lodges and clandestine student organizations.

page 215   *"An Hour of Thought"*
                a poem by one of the major Polish Romantic poets, Juliusz
                Słowacki (1809–1849).

page 215   *the one who died in Istanbul*
                the Polish national poet Adam Mickiewicz (1798–1855), born in
                Lithuania. After a tempestuous life, he died in Istanbul while
                organizing a legion to fight Russia.

page 215   *we and our Maryla*
                Mickiewicz and his beloved, Maryla, who was high above him in

social status, became a literary legend. She disappointed him by marrying a count.

page 216   *Understanding and pity*
            The poem alludes by its rhythm to Polish madrigals of the eighteenth century.

page 216   *the Zealous Lithuanian Lodge*
            the name of one of the Freemasonic lodges in Wilno around 1820.

page 218   *Basilian church*
            The religious order of St. Basil was Uniate, i.e., not Roman Catholic but Greco-Catholic. While Wilno was predominantly Roman Catholic and Jewish, large parts of the Grand Duchy of Lithuania were Uniate.

page 219   *King Otto and Melusine*
            characters in traditional stories from the late medieval period; they survived in cheaply printed books sold at fairs such as the one described here—the St. Casimir's Fair, held every year in Wilno on March 4 and featuring handicrafts made by peasants over the winter, as well as bagels and cakes baked in the shape of a heart.

page 219   *Tuzigoot*
            an Indian village in Arizona preserved as a historical landmark.

page 220   *parakeets from Samogitia*
            Samogitia is the northern province of Lithuania.

page 220   *Three Crosses Hill and Bekiesz Hill*
            The first was named to commemorate three Franciscan monks, according to legend crucified by pagan Lithuanians. The second borrowed its name from the tomb of a lord buried there in the sixteenth century, who since he was a heretic (anti-Trinitarian) could not be buried in a Catholic cemetery.

page 221   Noble Jan Dęboróg
            a tale in verse by the local poet Władysław Syrokomla (1823–1862).

UNCOLLECTED POEMS
page 254   *"To Raja Rao"*
            A poem written directly in English after a long theological conversation with Hindu writer and philosopher Raja Rao.

FROM THE RISING OF THE SUN
page 265   "L'Accélération de l'Histoire"
            "hands fighting for the people . . .": The last lines quote a poem written by Adam Mickiewicz in 1833:

Tongues shouting in the name of the people will bore the people,

And faces that amuse the people will bore the people,

And hands fighting for the people the people themselves will cut off.

Names dear to the people the people will forget.

Everything passes. After all the noise, the roar, the turmoil,

The inheritance will be received by silent, obscure, small people.

pages 291–308   *"From the Rising of the Sun"*
Unfortunately, the mixture of languages in "III. Lauda" makes a unified spelling practically impossible, and the author apologizes for switching from Lithuanian spelling to Polish and vice versa. For instance, "Kiejdany" and "Kedainiai" refer to the same place. The original, in fact, contains also fragments written in the language of the legal documents, Old Byelorussian. Translating "Lauda," the author and Robert Hass had recourse to English inventories and wills of the same period as the documents, i.e., the sixteenth century.

page 291   *This space is different*
This stanza evokes a traditional Polish Christmas carol, which we have tried to suggest in the translation.

page 292   *We were better than the yeomen of Lauda or Wędziagoła*
the rural gentry was stratified. At the top were the aristocratic families; in the middle, average landowners; at the bottom, but above the peasants, so-called gentry villages whose inhabitants tilled the land like peasants, yet were never serfs. Lauda and Wędziagoła are agglomerations of such free villages.

page 301   *his friend the poet Theodore*
Teodor Bujnicki (1907–1944) was, with the author, one of the founders of the Żagary or Catastrophist school of poetry in Wilno in the 1930s. He became a supporter of the Soviet authorities when they occupied Wilno around 1940 and was killed by young men from an underground resistance organization which opposed the Soviet occupation of Lithuania.

page 304   *Teodor Bujnicki*
See above note.

page 304   *Gustav in* Forefather's Eve
a hero of a major Polish dramatic work, a play in verse, by the Polish national poet Adam Mickiewicz. Gustav is an unhappy lover, much like Goethe's Werther; imprisoned for political activity against czarist Russia, he undergoes a change of heart

and, renouncing private concerns, dedicates himself to the political cause. The play was banned by the Communist authorities as recently as 1968.

page 306   *Mr. Norwid, for instance, and Mr. Gombrowicz, both from Samogitia*
The fact that important Polish writers used to come from Lithuania (not unlike important English writers coming from Ireland) contributed to a legend. Cyprian Norwid (1821–1883), considered the father of modern Polish poetry, bears a Lithuanian name (Norvidas). Witold Gombrowicz (1904–1969) always stressed the Lithuanian origin of his family.

page 307   *The bard Mickiewicz*
See note to page 215.

page 307   By the Great Kowno Highway
In this section, the italicized idioms and formulas are borrowed from sixteenth-century wills and bequests to Protestant churches, as well as from the privileges by which King Sigismund Augustus granted equal rights to the Catholic and non-Catholic nobility of the grand duchy. (According to *Monumenta Reformationis Polonicae et Lithuanicae*, printed by the Synod of the Lithuanian Evangelical-Reform Union, Wilno, 1911.)

page 313   *Then he reminisced about Count de Saint-Germain*
According to a legend circulating in Europe at the end of the eighteenth century, Count de Saint-Germain possessed the secret of eternal youth and perhaps of immortality.

page 313   *the lost Book of Hieroglyphic Figures*
work by a French alchemist of legendary fame, Nicolas Flamel (1330–1413).

page 315   *"i was not . . ."*
in Latin, *non fui, fui, non sum, non desidero.*

page 320   Nicola Chiaromonte (1905–1972), Italian humanist and critic, opponent of Italian fascism; Francis de Miomandre (1880–1959), a French literary critic; Sándor Petöfi (1823–1849), a Hungarian Romantic poet and national hero; Adam Mickiewicz (1798–1855), great Polish Romantic poet.

page 329   Introibo . . .
from the opening prayer of the Latin Tridentine Mass: "I will go up to the altar of God, to God who is the joy of my youth."

page 330   Memento etiam . . .
from the prayers for the dead in the Latin Tridentine Mass: "Remember therefore, God, your servants and handmaidens who preceded us."

HYMN OF THE PEARL

page 362   *The Separate Notebooks*
                Barbara, the princess: The king of Poland, Sigismund Augustus
                (1520–1572), fell in love with Barbara Radziwiłł and married her in
                spite of the opposition of parliament (she was not of royal blood).
                After her death he had recourse to magicians who presumably were
                able to bring about the appearance of her phantom.

page 379   *he reads: "Piłsudski"*
                Józef Piłsudski (1867–1935) is considered today as one of the
                heroes in the Polish national pantheon. In his youth he was a
                revolutionary engaged in daring attempts against the czarist
                authorities in Russian-occupied Poland and an editor of a
                socialist clandestine newspaper, *The Worker.* He organized Polish
                military units during World War I, created a Polish army in 1918,
                and was acclaimed marshal. In 1920, at the gates of Warsaw, he
                won the battle against the Soviet army. That victory was crucial
                for the existence of independent Poland in the interwar period.
                Piłsudski was from Lithuania. The correct Polish spelling of his
                name would be Piłsudski.

pages 381   The lines in quotation marks are taken from a long mystical
                poem, *The King Spirit*, written around 1849 by Juliusz Słowacki.
                Józef Piłsudski admired the poem and knew large parts of it by
                heart, but his enemy and compatriot from Lithuania, Feliks
                Dzerzhinski, the right hand of Lenin and the organizer of the
                police apparatus in Russia after the revolution, shared the same
                infatuation.

page 381   *Such then was the inheritor of the Boleslavian crown*
                Bolesław the Brave (967–1025), king of Poland, succeeded in
                consolidating his power over the territory freshly baptized in the
                Roman rite (in 966) stretching on the west beyond the Oder and
                on the east to the possessions of the princes of the Eastern Slavs,
                who took their religion from Byzantium in 988.

page 382   Józef Czechowicz (1903–1939)
                a poet and friend of the author, killed in a German bombardment
                in 1939. He was a soldier in 1920 at the time of the crucial battle
                of Warsaw. An eminent theater director, Wilam Horzyca, staged
                one of his plays in 1939, just before the out break of World War II.

page 384   *"The Wormwood Star"*
                from the Book of Revelation of St. John, 8.10–11:

                'And the third angel sounded, and there fell a great star
                from heaven, burning as if it were a lamp, and it fell upon
                the third part of the rivers, and upon the fountains of

waters. And the name of the star is called Wormwood: and the third part of the waters became wormwood; and many men died of the waters, because they were made bitter.'

They were informed by the schoolboy, Lebedyev's son, that "the Star that is called Wormwood" in the Apocalypse, "that fell upon the fountain of waters," was, by his father's interpretation, the network of railways that spread over Europe. Myshkin did not believe that Lebedyev did interpret it this way, and resolved to ask him about it at the first convenient opportunity. (Fyodor Dostoyevsky, *The Idiot*, Book 2, Chapter 10)

"Not railways, no," retorted Lebedyev, who was at the same time losing his temper and enjoying himself tremendously. "The railways alone won't pollute the 'springs of life,' but the whole thing is accursed; the whole tendency of the last few centuries in its general, scientific and materialistic entirety, is perhaps really accursed."

"Certainly accursed, or only perhaps? It is important to know that, you know," queried Yevgeny Pavlovitch.

"Accursed, accursed, most certainly accursed," Lebedyev maintained with heat. (*The Idiot*, Book 3, Chapter 4)

page 393   *"Bypassing Rue Descartes"*
"Water snake": In Lithuania, where the author grew up, many pagan beliefs survived, among them the cult of water snakes, which were associated with the sun. A strict taboo protected a water snake from any harm inflicted by man.

NEW POEMS
page 463   *"With Her"*
In 1945, during the big resettlements of population at the end of World War II, my family left Lithuania and was assigned quarters near Danzig (Gdansk) in a house belonging to a German peasant family. Only one old German woman remained in the house. She fell ill with typhus and there was nobody to take care of her. In spite of admonitions motivated partly by universal hatred for the Germans, my mother nursed her, became ill herself, and died.

page 475   *"Beyond the Urals"*
"Zdziechowski's lectures": Marian Zdziechowski (1861–1938), professor of literature before World War I at the Jagiellonian University in Kraków, then at the University of Wilno, where he was the chancellor (rector) when the author began his studies of law there.

PROVINCES
page 512   *"Mister Hanusevich"*
                           "sestritsas": Russian military nurse in World War I.

                           "A whole year in the saddle, in a cavalry regiment": In the 1920
                           war between Poland and the Soviet Union it was not uncommon
                           for women to serve in the cavalry.

FACING THE RIVER
page 602   *"To My Daimonion"*
                           "After his short life, they raised him on the altars": St. Stanislaus
                           Kostka.

THIS
page 668   *"My Grandfather Sigismund Kunat"*
                           Oscar Milosz: the author's cousin, a distinguished French poet of
                           Lithuanian ancestry.

page 707   *"Zone of Silence"*
                           Zygmunt Mycielski (1907–1987): a Polish composer and writer.

page 708   *"Selecting Iwaszkiewicz's Poems"*
                           Jarosław Iwaszkiewicz (1894–1980) was born of Polish parents in
                           Ukraine and became one of the most important Polish poets of
                           the Skamander group. During the war his home in Warsaw was a
                           main meeting place of intellectuals involved in the underground
                           movement.

page 711   *"What I Learned"*
                           Jeanne Hersch (1910–2000): a Swiss philosopher, translator of
                           Karl Jaspers's work into French, and professor of philosophy at
                           the University of Geneva.

page 714   *"Zdziechowski"*
                           Marian Zdziechowski (1861–1938): a Polish religious thinker,
                           professor of literature, and author of studies on Russian spirituality.

page 721   *"Aleksander Wat's Tie"*
                           Aleksander Wat (1900–1967), a sometimes futurist and dadaist
                           poet, escaped from the Nazis during the war to Soviet-occupied
                           Lwow, where he was immediately arrested as a suspected Zionist
                           and sent to Soviet Asia. Years later in Berkeley, Milosz persuaded
                           Wat to tell his story using a tape recorder. The resulting book is
                           called *My Life*.

page 724   *"On Poetry"*
                           Zbigniew Herbert (1924–2000) was one of the best-known
                           Polish poets of the twentieth century.

page 726   "Unde Malum"
            Tadeusz Rozewicz (b. 1921) is an important Polish poet of the
            postwar period. Both *"Unde Malum"* and "Rozewicz" mimic the
            poet's characteristic style.

page 745   *"Rays of Dazzling Light"*
            This poem resembles and quotes a well-known baroque carol.

INDEX OF POEMS AND TRANSLATORS

The poems were translated by Czeslaw Milosz and Robert Hass, except as initialed.

KEY TO TRANSLATORS:

DB	David Brooks
JC	John Carpenter
JD	Jan Darowski
LD	Lawrence Davis
JF	Jessica Fisher
BoG	Bozena Gilewska
BrG	Brian Glazer
RG	Renata Gorczynski
RH	Robert Hass
LI	Louis Iribarne
ML	Madeline Levine
RL	Richard Lourie
AM	Anthony Milosz
CM	Czeslaw Milosz
LN	Leonard Nathan
RP	Robert Pinsky
MS	Martin Sabiniewicz
JS	Jennifer Scappettone
PDS	Peter Dale Scott
LV	Lillian Vallee